A History of the

Brighton Workhouses

James Gardner

With Best Wishes

James Gardner

Jacket illustrations: (front) Elm Grove workhouse inmates begging on race day in the 1920s, *Daily Mirror* 9/8/1923; (back) *The Brighton and Hove Society* 9/1/1905.

Published by James Gardner, 5 East Way, Lewes, East Sussex BN7 1NG
www.jamesgardnerauthor.com

ISBN 978-0-9536101-1-2

Printed by Ashford Colour Press, Gosport, Hants PO13 0FW

In loving memory of two special friends

Marilyn Vrabez 1948–2010

Ted Burtenshaw 1948–2010

Metric and decimal equivalents

Weight
1lb (pound) = 454g
1 oz (ounce) = 28g
Liquid
1 pint (20 fluid ounces) = 568ml
Length
One inch – 2.54cm
One foot (twelve inches) = 30.5cm
Land
1 acre = 4,046 square metres

Monetary values

Before 1971 there were twenty shillings to a pound and twelve pennies to a shilling, so there were 240 pennies to a pound. There are two good websites which convert old money into today's monetary worth: *www.measuringworth.com/uk* and *www.nationalarchives.gov.uk/currency*. Using the latter, the equivalent 2005 price Brighton paid for its first workhouse in Bartholomews square in 1727 (£100), would have been £8,475. By the same token the £10,000 the town paid for the Church Hill workhouse in 1822 was equivalent to £419,200 in 2005.

Throughout the late eighteenth and nineteenth century there was very little inflation. For example, the two shillings which the parish paid to James Patching each week in 1790 "for the better support of his family" was worth £5.60 in 2005. In 1890 the same amount was worth only slightly more, £5.99. Wages also changed little in this period. In mid-nineteenth century Britain a farm labourer earned just under a pound a week. At the turn of the century it remained a pound.

CONTENTS

INTRODUCTION

'Regency Brighton', 'London-by-the-Sea', 'Old Ocean's Bauble', 'Dr. Brighton': all these are familiar titles that have been applied to Brighton, representing one side of Brighton's personality and identity. But it is only one side. As Graham Greene's *Brighton Rock*, Queenspark Books' *Backstreet Brighton* and many of the articles in Timothy Carder's *Encyclopaedia of Brighton* reveal, there was another side. In this book James Gardner adds an important new dimension to our understanding of that 'other Brighton'.

The history of the 'other Brighton', if not quite unknown, is largely detached from the Brighton of popular imagination. In popular imagination Brighton mainly exists in the forms associated with 'fashionable Brighton', the Brighton of the Royal Pavilion, the grand avenues and crescents and the high lifestyle of the rich and famous during the years of Brighton's royal patronage. The jarring reality of the poverty and the squalor of life for the many Brightonians who failed to share that lifestyle seems inconceivable.

The Brighton that James Gardner engagingly and carefully explores was a product of the polarization of British society in the eighteenth and early nineteenth centuries. Vast profits generated by the widening opportunities in commerce, banking, trade and manufacture, as well as public office and land, were increasingly funnelled into the pursuit of status and fashion. The accumulation of cultural capital became as important as the production of wealth itself. From the middle of the eighteenth century Brighton became one of the nation's chief engines for the production of cultural capital. Social status and prestige were no longer solely the consequences of birth into a family whose landed wealth could be traced back through the generations. Other avenues for establishing oneself in the social, cultural and political hierarchy emerged. By the end of the eighteenth century displays of wealth in various forms of conspicuous consumption became essential for the establishment and reinforcing of status. The exhibition of wealth, on which status depended, required venues in which such displays could be performed and admired by those whose opinion mattered. Resorts such as Brighton were especially well adapted to servicing that need. With its assembly rooms, ballrooms and promenades, Brighton provided the stage upon which the wealthy could flaunt, to its maximum effect, their elegant, refined and fashionable extravagance.

Yet fashionable, extravagant Brighton depended for its existence on an army of men and women who laboured day and night behind the opulent façade to service the needs of those whose successful enjoyment of Brighton depended on them doing no work at all. These were the maids and servants, the carters and livery boys, the road sweepers and the washerwomen without whom the glamour and glitter of Brighton would not have been possible. It was these men and women, whose survival depended on the brief flowering of the Brighton 'season', who constituted hidden Brighton. The reality of their lives, in the crowded and unhealthy slums of the lanes and terraces concealed behind the elegant and fashionable façade, was an ever-present threat to the imagined Brighton of the genteel visitor and the wealthy resident. In 1881, the Brighton newspaper *The Brightonian* described one part of this unknown and unacknowledged Brighton:

> Dirty, squalid and wretched, the district lying between Edward Street and Carlton Hill is not included in the attractions which the local guide books catalogue for the behoof [benefit] of the visitor. Brightonians themselves never, or rarely penetrate its shabby recesses; and officialdom, like a well-to-do relative, tries hard to banish from its mind the disagreeable fact that so poor a dependent exists. Tabooed, neglected and isolated, like a dark, noisome corner in a beautiful garden, the condemned district flourishes in a rank of luxuriance.

The author's failure to include the inhabitants of this district within the appellation 'Brightonians' reveals the huge gulf between the image and the reality.

Brighton's poor were casualties of the enormous social and economic change that had transformed Britain in the three hundred and fifty years between the mid-sixteenth and late nineteenth centuries. The commercialization and capitalistic transformation of agriculture, most familiarly associated with the various waves of enclosure, had forced hundreds of thousands of small holders and labourers out of the rural economy and into the towns. By 1851 Britain's population was, for the first time, predominantly urban. Many of the thousands pouring into the towns in the late eighteenth and early nineteenth centuries were hoping for work in the factories and workshops of the booming industrial cities. Although not an industrial city in the early nineteenth century, Brighton's expansion was on a par with the fastest growing of the northern industrial centres. During the 1810s Brighton was the fastest growing urban area in the country, doubling its population in the ten years between 1811 and 1821. Brighton's resort and tourist trade, hugely enhanced by the arrival of the railway in 1846, drew the poor, the unemployed and the displaced from far and wide, not just throughout the south-east, but even from the industrial cities of the north and west.

An ever-present fear of underemployment or unemployment was the day-to-day experience of many of Brighton's poor. The loss of seasonal employment in the homes of the wealthy could lead to starvation for oneself and one's family. Fear of unemployment, and the poverty which almost inevitably followed, was added to for many by the fear of the main alternative provided by the harsh realities of nineteenth-century welfare – the workhouse. The principle underlying the workhouse was that of 'less eligibility'. In practice that meant that no one in receipt of welfare should enjoy a standard of living better that the very poorest of those in work, a principle which has emerged once again as the basis for welfare provision. Clearly the distinction between 'minimum elgibility' and being punished for one's poverty is a narrow one. To accept that those of our fellow citizens who are unemployed, ill, disabled or elderly should suffer for their poverty is difficult to distinguish from a view that would blame them for their own poverty; that would see poverty as 'a lifestyle choice'. The frequent refrain that the basic human needs of the poor must always be set against the interests of the taxpayers, leads one to question just who these 'taxpayers' may be. Clearly they are not those who might, one day, find themselves ill, disabled, unemployed, elderly or impoverished.

In James Gardner's sympathetic and detailed narrative we encounter a wide range of individuals and the experiences that brought them to Brighton's workhouse. We meet the itinerant poor, the rootless, tramping poor who existed at the very margins of society, often with tragic stories to tell, constantly moving on, perhaps in hope of work, or perhaps escaping from a past that they prayed would never catch up with them. But many of those who came to the workhouse were part of the community of Brighton, some now too old or too ill to support themselves, but others whose precarious employment left them unemployed or underemployed when conditions were bad. These were members of the working poor, many involved in domestic and personal service – the cooks, porters, footmen, gardeners, washerwomen or charwomen who served the wealthy residents and visitors to Brighton.

Because of the seasonal nature of the resort trade many of the workers faced periodic unemployment, having no alternative but the workhouse when the hotels, restaurants, boarding houses and lodging houses closed at the end of the season. Others were part of the army of labourers who maintained Brighton's infrastructure or provided its services. Many worked on the railways, either on track maintenance or in the workshops of the Brighton depot. Others were involved in the construction industry that boomed in the early and middle decades of the nineteenth century. Alongside these were the labourers in a variety of industries and services such as brewers, iron workers, carters, draymen, porters, sweepers and workers in the brickyards and gasworks.

None of these employees enjoyed security of employment: they were often paid by the week or the day. In times of prosperity they could normally look forward to having a job for most of the year, subject to the important fluctuations of the weather and their own health and strength, but in 'bad' times their job outlook was bleak indeed – the weakest quickly went to the wall, and the strongest often were reduced to seeking casual labour. In addition there still lingered a dwindling number of fishermen and seafarers; the remnants of Brighton's once dominant fishing industry, now no longer manning a deep sea fleet, but dependent on local inshore fishing or provided pleasure trips for visitors.

What James Gardner has achieved is not only to reveal to us a hidden Brighton of abject poverty, despair and hopelessness. More than that, through his painstaking researches he has managed to give some of those poor a voice. In these pages they speak to us of their pain, suffering, frustration and anger, above all of their smouldering sense of injustice – of lives wasted and worn out by the mammoth struggle just to stay alive. They speak of the smallness of imagination and the poverty of compassion which underlay the system of relief and characterized many of those whom the authorities placed in command of the system.

These voices are important for us to hear, not only because they speak to us of a historical reality too often ignored, but because they speak to us of experiences and realities that are very much still with us. Who cannot avoid the contemporary resonance of the plea of Henry Hiles, published in *Lloyd's Weekly* in March 1867 in response to the refusal by the Board of Guardians of the Poor of his request for outdoor relief?

My poor though trifling request was only for three weeks outdoor relief, till I could get a little stronger after my severe illness so as to go to work again if I could get it. They have in the most unfeeling, and, as I consider, unjust manner, refused it to me, although I had the parish's doctor's certificate (their own doctor) to say I was, and should be unable to work for a month or more through debility caused by my late illness. I deem it right to make known to a Christian public this most unfeeling treatment in a Christian country, where, by law the poor are to be fed who are unable by misfortune to procure their own bread…

Yet Brighton's Guardians of the Poor were by no means the worst. For a long time during the nineteenth century, they retained a flexibility in the administration of the Poor Law that had been abandoned elsewhere, and which defied the demands of the 1834 Poor Law Act. In some respects Henry Hiles' request for outdoor relief was exceptional. Since 1834, in many parts of Britain, outdoor relief was no longer available as an alternative to the workhouse. It allowed individuals to obtain welfare while remaining in their home with their family. After 1834 Guardians were requested to withdraw it and force all on parish relief into the workhouse, where husbands and wives would be separated and children removed from their parents. That the Brighton Guardians were still offering outdoor relief in the 1860s perhaps indicates not just a stiff-necked refusal to be instructed in their duties by outsiders, but also, we can hope, an awareness of the damage to individuals, families and communities that could result from the inflexible imposition of the workhouse on those facing misfortune.

James Gardner's skillful and meticulous research brings back into our imaginary Brighton the 'house on the hill' and the 'place in the wilderness'. They and their predecessors played a dominant role in the lives, hopes and fears of Brighton's poor for over 200 years. We should be enormously grateful for the sympathetic attention he has paid to the voices of those whom their contemporaries so often failed to hear. His determination that, whenever possible, we should hear directly from those whose lives had been influenced, whether for good or ill, by a connection with the Brighton Workhouse is an important step forward in the recovery of Brighton's 'history from below'. He has brought out of the silence those who to ignore would be to inflict a double injustice.

Peter Jackson,
University of Brighton

We all arrived safely at Liverpool at about 3.30am…It seemed to me, as we traversed at that early hour, the silent streets of that great town, a very solemn thing, and I could not help feeling sad about it, although the brave young hearts who were so soon to part from what had been to them both home and friends, never flinched or faltered. At the last farewell, a few glistening eyes showed that the feelings were with difficulty restrained…May the undertaking, so far auspiciously accomplished receive the Divine blessing is the earnest wish of

Your faithful servant

Edward Sattin

(Letter from the master of the workhouse describing the last past of his journey escorting Brighton workhouse children emigrating to Canada in May 1871.)

The poetry of history lies in the quasi-miraculous fact that once, on this familiar spot of ground walked other men and women, as actual as we are today, thinking their own thoughts, swayed by their own passion, but now all gone, one generation after another, gone as utterly as we are ourselves shall shortly be gone like ghosts at cock-crow. [1] GM Trevelyan

PREFACE

As a young boy, I first became aware of workhouses through David Lean's film *Oliver Twist*. The opening sequence of a heavily pregnant woman staggering through a stormy night lashed by the rain before arriving at the forbidding gates of the parish workhouse was all the more haunting for being filmed in black and white. The woman gives birth and dies, and her son, Oliver, becomes famous for "asking for more". Later on, while writing a book, *Sweet Bells Jangled out of Tune*, about the Sussex Lunatic Asylum, I learned how paupers were often transferred like goods between there and the Brighton workhouses. More recently, an elderly aunt told me that one day her grandmother received a telegram from Brighton. She took the train there and on her return never spoke about the reason for her visit. Years later the aunt found out that the telegram had been sent by the Brighton workhouse informing her of the death of her husband.

Today the living memories of life in the workhouse have almost died out. If alive at all, they can only be through the memories passed down perhaps by parents and grandparents who witnessed their last days in the 1920s and 1930s. And yet, for much of the nineteenth and early twentieth centuries workhouses dominated our landscape. In Brighton's glorious Regency and post-Regency development period the largest accommodation in the town was not a hotel or a palace, it was the workhouse. It dominated the town, in its own way, just as much as the luxury hotels and elegant houses did.

In the second half of the nineteenth century you could hardly open a newspaper without reading about an incident or scandal connected with the workhouse system, the most horrific being at Andover where starving inmates were forced to eat the marrow from rotting horse bones to survive. It touched every town, every village. Families continually lived on a knife edge between employment and destitution, and entering the workhouse was often the only way of keeping alive. If you were an inhabitant of Brighton you were either paying for its upkeep as a ratepayer or were potentially an inmate. Then as now, there was a long-running debate about the "deserving" and "undeserving" poor and the difficulty of distinguishing between the two.

Of course, Charles Dickens' *Oliver Twist*, written in 1837, created huge public interest, and even Queen Victoria visited the Windsor workhouse. However, when royalty and the rich came to Brighton, they visited the Royal Sussex County Hospital, the Princess Alexandra Hospital for Children and the Royal Pavilion but never set foot in the workhouse.[i] Unless you had to, few people wanted to go there. It was a place to avoid at all cost.

Three workhouses were built in Brighton, each one bigger than its predecessor: Bartholomews (1727), Church Hill (1822) and Elm Grove (1867), latterly Brighton General Hospital. A workhouse for orphans, deserted children and the children of inmates, Warren Farm Industrial Schools, was also built at Woodingdean in 1862. Now only the Elm Grove building remains. It was by far the most important of the three, serving the town for over seventy years. The month before it opened in 1867, more than 12,000 locals visited it out of curiosity. And it is this workhouse, the one at Church Hill and the industrial schools at Woodingdean which this book is primarily about. Arguably, Brighton has hidden its poverty well under the image of a lively affluent seaside town, largely a legacy from when the Prince Regent set up court in the Royal Pavilion in the early part of the nineteenth century. But behind the town's façade there was a squalor equalled only by working class areas in industrial cities. One of Brighton's famous physicians, Dr William Kebbell, wrote in 1848:

> …the streets and districts of the poor, both in filth and general untidiness, and the squalor of the inhabitants are a disgrace to any civilized people. [2]

Growing up in Brighton, I occasionally came across this other face of the town: poorly dressed people queuing up outside the "doss house" in Elm Grove in the 1960s and 1970s. That overnight facility, next to Brighton General Hospital, was a reminder of the "casual ward" of the old workhouse

---

[i] George V did visit the Elm Grove workhouse in August 1915 during the First World War but it was then being used as a military hospital, not a workhouse.

days, a place where vagrants had a right to stay on their travels for one or two nights anywhere in the country.

Unfeeling, bleak and mean, many workhouses were profoundly inhumane institutions which cast a shadow over ordinary lives. Inadequate diets and brutality were commonplace. What I wanted to find out was: how accurate was this image in relation to the Brighton workhouses, particularly the one in Elm Grove? At the very least we know life there was pretty grim. In 1888, in a testimonial composed by the workhouse inmates and officers to Mrs Ellen Nye Chart, the owner of the Brighton Theatre Royal, they described their free admission to the Christmas pantomime as "one of the bright spots in the necessarily dull routine of workhouse life".

Today, if one wanders the corridors and stairways of the old Brighton General Hospital perhaps one can still feel Trevelyan's "poetry of history" where the inmates once worked, slept, laughed, cried, died and were even born. Sadly, many of the old workhouses' records are missing – destroyed by the Luftwaffe during World War Two – and the inmates left little record of their experiences. Nevertheless, I hope this book will reveal some of the names and unheard voices of Brighton's poor, as well as those of their administrators, and in the words of the great historian EP Thompson, enable us to rescue them from the "enormous condescension of posterity". [3]

ACKNOWLEDGEMENTS

Firstly, I would like to pay tribute to a dear friend, David Harrison, who died just as this book was being completed. It was David several years ago who started me off on this project by recommending Norman Longmate's book, *The Workhouse*. David was a kind, knowledgeable man with great integrity who will be greatly missed by his family and friends.

I am deeply indebted to the following people who gave up their free time to read parts or the whole of my manuscript and for their important observations and criticisms: Vic Baines, Andrew Bennet, Michael Burchall, David Crowe, Helen Devaney, Roger Gardner, Harry Gaston, Dr Peter Jackson, Dianne Jones, Mike Liardit and Suzi Mehmed. Next, I would like to thank the following for their valuable assistance, sometimes providing me with important material or memories about the institutions this book covers: Caroline Ann Carter-Adams, Jill Barlow, Sue Baxter, Edie Burt, Joyce Collins, Margaret Cronin, John Finnie, Anne Fryer, Sue Gillet, Sue Goodwin, Peter Groves, Chris Horlock, Eileen Jones, Laurie Keen, Joan Malik, Peter Mercer, Frank Mildreth, Sheila Parsons, Pam Piercey, Jaqueline Pollard, Peter Shannon, Sheila Sumner, Mick Toner, Adam Trimingham, Mary Wells and Barbara Westgate.

This book would not have been possible without the great assistance I have received from the staff at the National Archives; the staff at the East Sussex Record Office, who include Drew Boulton, Monica Brealey, Philip Bye, Andrew Lusted, Sarah Jackson, Jennifer Nash, Izabella Bicsak-Snitter and Sarah Woollard; and the staff at the Brighton History Centre: Kate Elms, Paul Jordan, Anna Kisby and Shona Milton. I have also received valuable assistance from Kevin Bacon and Kate Richardson at Brighton Museum; Ellie Thorne from the Berkshire Record Office and Marion Hyde from the Baptist Library in Brighton.

Great thanks to David Arscott for his skill, advice and help in producing this book. Over the last few years I have given talks on the Brighton workhouses and am much indebted to the many people who have shared their relatives' memories or their own about the workhouse system. They have been invaluable in helping me to understand the great fear that the word 'workhouse' engendered.

Special thanks to my brother, Steve Gardner. Over the last few years he has tirelessly supported me in this project and has read my various manuscripts more times than he cares to remember! His assistance, as it has been with my previous two books, has been invaluable.

Lastly, just a few words about the two people to whom this book is dedicated, my great friends Marilyn Vrabez and Ted Burtenshaw. Both bravely fought cancer and died of the disease at a relatively young age. Even up to the last few weeks of their lives, when they were seriously ill, they constantly encouraged me to write this book. May it be a memorial to their wonderful friendship.

PART ONE

Chapter One

POVERTY IN BRIGHTON

To be poor in Brighton in the early eighteenth century spelled utter desolation and helplessness. From being a prosperous fishing town of 4,000 inhabitants in the 1650s, by the turn of the century its population had halved and its fortunes plummeted spectacularly due to the foreshore's erosion and the fall in demand for fish. The destruction of many fishermen's dwellings below the cliffs in the terrible storms of 1703 – which nationally killed over 8,000 people – and 1705, added to the misfortune. With this decline came unemployment, homelessness and poverty.

Since the Elizabethan Poor Relief Act of 1601 the parish had become the administrative unit, with the parish officers, the Vestry – a kind of parochial parliament [i] – and an Overseer of the Poor appointed to collect the poor rate and allocate relief to paupers. The Act declared that no person should be left to die of hunger or cold. It gave a pauper – defined as anyone who was partly or wholly maintained by the parish – a legal right to live. Each parish was to look after its old, young or unfit to work, financed by taxing the wealthier members of the community. All landowners and tenants in a parish had to pay the poor rate, although some landowners paid the rate for a tenant and some did not. Anyone receiving parish relief was exempt. The rate could only be used for the specific purpose of supporting the poor and not for the parish's upkeep of lighting, roads and sewerage. The nearest modern day equivalent to the poor rate would be the national insurance contribution which is based on employment rather than property.

The Act gave paupers a chance for a more beareable life and some certainty about a roof over their heads and food in their stomachs, however bad either was. Like most legislation about the pauper, it was aimed at the deserving poor, those too old or too young to look after themselves or those who through physical disability could not earn a

---

[i] It was theoretically composed of all the ratepayers. In Brighton's case it was often dominated by a small clique, including the vicar of Brighton, churchwardens and the chief constable.

3

living. It was run by individual parishes looking after their own, using the unpaid services of sometimes illiterate churchwardens and overseers, often parochial officers detested by both pauper and rate-payer. [i]

In Brighton in the seventeenth century, recipients of parish relief were usually maintained in the community, although there was a tenement in East Street which housed the homeless. Relief was meant to be a temporary subsidy until their situations improved. Paupers had to wear a badge with the letters BP (Brighthelmstone Pauper) proclaiming their poverty. There is a record of one woman, Susan Stone, refusing to do so, and she was thrown out the parish by the overseer.

Costing £100, the first workhouse in Brighton was opened in 1727 on the town hall site in Bartholomew's square. It was also called the townhouse or poorhouse. Bartholomews was small and could only accommodate up to 35 paupers, but it included a workroom with ten spinning wheels, a brew-house and bedrooms with 18 feather beds. In 1744, there were 20 inmates and the inventory included four "live hoggs". The inmates were expected to work if they were fit enough, to make their own clothes and prepare their own food. They also made mats which, when unsold, were taken to auction. Sweetened food or hot beverages were forbidden, although beer was allowed as it was considered a basic necessity. On leaving, inmates were often given one shilling a week for a short period and some new clothes.

In the 1740s inmates picked oakum – a chore inherited from prisons that would become the one most closely associated with workhouses. Old ropes, some of them tarred, some knotted, were unpicked and sold to ship-builders to seal ships' bottoms. Paupers had to twist and unravel the rope inch by inch with their bare hands [ii], which frequently left their fingers sore and bloody. During the winter months they collected and crushed oyster shells in a large iron mortar. The resulting mixture was sold to farmers for fertilizer or used for constructing paths in parks. When the Town Commissioners became responsible for maintaining local highways, paupers were reported to have been harnessed by ropes to muck and barrel water carts and used as town scavengers, removing animal dung and refuse

---

[i] Paraphrased from email received from M.J. Burchall 2/10/2011.

[ii] Sometimes a spike was used, which may account for the workhouse nickname, "The Spike."

4

from the street. They were treated like convicted criminals and there was a public outcry. This practice was stopped only to be replaced by the hauling of barrow loads of sand and pebbles from the seashore to the workhouse.

By 1777, Bartholomews could accommodate up to 70 inmates, including the sick, aged and young. It also included pauper lunatics:

> Ordered that the said Robert Burgh be taken into the townhouse and there confined under the care of the Governor, Sicklemore, it being represented by this Vestry that the said Robert Burgh is greatly deranged in his intellect and becomes very riotous and troublesome to many inhabitants of the town. [1]

On application, the Vestry also granted help in "kind and money" [outdoor relief] to families and individuals on very low wages who needed periodic assistance with clothing, coal, food, medical care or funeral expenses. In 1790, it voted "to allow two guineas towards clothing the children of James Patching and 2s per week for the better support of his family". [2] Outdoor relief was also given to families during the month their male was away on militia duty, widows, people whose parish was unknown and even to young girls who needed clothes in order to go out to service. Relief in "kind" was given in the form of tokens which could only be used in certain shops.

On the whole, the Vestry was flexible about relief and often paid money to unemployed relatives or friends for looking after children or old people. The alternative was to be ordered into the workhouse which was potentially more expensive if it was a whole family. If you were single, like Jane Tucknott, who applied for an allowance for clothing, the Vestry was less sympathetic. They refused her application "but it is ordered that if the said Jane Tucknott chooses to come into the poorhouse she shall be admitted." [3]

With relatively few ratepayers in the town, any unexpected expense was a blow to the parish finances. In November 1799, when ten Brighton fishermen fishing near Seaford were seized by two French privateers and carried off to France, the Vestry petitioned the Government to get their release and to restore them to their wives and families who otherwise would have become a long term burden to the parish. And in 1800, when the Hampshire Cavalry were disbanded in the town several soldiers were too sick to leave. To transport them to their parishes, which were a long way off, would have been expensive and if the soldiers couldn't get home the parish would have to keep them. So, the Vestry petitioned the secretary of war to put pressure on the soldiers' parishes to pay Brighton money to maintain them. The Vestry did not want the expense of a removal order to force the soldiers' parishes to take them back.

After 1795, a removal order was granted to a parish when one of the people living there (but who had settlement in another parish) had become, or was about to become, in need of poor relief. Before someone could be removed they had to be taken before a magistrate and examined as to their place of settlement. The settlement officer had the job of finding out which parish was responsible for paying the pauper's maintenance if he/she did not have proper residence. [i] This applied to outdoor relief [ii] as well as to relief in the workhouse. However, often the order was not acted upon because of the expense. [iii]

On the whole, Brighton, like many other parishes, tried to avoid any legal costs and preferred to contact the parish concerned and give them the option of either removing their pauper or paying the town to keep them in their workhouse. In 1829 the town's overseer wrote to Rev Walsh of Hailsham concerning a woman from there expressing the hope that the settlement can be agreed "without the expense and trouble of an order of removal" and asking to be informed about "the sentiments of your parish on this subject". [4] However, from 1835–1842 Brighton did apply for 570 removal orders for the removal of paupers to other parishes. During the same period, other parishes only applied for 82 paupers to be removed back to Brighton.

The settlement laws made sure that only the really desperate would apply for relief (if they did not have settlement) as they risked being

---

[i] There were various ways of obtaining settlement in a parish. It could be through marriage, length of residency, holding public office, employment through apprenticeship etc.

[ii] As late as July 1910 a woman and her four children receiving 5s outdoor relief a week were forcibly dragged by the settlement officer and police and taken to a workhouse near Norwich which had refused to pay their maintenance.

[iii] Brighton appears to have lost more appeals than it won, and often the expenses involved were more than a year's maintenance for the pauper in the workhouse.

removed from their families and friends to perhaps an area where they had not lived for many years and knew few people. The laws also discouraged the unemployed from seeking work outside their town. When the settlement laws were relaxed in 1846 and 1865, those claiming relief in Brighton dramatically increased.

*   *   *

The parish regarded vagrants and beggars as their biggest problem. At a Vestry meeting in 1796 it was decided that they were to be apprehended by the town crier who was to receive 1s per head for their capture and that they should be sent to the house of correction [i] in North Street, Lewes. Another target was men who abandoned their families and left the parish. Their names were publicly advertised and rewards were offered for their return to make them provide for their families. Unmarried mothers were also pressurized into giving the names of the fathers so they could be charged child maintenance.

Vagrancy and desertion were both treated as crimes because they were thought to deliberately foist costs onto the local community. The *Brighton Gazette* reported in 1821:

> The Bench expressed a determination of putting a stop to the infamous traffic carried on to the great injury of the parish, by the harbouring of vagrants, and several habitations were named to them, as notorious in that line. These are to be looked to, and rigidly proceeded against, as occasions may occur. One man, against whom a conviction was open, was searched for but could not be found. This man is the cripple and ingenious fan-cutter, etc. we have spoken of, and of whom, we conclude, we shall shortly have to speak again. [5]

The man, Thomas McDermot, who was described as having "no arms and hardly any legs", was frequently mentioned in the newspapers but was an elusive figure. In court, a woman calling herself his wife turned up instead of him and was warned that his house would be watched and that he

---

[i] Houses of correction were for the confinement of short term minor offenders for less than a year. Local magistrates could impose hard labour, whipping and a minimum diet on them.

would be fined forty shillings for every vagrant he could be proved to have harboured. In addition, if any of 'his' vagrants ended up claiming relief, the parish would claim back every farthing from him. A few months later one vagrant was given the choice of one month's hard labour or quitting the town for ever. A vagrant then had a right to stay one night in the workhouse and was usually given 1s in the morning.

Pursuit of men and women who deserted their families could be relentless. On one occasion a Signor Waldini, an entertainer and magician performing in Tottenham Court Road, London, was arrested during a performance. He was then brought back to Brighton where under his real name of Watson he was given three months imprisonment for abandoning his wife and three children four years earlier and for not sending them any money.

Orphaned or deserted children were, if suitable, apprenticed to local tradesmen who were paid a premium. In 1805, a large group of children from the Brighton workhouse – some as young as seven – were actually dispatched to "Blackborough" in Lancashire to work in the cotton mills as cheap labour. The children became known as pauper apprentices – by the late 1790s about a third of all workers in the cotton industry were pauper apprentices – and signed contracts that made them virtually the property of the factory owners. By sending them a long way away, the Vestry hoped the children would eventually settle there and not return to be a burden on the parish.

When two members of the Vestry sprang a surprise visit to the mills without informing the owners, Messrs Birch and Robinson, they found the children working fourteen hours a day, six days a week. They described this as 'far from laborious'. The children were poorly clad and the diet consisted of alternate days of milk and animal food and some very sour brown bread which the members found inedible. They only received two hours of education from a clergyman every Sunday. As there were 140 children, there was little chance of learning, and none of the children from Brighton had been taught how to write. The members complained about this and the bread in a letter to the owners who replied that "if the parish was not perfectly satisfied, they could take them away at a moment's notice". [6]

* * *

Between 1750 and 1821 Brighton's population increased from 2,000 to over 24,000. Ten years later it was 40,000. Of the resorts, only Bath grew faster. During this period Brighton was transformed from a decaying seafaring village into a prosperous resort by the well-documented influence of Dr Russell who promoted the town as a place for health cures; the Prince Regent's decision to set up a royal court which attracted fashionable society; improved transport communications and Brighton's proximity to London.

However, this great expansion came at a price. As the large seafront houses for the well-off sprang up, so too did the densely packed streets and homes behind them for the lower classes. To economise they were built using sand from the beach with the result that they constantly suffered from damp. These houses became the new slums of Brighton. Compared with industrial towns, Brighton's manufacturing sector was small and its population became mainly dependent upon seasonal expenditure by visitors for their employment. Often the visitors brought their own servants with them and took them away again when they left. All sectors of the employed population were vulnerable to seasonal unemployment and reduced earnings when the number of visitors fell. Barely surviving at the margins of respectable society, a large proportion of the population often depended on charity with the haunting fear of the workhouse always present. Soon the town's administration were overrun by people claiming relief as those unable to find work – often poor fishermen – became the paupers of Brighton.

In 1800 the workhouse in Bartholomews Square was enlarged to accommodate 150 inmates who now wore thick brown coarse uniforms and hats. It was often full, and wherever possible the parish tried to recoup the money from relatives who it believed should contribute towards the care of their family. In January 1806 an order was made for Richard Chapman, a stonemason, to contribute 4s a week towards the maintenance of his father, John Chapman, "a poor, impotent and aged person unable to maintain himself residing in the workhouse and a great burden". [7] Six months later the stonemason appealed against the order and won.

In 1810, responsibility for the workhouse passed from the Vestry to a board of thirty Directors and Guardians of the Poor elected by the town commissioners. In 1825, they were to be elected by the ratepayers. The new Guardians found the old workhouse contained a hundred people, a figure they immediately reduced to 82 on the grounds that it was a "workhouse not a playhouse" and should not "support idle and drunk fishermen". They accused the latter of using it as a winter retreat and of only leaving when the weather became milder. The diet then was beef, split peas, oatmeal, bread, cheese, beer but no fresh fruit or vegetables or hot drinks, and the new Board decided to reduce the consumption of bread (an expensive commodity during the post-Napoleonic period) and substitute rice or herring in its place.

By 1818, the Guardians had decided a new larger workhouse was needed to cope with the increasing number of paupers. But they also wanted to remove the old workhouse from the centre of town, as it was becoming an eyesore to its fashionable visitors. Two years later, a nine-acre site was purchased for £1,400 on the east side of Church Hill. It was situated just north of St Nicholas churchyard in Dyke Road and was surrounded by fields, with a soap factory and artillery range nearby and virtually no houses. The new building, costing £10,000, was designed by a London architect, William Mackie, and built by a local builder, John Cheesman. It could accommodate up to 450 inmates and commanded a view of the channel as far as Beachy Head to the east and the Isle of Wight to the west. If you were not in a workhouse, you might have described the view as picturesque.

The Bartholomews workhouse had lasted almost a hundred years, and few records exist about what life was like there for the inmates. One famous person there, though, was Phoebe Hessell – the reputed woman soldier – who arrived in 1797 and left in 1806 after being granted a pension by the Prince of Wales. She eventually died in 1821 at the age of 108. The same year a seven-year-old abandoned boy found begging at the door of the town hall was whipped with a birch and told to go away.

In the year that Phoebe Hessell died England was still recovering from the long years of the Napoleonic wars. The victory over Napoleon was a bitter-sweet victory for the nation's poor. Swelled by the vast hordes of demobilized soldiers, real economic and social distress became distinct realities as the unemployed and semi-employed numbers soared, particularly in the grain-producing counties of Kent, Essex and Sussex, which suffered a string of poor harvests. With little industrial development in the county, the Sussex labourer's only alternative to farm work was parish relief. Despite there being more seasonal work in Brighton, poverty and ill-health were just as prominent there as in the countryside. In 1821, the chemist of the town, a Mr W.M. Gregory, did a statistical analysis. He concluded that almost 50 per cent of children died before the age of eight, and that only 78 people out of a thousand had a chance of reaching old age.

Fig 1 1820s map showing the 'H' shape of the Church Hill Workhouse.

Chapter Two

A HOWLING WILDERNESS

In late September 1822, with the rain pouring down, ninety-five paupers were transferred from Bartholomews to the new workhouse at Church Hill. Because of the weather, those who were old, infirm or small children were conveyed in a covered van. So far up the hill and out of town was their new abode that some called it a "howling wilderness". As Bartholomews had averaged 150 paupers, it was clear that many paupers had decided to find other means of subsistence. They probably feared their relations might not visit them or that they might be subject to more rigid regulation.

Fig 2 Church Hill 1822 – John Erredge's History of Brighthelmstone *(1862).*

The new building was 191 feet long and had an 'H' shaped layout which divided the workhouse into sections. Inmates were segregated on the basis of their sex, age and whether they were capable of work or not. The authorities described it as "fitted up with every convenience requisite to ensure the cleanliness and health and comfort of its inmates". [1] There was also a school which provided compulsory lessons for younger children and intended to provide industrial training for the older boys [over 14], the idea being that they then might be started on an apprenticeship if the Guardians paid the premium.

The building included a committee room where new applicants could be examined, sick wards; a "lying-in"[i] ward and a nursery. There was a brewhouse, bakery and spacious laundry. Within its yards there were workshops for dressing flax, making shoes and clothes; door mat and sack-making; weaving and the carding of wool and a corn mill for grinding corn. The whole building was surrounded by a high prison-like wall. Outside a garden, a "parish farm" of six acres, was to be cultivated by inmates under the supervision of a gardener. Vegetables and fruit could be grown and sold in the market. A separate building for an infirmary with 90 beds was added in 1831 and later enlarged to contain 160.

The idea was to make the workhouse as independent and as self-sufficient as possible. There was also another aspiration: to reduce the poor rates. The *Brighton Gazette* was convinced that "the manufactories which are to be carried on will tend to lighten considerably the burden of their maintenance".[2] The Guardians produced their own rulebook for the new workhouse: Rules of the Brighthelmstone Work-House.[13] It declared that the governor:

> must be frugal in house-keeping, exact in his accounts, humane and attentive to the sick; firm and positive in his commands; but first consider they are just; he will have to bring into action all the various duties of a Christian, and on all occasions to "do as he would be done by;"…he must watch every action and not let any crime go unnoticed.

The matron was expected to make sure the children were "combed and washed" before breakfast and the sheets of the inmates changed every twenty-one days. She was also to see that "the girls who were capable of learning be instructed in knitting and plain work". In fact, they knitted all the stockings and made straw bonnets for the inmates. Both the governor and the matron were required to visit all the wards once a day to check they were clean and to go round at night to "see that all is quiet and that the fires and candles are extinguished".

On arrival the paupers were to be "admitted into a convenient apartment and washed with warm water" and have their hair cropped. Their clothes

---

[i] Maternity.

and possessions were taken away from them – to be given back on discharge – and they had to wear a plain uniform. The first bells of the day tolled at 5am summoning them to prayers, followed by half an hour for breakfast. In the summer, the able-bodied were expected to work from six in the morning to six at night and from daylight to dark in the winter with one hour for lunch. After supper, the inmates were read prayers by the governor or matron and then had to be in bed by 8pm in the winter and 9pm in the summer. They could only get leave with permission but then had to be back by bed-time. Visitors were permitted on two afternoons per week but were not "allowed to stay in the house longer than is absolutely necessary".

No inmates could be discharged without the permission of the Guardians. Neither could a woman giving birth in the workhouse be discharged before the child was one year old. The punishments for transgressions included "hard labour, solitary confinement, abatement of diet [bread and water] or distinction of dress, at the discretion of the Guardians or the assistant overseer". They could also be sent before a magistrate. If any inmate felt he was being treated or punished unfairly, he/she could appeal to the Guardians at their next meeting.

The rulebook also included a "Weekly Bill Of Fare" which, surprisingly, shows that even children received beer as part of their daily diet. (This may have been more to do with safety than generosity, for, with water supplies often being contaminated and the fear of cholera, beer was a lot safer and considered to be a basic necessity.) In addition the older men received a pint of beer at 11am, and men that worked at the well pumping water also received an extra pint. But it was the quality of food rather than the quantity that made workhouse food notorious. As the table overleaf shows, gruel – a thin oatmeal porridge made with water and unsweetened with milk or sugar – came to symbolize the poverty of the diet.

The Guardians particularly favoured gruel. Containing less oatmeal than porridge, it was cheap, easy to prepare and was, although completely unappetizing, filling. But after only two weeks, the women and old men protested so much about the gruel and milk porridge for breakfast and supper that the Guardians decided they should only have it for breakfast. Supper was changed to bread and butter or cheese every day.

Church Hill got off to an inauspicious start when the governor, John Hayward, disappeared after a few days. His replacement, a Mr Nuttal, only lasted a few weeks before he was dismissed for immoral conduct. He was replaced by the assistant-governor, Samuel Thorncroft, who was only 23 years old and for the first few weeks was, surprisingly, to be under the supervision of John Cheesman, the builder who later became a Guardian. And of all the figures involved in the implementation of the Poor Law in Brighton, it would be Thorncroft who would controversially dominate it for almost fifty years. For the next twelve years he remained at Church Hill before taking on the post of assistant-overseer, replacing John Harper who was sacked, although not prosecuted, for fraud.

WEEKLY BILL OF FARE.

	Breakfast.	Dinner.	Supper.
Sunday.............	Milk Porridge	Boiled Beef or Pork	Cheese or Butter.
Monday............	Gruel.............	Pease Soup made with the preceding day's liquor, and 1lb. of fresh beef to 4qts. of liquor....	Milk Porridge.
Tuesday.......	Milk Porridge	Beef Pudding...........	Cheese or Butter.
Wednesday....... ..	Gruel.............	Boiled Beef.... ....[day.	Milk Porridge.
Thursday......	Milk Porridge	Pease Soup, same as on Mon-	Cheese or Butter.
Friday.......... ..	Gruel.............	Meat Pudding.	Milk Porridge.
Saturday........ ..	Milk Porridge	Irish Stew.......	Gruel.

With Bread and proper Vegetables in season every day.

Adults allowed one pint of Beer per day for Dinner, and Children half-a-pint : and also the same quantity for Supper when they have Bread and Cheese.

Christmas Day.. .Roast Beef & Plum Pudding.	✴	Midsummer Day....Pork & Beans (if any).
Good Friday......Bunns.	✴	Michaelmas Day .... Roast Pork.

In 1826, Church Hill was still sometimes referred to as the "Poor House" although some of the Guardians – a mixture of shopkeepers, landlords and tradesmen – had other ideas about what it should be. The following year the *Brighton Gazette*, revealed that they had secretly, at a late night meeting with few members present, decided to get a treadmill for the workhouse. It called it:

…a cruel, unequal, and unjust punishment on such unfortunate persons as might be placed under their hard hands by the pressure of the times, whose last resource is the workhouse, who are driven for temporary relief to the charity of their fellow townsmen and fellow Christians.

A committee appointed by the Guardians had visited the house of correction in Lewes and Brixton Prison to see how a treadmill worked. However, when the Brighton press got wind of this "improvement" it was hurriedly dropped in its embryo state by the committee which claimed it had not actually ordered one. But the next year it received a letter from a solicitor representing a treadmill maker of Greenwich demanding £555 for a treadmill that had been ordered! Initially the committee denied it, until one of its members owned up and admitted that "a kind of order" had been made. The newspaper article calculated that the Guardians would have needed to spend another £1,500 on erecting a house and building for the treadmill. It advised the Guardians to "stick to their cucumber and asparagus beds, but not to inflict on the parish an expenditure of £2,000 to incur a positive loss; by preparing as instruments of torture which some of themselves or children may perhaps be doomed to be punished with, at the instance of some more fortunate Guardians than themselves".

However, the newspaper did not object to it merely on economic grounds:

> …we detest it on principle. We have an objection to treadmills even in prisons, because the punishment is much more severe to some men, than it is to others…It is alright for the young and fit but not for the elderly who have been sedentary who have suffered dreadfully. To have tread-mills in poor houses is most objectionable on every ground. Firstly, poor houses are not houses of correction, but what their name implies:- houses of asylum for the poor. If punishment is be to be inflicted on any person, however depraved, let him have a public hearing before magistrates, and if deserving of it, let him be sent to a House of Correction.
>
> We prefer magistrates to the ungracious mode too frequently practiced by an upstart, purse-proud Jack-in-office. We have ourselves been often struck with the kindness shown to poor ragged prisoners, arraigned perhaps for great crimes, when compared to the rude and unfeeling rebuff a wretched woman supplicant for relief has often received from a hard-hearted overseer. Merely because a man is reduced to a state of destitution, he is to be sentenced to the degradation of the torture mill at the caprice of some Guardian who has perhaps scarcely reached manhood. Who has never been beyond the bounds of his own county and who has never experienced the sorrows of poverty. Who is unfitted by his education, by his manners, by his sphere of life, by his very inexperience, to be a judge? Will any one dare affirm that such a man… with all his prejudices and ignorancies, all the self-importance of a narrow selvish mind, operating in full vigour, ought to have this power? Ought such a man to be invested with a power to condemn others, and for no crime but poverty, to a Tread-mill?!!!

The article concluded by asking by what right had the Guardians in expending money "wrung from the hard hand of industry for the relief of the destitute in such a way as this? In a way disgraceful to themselves, dishonourable to the parish, and calamitous to the poor?!!!" Surprisingly, the *Brighton Gazette,* far from being a radical newspaper was a conservative one. [4] The Guardians cancelled the order and probably settled with the treadmill maker out of court.

The *Gazette* reporter's belief that magistrates were often more sympathetic to paupers than the Guardians were was sometimes borne out by their actions. Magistrates "were a sort of court of appeal against the refusal of relief by some stoney-hearted parish official". [5] On one occasion a married woman with seven children was refused outdoor relief despite claiming that her husband's 15s a week was not enough to live on. The Guardians ordered her and her children into the workhouse. However, the magistrates[i] ruled against this and ordered the Guardians to give her outdoor relief. On the other hand, if the appeal by the pauper failed, the magistrates could punish them. Later, when local fishermen went as far away as Plymouth to catch mackerel, the magistrates and Guardians often clashed about whether it was legitimate or not to charge the fishermen with running away and abandoning their families to the parish. The magistrates tended to support the idea that their families should not be broken up and sent to the workhouse but should be given temporary outdoor relief and the fishermen repay the money when they returned. Often the Guardians wanted the families to be sent straight to the workhouse and the returning fishermen arrested.

For the next three years, from 1826-28, the workhouse substantially increased its manufacturing output of sacks, rope, straw bonnets etc. and almost doubled their sales. Some of the work was done by able-bodied paupers with families on outdoor relief. They were made to come in daily but did not have to live in. The *Gazette* published the accounts for this period – see Appendix 1 – because it wanted to let the inhabitants know what products were being sold there.

---

[i] This power was taken from them by the 1834 New Poor Law Act.

The newspaper declared:

> … the employment of the inmates is of the utmost consequence in order to stimulate them to acts of industry, as well as to correct idle habits, and materially assists in maintaining regularity and good discipline. [6]

In this period, every Monday evening the thirty Guardians met in the magistrates' room at the town hall to interview applicants for relief. The paupers were called in individually to state their case and were either granted relief the next day or a committee was appointed to examine their statement. A foreign visitor, Ollapod Ochlensloeger, in a letter to a friend, described the waiting room the applicants were kept in. It was:

> …a mean, low kind of shed, covered with red tiles, about twenty feet high to the ridge of the roof which slopes to the street. The interior is as miserable looking a place as it is possible to conceive. There is but one window, near the roof, no ceiling, and a brick floor, and but one bench against the wall. This room is frequently used as a "dead house" for persons who have been accidentally killed, and sometimes as many as eight or nine bodies have been put there together…It is in this room that the paupers wait their turns to apply for relief. The hour of application is six oclock, after which the door is locked and no more are admitted that night. You must possess greater powers of imagination than I pretend to lay claim to, if you can conceive anything more distressing or disgusting than the fact of men and women of every age being thus shut up from the above hour till perhaps 11 or 12 at night, or later. Fishermen, labourers, women with child, diseased and hale, are indiscriminately mixed together… as many as one hundred have been waiting for relief in one night. And this, gracious God! in a town which is made the seat of pleasure for the affluent and luxurious. [7]

As the 1820s ended, the national tensions over political reform and the plight of the agricultural worker thrown into unemployment by enclosure and industrialization threatened to destabilize society. The Brighton Guardians were not unaffected. On one occasion, during a meeting, several windows of their board room were broken by stones thrown by an angry mob. Two men were arrested and put in a dungeon known as 'The Black Hole' – located just behind the town hall – and another bound over to keep the peace. One of the Guardians exclaimed that "our lives are in danger". In exchange for outdoor relief, 200–300 paupers were employed at digging holes at The Level – a public park – and 40 were used to collect and break stones on the beach. More controversially, occasionally pauper labour was auctioned off to local farmers at wages which undercut those of the agricultural worker, further worsening his conditions.

* * *

By 1832, with national relief costs spiralling out of control, especially in Sussex where it was twice the national average, the government set up a Royal Commission of Enquiry into workhouses. The investigation was based on two premises: that outdoor relief was ruining the country and that workhouses were ineffectively run by the parishes. The Commission believed that pauperism arose from fraud, indolence or improvidence and that the cause of destitution was the moral fault of the individual. In the long term it recommended that there should be separate institutions: for able-bodied men, for able-bodied women, for the aged, for the sick and for children. In reality, this never happened.

The result of the enquiry was the 1834 Poor Law Amendment Act, which recommended the gradual abolition of outdoor relief. Its chief target was the able-bodied claimant – physically fit and aged 16–70. From now on, if he/she wanted relief they would have to enter the workhouse with their family and be segregated from their children and spouses. Outdoor relief was only to be granted in cases of sudden and urgent necessity, sickness or to meet funeral expenses.

Economy and discomfort were to be the new watchwords. Workhouses were not to be more comfortable than paupers' own homes and inmates were to wear prison style uniforms and do hard and tedious work. There were to be six model diets of 137–182 ounces of solid food per week, on the whole less than that received in prison. Women were to receive less bread and meat than men. The workhouse 'test' was that anyone willing to accept a place inside one must be lacking the strength of character to survive outside. Above all, "the workhouse should be a place of hardship, of coarse fare, of degradation and humility; it should be administered with strictness, with severity; it should be as repulsive as is consistent with humanity[i]". [8]

---

[i] A letter from Rev H.H. Milman in 1832 to Edwin Chadwick, who sat on the Commission of Enquiry.

Some saw an irony in the fact that in the same year as the Act, Britain abolished slavery in its colonies. Now there appeared to be a new kind of enslavement.

The Act allowed the uniting of several parishes into Unions[i], each with its own workhouse. As the Brighton Guardians had built a new one only twelve years earlier, they were against it. They also objected to being supervised by "autocratic" Poor Law Commissioners, men with often a legal background, appointed by the Government – but not directly responsible to Parliament – whose assistant commissioners would regularly visit to supervise the new system. The Guardians wanted no interference in the dietary or management of Church Hill. In addition, they did not want to abolish outdoor relief in money completely, because it would have affected local businesses which depended on it. Finally, they argued that their workhouse was not large enough to contain all the town's paupers in times of economic hardship. The Vestry called the Act "uncalled for and calculated to cause great and general dissatisfaction and discord among all classes of the inhabitants".[9] Brighton sent in a petition to the Commons claiming that they had already saved money under the old law without oppressing the poor.[ii]

By 1836 all the parishes of East Sussex, with the exception of Brighton, had combined to form Poor Law Unions. However, Brighton, with its own workhouse already conforming to many of the requirements of the new act, was allowed to carry on as before, administered under a local act. For example, already (as far as possible) the sexes and ages were separated, and even categories within the sexes, such as expectant unmarried women, had their own ward. In the early days of Church Hill several small cottages had also been built in its yards where old couples could live together. After a few years though, as it became more crowded, they were knocked down or used for other purposes. So, although the Guardians were in principle against old couples being separated, it became inevitable.

From 1834–39 the *Times* reported almost every week the cruelty of the New Poor Law to the agricultural worker. In the Sussex parish of Cowfold, where the poor had previously received 1s per week, 10s a year for wood

---

[i] Over 15,000 parishes were merged into 600 Unions.

[ii] Brighton's poor rates had gone down from £28,323 13s in 1832 to £15,829 9s 8d in 1834.

and £1 for rent, they now only received a gallon of flour a week for their outdoor relief. Popular protest against the new law was particularly strong in the county. The red flag was hoisted above the workhouses at Seaford and Alfriston along with banners declaring "Death or Liberty". At Eastbourne an attempt was made to burn the workhouse down, and throughout the county relieving officers and workhouse guardians were attacked. In November 1834 there was a rising of agricultural labourers in Goring, and in September 1835, a riot in the Steyning workhouse. The labourers were punished particularly severely for any transgression. That year John Coleman, only fourteen years of age, was transported for seven years for stealing a dead rabbit worth one shilling. These protests must be seen within the wider context of the working classes venting their anger over industrialization and the ruling classes needing to re-assert their authority.

Opposition to the New Poor Law came from many quarters. The medical profession, through the mouthpiece of the *Lancet*, predicted that lumping the poor altogether in large institutions would increase sickness and mortality. It believed sickness was one of the most active causes of pauperism A few years after the law came into force, the medical journal was claiming that the annual death rate in workhouses was over 20 per cent as opposed to 1½ per cent in prisons, and that the law:

> …was more revolting in its results than anything that has been witnessed in England for many centuries…It is all machinery…a faceless machinery; it neither has hands to help…nor eyes to see the poor and afflicted; it has no living blood in its arteries, no throbbing heart, no voice of tenderness, no human soul. God never made it; humanity never blessed it. [10]

Ironically, the New Poor Law was successfully resisted only in places where the Guardians were against it (as in Brighton), rather than by any violent disturbances by the poor. There were public meetings in the town, where the new law was seen as a way of making savings by oppressing the poor. Under the new standardized guidelines you could be punished for speaking to your wife. One Brighton Guardian, Mr Nute, was cheered at a meeting when he said that "should misfortune bring him to the workhouse he would, if he had a pistol in his hand, blow out the brains of the first man who attempted to separate him from his wife". [11]

Public meetings against the New Poor Law in the town drew huge audiences. In 1841, a thousand people crammed into the town hall to protest. One of the speakers, a Chartist, declared that "the system was one of the effects of a want of representation of the people and that nothing but 'universal suffrage' would remove the evils under which they laboured".[12] In the event, Brighton continued to provide discretionary outdoor relief partly in money and partly in kind well after the Poor Law was abolished in the twentieth century.

Under the new workhouse system there were to be seven categories:

Men infirm through age or any other cause
Able-bodied males over fifteen
Boys from seven to fifteen
Women infirm through age or any other cause
Able-bodied girls over fifteen
Girls from seven to fifteen
Children under seven

The last category was particularly poignant, for under the old legislation a child under seven could not be forcibly separated from its parent. It could now.

* * *

With the Brighton Guardians suspicious of any interference, in March 1836 William Hawley, the assistant commissioner responsible for introducing the new law in Sussex, visited Church Hill. He reported that:

…weaving manufacture only provides employment for a few hands…They [the hands] should be seeking an honest and independent livelihood elsewhere. Thirty able-bodied paupers cultivate the "parish farm" …as this is merely day work, and by no means of an uncomfortable nature, it results that numbers of able-bodied paupers are the constant inmates of the house. Another inducement to their sojourn here, is also to be found in one of the highest and most objectionable dietaries I have hitherto observed. [13]

The *Brighton Guardian* alleged the following conversation during his visit:

> He [Hawley] asked what savoury dish he smelt; the Governor replied "Pudding; if you'll walk this way, Sir, I'll show you the room." "Why, who is dining?" asked he, "The paupers, Sir". "Paupers dining? What have they got?"
>   "Beef steak puddings, Sir".
>   "Beef steak puddings for paupers!" exclaimed he; "good God I never heard such a thing in my life. Monstrous. What! Think of giving paupers beef steak puddings?"
>   "Yes, Sir", replied the attendant, "we have done so for a very long period and the poor have been very satisfied and what is more, the parish have been satisfied too; therefore we see no reason to depart from that practice."[14]

Hawley recorded that Brighton was still offering outdoor relief – partly in kind and money – to married people and the aged poor. It was generally only using the workhouse 'test' for single people rather than the Commission's preference that all able-bodied paupers and their families should be ordered into the workhouse. He found that, out of a population of 40,000, Brighton had over 2,000 people on oudoor relief [i] and 403 inmates in its workhouse. Hawley concluded that the Brighton Guardians had "no sufficient cause" to not implement the Commission's rules and regulations for the "future ordering of relief in the parish".

Under the Commission's guidelines food had to be weighed and the meat reduced, but for the time being Brighton resisted. One Guardian, Mr Streeter, said that he would like to see the Commissioners "placed upon their own diet for six months". [15] Another, Mr Lewis, at the mention of their name, exclaimed: "Oh pray, do not mention the Poor Law Commission. I like the poor much better than them". [16] The Commission also tried to discourage parishes and Unions from providing the traditional roast beef and plum pudding at Christmas, but this was fiercely and successfully resisted.

However, it was not long before the weighing of food and a reduction in diet did take place at Church Hill. Soon 6oz and 5oz of bread plus gruel

---

[i] 109 able-bodied men; 156 wives of able-bodied men; 653 children of able-bodied men; 177 aged infirm men; 214 aged infirm women; 214 widows; and 525 parish children.

were given to male and female inmates respectively every breakfast. For dinner, the meat was reduced to three cold meat days, three days of soup and one day of suet pudding. Supper was bread and cheese four days a week and broth on the other days. Only the sick or inmates over 60 were given extras of tea and butter.

No. 4.—DIETARY for ABLE-BODIED PAUPERS of both SEXES.

		BREAKFAST.		DINNER.					SUPPER.	
—		Bread.	Gruel.	Pickled Pork, or Bacon, with Vegetables.	Soup.	Bread.	Meat Pudding, with Vegetables.	Rice or Suet Pudding, with Vegetables.	Bread.	Cheese.
		oz.	pints.	oz.	pints.	oz.	oz.	oz.	oz.	oz.
Sunday	Men	8	1½	-	2	6	-	-	6	2
	Women	6	1½	-	1½	5	-	-	5	1½
Monday	Men	8	1½	-	-	-	-	12	6	2
	Women	6	1½	-	-	-	-	10	5	1½
Tuesday	Men	8	1½	-	2	6	-	-	6	2
	Women	6	1½	-	1½	5	-	-	5	1½
Wednesday	Men	8	1½	6	-	-	-	-	6	2
	Women	6	1½	5	-	-	-	-	5	1½
Thursday	Men	8	1½	-	-	-	-	12	6	2
	Women	6	1½	-	-	-	-	10	5	1½
Friday	Men	8	1½	-	2	6	-	-	6	2
	Women	6	1½	-	1½	5	-	-	5	1½
Saturday	Men	8	1½	-	-	-	12	-	6	2
	Women	6	1½	-	-	-	10	-	5	1½

The vegetables are not included in the weight specified, which is for the meat when cooked.
If it be thought desirable, half an ounce of butter may be given to the women in lieu of cheese, for supper.
Old people of 60 years of age and upwards may be allowed one ounce of tea, five ounces of butter, and seven ounces of sugar per week, in lieu of gruel for breakfast, if deemed expedient to make this change.
Children under nine years of age to be dieted at discretion; above nine, to be allowed the same quantities as women.
Sick to be dieted as directed by the medical officer.

Fig 4. One of the official six dietary sheets under the New Poor Law Amendment Act. Gruel and bread dominated, and any meat was boiled. Eating it was a particularly difficult chore for inmates with poor teeth.

The letter below, published by the *Brighton Patriot* [17] in 1837 with the title 'A Workhouse Bastille' ,may have been written in Church Hill and reflected the reduction in diet. It was thrown out of a workhouse window by Ann Stapley and was addressed to her husband, Henry, who had been sent to prison:

My dear husband,

I have rote a few lines and hope they will find you quite well. The children are better than they was altho Caroline is very poorley and has a little port wine and the doctor ordered a half pint porter a day for me. I am better than I was.

He said I was very weak. We have not so much to eat as we had when you was heare. We have 5 oz of bread in the morning and half an ounce of butter and 6 oz of bread at noon and one oz of cheese and 5 oz at night and cheese with as much water as we choose. The children would eat more if they could have it. The children often cry for bread heare and the mothers have none to give. We have so little our elizea asked me for bread and cheese long before daylight this morning. We have 10 oz of pudding too days a week. Mrs Clapson has lost her youngest child, Mary…Mrs Miller is very ill. Several children are as bad as bad as can be alive. There has been 2 boks [books] made since you was heare. One is the black book. If we do a fault or will not work when master tell us it is put down in this bok and took up before the rouges [magistrates] every Friday and we are to be punished as they think proper and there is a new lock and boult put on the women's black hole and if we disobey what master say or speak what he calls sausy to him he says don't say more I will shut you up. We really have not strength to work. Not more than quarter lb of meat in five weeks…

Ann Stapley finished her letter by saying that the next time she left she would rather beg than return.

In 1839, the Commission also criticized the Guardians for not providing sick relief to a man, "P", from Chailey, who was living in Brighton, and for their medical officer's exorbitant charges. There had been a general understanding that although a parish did not have to pay for the relief of non-residents, it did pay for their medical treatment. The Brighton Guardians responded angrily:

…affording all such paupers medical relief indiscriminately at the expense of this Parish is offering a premium to the surrounding parishes to send their paupers to this place, to live, at the same time that it [the Commission] is countenancing a practice condemned by the Commission, namely that of giving relief to non-resident paupers, and if sick die in this Parish, the additional expense is incurred of burying them, as has been the case with "P", belonging to and relieved by the Chailey Union. They have refused to bury their paupers in Brighton. This is a large burden on the ratepayers of Brighton and contrary to the principle that each Parish should support its own poor…The allegation that these heavy medical charges are made to supplement the inadequate remuneration of the medical officer from other sources is equally without foundation. [18]

* * *

If one looks at just one year – 1836 – in the life of Church Hill, it was full of incidents reported by the local newspapers. In January, in freezing temperatures, three inmates refused to work because the fire was not lit (after they had returned from work), and they threatened the governor, Callington, who had replaced Thorncroft in 1834. They were given 21 days hard labour in the house of correction at Lewes, where they would be expected to spend long hours on a treadmill driving a corn mill. In the same month a workhouse girl was snatched by gypsies. In February there were complaints that the bodies of paupers were brought for internment in a vegetable cart. In March, there were rumours that some of the overseers had written to the Poor Law Board complaining about the new workhouse diet. A Guardian, Paul Hewitt, a lodging house keeper, responded by proclaiming: "They [the Guardians] could treat their paupers as they liked".

In April, George Martin applied for relief for himself. He was told to come to the workhouse with his wife and three children. He took his children there, had dinner and then absconded. He was arrested and brought before the bench. Martin told them he wanted to work but did not want to be separated from his wife. He was sentenced to three months on the treadmill at the house of correction.

In May, Callington had his annual salary increased from £60 to £80. One Guardian, Patching, objected and wanted to have a committee to enquire into his past conduct as he had heard "he had a very violent temper and was cruel to the inmates". The year before, Callington had refused to admit a young pregnant woman on a cold November night. When he had eventually let her in, she had had a child but it had died soon afterwards. Not long after he had been found guilty of brutally beating an eleven-year-old boy called Lewis with a thick stick. A vote was taken, 12 for and 12 against Callington. The chairman decided to support Callington who, surprisingly, requested an enquiry himself to "stop the innuendoes". Thinking he had been accepted for another job at twice the salary, he resigned. A few days later when the new job failed to materialize he asked for his job back, but after another close vote his original resignation was accepted. Despite being married with two children, John Bartlett, a relieving officer, was appointed. Being single was a usual requirement.

In June, a Guardian complained about the religious instruction at the workhouse, claiming that "the inmates were called upon to attend more religious exercise on a Sunday than their understandings could bear".

Apart from twenty minutes of prayers before breakfast, they afterwards had to listen to the schoolmaster, mounted on a rostrum for at least three hours, and only then could they attend their own church services outside. Another Guardian said the sermon had "tired him to death" and he thought it would never end. A motion to have shorter sermons was carried. Despite the length of religious instruction at the workhouse, it seems to have made little impact on the children. When tested, none of them could repeat the Lord's Prayer or knew why it was called that. Only eight out of eighty could write properly.

The major talking point of the year was the question of whether a chaplain should be appointed. Previously, visiting clergy had taken the services, but now the Poor Law Commission were putting pressure on Brighton to appoint a permanent one. In July, contrary to public expectation, Rev Henry Mortlock was appointed at £100 a year. There was a public outcry, as many felt that the vicar of Brighton, Rev Henry Wagner, should pay the salary out of his own income, which was over a thousand pounds a year. Mortlock was dismissed amid an acrimonious debate about who should be paying his salary, but he decided to carry on with his duties and was temporarily paid by Wagner. To prove his worth, Mortlock let his chaplain's journal for a two week period be published in the *Gazette*. [19] Below are extracts:

August 4th Thursday, from 2 to half-past 4; visited the sick and paid particular attention to S _____ and others, who seem to be in a dying state, and found both in the infirmary and workhouse, the greatest attention and readiness to hear the word of God. Read the Scriptures, expounded and concluded with prayer.

August 6th Saturday, from seven to a quarter before nine; visited two women in apparently dying state; also a poor widow and a sick child; both died in the course of the night; also, at the request of the matron, visited an aged woman in the workhouse.

August 7th Sunday, Named a child Philadelphia, daughter of _____, a single woman, at the request of the matron, in consequence of her considering it to be dangerously ill.

August 10th Wednesday, from half-past eight to nine, morning prayers and exposition of Scripture in the boys' school-room… found them exceedingly attentive and thankful for extra service. Weekly lecture, Epistle to Phillipians.

August 13th Saturday, From nine to ten; visited the sick, especially Mrs_____, for the last time. She expressed much hope at acceptance with God through faith in a crucified Redeemer, and, I verily believe, died a sincere Christian. She expressed to me in the ward much comfort from the ministrations of the word of God and prayer.

August 14th Sunday,... From half-past ten a.m. to half-past one p.m.; visited the girls' school; also read prayers and the Scriptures with short exposition in lying-in ward; the same with many aged persons confined to their rooms up-stairs...From five to seven, visited the sick, and also performed service in the infirmary.

The following year Mortlock, a dedicated[i] man, resigned due to ill health and died at the age of 47 leaving a wife and seven children. He was replaced by Rev Spencer Drummond who started to be paid by the Guardians.

In September, the *Times* reported that a policeman in Brighton, on hearing the rattle of chains in the town centre, found a shaven headed man with his legs in fetters riveted by a chain to an iron band around his waist. In his pocket he had a pair of handcuffs. His name was Thomas Tidy, a twenty-six-year-old candle seller. When he was taken before the magistrates he explained he had broken out from the Dorking workhouse where he had been chained up for the last seven years. The magistrates thought he was insane and sent him temporarily to Church Hill. They then complained to the Poor Law Commissioners about the Dorking workhouse, as by law a dangerous lunatic should have been sent to a lunatic asylum within fourteen days rather than be chained up in a workhouse.

In November, John Hedgecock, a fourteen-year-old workhouse boy, was brought before the bench for absconding and was given twenty-one days in the house of correction. A week later another inmate, Robert Pentecost, was before the bench for refusing to wear a pair of shoes – made in the shoemaker's shop – which hurt his feet. He went sixty hours without food as punishment, still refused and was given slippers to wear but wore them out. While the governor was absent he laughed at the clergyman during prayers. He told the bench he had laughed because his stomach was empty: "I have a piece of beef as big as a walnut to do my work upon – I could eat a pound of beef. (laughter)". He was given 14 days' hard labour.

---

[i] On being told that he was to receive no salary, Mortlock allegedly told the governor: "I shall not leave you, Mr Bartlett. I care nothing about salary in comparison of immortal souls." (*Evangelical Magazine and Missionary Chronicle*, volume two.)

In December, a pauper woman, Mary Warmington, on relief in the community, claimed she was carrying the child of the assistant overseer, Samuel Thorncroft. She had lost her husband in 1835 and Thorncroft had helped her to open a greengrocer's. In June he had started to invite her to his home and had visited her at suspicious times of the night. When she fell on hard times he managed to get her 7s relief money a week. Witnesses claim to have seen him reading a book to her – *The Means to Avoid Pregnancy*. When she told him she was pregnant he threatened to have her money stopped. Thorncroft was charged in court for failing to support a "female bastard child", but was acquitted through lack of evidence despite one of the female witnesses claiming that Thorncroft was "such a man to kiss and pull you about". The Poor Law Commissioners wanted him to be suspended but the Guardians refused. Assistant overseers and relieving officers had tremendous power in the community. They had the power – through their recommendation to the Guardians – to decide whether a pauper should be admitted into the workhouse or how much, if any, outdoor relief they should receive.

The year ended with terrible snowstorms and an influenza epidemic breaking out in Brighton where a General Relief Fund was set up to raise money for the distribution of food, clothing and coals to the needy. "The newspapers reported that persons of all rank and age, and of both sexes, suffered under its blighting effect till all business, and even domestic duties, sustained serious interruption". [20] Back at the workhouse, the governor, Bartlett, claimed he was overrun by new admissions and said he often found himself working till 10pm.

In this period the *Brighton Herald* was declaring that "nothing can be so wretched, nothing so degrading, as the present state of the poor". [21] During the winter months bricklayers, carpenters, labourers and other workmen were often unable to work because of the snow and frost, and became paupers. In the past as many as 500 paupers on outdoor relief had been put to work by the parish, including a hundred working on the sea wall at Marine Parade. However, by the end of 1836, under pressure from the Poor Law Commission to discontinue outdoor relief to able-bodied paupers, only fifty were employed on parish work until a place could be found for them in the workhouse. The Guardians were mindful that cheap pauper labour could undermine the ordinary labourer, and they were heavily criticized for using it to excavate the Victoria wing of the Royal Sussex

County Hospital. As outdoor poverty grew, in January 1837 the Guardians started to raise subscriptions for a soup fund and to sell soup at a penny for two pints.

Although the workhouse was no longer at the town hall site, applicants for outdoor relief still had to go there and be examined by the Guardians:

> Scores of the very lowest class of persons i.e. men, women, children, young boys and girls, have been huddled together for hours at night, indulging in loose and licentious gossip; coming again the next morning sometimes to receive a negative answer. [22]

If relief was granted, even the old and the sick had to walk up the hill to Church Hill to collect it. Outdoor relief in kind often meant a loaf of bread for each child and some meat. It was rumoured that sometimes the bread was swapped for potatoes or even gin. A minority of Guardians did favour all outdoor relief being paid in money so that a pauper could spend it how he wished. However, often a pauper was not given any food until after he had worked and, as the above newspaper noted, "it was heart-breaking to be working and starving".

Although in theory paupers could leave the workhouse as long as they gave reasonable notice, in practice they were unlikely to be given permission if there was a danger of their becoming a public nuisance or of coming back too soon. In 1835 an elderly pauper appeared before the magistrates complaining that he was being kept a prisoner in the workhouse. Thorncroft told them that he was always drunk and extremely discontented:

> Pauper: How can that be? I've took a hoath against liquor. I don't drink nothing now.
> Magistrate: Why, man! You are half drunk now. Case dismissed.(*idem.*)

And the following year a female inmate who absconded with her workhouse clothes was also brought before the magistrates. She had slipped out and had joined a passing funeral cortege:

> Magistrate: So you went out with parish clothes on?
> Pauper: Yes, to be sure I did. You wouldn't have me go out naked, would you?
> Magistrate: Why did you go out at all?
> Pauper: I asked to go out and they wouldn't let me. I've been there these six years and can never get out.

Magistrate: No, not till you can get your own living.

(The Governor, Bartlett, explained that she had gone out before and had sold her clothes).

Magistrate: You should be sent to Botany Bay.

Pauper: Well, I'd as soon be there as remain here.

Magistrate: Three months House of Correction! [23]

A few months later it was discovered that an inmate, Charles Willard, with the help of friends on the outside, had removed stones from a workhouse wall and replaced them with bricks, thereby forming a series of steps. Willard was caught returning drunk at 4am one morning and received twenty-one days in the house of correction. The following year the walls were heightened to stop inmates talking to outsiders, boys passing provisions to their friends and people coming in just for dinner!

However bad conditions were in the workhouse, they were often worse outside. During this period a young boy, John Chandler, living in a "fearfully cold" attic with his parents, later recalled:

> I well remember how I used to go up North Street and look into the confectioners shops and squeeze my nose against the windows and long for a piece of bread, and then I would stand over the areas [grilles] and smell the cooking below. This was all I got for I had to go away with an empty belly...Sometimes I would pick up a piece of orange peel which I thought was a treat. [24]

In 1835, four women were sent to prison for stealing cinders from an ash heap near Brunswick Terrace. Five years later it was reported that in the neighbourhood of Edward Street and Church Street, "hundreds and hundreds of poor children were actually famishing from cold and starvation, and were seen five and six together endeavouring to impart heat to each other upon a wretched parcel of straw in the corner of some miserable garret". [25] Although the numbers at Church Hill had increased to over 500, in 1841 the *Brighton Herald* believed "the poor have a greater fear of the workhouse than ever before. They would rather die than go into it". [26]

Chapter Three

THE GUARDIANS AND THE
CHILDREN OF THE WORKHOUSE

The Brighton Guardians were mainly local successful tradesmen, businessmen and occasionally "gentlemen". Thirty were elected every April [i] by the ratepayers and could only stand if they had property worth at least £25, later raised to £30 in the 1880s. Some *ex-officio* dignitaries such as the vicar of Brighton, Henry Wagner, were appointed. The Guardians automatically lost their position if they failed to attend a meeting for more than six months, were made bankrupt, moved outside the parish or if they themselves became paupers. They met weekly or fortnightly. Their chief duties were the appointment of salaried officers, settling relief applications, the supervision of the workhouse and the expenditure though not the collection of the poor rate. [ii] Individual Guardians could not visit the "house" without the governor's permission.

Their public face was the clerk to the Guardians, who often had a legal background and was usually their most educated and highest paid employee. The clerks knew the legal niceties and loopholes and dealt with all the correspondence with the Poor Law Commission [later Board] and with any other bodies or individuals, including inmate and staff complaints. Whatever the decisions the Guardians came to, it was the clerk who publicly represented them. Often, after consulting with the Board's solicitor, he would advise the Guardians about what they could or could not do. It was a demanding and pressurized job. In 1858, Robert Becher, the clerk for twenty years, went to Brussels for a holiday and seemed reluctant to come back. Despite earning the huge sum of £400 – although from this he had to pay assistants – he had somehow run up debts of nearly £5,000 in the town, including £300 to a Guardian. Becher was dismissed and made bankrupt,

---

[i] Increased to 36 in 1894.

[ii] They did take over its collection in 1888.

and he was replaced by his assistant, Alfred Morris, who would go on to hold the post for most of the century.

The Guardians reappointed important staff annually, such as the assistant overseer and relieving officers. The former, Samuel Thorncroft, whom we have already come across, was re-appointed thirty-five times before retiring due to ill health in 1870. Thorncroft supervised the relieving officers and the collection of the poor rate. He could grant someone relief without the permission of the Guardians only in an emergency. The relieving officers visited applicants in their homes to assess their situation. They reported back to the assistant overseer and the Guardians and made regular checks if relief was granted. If they found someone was sick they could give an order to the district medical officer to visit. As they were constantly handling money they were subject to temptation. More than one relieving officer from Brighton absconded and was never seen again.

The exception to the annual re-appointments, were the part time posts of visiting chaplain and visiting medical officer. They were both lifetime appointments. The main job of the former was to comfort the sick and provide religious instruction for the children and to read prayers and preach a sermon every Sunday, at Christmas and at Easter. The medical officer had to go daily to the workhouse to prepare prescriptions, dispense medicines and visit the sick. They rarely stayed more than two hours and were not particularly conscientious.

One Brighton medical officer, Dr David Richards, went nine years without recording any report in the workhouse medical book. Both posts were better paid than that of the most important officer the Guardians had to appoint: the governor. Extremely poorly paid compared to prison governors and superintendents of lunatic asylums, it was a twenty-four hour a day, seven-day week job with little relief. Apart from dealing with the daily grind of workhouse life, the governor had to regularly report to the Guardians. And even after his appointment he could be constantly undermined by those who had not voted for him.

The Guardians on the workhouse visiting committee[i] were regularly taken by the parochial van, often driven by a pauper, to the workhouse to inspect the latest reports of the governor, the chaplain and the medical

---

[i] There were other smaller committees such as the stock and management committee.

officer. They had to investigate any complaints by the inmates and record their investigations in the visitors' book which was produced at the full board meeting. The Guardians also held weekly sessions at their parochial offices in Church Street, where female applicants applied for relief in the morning and males in the afternoon

Despite being time consuming and unpaid, often the same people were re-elected year after year. [i] But there were perks. Once a Guardian, it was possible to make useful business and social contacts and, as their meetings were regularly reported in the local newspapers, a chance to become a well-known figure in the town. They were often accused of feathering their nests by handing out lucrative workhouse contracts and tenders to their friends (or sometimes to themselves). In the early days they were frequently under fire for their reputation for wining and dining at the parishes' expense. In 1836, after the resignation of Callington, the governor, the *Brighton Patriot* had lampooned their reaction:

> Guardian: He ought not to have resigned at all. What can we do without him?
> Guardian: They tell me that Bartlett [his successor] knows nothing at all about cooking. He may perhaps put meat into an oven, but as to cooking it, it is out of the question.
> Guardian: Shocking. I shall resign.
> Guardian: There is no man that can get up a dinner like the present Governor. Did you ever see a ham better done than it was today? The veal was delicious, and what excellent asparagus, and the cucumber sliced so divinely. Oh, what use is a Governor of a workhouse if he can't cook a good dinner every day for the Guardians? (A laugh, and hear, hear.) These cigars gentlemen, this excellent port and sherry, these brandy grogs, all prove how well our Governor under-stands his business, and I beg to propose his health. (Hear, hear!)
> Guardian: Mr Governor, I shall do my best to retain your services. As to Bartlett being Governor, it is horrible . . . Call in the paupers [requesting outdoor relief]. How old are you?
> Old woman: 89.
> Guardian: Oh, you are in good health. What pay has she?
> Guardian: 3s 6d a week, but it has been reduced to 1s 6d.

---

[i] For example, in 1881 twenty-six Guardians offered themselves for re-election and only four were rejected.

Guardian: That's plenty. It is 2½d a day. In Scotland they only allow one penny. (Aside to the Governor) What did you pay for that wine?
Governor: Six shillings a bottle. It is Chateaux Margaux.
Guardian: It is capital.
Guardian: It is put down, I suppose, as port to the sick list.
Guardian: Of course.
Chairman: We can do nothing for you, woman.
Old woman: Shilling a week rent. I can't live on 6d.
Chairman: Then you ought to be ashamed of yourself. You must be economical in these times, my good woman, or we shall have the Poor Law Commissioners here. You may go. [1]

The following year, after one particular extravagant bit of 'feasting and guzzling', there was an outcry from the ratepayers about their abuse of privilege. Many Guardians were found to be drunk after their meetings at the workhouse and were criticized for coming for the refreshments not the business. Often their first question on arrival was "What's for lunch?" They were accused of wandering around the house for one hour before "feasting." In just one eight-week period the visiting committee of three to five Guardians had consumed 160 cigars and 48 bottles of sherry. At an enquiry, the governor testified that the paupers had gone two months without any vegetables but the Guardians had always had them. Below are some selected verses from an anonymous poet in the *Brighton Herald* [2] which captured the public mood:

"The Good of the Poor!!!"
A Defence of the Directors and Guardians, by one of the Body

Dear Brother Electors, when chosen Directors,
In order your suffrage next year to ensure;
We all began eating and drinking and treating,
At the parish expense – for the good of the poor!

At first our suggestion was call'd into question,
And objections were made by the low and obscure,
But we carried our points for fish, fowl, and joints,
And feasted away – for the good of the poor!

36

Then we order'd fresh brandy, we found twasn't handy
To drink common brown like the low or impure,-
'Twas thick and looked dirty, so we got some at thirty-
Five shillings a gallon – for the good of the poor!

We next gave up port and all the wines of that sort
As only designed the vile paupers to cure;
And resolved to be merry, got glorious with sherry,
And staggered to bed – for the good of the poor!

And for fear that our banker should bring us to anchor,
"Cut off our supplies," and refuse to give more;
We resolved to raise money like bees making honey,
And spend it in feasts – for the good of the poor!

So we sent our letters to poor parish debtors,
To tell them that, brimful of anger and fury,
We'd sell all their chattels, their goods and their cattles,
If they didn't pay up – for the good of the poor.

Thus, Electors of Brighton, we beg to enlighten
Your minds on our merits; we now say no more;
But we hope that next Easter, each jolly good feaster
Will be chosen again – for the good of the poor!

For with feasting and dining and drinking and shining
We've the Scripture fulfilled, our election made sure,
And, in spite of the papers exposing our capers,
We shall claim all your votes – for the good of the poor!

This latest publicity resulted in a Guardian being attacked in the street by 20 to 30 angry ratepayers. Another, Hewitt, charged the parish for transporting a non-resident pauper to Bridgewater in Somerset where Hewitt had a house, kept his dog at the workhouse when he was on holiday and sent his boots to be polished! All of them were lambasted for having a summer house built where they could smoke their cigars and drink spirits in full view of the paupers working in the gardens.

In retaliation, the Guardians withdrew their adverts from the highly critical *Brighton Guardian*, whose editor responded:

> We certainly did not look for a compliment from these gentlemen whose cosy afternoons in the agreeable summer house erected by their own order we broke in upon so unceremoniously. [3]

After this bad publicity, the Guardians moved their board meetings to the new offices in Church Street and voted to exclude the press from them anytime they wanted to – as they frequently did. However, even there it was rumoured that they were still feasting away on lobster and salmon and had ordered new cutlery and cut-glass decanters as the workhouse crockery had been "too inferior" for their use.

Some newspapers certainly seemed to take a delight in exposing their "capers" and knew that their readers enjoyed the stories. In 1856, they gleefully reported on the case of a Guardian, Augustus Picket, a coal merchant. Picket was seen talking to a well-known prostitute, and when a policeman asked him to move on Picket enraged him by saying that he was his "master". The policeman knocked him down, sat on him and hauled him to the police station where he was charged with an offence. In court, fortunately for Picket, he managed to get the case dismissed, but the public perception that guardians could be pompous and arrogant was enhanced.

Year after year often the same Guardians were re-elected in April, mainly due to the limited number of people – eligible householders – permitted to vote. Even later on in the century when the franchise widened to include more working people, they were handicapped by the fact that they had to vote during working time. If we look at local newspaper reports of their meetings, the Brighton Guardians come across as a very self-opinionated group of men – the first female Guardian in the town was not elected until 1884. There was rarely total agreement. But however much the Guardians might argue amongst themselves, when they were faced with outside criticism they closed ranks and became defensive.

As we have seen, the Brighton Guardians successfully resisted the full implementation of the New Poor Law Act of 1834 and continued to pay outdoor relief throughout the century. Whenever the Poor Law Board (the Local Government Board after 1870) criticized the Guardians, they reacted indignantly and aggressively. Occasionally, workhouse inmates complained directly to the Board about their treatment and were met with the wrath of the Guardians who usually condemned them as "ungrateful paupers". The allegations were often difficult to substantiate. When questioned by the Guardians, the inmates often withdrew their complaints because they feared the consequences. For example, in the late 1850s two female inmates wrote a letter to the Poor Law Board complaining about being beaten by sticks and the number of vermin in their ward. However, when questioned by the Guardians they denied writing the letter. Described as "low prostitutes", they were visited by a Poor Law inspector and repeated the denial. While the Guardians reluctantly accepted the Board making its own enquiries – and even on occasion invited it in to allay public suspicions – they were absolutely against local, public enquiries and were often criticized by ratepayers for not being more open.

* * *

By 1840 one in fifteen of Brighton's population was in receipt of relief, although the national average was one in eighteen. Apart from the 531 inmates in the workhouse, 854 families – 2,679 individuals – in the town were receiving some form of relief. It was estimated that almost a quarter of the population received only one good meal a week. When the wealthy and middle classes visited for their health and amusement, in their wake came the poor hoping to get work as domestic servants or labourers. When the visitors left, unemployment rose dramatically. For this reason, according to Samuel Thorncroft, the workhouse had most inmates in March when the winter season for the visitors was over.

Sometimes paupers openly stated that they preferred prison to the workhouse, especially when it was rumoured that there were not enough facilities to do 'hard labour' in the former. In fact, the chaplain of the house of correction in Lewes admitted that he was embarrassed that "with the workhouse being so nearly connected to the prison," [4] the latter had a library and prisoners were allowed to read whilst workhouse inmates, with the exception of the children, had no access to books except for the Bible. And sometimes the work of a pauper was harder. The use of pauper labour to bring up a bushel and a half [i] of shingle from the beach to the workhouse – uphill all the way – was back-breaking.

---

[i] 54 kilos.

It is distressing to see these poor wretches labouring up the hill with their burdens. Every now and then they are compelled to stop and take breath. On these occasions they seat themselves a few minutes on one of the handles of their barrow, whilst the perspiration bursts from every pore in their body. "It is killing a man by inches," as one of them said when questioned on the subject. These men are guilty of no crime except that of being poor, and yet they are subjected to severer labour than persons sentenced to the tread-mill, and convicts who work in the dockyards are much better off . . . The Aristocracy knows nothing about the people, and care as little, but what a mass of discontent must exist when man, even in a fashionable and gay town like this, finds himself, like our paupers, degraded to the condition of brute beasts of burden. [41]

The moral was that if you broke the law you would be better treated. At least in prison you served a determinate sentence and were then freed. In contrast, it was not always easy to get permission to leave a workhouse.

Thirteen years after the 1834 Act, contrary to its intention, those claiming outdoor relief in Brighton had dramatically increased. For the week ending 16th Feb 1847, 1308 families were on outdoor relief costing £339 11s 10d, almost double that of the previous year. Seven years later Brighton was spending more than £5,000 [i] a year on outdoor relief. Alongside official relief existed several trade societies which encouraged people to be more self-supporting by making small deductions from their weekly wage to provide against hard times. However, these only protected a small proportion of productive workers. Many were too poor to contribute. There were also a number of charities which undoubtedly saved people from the work-house and offered temporary relief, but again these were small. On the whole the poor tried to make ends meet in any way they could. In 1844 Edward Burn, a tailor from Dublin "with a large quantity of hair", knocked on doors in Brunswick Square with a card proclaiming he was a deaf and dumb fortune teller. He had no luck and one wonders whether he foresaw his own destiny: one month's detention in the house of correction for his activities.

*   *   *

---

[i] £4,210 19s 5d in money; £1,354 in food and £51 11s 10d in clothing. (TNA/MH 12/12773)

With so many old people in the workhouse and its infirmary, death was never very far away. Dying in a workhouse and being buried in a pauper's grave was a nightmare scenario for people living in Victorian Britain. In Brighton's case, paupers were buried in the nearby burial ground – for them depressingly in view of the workhouse – and when that became full they were taken to the Extra-Mural Cemetery in Lewes Road.

If a poor person had an accident in Brighton they were usually taken to the Royal Sussex County Hospital for initial treatment, but as it was a fee-paying voluntary hospital they were quickly transferred to the workhouse infirmary. If a pauper died in the county hospital, inmates from Church Hill had to collect the coffin and transfer it to a pauper's grave in the burial ground. On one occasion they commented that the coffin was very light and were told by the hospital staff that "she was very slim". After the coffin was buried, with rumours rife, it was lifted out and found to be empty. Back at the county hospital the body was found on a mortuary slab.

Most deaths in workhouses were from natural causes, but there were also a few suicides – proportionally probably no fewer than in the wider society – usually by hanging in the nineteenth century. For example, in the winter of 1849, Thomas Aldridge, a journeyman printer, hanged himself from a bedpost in the workhouse, leaving a wife and child.

In 1846, the first and only ever recorded murder at the Brighton work-houses occurred at Church Hill. A thirty-six-year-old woman, Catherine Norman and her three children, Henry (9), Robert (7) and Thomas (3 months) entered the workhouse in April. She had been forced to do this as her husband, Alfred – a former grocer and clerk – had been sent to prison for breaking into a house near Uckfield. She had another child living in London. According to workhouse witnesses, she appeared to have "notions above her station in life" and said she could not bring up her children without a servant. It transpired that she had been brought up in a boarding school and that her father was a journalist on the *London Pictorial Times*

Soon after her admission, Catherine was complaining she did not have enough milk to suckle her child and was depressed. The matron, Mrs Bartlett, appears to have treated her well and the governor believed his wife was "too foolishly indulgent" towards her. Nevertheless, Catherine requested to be transferred to the workhouse of her place of settlement, St Mary's in Islington, London, where she felt she would be better off.

Because of her depression, she and Thomas were placed in a bedroom with a young inmate, Deborah Jenkins, who helped her look after him.

One Monday evening, Catherine asked Deborah if she would be kind to her boys if she died and told her that her own mother had been burnt to death. Holding a Bible in her hand, Catherine said she must die and would not be here this time next week. She then sent Deborah to ask Mrs Bartlett if her two boys could come up and see her, but her request was turned down. Deborah took charge of Thomas for the first part of the night before, at 3am, Catherine said she felt better and took the baby into her own bed. At 5.30am, Deborah dressed herself and fed the baby and Catherine told her "Bless your sweet lips". She had a Bible in her hand and said she had been praying all night for her baby to die.

At 8am, Catherine complained of feeling unwell and said she could not get up. At 9.45, an inmate nurse found her standing in her room bleeding from her throat. On the bed, Thomas was lying in a pool of blood as if asleep. Next to him lay a blunt, bloody knife. Catherine lived for another twenty minutes but could not speak. The surgeon decided not to put stitches in Thomas's wound and he died five hours later. At the inquest, the jury concluded that Catherine had murdered her child in a "fit of insanity".

* * *

While adults voluntarily entered workhouses, children had no choice. Those with parents entered and left the workhouse with them. But if deserted or orphaned they became the responsibility of the Board of Guardians and literally grew up in the workhouse. Some children even regarded it as their natural home

As early as 1821, the *Brighton Gazette* was describing workhouse boys as "rude and abusive". A few years later, three boys from Church Hill were brought before the magistrates' bench for disorderly conduct. They had refused to get out of bed at 7am and were very abusive to the gardener when he tried to get them up. They were sentenced to two weeks 'hard labour' in the house of correction at Lewes. Other boys received the same punishment for absconding to the races, refusing to turn the corn mill or turning it deliberately the wrong way. They were regularly beaten and one boy, George Slaughter, died later after being kicked, allegedly by a governor. These were violent times. Even the vicar of Brighton, Henry Wagner, was fined four shillings for flogging a seven-year-old boy five times in the street. The prosecutor, S.W. Bennett, said of the conservative Wagner that "you could not look at him without imagining that every evil passion that haunted the human mind dwelt there". [6]

Fig 5 Workhouse children, Illustrated London News, *date unknown.*

Where possible, boys were found apprenticeships that often lasted seven years or until they were twenty-one. A record of placements from 1828–1865 [7] showed that the Guardians found over a hundred in this period and that most children were placed with local tradesmen. The usual payment was £5 as a premium to the tradesman at the beginning, and another £5 when the apprenticeship was halfway. It could be cancelled during it if either party was unhappy. By the late 1840s the Guardians also used to provide money for clothes, usually £3. But the apprenticeship was not compulsory and in 1837, a young boy, William Cripps, who was offered an apprenticeship by a baker, refused to go. The Guardians' clerk wrote: "Apprenticeship not executed, boy refused to be bound over". [8]

Workhouse girls were just as spirited as the boys. In August 1838, six girls aged 14–20 threw cocoa fibre – which had been sent to them to pick for mattresses – over the workhouse wall. The governor locked them inside a cottage in the yard. They then knocked two door panels out, put their heads through and 'abused him with terrible language'. They eventually smashed the door down, broke six windows and encouraged other inmates to do the same. Forty-two windows were broken in all. They were sentenced to 'hard labour' by the magistrates and were threatened with transportation if they came before them again.

A lot of the disorder at Church Hill was attributed to the children being mixed with adults or in the terminology of the New Poor Law, to the "lack of classification". In April 1841 the workhouse chaplain, Rev John Allen, concentrated on the children in his report, 'The Training and Religious Instruction of the Poor at the Brighton Workhouse'. [9] He started with the boys' school. Their schoolroom, which was underground, was excessively cold in winter, and in wet weather it flooded so much that holes had to be made in the floor to carry off the water. In the summer the room was too hot because of poor ventilation. In the playground there was "barely room for walking about; the consequence is, that the boys instead of acquiring energy by recreation, become listless and indolent, and the more depraved among them embrace the opportunity to corrupt the better disposed". Allen claimed that tradesmen who took lads on trial frequently brought them back complaining that they were "incorrigibly indolent".

The girls' schoolroom was also "grossly overcrowded":

> The physical exercises, too, which form an important and indeed integral part of infant training, are hereby rendered almost unavailing, and the elder girls hindered from pursuing their proper occupations and studies without interruption.

He argued that as the "the prevailing character of the inmates of the workhouse is vicious", the children were contaminated by their association with them. Allen claimed that whenever a child was punished, the parents complained loudly, which created a spirit of insubordination in the child:

I have known a drunken person who almost starved her children before her misconduct forced her into the Workhouse, bitterly complain and rail against the master if all her requirements in reference to her children were not complied with.

Allen believed most of the children were entirely dependent on the Guardians as they were orphans or had "dissolute parents". The few able-bodied inmates in the workhouse tended to stay for short periods so their children's presence in the school was "rare and transient". Allen concluded:

No system will be effective unless some provision for removing children from the sphere of evil influences and bad example. At the moment the children are not sought after by Masters but regarded with a suspicion and a burden on the parish.

The year Allen made his report a nineteen-year-old was appointed to the responsible position of schoolmaster, a position which became frequently vacant. He was assisted by monitors who Allen described as "indolent and inactive". He believed that only 50 out of 79 boys received a "constant and regular course of education", and that the only industrial training they received was in shoemaking and tailoring. He concluded that they needed an "entire reformation of character and conduct".

Education in workhouse schools was extremely basic. On one occasion, guardians in Bedford had even asked the Commissioners if their children could only be taught "reading" as to learn to write would give them an unfair advantage over the children of local agricultural workers. Their request was turned down. The teachers were lowly paid, often unqualified and had to live with restrictive conditions on the premises. It was small wonder that the positions were sometimes hard to fill. In reality, guardians did not want to give child inmates a better education than that received by poor children on outdoor relief. [i]

Although the Guardians decided to spend £2,000 on enlarging Church Hill, particularly the school facilities, conditions in the schools remained

---

[i] Until 1855 guardians were not allowed to pay for the education of pauper children on outdoor relief.

particularly bad. One Guardian was shocked to find the girls in a dirty state with no bath and a quarter of them having no change of clothes. Lack of bathing facilities led to a Mr Wisden being employed to bring his mobile "bathing" machines near the workhouse for the children. Their main exercise was when a lame inmate led them on walks through the town. One observer commented that "their degraded appearance made them look like pariahs". In fact, even the ex-workhouse chaplain, Spencer Drummond, tried to bar them from attending his church, St John the Evangelist. That children such as the fourteen-year-old Henry Ade absconded frequently was no surprise:

> Magistrate: How do you know you are fourteen?
> Ade: Because I was nine when I went to the Workhouse and I have been there five years.
> Magistrate: How do you know you were nine when you went to the Workhouse?
> Ade: My mother told me so.
> [Bartlett, the Governor, thought he was no more than thirteen.]
> Magistrate: We shall treat him as under 14. How long has the boy been in the Workhouse?
> Bartlett: The last time about three weeks. He spends about half his time in the House of Correction.
> Magistrate: Are the clothes he has the property of the Parish?
> Bartlett: Yes.
> Magistrate: How many times has he run away from the Workhouse?
> Bartlett: I should say twenty times.
> Magistrate: How many times has he been sent to prison?
> Bartlett: Oh, several times.
> Magistrate: Well, imprisonment seems to have little effect on you, so we will try what effect a little addition in the shape of bodily punishment will do. You are sentenced to three weeks' hard labour, and to be once privately whipped. [10]

Despite the improvements in the children's accommodation a report in 1847 concluded that "the lack of separation exposed the children to bad examples from persons of more mature age (who) were likely to exercise a baneful influence over their minds". [11] Only the schoolrooms and bedrooms were for separate use, and the *Brighton Herald* was declaring that for children "at present the workhouse is the road to the brothel and the gaol". The *Gazette* commented that "the children of paupers were generally paupers to the end of their lives". In 1851, over half the young men in the able-bodied ward had been brought up in a workhouse. Of the older boys, fourteen had been in prison once, eleven twice, seven three times, six twelve times and one young man of 22 had been in prison for every year of his life.

According to E.C. Tuffnell, a Poor Law Commissioner, most of the children turned out badly. He believed the objectives of a workhouse school – to reform and educate – were completely opposed to those of a workhouse and that you could not carry out the two under the same roof. After the age of 14, the children were given no schooling. The boys were sent to the labour yard to do shoemaking and tailoring and were only separated by a railing from the able-bodied adults. The girls were sent out into service where they were plunged into work for which they were physically and mentally unprepared. Working long hours, they were often poorly fed and mistreated. One Guardian estimated that nine out of ten of the girls returned to the workhouse.

One such girl who returned was a fifteen-year-old orphan, Louisa Abinett. She had been placed as a servant girl with Joseph Bowtell, a married shoemaker with four children of St James Street. One evening he raped her and the next day she ran away and showed her injuries to an aunt. Bowtell was brought before the magistrates, but although he was found guilty they decided that, "in consideration for the prisoner's position and the feelings of his wife" [12] , not to imprison him and to release him on the payment of a ten pound fine. Louisa was returned to the 'care' of the institution. Significantly, there was no public outcry over the leniency of the sentence. Workhouse girls were usually groomed for domestic service and were frequently subject to unwanted sexual advances.

Although the Brighton Guardians had been reluctant to have anything to do with the Poor Law Board if they could help it, monetary inducements, especially with regards to paying the wages of schoolteachers, altered their perspective. Once they allowed the Poor Law Board to sanction the appointments and salaries of their medical officer and teachers in 1851, they were entitled to a Parliamentary grant which paid half the salary of the former and the full salaries of the latter if they had teaching certificates.

The highlight of the children's year began to be a "treat" at the Swiss Gardens, Shoreham, where the owner, a Mr Goodchild, let them in free and the local railway company provided free transport. The Gardens – opened in 1838 – were a fantasy land of entertainment. They had lakes with tub-like gondolas, swings, roundabouts, sea-saws, a shooting gallery, a ballroom, a theatre, magic lantern displays, bands and a photographic gallery and studio. They also had a temple of the oracle where a mysterious voice emanated from nowhere "predicting the future more or less accurately". On the children's first visit on 28th August 1851, the *Gazette* even published the song they sang at the pleasure dome:

> Now wreath we, of song, a sweet garland to lay,
> At gratitude's shrine, on the year's brightest day,
> Whilst through beauties unnumbered we joyfully stray,
> And care, pain and sorrow are banished away.
> Oh, well we'll remember the joys we now share,
> Waters, flowers, trees, music and soft balmy air,
> And along with all these, and our sports, and good cheer,
> The approving kind faces surrounding us here.
> So wreath we etc.
>
> To our Guardians so good first our gratitude's due,
> Again and again we'll recall it anew,
> And to show it more plainly than words can er'er do,
> We'll strive to be careful, hardworking and true.
> In the great Book of books the bright promise is plain,
> "He that waters himself shall be watered again;"
> And as good, wise, and happy you'd fain have us grow,
> We pray you may ne'er aught but happiness know.
> So wreath we etc.
>
> And oh! far too much for expression in song,
> Do we owe the kind friends whose sweet bowers we're among,
> To the lovely Swiss Gardens may merry crowds throng,
> Enjoy them as we, and remember as long.
> For the gentlemen too of the railway three cheers,
> As hearty and loud as e'er greeted their ears;
> May nought in this world their prosperity mar,
> And the shares of the line rise a hundred 'bove par.
> Then wreath we etc.

Fig 6 The Swiss Gardens, Shoreham, "The House of Gaiety, Love and Drama", an 1876 design, Brighton Herald 2/6/1934.

In 1860, a juvenile band was formed, despite one Guardian's comment that music was "too much for them". The following year, carrying a banner which read "Poor but Happy", the children were once again off to Shoreham, led by the band and accompanied by some of the Guardians and officials:

On emerging from the house, the brass band, comprising fifteen boys, struck up the "Allambra quick step", which they played with remarkable precision to a marching tune. The children proceeded down the hill to North Street, thence through the Queen's Road to the Terminus, the band playing the whole distance. Their cleanly and neat appearance excited the admiration of the hundreds, who lined the road to witness the procession…During their progress to the Railway the band played "Nelly Grey" and "Ever of Thee". They were provided with second and third class carriages, and in a jiffy, they were taken to Shoreham. They were marched in the same order as they came out from the Shoreham Station to the Gardens…

For about an hour and a half, most of the children, under the watchfulness of the officials, rambled about the gardens, whilst others enjoyed boating on the lake. One little creature fell overboard, but was immediately rescued. She had a good ducking. Her wet clothes were taken off, and care taken of her. Fresh clothes from the poor-house were provided, and, in a short time afterwards, she was the gayest of the gay. This was the only mishap that occurred in the course of the day. [13]

The children were then served lunch by the officials and the Guardians. In the afternoon, they attended a concert in the theatre and a staged scene, 'To India and back in half an hour'. After tea, they attended a farce and then had races on the lawn. The winners received a toy, and all the children received a tin whistle. The band played all the time and collected money from the spectators. The evening finished with dancing. At 8.30pm a bugle signalled their departure and they headed off to the station. They reached home before ten "with nothing to mar the pleasures of the day, but with everything for their young minds to remember with gratitude". [14]

As early as 1843, the vicar of Brighton, Henry Wagner, had argued that Brighton should have an industrial school for their children, institutions which already existed in Liverpool and Manchester. These schools, also called "barrack" schools, were designed to install the habit of work into destitute children and to remove them from bad influences. Almost ten years later, an Assistant Poor Law Commissioner was still reporting that at Church Hill "many children suffer greatly in every subject through want of sufficient separation from adults". [15] With a population varying between 500 and 700, at times it was vastly overcrowded with four or five female paupers often having to share a bed. A major aim of the new industrial schools was to prevent pauper girls ending up as "girls on the town". But there was a difficulty: many prostitutes were in domestic service, the main occupation the girls in these schools were prepared for.

By 1854, with pigs and cows being kept in the garden at Church Hill, and with the workhouse becoming more and more central as the town expanded, the Guardians decided to plan for alternative accommodation. They could get a good price for the Church Hill site and remove their paupers to the edge of town, far enough away so as not to disturb fashionable visitors. That year, the Poor Law Board gave the Guardians permission to buy land for an industrial school and a new workhouse. Land was soon acquired at Warren Farm in Woodingdean and on the top of Elm Grove respectively. The land for the industrial schools occupied twenty acres of arable land immediately north east of the race course and cost £2,000, while the proposed new workhouse was to be built on a seven-acre plot near Race Hill, costing £2,205. The predicted cost of the buildings was around £10,000 for the schools and £30,000 for the workhouse. Despite buying the land and getting the go-ahead from the government, the Guardians now faced opposition from their own ratepayers. Some were determined that these buildings should never be built.

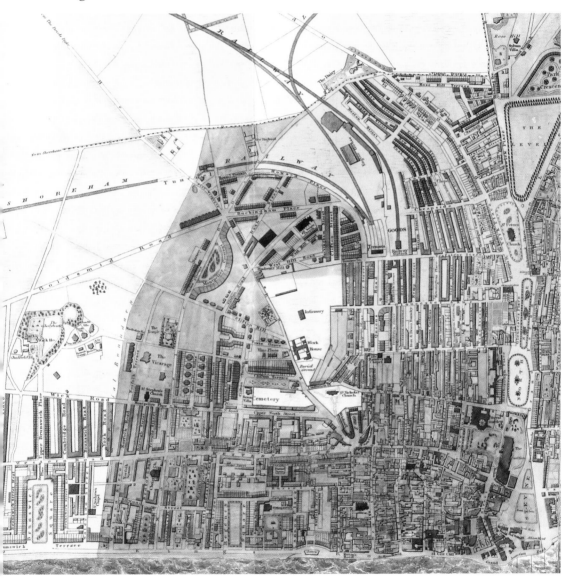

Fig 7 Map showing the development around Church Hill circa 1850.

Chapter Four

THE GOVERNORS

J.A. Erredge, in his *History of Brighthelmstone* (1862), looked back at the new workhouse system and saw it as a success. He believed:

> many a man who considered the 'house' his birthright, because father and grandfather from time immemorial wintered there, has taken to provident and industrious habits, and learned the sweet uses of adversity.

From the system's point of view, he was right. The poor rate had started to fall, which had pleased the ratepayers, and more paupers were being helped at a cheaper rate. However, the truth was that its regime had become so oppressive that some people preferred to starve rather than to enter it. Less productive work was being done there, and task masters and mistresses ensured the able-bodied did more arduous work, such as the breaking and pounding of stones etc. which made the atmosphere more confrontational. Since the appointment of Callington as governor in 1834, the workhouse appeared to have been for many years a place of violence and strife.

After Callington's short but brutal reign, he was succeeded by Mr Bartlett in 1836. He was just as violent. In 1838, an inmate, James Turner, aged 69, was employed at the town hall in the clerk's office during the day but stayed at the workhouse at night. He usually arrived back late in the evening and went to the kitchen to collect his supper, beer and breakfast. One evening he bumped into Bartlett, who accused him of being drunk and, according to Turner, viciously attacked him and refused to give him anything. Ordinarily the complaints of an inmate were rarely taken seriously. However, Turner was different. He had been working at the town hall for ten years and was a popular figure with the parochial staff. As his face was swollen and bruised all over, his head bandaged and a couple of his teeth missing, the assault was impossible to cover up. The Guardians suspended Bartlett for a week – with Thorncroft taking over again – and launched an enquiry.

At the enquiry one or two of the witnesses said that Bartlett had been known to beat the boys regularly. Evidence suggested that Bartlett had hit Turner while he was on the ground. In his defence Bartlett claimed Turner had been insolent to him. Brought before the magistrates, Bartlett was surprisingly found "not guilty". Afterwards he apologized for his conduct and was reinstated. But not everyone was happy with the verdict. The *Brighton Patriot* declared: "Will not the Guardians step in and shield the poor from such disgraceful, brutal attacks in the future?" [1] and demanded they protect the poor. After Bartlett's acquittal, the same newspaper claimed that there had been 14 cases against him in all. On one occasion he had dragged a female inmate, who was drunk, out into the street at night and had left her there. On another, a local baker who supplied the parish with flour claimed that when he had gone to collect his sacks from the workhouse, Bartlett had called him a rascal and had tried to run him through with a six foot iron rake.

Bartlett finally retired in 1848 along with his wife, who was the matron. There were fifty-five applicants for the joint posts of governor and matron, many from the prison service. Surprisingly Henry Barnes, the workhouse porter, also applied. It may seem strange to us that Barnes should have done so, but the Guardians considered his post to be an important one and paid him almost as much as their matron. [i] Porters and portresses, stationed at the workhouse gates, were the public face of the workhouse and often worked seventeen hours a day. They had to be physically strong and had to prevent any unauthorized entry or exit and keep a register of all those leaving and entering. An overzealous Brighton workhouse porter once recorded the entrance of a donkey! They also searched everyone on arrival for prohibited articles such as alcohol, dice, cards, and matches. They had to take the keys to the governor at 9pm and get them back at 6am. Porters were often cantankerous figures, and there were rumours of them taking advantage of female paupers. Up until 1852, the porter at Church Hill was allowed to search them.

Henry Barnes failed to get an interview. Instead, a Mr and Mrs Cuzens from the Shipley workhouse narrowly beat a Mr and Mrs King who had

---

[i] Even in 1871 the porter was receiving £40 per annum, the same salary as the head nurse.

worked in a workhouse near Sandwich, Kent. Despite King having 80 testimonials, some Guardians had discovered that in just one year he had committed 318 paupers to the magistrates' court. One Guardian, Lambert, predicted that the "workhouse would be in a state of insubordination for years under King". They soon discovered John Cuzens, too, regularly brought paupers before the magistrates.

In 1849, a pauper, Henry Holland from Number 19 Ward[i], sat in the wrong seat during chapel. When Cuzens told him to move Holland replied he would not sit anywhere else and would go back to his ward. When he left the chapel, other men followed. George Pitt, the superintendent of the ward, tried to stop him leaving and Holland hit him. Cuzens told him he would place him in solitary confinement and take him before the Guardians. Holland swore at him and said he wouldn't go. The *Herald*, under the title, *A Revolt in the Workhouse*,[2] reported Holland's appearance at the magistrates' court. Holland questioned Cuzens:

Prisoner: Why did you refuse us the privilege of attending divine worship in the chapel?

Governor: You were not refused.

Prisoner: Why, we are seated in the dining room; and my seat was eighteen feet from the chapel door, so that it was impossible to hear the minister, who has not the strongest of voices; and I do not see why we should not have a seat in the chapel.

George Pitt corroborated the evidence of the Governor.

John Funnell, a pauper in the No 19, deposed that Holland told the paupers in No 19 that he would not sit in the dining room, but would take his seat in the chapel with the rest; and if anyone refused to follow his example he would "turn to at them."[ii] He said he would be the first to go into the chapel, and that if anyone "turned tail," they deserved to be hung up by the thumbs. (*Laughter.*)

Prisoner: What answer did you make to the proposal when a question was asked if you would support the cause? Didn't you say that if anyone refused to go into the chapel he should be "whopped with a wet towel?" (*Laughter.*)

Witness: I said, I did not want to have anything to do with it. I dreaded Sunday coming on account of it.

Magistrate: Now, prisoner, what have you to say to this charge?

---

[i] The Refractory Ward.

[ii] Threaten them

Prisoner: When I applied for admission to the house, they gave me No 19 Ward. I enquired the reason why, but could not get any satisfactory answer. In the 19 Ward the pauper has inferior clothes, limited diet, and hardest work, and above all, they are denied the privilege of seeing their friends. We all agreed to take our seats in the body of the chapel as we could not hear in the dining room, and we cast lots to know who was to take the lead, and it came to the tallest, and I being the tallest, I was the first man to go into the room sooner than give up the cause in which we were engaged…the others followed. The Governor came in, and seeing us seated in the chapel, immediately said, "Front seat arise". We all sat still. He repeated his command; and we got up. I was going out, when the Governor said to me, "You go back my man". Pitt then came, up, took hold of me, and used me very roughly; and if I struck him it must have been in the struggle. The Governor sent for me afterwards, and I told him then I should appeal to the Magistrates, and he immediately said, "The Magistrates be_____!; this is no case for a Magistrate". I assure you gentlemen, these were the words.

Cuzens, backed up by Pitt, denied he had said this. The magistrates sentenced Holland to 21 days' hard labour at the house of correction.

Even in these turbulent times some inmates were by no means cowed by the workhouse regime, and there appears to have been a constant battle of wits between them and the officials. On one occasion, at a magistrates' hearing, two inmates were accused of skimming fat from the soup and selling it outside. The wardsman on the able-bodied ward, John Body – who was described in court as terribly thin – testified that he had found a cat's head and a mouse in the soup. Another witness, Robert Redding, said the soup was impossible to eat when it had black beetles in it. The two inmates were found "not guilty".

The Guardians immediately ordered an enquiry. They called Body, Redding, several inmates, the cook and the workhouse medical officer, Richard Rugg. Rugg examined the cat's head and thought it had been dead many years and that it could have been the head of a rabbit. The Guardians concluded that it had been a practical joke concocted amongst the inmates of the able-bodied ward. Afterwards, one Guardian said that whenever he went into company and was recognized as a Guardian, there was immediately a cry of "meow"!

During Cuzens' reign there appears to have been almost anarchy. On one occasion four females in the refractory ward broke nearly 50 panes of glass and barricaded themselves in with bedsteads against the door. When Cuzens finally got in he found the contents of mattresses spread around the room. They were given six weeks' hard labour in the house of correction at Lewes. One young woman on crutches, Eliz Willard, broke 24 windows and was given one month's hard labour. On another occasion Cuzens told William Mowbray, an inmate of the refractory ward, to wheel some wood to the cattle market. Mowbray struck him so hard he broke his glasses and Cuzens had to stay in bed for a day. Mowbray was sent for trial. Cuzens also had to bring his own schoolmaster, Mr Baber, in front of the Board for thrashing a boy without requesting his presence, which was a requirement. The boy, named Buddle, was brought in to show his bare back. Baber was given two weeks to resign or be sacked.

Cuzens was also finding it difficult to get inmates to work. He reported that the male inmates of Number 19 ward were refusing to grind more than three bushels of wheat per day. He took eight boys from the playground and found they ground half a bushel in thirty-three minutes. Cuzens told the inmates they should do eight bushels a day though he would be happy with six. They replied they couldn't do more than four. Cuzens appealed to the Guardians, who ruled that they must do six bushels a day or be punished.

In the past, the numbers of tramps/vagrants using the casual ward had been small: 632 in 1843 and 847 the following year. But quite dramatically, due to a serious economic recession, it increased to over 3,000 by the time Cuzens took charge in 1848. A year later, it was almost 5,000, with sometimes as many as 70 vagrants coming every night. The Guardians feared they were becoming an annoyance to the visitors and inhabitants and that their workhouse was becoming a home for professional beggars. Not for the first time the idea was mooted that they should be made to work for their "lodgings". One night Cuzens refused several strong looking men admission. One of them:

> Henry Terry, called out, "The Governor must pay for damages tomorrow if he does not admit us tonight." Terry pushed aside the porter, Henry Barnes, and rushed in saying, "Come along, my lads".[3]

Terry received one month's hard labour. Cuzens decided only to let women, children and first-timers in. The Guardians then insisted that the vagrants could be admitted only if they had a "travelling pass" from the last parish they resided in and the numbers dropped temporarily.

The porter, Henry Barnes, was also involved in Cuzens' own departure. In June 1849, the governor told his wife he was going to see their son in London and strangely left by the back gate. He never came back. It transpired he had borrowed £3 from Barnes and had repeatedly refused to pay him back. In desperation, Barnes had decided to write to the Guardians about the debt and other "irregularities". Then Cuzens had fled, leaving his distraught wife and a leaderless workhouse.

The Guardians discovered that he had embezzled almost £120 from workhouse funds – fortunately for them the same amount as the surety they had demanded from him on his appointment. However, they found Cuzens had even borrowed 5s 6d from one small pauper girl who had saved up her "small rewards" over time. It was not recorded whether she was recompensed. Surprisingly the surveyor/architect George Maynard and his wife were put in temporary charge, and Mrs Cuzens was dismissed along with her husband. One of the first things Maynard did was to ask a pauper to tidy the bed of the former governor. Shortly afterwards, Maynard was surprised to find the pauper drunk. He had found a bottle of brandy hidden under Cuzens' pillow. According to Henry Barnes, Cuzens had frequently been drunk. Before Mrs Cuzens left, she wrote to the Guardians saying she feared her husband had been lost at sea on an emigrant ship.

After Cuzens' departure the Guardians raised the sureties: £200 for the husband and £100 for the wife. They also started to advertise the post in the *Times*. They interviewed six candidates and narrowed the choice down to two. On a casting vote of the chairman, the Guardians appointed Henry and Martha Hodge from the Gravesend workhouse. The other candidates had again been the Kings. This time the Guardian, Lambert, claimed that John King "did not know how to handle paupers" and that he had recently failed in business. In September 1850, barely a year later, the Hodges left and, third time lucky, the Kings were made master and matron.

Under the Kings, the violence continued. On one occasion four young men attacked a wardsmen, Joseph Gorringe. They hit him with a candlestick and he locked himself in his room. They broke the panels of the door with large flint stones, but he was rescued by other staff. The other eighteen inmates of the ward just went to bed and laughed. Brought before the bench, the four men were each fined 12s and costs or six weeks hard labour. Not having any money, all the paupers went to prison. On another occasion the schoolmistress was reprimanded for severely flogging one of the children, and she resigned shortly afterwards. The schoolmaster also resigned, complaining about his treatment by the Kings. In all, seven teachers resigned during their tenure. King had fights with inmates and even with visiting tradesmen, proving the Guardians who had feared he would be too confrontational to be right.

In 1854 the Kings left and were replaced by Philip and Elizabeth Passmore from the Totness workhouse in Devonshire. By now it was getting terribly overcrowded and its average population, excluding the vagrant wards, had gone up from 356 in 1835 to 616 in 1855. In one week alone in the last year there had been 743 inmates. The ratepayers put the dramatic increase down to the leniency of the Guardians. It was rumoured that surrounding parishes were refusing to give outdoor relief – thereby applying the workhouse "test" – and so their paupers were coming to Brighton. The Brighton Guardians were left with three choices. They could allow these paupers to starve, provide them with outdoor relief or send them back to their parishes at great expense. At this stage, the Guardians were reluctant to use the "test" and were still giving outdoor relief in winter to resident able-bodied paupers with families.

In December 1857 Cecilia Brown, the assistant-matron who had been working at Church Hill for nine months, started to complain of feeling unwell. Dr Rugg, the workhouse surgeon, visited her but did not make any diagnosis. During the early part of the following week it became more serious and she was confined to bed. After she returned to duty, an inmate who acted as a nurse made a gruesome discovery in Brown's room. Inside a cupboard she found the body of a newly born female child. She told the matron who confined Brown to her bed. When she was better she was placed in custody and charged with "concealment of birth". She intimated to the court that the father had gone to Australia.

In the summer of 1859 the Guardians were surprised to receive a letter from the Passmores asking to resign and requesting testimonials. They had considered Philip Passsmore to be one of the most efficient governors they had ever had and had even given him a rise. At their next meeting the chairman of the Guardians, in the presence of Passmore, had some "painful business" to relate. He claimed that, according to many of the officials and inmates at the workhouse, Passmore was the father of the dead child found in the cupboard in Cecilia Brown's room. Not only that, he was suspected of having had an affair with the infant school-mistress, Miss Emma Wells. Lastly, there was "positive evidence" that he had also been the father to an inmate pauper woman's child that had died. After Passmore had listened to the allegations he went straight to the railway station and was never seen again.

With Mrs Passmore still at the workhouse but clearly unwell, the Guardians launched an enquiry. Calling fifteen witnesses, including staff and inmates, they heard conflicting evidence. Despite the workhouse chaplain and medical officer not noticing anything immoral in the governor's conduct, the Guardians concluded that the charges were proved. They sacked Passmore in his absence but let his wife resign and gave her a good testimonial.

Bearing in mind the last few disastrous appointments, who were the Guardians going to appoint next? A letter in the *Brighton Herald* [4] gave some advice:

THE GOVERNOR OF THE WORKHOUSE

To the Editor of the *Brighton Herald*

Sir,
The class of persons from whom Governors are chosen is limited and utterly worthless. Men that have failed in every other pursuit are thought good enough to be Governors of a Workhouse; and accordingly, duties demanding the soundest judgement and great energy and intelligence are, in nine cases out of ten, committed in cold blood to insolvent tradesmen and broken-down schoolmasters....

It is perfectly well known who the last four Governors of our Workhouse were. Two were insolvent tradesmen, and two were unsuccessful schoolmasters. The miserable man who has fled from the town with so much precipitation was of the latter type. What course, then, are the Board of Guardians about to take in the appointment of a new Governor? Surely they do not intend to pursue the same vicious circle! Yet this is the conclusion to which we are led by the advertisement they have just issued. The Governor to be appointed must be above 35 years of age. This limitation shuts out, in my opinion, at least one third of all who might become candidates for the office; and why a man at the age of 30 should not be as judicious or efficient as a man at the age of 35 or 40, it is impossible to conceive.

Then the Governor must be a man "without encumbrance: "a euphonic expression, I presume, for having no children: in other words the best pledge for good conduct and sustained exertion is to be a disqualification for the office! Do the Governors remember that the only Governor who was worthy of his office…was a man with several children?

What we do want is an honest, intelligent man; and whether he is married or single – whether he has "no encumbrance" or three or four children – whether he is five years older or younger – ought to be matters of secondary importance….

A RATEPAYER

The Passmores were now temporarily replaced by Edward Sattin, the accountant/clerk at the workhouse and Miss Tomkins, the assistant matron. Ten couples applied for the new vacancies, six were interviewed and three made the short list:

Mr and Mrs Bryant of the Royston Union, Herts
Mr and Mrs Feist of the St Mary's, Newington workhouse
Mr and Mrs Sattin of Brighton

At their next meeting, the Guardians quickly eliminated the second couple. It transpired the Feists had "resigned their situations" from the Newington workhouse after they had been charged with trafficking in the bodies of paupers. The latters' friends found out that at their funerals they had been following to their graves coffins full of the remains of paupers who had undergone dissection at the local hospital. So now the choice was between the Bryants and the Sattins.

The Bryants had 53 testimonials praising their conduct. The appointment of the Sattins was proposed by one of the Guardians, Mr H Saunders:

Mr Sattin was a native of this town, and he (Mr Saunders) had known him from childhood, and believed him to be an honest, upright, and deserving young man, and would make his way in life. It had been the order of things in Brighton, when they saw a deserving young man, to promote him, if possible.[5]

In contrast to the Bryants, the Sattins only had five testimonials, but they had one huge advantage: both were already working at the workhouse. Emma Dawe and Edward Sattin had met and married there in February 1857. She had formerly been a cook at the Totness workhouse, Devon, where her father was the master, but was now at the age of twenty-five the assistant matron at the Brighton workhouse. Edward – who in fact had been born in Lewes in 1825 – had been working there as a clerk since 1855. His own father was a well known broker in Brighton and sat on the town council.

The Sattins were clear favourites for the job – even though they had two children – but one Guardian, Mr Lamb, was not happy with the prospect. He claimed that for at least two years Sattin had known that Passmore had been taking advantage of female inmates but had not reported it. In fact, at the enquiries into Passmore's conduct, Sattin had stated that he had often seen the governor come into his office and put his hand on the breast of the infant schoolmistress, Miss Wells, and that no one seemed to mind. He had also witnessed the same thing happening with Cecilia Brown, the mother of the dead child found in the cupboard. When there had been an investigation into the latter, Sattin had not said a word. Later, he told the two enquiries that he "really took no notice" of what the governor did in his office.

However, another Guardian rose to Sattin's defence, claiming that "those who fill inferior situations know how dangerous it was to make statements which would jeopardise their situation… his sins were of omission and not of commission". Another Guardian, Lucas, disagreed. He felt that Sattin was all right for a small workhouse such as Bridgewater in Somerset – which he had applied to two years earlier – but not for a large one like Brighton's. Also, because the Sattins were young it was likely they would have a large family which would result in Mrs Sattin being distracted from her duties. He concluded that:

> Sattin was no more fit for this office than a person who had never seen the duties at all. He objected also to the appointment of a Master with children …Even without children he did not think Mrs Sattin would be fit for our Matron…He believed that Mr and Mrs Bryant were well qualified for the situations, and persons who managed matters in that house ought to have no connexions in the locality at all. [6]

Lucas also accused the Sattins' proposer, Saunders, of suggesting them in order to visit the 'house' whenever he liked. After more discussion there was a vote. The Sattins won by twenty to ten. Their appointment was due, no doubt, to the fact that they were well known in the town and had good connections. Their salary was £90 and £50 respectively. It was around this time that the governor of a workhouse was more often than not called the "master".

* * *

At the beginning of this chapter Erredge commented about the success of the new workhouse system where men no longer "considered the house his birthright". But this "success", as we have seen, came at an enormous cost. For, since at least from the time in the 1830s when the diet started to be reduced, the Brighton workhouse, like virtually all other workhouses, became a place synonymous with degradation, demoralization, humiliation and, above all, the loss of freedom and hope. Although there was not the bone-crushing[i] which took place at the nearby Eastbourne workhouse, a significant number of Brighton paupers preferred living in far worse conditions outside, even starving to death, rather than being separated from their families in the workhouse. Wearing its uniform had become a mark of failure. However, by 1859, with upwards of 140,000 paupers – including 40,000 children – living in workhouses in England and Wales, there was a glimmer of hope, for some Victorian philanthropists were determined to improve conditions for the inmates.

In the 1850s, Louisa Twining (of the famous tea family) organized ladies' committees to visit workhouses. After initial opposition from workhouse Guardians, some ladies were allowed to visit. Even then, they were often treated badly at the workhouse gates by the porters, who Louisa Twining found to be "rude and insolent". She first visited Church Hill in 1853 and continued to visit Brighton's workhouses over the next thirty-six years.

In 1859, Twining formed the Workhouse Visiting Society and a journal to go with it. It was to promote the moral and spiritual improvement of workhouse inmates. She explained its specific aims to a Parliamentary Select Committee on Poor Relief in 1862.[ii] It was to "befriend destitute and orphan children; instruct and comfort the sick and to be useful and beneficial to the ignorant and depraved". Although the journal contained rather paternalistic articles about inmates from a middle and upper class point of view, it did aim to improve their plight. The society took a particular interest in ex-workhouse girls, and Louisa Twining set up a girls' home in London to dissuade them from a "life of vice and depravity" and from returning to the workhouse. (Brighton was a suitable place for her to target as in 1859 there were 97 public brothels and 325 prostitutes, twenty-five of whom were under sixteen).

---

[i] It was used as fertiliser.

[ii] *Workhouse Visiting Society Journal*, January 1862 p. 535.

Twining started to encourage groups of ladies to visit workhouse inmates and initiated the promotion and enlargement of workhouse libraries, two advantages prison inmates already had. In 1859, she wrote to the Brighton Guardians requesting that her "ladies" might be allowed to visit Church Hill:

> Amongst many inmates, a large number of whom are sick and infirm and unable to read for themselves, there is obviously an extensive sphere of work; and however zealous the Chaplain may be, there must be much to be done, especially among the women, which might be undertaken by lady-visitors. The sick and aged are cheered by a little sympathy and consolation, and with the younger women we have found much good to result from the influence obtained over them by the visits of ladies. In some instances they succeed in finding places for such persons, and by keeping up a little knowledge of them have prevented their return to the workhouse…From an experience of many years in the London workhouses, I may say that I believe such plans are calculated to assist the officers of such establishments and to promote good order and discipline among the inmates.
>
> Suitable visitors could no doubt be selected by the Chaplain and some of the clergy, from amongst those ladies who are accustomed to visit the poor. As a stranger, of course I have no wish to interfere with this part of the question; but I may perhaps be allowed to mention one lady who, I think, is well qualified for the work having already had experience of it in a country workhouse, Miss Wake, 39, Brunswick Terrace, who was admitted to visit your Workhouse some years ago, with much satisfaction to herself and the inmates, and would gladly now resume her visits, should they be sanctioned by you.
>
> In one workhouse which I visit in London, the master has expressed himself indebted to the ladies (about twelve in number), who each take a ward; and the Guardians have also acknowledged their assistance.[i]

Louisa Twining suggested an experiment for six months and ended her letter, "I shall be truly glad if success should attend this proposal for the benefit of the large number of our afflicted and often ignorant fellow creatures".

Although the vicar of Brighton, the chaplain at the workhouse and several of the Guardians approved of her plan, the majority of Guardians

---

[i] *Brighton Examiner* 31/5/1859.

were against it. They were worried that the "lady visitors might act at variance with the regulations of the House". [7] They argued that if they admitted the ladies in, it was tantamount to admitting that they, the Guardians, weren't doing their job. They claimed visiting ladies were not necessary in such a well-run workhouse. And they feared they would want the sick removed to separate wards – something that was not possible at Church Hill. The Guardians maintained this position for the next few years but eventually let Twining and her friends in. They needn't have worried about the ladies challenging their authority for, as Twining had told the select committee above, if they complained about conditions she knew they would be "turned out as visitors". [8]

The 1850s ended with a pauper, James Bannister, aged 55, a bricklayer by trade, collapsing dead of a heart attack while carrying a basket of boulders on his back from the beach to the workhouse. He had previously complained to another pauper that the work was "enough to kill a horse". He had been living on outdoor relief of bread and just enough money to pay his rent. At the inquest a doctor said that it was not the kind of work an unfit person should do. The coroner added that "such hard work seemed incompatible with such a low diet". The jury's verdict was "death from a diseased heart", but they added that "his death was accelerated by the extreme laborious work and low diet to which he was subjected to by the Directors and Guardians". The Guardians decided to stop the wheeling of material from the beaches.

FELLOW
RATE PAYERS.

An attempt will be made at the Vestry Meeting, on Thursday next, (the 17th,) to foist upon you the old plan for the removal of the present Workhouse.

ATTEND THE MEETING

And do not let the late Guardians, and their Friends, the Builders, run you to the enormous expence of

£100,000

for such jobbery and folly.

If alterations are wanted, there is plenty of room on the site the present Workhouse and Garden, with perhaps the exception of the INDUSTRIAL SCHOOLS.

Do not fail to attend the Meeting at Twelve o'clock

On Thursday next

July 16th, 1856.

Fig 8 Poster against the building of a new workhouse.

Chapter Five

NEW BEGINNINGS

Two years after the Guardians had bought the land for the new workhouse and industrial schools not one brick had been laid. Instead, it had been rented out for the growing of mangelwurzels and the production of hay. By November 1854, the Guardians had "wasted" almost £1800 on private tendering for the project.[1] In May 1856, the Poor Law Board were declaring that there must be no further delay in erecting the new buildings and were threatening to intervene unless something was done. That year the Vestry finally gave their consent to the selling of the Church Hill site. The delay was caused by the anger of ratepayers over the expense of the project; their suspicions, not unfounded, that some of the ex-Guardians were out to make a killing on the old site; and by the election of new Guardians against the plans. As the plans stood, the Guardians would have to borrow a considerable amount of money from the government: £24,205 plus interest of 4 per cent repayable in ten instalments over twenty years from the Public Works Loan Board. For this reason, the opposition brought out alternative plans.

One proposal was that the new industrial schools should be built in the middle of the garden at Church Hill and that the space vacated by the children could provide extra accommodation for the adults. The cost would be around £8,000 instead of the £40,000 needed for the original plans. However, this would still make it hard to stop "improper communication" between the children and the adults, one of the main reasons for building a separate institution in the first place. As one of the Guardians, Tennant, pointed out, remaining at Church Hill meant:

> innocent orphans and the offspring of unfortunate and respectable tradesmen who by the teaching at present practiced in the old house, would be carried away in the vortex of pauperism, generating pauperism from generation to generation.[2]

Another proposal was that instead of building the schools just outside of Brighton at Warren Farm in Woodingdean, why not build them on the land bought for the new workhouse at Race Hill and just enlarge the accommodation at Church Hill? The *Brighton Gazette* favoured this latter plan rather than building the schools "in a desert of a place, almost unapproachable for six months of the year and left to the mercies of the Parish officials".[3] Others thought the site's remoteness was its greatest recommendation.

The Warren Farm site, nestled in a hollow of the Downs surrounded by undulating pasture land and downland of flashes of white cliffs and glimpses of blue sea along the Sussex coast, was a beautiful place on a summer's day but was horribly exposed in winter. Despite the building of a new road in 1857 connecting it to Brighton, it would still, at times, be hard to get to. One local journalist who went to visit the site on a foggy day got lost and never found it. Just as Church Hill had once been described as a "howling wilderness", so too was the site at Warren Farm. So remote was the area that, according to the *Gazette*, some of the locals referred to it as "East America".

The most prominent critic of the original plans was a new Guardian, Richard Edwards. He claimed the whole town was against the Warren Farm site. He was thought to be responsible for the printing of 100,000 scaremongering handbills warning the town against the proposal. The Poor Law Board quickly rejected the idea of building the schools on Race Hill, as they considered the seven-acre site a completely inadequate space for the needs of the children. Despite this, in August 1858 a petition signed by 121 ratepayers was sent to the Poor Law Board arguing against the original plans. It stated that:

> A majority of the elected Directors and Guardians of this Parish are strongly opposed to the Warren Farm as the most unsuitable spot to be found in the vicinity of Brighton for the site of these Schools; but their opinions are rendered nugatory [worthless] by the votes of the Parish officers who are ex-officio Directors, and over whom the ratepayers have no control…The proposed site for the Schools is difficult of access and is situated at such a distance from the town of Brighton as to preclude the probability of their being visited by the Directors and Guardians generally.[4]

The petition went on to urge the benefits of the Race Hill site for the schools and requested that the Poor Law Board institute an inquiry. The Board refused, as the previous Guardians had already incurred considerable expense with the plans and had entered into contracts for the erection of the schools. Besides, the workhouse infirmary was getting dangerously over-crowded, with beds only sixteen inches apart.

In March 1859, five years after the land had been purchased, the first stone of the Warren Farm Industrial Schools was finally laid. George Maynard, the parish surveyor, was the architect and John Fabian of Brighton, the builder. It was to house 250–300 children. As the Guardians were reluctant to pay for piped water from the local pumping station to supply the new workhouse and the schools, workhouse labour and paid labour was used to dig a new artesian well at the farm. By December 1859 the buildings were completed at a cost of £8,270 14s 9d. Fabian also erected farm buildings at a cost of £1,514 16s and another £560 1s was spent on a boundary wall. But there was no sign of water in the well – started in March 1858 – as arid strata upon arid strata piled up beside the spot chosen for the operation. The contractor, Mr North, had predicted that water would be found after 400ft, and when it was not he had resigned out of frustration. As time passed the Guardians were heavily criticized by the ratepayers for their expenditure on "that bottomless well". On one occasion a rumour spread through the town that six workmen had been suffocated in the excavation. Their wives rushed to the site only to find them alive and well.

George Maynard, the parish surveyor, replaced North and was soon making regular trips to the Institute of Practical Geology in London to get advice from the experts – advice that was usually overly optimistic. By the beginning of March 1862, with the schools still empty and the dry well costing up to a £100 a week to excavate, with workmen working around the clock, the Guardians were faced with three options: they could be further overdrawn on their treasurer's account, introduce a new special rate or abandon the well altogether. With the last option a real possibility, in desperation they instructed Maynard to again visit Professor Ramsay at the institute in London, which he did on Friday 14th March. He took with him specimens of the recently dug strata. Ramsay said he could not tell if the water was near or not and asked Maynard to send him shells from the excavation. The following day Maynard collected the shells which he was intending to send Ramsay on the Monday. Then, to everyone's amazement, on Sunday evening there was a loud bang and water started gushing up from the bottom of the well. It rushed in so quickly that the men who had minutes earlier been working at the bottom would almost certainly have drowned if they had not just reached the top to change shifts. To the cheers of the workmen, the first pailful of water was drawn up at noon the next day.

To one of the men, the water looked like "soapsuds in which dirty green baize had been washed". [5] However, it tasted "excellent" and Maynard took a bottle to a chemist in North Street who "pronounced the water pure and good, the specific gravity being scarcely greater than distilled water". [6] The news of water in the well spread like wildfire throughout the town and the bells of St Nicholas rang forth peals all day. The engineers were feted with a parade and a banquet was given by a Guardian, Henry Catt, at a large room at the town hall. Over the entrance was an emblem consisting of a number of picks and shovels which had been used in the sinking of the well. The 45 labourers used in its digging were rewarded with inscribed silver medals whilst Isaec Huggett, the engineer, received a gold one. The medals bore the inscription: "By the blessing of God, on hard work, patience and perseverance" and "Warren Farm Well, Brighton, water found 16th March, 1862". Catt calculated that any workman who had worked on it for a year had had to walk 2,200 miles to and from work. The toast of the evening was to "The Health of the Working Men".

On Maynard's weekly visits to the site of the well, and when he had taken the sample to the Brighton chemist, he had been accompanied by his young grandson. When this boy grew up he would lay his own claim to fame, for he was Magnus Volk, inventor of the world's first electric railway.[i]

The well was in the engine room, encircled by iron railings and covered with an iron grating. The water was 425ft below, 855ft of water in all with a capacity of 3,800 gallons. It had eventually cost just under £6,600 – out of a total cost of just over £21,000 for the schools – instead of the several hundred pounds of the original estimate. A man called Marsh, aged 24, had actually died during its digging after falling 150ft. His workmates had collected £6 for his wife and recently born child, and the Guardians had resolved to have a subscription for him. The workmen's achievement was immense, for they had managed to dig the deepest man made well in the world, 1285ft – longer than the Empire State building is high – and they still hold that record.[ii]

---

[i] Volks Electric Railway (1883).

[ii] It was ironic that just 16 years later the well was abandoned in favour of the Corporation's piped water supply.

*Fig 9 Medal struck to honour the men who
dug the well at Warren Farm.*

With the opening of the schools imminent, there was now genuine optimism that the maxim "once a pauper, always a pauper" might not now apply to children considered to be a degraded caste who seldom rose above the pauperism into which they were born. The alternative to being a child of the workhouse in Brighton, was to be a child of the street, a "street arab":

> You see them in the back streets – those dirty ragged objects, more like animals than children. You find them at times emerging from their burrows into the town, flitting fast in wild battered herds, or crouching in pursuit of their mysterious pleasures about the filthy gutters.[7]

* * *

On August 14th 1862, led by the governor of the workhouse, Edward Sattin, his wife and the Industrial Schools Committee, a procession of 77 boys and 65 girls with flags and banners accompanied by the juvenile band, marched from the Church Hill site in Lower Dyke Road, down North Street and along Grand Parade. It was reported that the children "looked well and happy". From the bottom of Elm Grove the youngest were taken up in vans and the rest straggled up the hill. After a walk of an hour and a half they arrived at the Warren Farm site situated on the slope of a hill on the east side of Brighton racecourse. They faced a plain two-storey-high building broadly T-shaped in layout, with the boys accommodated on one side and the girls on the other. It was surrounded by a high wall. Sattin handed over a list of the children to the newly appointed superintendent and matron, Mr and Mrs Hales.

On entering the gates the children were lined up outside the main building to listen to a speech by Mr Marchant, the chairman of the Guardians' schools committee. He told them he had brought them there in order to prevent them ever again returning to a workhouse and that they should be grateful for the education they would receive in the schools. The children were marched into the building, according to the *Brighton Examiner*, looking "both pleased and astonished whilst the band followed afterwards". That evening, the Guardians threw a party for themselves.

A few days later, a reporter from the *Brighton Guardian* came to visit. In front of the schools "there are grass banks, a shrubbery skirting the road, and a lawn of some extent, relieved by flower beds...altogether a pretty piece of pleasure ground". He was met at the entrance by Mr Hales' clerk, "a bright, intelligent-looking lad, with a pen in his hand – albeit he was clad in pauper uniform". He found the rooms not luxurious but neat and

Fig 10 *Warren Farm.*

tidy and listened to children singing a "well-known Spanish Chant with most creditable precision and harmony":

> Give these pauper children but a tolerable education and there is at once engendered in their minds enough self-respect, self-pride, if you like - to act as a powerful means of saving them from falling into that slough of vicious degradation into which it is well-known too many workhouse-reared girls have sunk when assailed and overcome by temptations they meet on being thrown on their own resources. The children all looked happy and those who were asked unhesitatingly replied that they much preferred their new quarters to the workhouse.[8]

In the centre of the building were the dining room and the chapel. In the former the food was brought up by a hoist which rose through the floor from the basement. The chapel was "plainly fitted up". However, both rooms had "a most objectionable arrangement":

> … a high wooden screen runs down the centre of each room and completely divides the male and the female children. Why, in the name of common sense is this so? Do the most sapient members of the Board of Guardians imagine that the boys in these Industrial Schools are to be kept unaware of the fact that there are such beings as girls in existence? And even conceding the impossibility, what good can come of the oblivion? If, on the other hand, the lads are to be made aware that girls are in the building, what is the use of shutting out each sex from the sight of the other? Will any object be served; will the morality of the inmates be more assured? Those who answer in the affirmative are regaling themselves on worse than nonsense. It is not too much to say that those unfortunate screens in the chapel and refectory will have almost the same, if not a greater, effect on the children than even the contamination of a workhouse.
>
> Will not a moment's thought convince the most prejudiced that the first query Jem Baggs puts to himself on one side of the screen is why such a separation is raised between himself and little Sally Scriggins on the other? And does not the question, thus induced, call up, even in Jem's untutored mind, a train of consideration that had, far better be allowed to lie dormant? If Sally's juvenile charms were exposed to his gaze, undoubtedly custom would so dull them that the number of stitches in the back seam of Tim Bobbin's jacket would be a far more alluring study. But, when he finds Sally so jealously hidden from him, will he not, in his rough way, jump to the conclusion that the fruit so carefully forbidden must be very sweet, and at once, boylike, compass measures for having a taste by hook or by crook? Bedsides, Messieurs Directors and Guardians, are you dealing with criminals, with children who have plunged

into depravity, or with poor unfortunates whose trials and griefs have but sobered the exuberance of youth and blunted the impetuosity of childhood? Is your establishment to be a school or a reformatory? If the former, would you in the social education of your own individual family divide the sexes by a firescreen across your mahogany, leaving only yourself and your good wife tete-a-tete? No, no; away with those screens! Let the seats be placed at each side, close to the walls, so as to leave a wide pathway in the middle of the rooms, if you like; but do get rid of the screens. Depend upon it they will only engender sin every day you allow them to stand, instead of, as you imagine, conserving morality.

Granville Pigott, a Poor Law inspector, had also objected to the screens when he had first seen the plans, but the Guardians had ignored his advice. The idea of a screen was nothing new as one had already been placed in the chapel at Church Hill in 1854 after "disgraceful conduct" between the able-bodied males and females during a service.

After looking at a ward where all newcomers were to have their clothes disinfected, the reporter visited the schools infirmary and found:

> …a poor girl in a decline whom we found sitting lonely on a chair at the head of one of the beds in the dormitory. Poor creature, she looked very lonely, and we could not help thinking that in such cases, above all others the path to the grave of the poor orphan should be smoothed as much as possible. We feel sure this will be so; but that dying girl with the crooked shoulders, and the convex chest, and the hectic flush, and the bright eyes, and the hollow cheeks looked very sad as she sat by the head of her little bedstead.

In each of the dormitories, there was a curtained-off space set apart as the bedroom of an adult official in charge. "The children lie on mattresses stuffed with cocoa-nut fibre, and are covered with a blanket and counterpane, the latter prominently marked with the title of the establishment". The reporter finished by visiting the farm buildings which he described as "a model farmstead, with a piggery with windows in its walls and twenty acres of land with a coach house and stables and a good crop of oats…The ratepayers may be proud of themselves".

The fundamental idea behind industrial schools in mid-Victorian Britain was that they were to be places of education and industrial training but also of stern discipline. After the 1857 Industrial Schools Act, magistrates could sentence children between the ages of seven to fourteen to these schools. Apart from being abandoned or orphaned, children could be sent to them if they were vagrants, out of control or if their parents were a bad influence. Their objective was to ensure that children of workhouse paupers did not become habitual criminals or new fodder for the workhouses and therefore a long term expense for society. Life was therefore to be based on an almost barrack-style military existence. Although some trades were taught, many believed these schools merely trained children to join the servant classes. In theory, the schools were to be funded by parents, but as so many of the children were homeless the ratepayers bore most of the expense.

Fig 11 Warren Farm Industrial Schools main building.

Before entering Warren Farm, all children had to enter the receiving and quarantine wards at Church Hill. Their heads were shaved and they were placed under medical observation for a period of time. Once sent to the schools – only those aged two or under could not be separated from their parents under the New Poor Law Amendment Act of 1834 – their parents could only visit after obtaining permission from the Guardians. They saw them in a special room with staff around unless the child was sick. Children could leave before they were sixteen only if they were placed in employment or if their parents were granted their "discharge" from the workhouse.

The new schools strictly followed national rules. Every boy above the age of ten was to have his own bed. The children, half an hour after the bell for rising, were to have their names called out by the schoolmaster before having their breakfast of mixed gruel and bread. Silence was to be observed at all times during meals. All the children were to have 18 hours education a week – the Guardians had to approve of all the literature used – and be drilled by a drill-master. The older children had to do housework and instruct the youngsters. The boys were groomed for military bands, trades such as tailoring and boot making and agriculture, while the girls were taught sewing and encouraged to go into service. If any girl who was put out to service returned, she was not entitled to any education in the school. Offences such as the playing of cards could be punished by a bread diet for 48 hours. More serious misbehaviour led to a 24-hour confinement or a beating which could only take place two hours after the offence in the presence of two staff. Girls could not be beaten but could, like the boys, be sent back to the workhouse which was considered to be the severest punishment.

A year later, on the anniversary of its opening, 14th August, 150 children with their band arrived under the grandstand of the Brighton racecourse shortly after 2pm, formed into a square and sang "God save the Queen". There followed games, tea and some free toys sent by a Guardian, Henry Willet, before they started for home at seven singing "Home Sweet Home". It was reported that "there were 24 in the band although only 12 played properly". This was their holiday that year.

* * *

As plans for the new workhouse in Elm Grove developed painfully slowly the Poor Law Board complained bitterly about Church Hill. In 1860 Commissioner Lutwidge said that "the whole house had an aspect of discomfort, not just the infirmary, and that it was not meeting the needs of the inmates in winter and its internal arrangements are very defective".[9] One of the male assistants claimed that he could not visit the infirmary wards without needing a drink before and after. In 1861, out of 689 inmates 393 were "sick, old or disabled" and only 16 men and 35 women were considered to be able-bodied and they had to do their labour inside.[i] Sattin

---

[i] In 1860 Florence Nightingale wrote: "Every year our workhouses are becoming more and more receptacles for the sick, rather than for the able-bodied". *Workhouse Visiting Society Journal*, April 1860.

admitted that sometimes there were not enough able-bodied men to work the water pump. Only the old and infirm worked outside on the shrubberies. Three years later, Edward Sattin wrote to the Guardians explaining why the maintenance charges had gone up:

> Never during the nine years I have been connected with this institution have there been so many aged and sick cases, all requiring extra dietary, clothing, washing and attendance. I am frequently at my wits end to provide private accommodation and attendants, and often wish myself in some other office than that of Master of a Workhouse.[10]

The Poor Law Board complained that "the proposed new workhouse was preventing all improvements on the old structure which has become more dilapidated and uncomfortable…there is not a cheerful well-lighted room anywhere; and the ordinary dayrooms, as well as the basements, abominable".[11] And there was another problem: the stench of the cesspools in the garden at Church Hill. There was no drainage to the sea. It was annoying the neighbours:

> This morning it has been worse than ever – enough to drive us all out of the house, for, notwithstanding closed windows, it has permeated the cracks, crevices and keyholes, filling every room, and causing us to inhale gas most destructive to health for every person living in the neighbourhood. An occupant of Buckingham Road has moved because of it.
>
> *A letter from James Howell* [12]

Despite the opening of the industrial schools in 1862, Church Hill continued to be overcrowded, with an average of over 650 inmates. In 1864, a Guardian, Henry Willet, proposed emigration as a solution as he believed the workhouse encouraged dependency. When it was full they were forced to give outdoor relief, which caused "hereditary pauperism". In fact, that year, with a population of just under 78,000, Brighton spent £12,000 on outdoor relief supporting 9,000 people. Willet joked that some workmen came out of the pub saying "Oh! We'll go and see Sammy[i] [and get some money]". Other Guardians believed most paupers did not want to emigrate and that a new enlarged workhouse was necessary, particularly in winter

---

[i] Samuel Thorncroft, the assistant overseer.

when unemployment was high. Also, they claimed it would enable them to have more accommodation for lunatics instead of having to send them to asylums. To keep them at the workhouse cost 5s a week as opposed to 10s to 14s in an asylum.

To combat "hereditary pauperism", another Guardian, William Day, argued that the names and addresses of all those claiming outdoor relief should be published in order to detect fraud. The Poor Law Board refused to give any guidance on the matter. Conditions outside the workhouse were still hard. In March 1864, a young girl, Marion Jane Pearce, was found in a shed near the racecourse in a destitute condition, soaked to the skin lying on wet straw. She had been refused admission to the workhouse and had stolen a petticoat. The magistrates sentenced her to one month's hard labour and told her she must then go into the workhouse.

* * *

On Twelfth Night 1865 the following invitation was sent out to ratepayers:

> By permission of the Directors and Guardians of the Poor of the Parish of Brighton, a Musical Entertainment will be given to the Inmates at the Workhouse, on Thursday evening, January 5th 1865. To commence at half-past six o'clock precisely. [13]

A hundred parishioners took advantage of the invitation and arrived at the Boys' School Room at Church Hill which was decorated with illuminations and messages of welcome. On one side of the room was a raised platform where the local dignitaries and Guardians sat, the other being filled with adult inmates. Edward Sattin introduced the proceedings:

> For the sixth time we are permitted to assemble for the purpose of passing an evening together…The propriety of these gatherings has been questioned… but by these meetings you may feel that not only the aid the law requires is given, but that the hearts of the givers go with it; and we aim, by inducing you to think kindly of your fellow creatures, to lead you to think also of Him who is the Great Keeper of us all…. During the last five years there have been 5,515 admissions; 177 births; 5018 discharges; 604 deaths and about 16,000 tramps relieved…One must also bear in mind that service in a House of this kind

involves seven days a week, and long days too. Surely, then, our endeavours to relieve the monotony of this life should be kindly looked upon. Permit me to wish you all a "Happy New Year".[14]

A Mrs May led the singing of "Jolly John Bull" accompanied by a Miss Wood, followed by a rendition of "Happy Sunshine" by Miss Brook and "Richard and Kate" by Rhoda Martin, a sixty-three year old inmate. At the interval they had oranges, cake, coffee and tea. Lt Col Moorsom, chairman of the Guardians, then made a speech which he concluded by saying that "happiness did not depend on wealth or station, and that contentment and real enjoyment were to be found in the workhouse as well as the palace".

That year a Dr Foreman asked if he could give amusing and instructive "readings" to the inmates for an hour. He wanted to "break the monotony of their cheerless lives". One Guardian objected because "some people thought out-of-doors that the poor in the house got much better entertainment than those out of the house". Another believed "instead of being a workhouse it would become a playhouse or a place of amusements". Foreman's proposal was rejected.

Since 1860 the aged inmates had enjoyed a summer treat at the Swiss Gardens in Shoreham. In July 1865, 160 of them between the ages of 60 and 94, were marched down to the station and taken to Shoreham. When they arrived, they were allowed to drink beer and smoke their pipes. They were given tea on the lawns, served by the Guardians, and then attended the theatre. When they got back to Brighton they were led by the Industrial Schools' Juvenile Band playing "Home Sweet Home", and marched to Church Hill. There the band struck up the national anthem before returning to Woodingdean.

On Thursday 11 May 1865, with the rain falling fast, a group of well-dressed women, councillors and Guardians sheltered under a temporary shed erected over the site where the first stone of the new workhouse was to be laid in Elm Grove. At the entrance flags flew and the brass band of the industrial schools kept them entertained whilst they waited. The ceremony began with the choir of All Saints Church singing the 127th Psalm, followed by prayers from the workhouse chaplain, the Rev J. Allen. Then Moorsom carefully prepared the bed of the stone, which was lowered into its place.

As he struck it with a mallet made of American birch he said:

I lay this stone in the name of the Father, and of the Son and of the Holy Ghost, the holy and undivided Trinity. And may this house, here to be erected, be a blessing to the poor of Christ. [15]

He placed a bottle containing an engrossed document into a hole cut in the stone, covered it with fine sand and fitted a thick slate slab over the hollow. It contained the name of the architect, George Maynard, and the builder and all the names of the Guardians. Moorsom declared:

They were about to raise a workhouse for above 800 persons and he trusted that the social conditions of the lower classes might be so far improved that the number of persons who would apply for admission, would not increase in proportion to the usual increase in the population of the country. (*Hear, hear*). But, even supposing they should have as many in the house as there had been during the last winter, and 696 was the largest number at any one time, what a history it would be, provided that a record of their lives could be written! (*Hear, hear*).

Perhaps a large number of them might not have needed assistance had it not been for their own improvidence or vice. (*Hear, hear*). But he was not there to cast a stone at any unfortunate fellow creatures….there were also a great number who were there not through any fault of their own, but from misfortune. He would take first the old soldier, perhaps a Peninsular or Waterloo man, who with all his friends dead, gave up his pension to enter the Workhouse to end his days, and he passed those days calmly, peacefully, and contentedly, awaiting that great change which must come upon all. (*Hear, hear*).

Then there was the old servant, whose employers were gone. Her eyes were dim, but she could see sufficiently to read some portion of the Holy Scriptures during the day, and these were sufficient to give her comfort in her old age; and she, too, awaited, in this place of refuge, that great change that must come upon all.

After giving a brief history of the Poor Laws, he turned to the question of the able-bodied poor:

….there was great difficulty; for to deal with them required great discrimination (*hear, hear*): and the longer he was in office….the more he was convinced of the great liability of the Board to be deceived. Even Mr Thorncroft, who had been in office between 30 and 40 years, he believed was occasionally misled. There were many men who might say, "So and so has relief, why should not I? He is not worse off than me". And so, when he came to the parish, it was difficult to discriminate between the two – between those who can support themselves and those who cannot. (*Hear, hear*). It seemed, then, that the workhouse was the necessary test, and that was why the present ceremony was taking place – to lay the first stone of a new Workhouse, in order to apply that test.

Moorsom then spoke about the lack of trained or paid staff at the workhouse infirmary where "the aged and infirm lived, with no hope of recovery as in the hospitals, their only passage was to the grave". He believed the local hospital had a 'competent staff' whilst in the workhouse infirmary there were no nurses or assistants and the inmates had to do make do with 'nurses' selected from themselves. He ended by hoping "that the step which had been taken that day in laying the first stone of the new workhouse, would be a step towards ameliorating the sufferings of a large class in this important borough. (*Loud applause*)".

The national anthem was sung by the choristers and the party wended its way to the Park Tavern, Queen's Park cricket ground, where luncheon was served. Much drinking followed, interspersed with occasional speeches. When it came to the chaplain's turn, he compared "the present comfortable state of the inmates of the workhouse with that in which they were fifteen, twenty and twenty-five years since, when it was thought necessary to rule them with a rod of iron, and violence was being constantly committed – when there was but little pity, less sympathy, and no love to lighten up the gloom of their desolate minds, or to relieve the monotony of their destitute hearts (*Applause*)". He then proposed a toast to a man who he respected very highly, "a man whom he had heard it said that there is a thin crust of severity overlaying the native generosity of his fine character....but he believed that a more considerate mind for the interests of the poor, and a tenderer heart for them, did not exist than that possessed by Mr Samuel Thorncroft. (*Loud applause*). "To the Health of the Assistant-Overseer!"

Thorncroft stood up to respond and was described as "emotional" – a euphemism for drunk. He spoke about how he was always kind to those in distress but harsh with those who were not. He finished by saying:

> . . . he had had 14 years' experience in the workhouse, and he knew that it happened sometimes that for a nurse they were compelled to have a dissipated pauper who had spent her whole life in debauchery and sin….he hoped to see the day when those who were sick, would not have the attendance of dissipated paupers, but the consolation which can be afforded by feeling and kindhearted nurses.

After several more speeches, the proceedings ended with Moorsom giving three pence each to the 140 men involved in the construction of the new workhouse and to the Industrial Schools Band. A few days later, the Guardians censured Thorncroft for his remarks, although it was common knowledge that most workhouse "nurses" were over sixty and either physically incapable of doing the job or were drunk. Indeed, pauper nurses in workhouses were often rewarded for their work with gin. His claim that he was "always kind to those in distress" was more debatable. In 1860, a lodging housekeeper had brought a sick man to him in a wheel-barrow and Thorncroft had refused him relief. So the housekeeper had left him outside Thorncroft's house till the magistrates ordered that he be given temporary relief.

However unpopular Thorncroft was with some of the Guardians, they knew he was indispensable because of his vast knowledge and experience of the poor laws. He had even, on one occasion, been called by a Parliamentary Committee to give his views on them. He was a churchwarden of All Souls Church and in 1853 became the registrar of births and deaths for the St Peter's district of Brighton. It was a paid position and although the Guardians allowed him to do the two jobs, at one stage they cut his assistant overseer's wages in the hope he would resign from the other post: much to their amazement, he did not. However, he did write a series of anonymous letters – signed "inhabitant" – to the *Brighton Herald* which criticized the policies of the Guardians. Even though he eventually admitted authorship, he was not reprimanded.

* * *

From 1859 to 1864, more than 20,000 people had been admitted into the workhouse, three quarters of them as vagrants. In January 1866, a Poor Law inspector, Mr R.B. Cane, criticized the Brighton Guardians' laxity towards vagrants who used the workhouse as a "good hotel …considering the great attraction of Brighton and considering the Guardians were so lenient, he wondered they did not have more vagrants." [16] Crane covered the southern district of England consisting of sixty-eight Unions and pointed out that Brighton was one of only four Unions which did not require its casuals to work. Whereas the general trend in his district in 1865 had been a decrease in vagrants, Brighton's had gone up.[i] Furthermore, usually the number of vagrants was less in summer than in winter but this was not the case in Brighton. Crane recommended that after breakfast the able-bodied ones should be sent to work for four hours and suggested oakum picking as a task. Unlike stone-breaking, it could be done inside during bad weather and was more profitable. [ii]

Following Crane's visit, Lt Col Moorsom, declared:

> There is a population growing up which does not work at all. It wanders about from one place to another in idleness and sin…There is no education for the children, except an education in evil…We see a man and wife wandering about the streets making some horrible noise which they call "singing" and dragging about with them a number of poor children. A maidservant goes out and gives them a penny; a lady or gentleman passing by gives them six pence, an act of very great cruelty.[17]

But some Guardians were against the idea of making vagrants work as it might induce them to stay or they might become ill. Their wives and children were often in cheap lodging houses nearby, and if the vagrants were made to work they would be begging in the streets. It was far better that the vagrants left first thing in the morning, 6am in summer and 8am in the winter. Besides, if they worked they would have to be fed extra food – more than the 4oz of bread for breakfast and 6oz for supper they were receiving – and be supervised. Although the Guardians rejected the idea of making vagrants work for the first night, they decided to require those who came more than once in any week to pick two ounces of oakum. They sent Sattin to the Government stores at Woolwich to buy £50 worth of oakum.

Despite the view that the vagrants ward – or casuals ward as it was now called – was "a good hotel", this was not how the vagrants themselves saw it. In 1857, Richard Neale, a sixty-two-year-old shipwrecked sailor who had been picked up from an Australian beach, had eventually made his way to the Brighton casual ward. He was suffering from bronchitis and dysentery. In a letter to the Poor Law Board, he described the ward as "a travelling menagerie for the exhibition of wild animals" and that he had to sleep on

---

[i] 1,997 in the second half of 1864, 2,503 in the corresponding period for 1865.

[ii] Crane said oakum could be bought at 15s and the finished product sold at one pound.

loose straw "in a kind of cell without fire".[18] He complained about the "scandalous treatment in this place", which included bread and gruel for breakfast, and cheese and bread for dinner and supper. The only drink he received was cold water. Neale protested about "an old man rolling in pain on loose straw for 41 days and nights. The stench became so great, a man volunteered to remove the wet straw. He was so overcome when he wheeled it away he had to have restoratives". One man told Neale he would sooner be in prison than submit to "such tyranny" and tore his clothes[i] and received one months' imprisonment. Neale ended his letter by saying that, although sick, he found he was "mixed up with the vermin and filth of travellers who came in at night from all parts of the country" and that the "instances of petty tyranny here have been so numerous that I have omitted to say them all".

The Poor Law Board asked the Brighton Guardians to enquire into Neale's allegations. They replied that the ward had clean straw every week; that it was cleaned out every morning; that the vagrants were given a blanket and rug; and that the ward was heated. They did admit, however, that the medical officer was reluctant to put vagrants into the infirmary.

In March 1863, four inmates wrote to the Poor Law Board complaining of the quality of the bread and cheese diet and that:

> instead of giving us work outside or an order for the House, they place us in the Tramps Ward where we have been for several weeks.[19]

A Guardian, Lucas, at the next meeting moved the following resolution:

> That the Poor Law Board be informed that the four persons who have complained of being placed in the Mendicants Ward are idle and disorderly characters, preferring to pass their time in the workhouse rather than to be obtaining their own livelihood ....[20]

There was no law against the Guardians putting who they liked in the vagrants ward – by far the worst accommodation – and they were not averse to placing able-bodied inmates there to make them leave quickly and find work. In 1865, an inmate, James Backing, wrote to the Board to complain.

---

[i] A traditional way of protesting against conditions.

For two weeks I was kept in the tramps' ward, lying on the boards with a little straw, an old blanket and an old rug full of vermin. I had a bad leg and was attended by a doctor who ordered me poultices for my leg. I was kept there with very little food to eat. Two days later the doctor laughed when he saw me and I told him about the vermin, the cold and the lack of food…It is a miserable place full of sick people. We can make no complaint as no visiting gentlemen have been here since I have been here… There is a law for cruelty to dumb animals and I hope that there is for a poor man. Let the public know…[21]

The Board wrote to the Guardians. At an enquiry, Richard Rugg, the work-house surgeon, said that he thought that Blacking was "well-able to tramp out of Brighton as into it".[22] However, Blacking was transferred to the able-bodied ward.

*   *   *

One cold wintry evening in November 1866, a solitary figure of a tramp could be seen climbing the steep hill on the summit of which stood Church Hill. He was wearing:

> …a hat that could have been spared a little of its "ventilator", a coat with sundry slits in the back and at the elbows, collar turned up and buttoned up to the chin, trousers that might have been the "cast off" of the most woe-begone navvy, and boots that from encrusted dirt upon them belied the idea of any very recent lengthy journey – this was the costume of the individual striking enough, surely; but his actions were even more singular. An irrepressible desire seemed to possess him, when no other person was near, to give vent to fits of uncontrollable laughter and glee; although, on passing either shop, lamp, or passenger, demure was his look, and a hand was constantly raised to pull some of the shaggy locks that escaped from under the brim of his hat with the evident intention of concealing identity. After many a pause, and with a limp as though the boots were strangers to his feet he …[23]

But this was no ordinary tramp, it was, in fact, a young reporter from the *Brighton Examiner* and he was on his way to the casual ward at Church Hill. Earlier that year, a respected journalist, James Greenwood, of the *Pall Mall Gazette*, had similarly disguised himself and had entered Lambeth workhouse. He had found that pretending to be a tramp was no easy part to play. How would the young Brighton reporter get on?

An 1869 study entitled 'Houseless and Hungry' by Luke Fildes, depicting homeless paupers queuing outside the casual ward of a London workhouse. A policeman stands at the left of the scene. [Mary Evans/Peter Higginbotham collection]

Chapter Six

A NIGHT IN THE CASUALTY WARD

When the reporter arrived at Church Hill, he and three other tramps obtained the necessary admission tickets and "set out to tramp over the hill to the place, "three lamps above", where the casual ward was situated. When the workhouse had first opened the ward had been in the main building, now as shown on the map,[i] it was to its north. After ringing the bell and a kick at the door the four were let in by a little old man "dressed in the garb of an inmate of the House". He collected their tickets and showed them into a little office "round the wall of which were ranged shelves covered with official looking volumes, and also a large card headed 'Government Rules for Vagrants', setting forth that the dietary was 'Evening, six ounces of bread; morning, four ounces ditto'." The reporter was interviewed by a little girl about fourteen years of age. Believing that "the end justifieth the means", he had the following conversation:

> What is your name? – Henry Jones
> What is your age? – 22
> Where were you born? – Portsmouth
> Where do you belong to? – Portsmouth
> Where have you come from today? – Newhaven
> Where are you going to? Portsmouth
> Can you read and write? – Yes
> What trade are you? – Well, I ain't any; labourer I suppose

After emptying their pockets of all possessions, the porter conducted the men across the yard and pushed three of them into a little stove room while the fourth was taken to the bathroom. While waiting, not wanting to give the game away, the reporter kept as silent as he could, and "gave an affirmative nod to all questions".

---

[i] The map for the 1850s on page 51.

[ii] Giving a false name made it difficult for Guardians to "ration" tramps to a certain number of nights.

His turn came:

I followed my Mentor, and soon found myself in the "bath-room," an apartment of about 10ft by 7ft, containing two baths, although but one was in use on
the occasion of my visit. "Take off all your clothes, my man, and tie 'em up in
a bundle," said old Cerberus.[i] After complying with this order, though my
awkwardness in the tying-up process was made the subject of some deprecatory
remarks, I plunged in, but almost immediately regretted my haste, for that
which I supposed to be clean warm water turned out to be a most dingy hue,
of exceedingly questionable purity, and I had the uncomfortable belief in my
mind that the three bona fide casuals in whose company I had arrived, had
previously washed off the dirt, and other disagremens consequent on a day's
tramp across country, in the identical water in which the old porter requested
me to "well wash your face, young man"; and afterwards added, "you should
be very pertickler about your feet, my man ,'cos they's very important." With
a feeling of nausea rising within me, I quickly emerged, and having passed
muster, was wiping myself with the towel there provided, when another was
ushered in, no doubt to enjoy an "invigorating bath" in the same doubtful-
looking liquid from which I had risen…

Old Cerberus handed me a long blue shirt, on which was displayed, in large
letters, the word "Brighton," (all my own clothes – boots and all – having
previously vanished under the guardianship of the old fellow), and having
arrayed myself in it, the door was opened, and out into the piercing cold night
air, from the comparatively warm atmosphere of the bathroom itself, with
nothing on but the long shirt, and an old, worn out pair of slippers…

He shivered and trembled as he walked twenty yards or more across the
yard, "the cold night wind whistling round my bare head", before arriving
at a shed. It was about 12ft in height, 50ft in length and 9ft wide, with three
separate entrances. On opening the door he was startled to see two rows of
bedding running the whole length of the shed: one about a foot from the
floor, the second about four feet above the other. They were covered with
a few inches of straw. As he entered he saw "five or six occupants crouching
in all manner of postures" and gazing at every new arrival.

---

[i] A monstrous watchdog in Greek mythology.

"Get in here, my man; close up to him," said old Cerberus, "and here's your blanket and rug". Mounting over the foot-board, I clambered amongst the straw, and here for the first time almost disclosed my incognito. The blanket that was thrown to me I spread out entirely, and somewhat clumsily (being no chambermaid), and knowing I was altogether ignorant of the proper manner of the arrangement, I became confused and was doubling it somehow, when, in consequence of the exclamations of my confreres who were already in bed, the attention of the old porter was attracted, and he considerately volunteered me some information. Feeling the blood rising in my cheek, and everything depending on my playing my character out to the letter, I gave utterance to an exclamation, which, without exaggeration, I may describe as "hanging in my teeth,"… "— the blanket, and the parish, too," said I; and as I spoke, my keen furtive glance showed me that my words had dispelled any doubts that might still lurk in the minds of either my brother "casuals" or in the old porter himself. Down I huddled; and, after a short time in came the two others, and from the manner in which they adjusted their blankets and rugs, I easily guessed – "amateur" that I was – that these at least might justly claim the appellation of vagrants, and a berth in a refuge for a wandering destitute.

"Hoi, you old curmudgeon, bring this 'ere child a drop o' water, will ye," shouted the last comer to the old porter, to invent a name for whom I do not care to starch my imagination as did a prototype of mine.

"The Guardians don't keep servants to wait on such as you my man," was the reply of the old porter; "if yer wants any water, ye'd better get up and fetch it, my man. However, I'll bring it this once," and suiting the action to the word, he went to one corner of the ward, where there was a large can full of water, and fetched some in a tin hat that would hold comfortably a quart or more.

"You're worth a 'jew's eye,' old bloke; I'm – if you ain't," replied the first speaker, but with such a peculiarly telling emphasis, that the old gent alluded to at once took up his lamp, slammed the door, and left us all in total darkness, with the tin full of water in the hands of the one furthest from the can, who, after a "swig," passed it down until it reached one more thirsty than the others, who, having first drained it of its contents, after a short consultation, aimed it against the wall, in the direction where the can was supposed to be, for the darkness was so intense that it was impossible to see one's hand a few inches off.

And now the real fun began – all had something to relate; where they came from, where they were going, what success had attended their "cadging" operations, what "pals" they had seen, and other matters incidental to the "profession". One, reposing two or three yards from myself, a big, unshaved, matted-haired sort of fellow, more loquacious than the rest, commenced the general conversation, after a volley of oaths at the head of the offending official, with a narration of a cure of a certain skin disease, which he had seen recently effected by cramming the mouth of the sufferer with brimstone; this elicited from another further down, the assertion that "I'm cursed if I didn't have it once," which in fact no doubt added greatly to the comfort of the next sleepers. This talkative fellow alluded to what was evidently as much as a parvenu in his way as ever was a wealthy tallow-chandler[i] among the "upper ten thousand," and it was amusing to witness the manner in which my right-hand neighbour cut the ground from under him in some of his bombastic statements.

"That D_____d fellow Jeffery, him as 'peached'[ii] on the safe robbery, and 'split a nut'[iii] in the presence of the whole Court," remarked the hero, continuing the general conversation, by breaking entirely new ground. "I saw the sneaking villain in Millbank t'other day. I'd like to tickle his feet with a straw till his eyes bolted out of his pate, the cuss!"

"How did you see him?" queried the fellow on my right who was called, most inappropriately it seemed to me, "Softy," for he was of all there the most cute and seemed more accustomed to the routine than any, while his closely-shaven head was suggestive of something even worse than a "casual ward".

"Oh, I know the Governor; he's an old friend of mine. He served a twelve month along with me in Derby gaol once," replied the fellow, with all the impudence imaginable.

"What's his name? How long ago was it? Was it on a visiting day, at the reg'ler hours?" quietly asked the other, yet loud enough for all to hear.

"Austin his name was, and its about three months ago, and it was on a visiting day," replied No.1, after a little hesitation.

"Then it's all a ----lie, for I know Captain Redgett has been Governor there for nigh twelve year; I served four years there myself for 'cracking a crib' (committing a burglary), for which I got 'lagged' (apprehended and convicted), was the extinguisher of No. 2.

Nothing daunted, the above loquacious fellow after sleeping off the effects of this, in a few moments commenced again, and made a running commentary on the prospects of "old Moses," who is awaiting his trial in London on several charges of receiving stolen goods, and on two others in the provinces awaiting sentence for a similar offence. At this point – it seemed to me about seven o'clock two or three more casuals came in, wearing their shirts, which gave a great similarity to their appearance, swearing and cursing the old porter,

---

[i] Candle maker.

[ii] Gave information.

[iii] Break open an iron safe.

because he would only allow two of them who were "pals" and thus slept together, but one blanket. His entrance, too, seemed to elicit a fresh volley of oaths from all, and some most uncomplimentary remarks were passed on him, some of which I could not, at the time quite understand. Omitting the disgusting epithets that were so profusely interspersed with their remarks, this is a specimen of the lingo that was shouted from one end of the ward to the other:-

"You cursed whelp, son of a dam, what --- time do you bring round the d----d 'stark naked?' I'd like to get at ye; I'd spile your cussed carcas, s'help me, I would!"

"Now, my men; now my men;" remarked the old man, in a weak, trembling sort of voice, occasionally found in persons of his class and occupation; and then he would alter, and speaking in as commanding a tone as he possibly could, would add, "If you're not more quiet, I'll stop your 'lowance. The Guardians 'as given me my orders, an' them I follers".

"You cursed psalm-singing hound, you don't foller your orders. That water in that bath ought to have been changed, but you lazy lubber, it was like so much soft mud to pitch your carcass into it, a-opening that door on me four times as you did when I was having my bath; " shouted one of the latest arrivals.

" Now, my men; be quiet, will you?" and away went the old porter, leaving his lamp on the edge of the footboard.

An animated conversation followed his departure as to what would be the next penalty of "pitching into" the old porter on his next appearance, some contending that as he was but an assistant and a pauper, no punishment could be inflicted for so doing; while others as stoutly maintained that it was a "matter of six months in the crank," but all dispute was put to an end to by "Softy," who said, "You'd better not try that game on; I'd four months myself last year for tapping a pauper on the head down at Ripley, in Yorkshire."

Being altogether unable to withstand such an overwhelming fact, the advocate of a slight corporal punishment on the old porter gave in, and other topics were discussed, among which were the stoppage of gruel and substitution of the "stark naked" in its place, and the recent commencement of the bath, which was, it appeared, abandoned at the time of the Races; a comparison being instituted between their present apartments and the accommodation in other parishes, the different kinds of employment in which they had repaid their night's lodging, the various ways in which they had successfully shirked their "labour task," and congratulation that Brighton was an exception in that matter.

"Softy," said I, turning to my right hand neighbour – he who had "done" four years in Millbank, and who now told me that he had been in the present quarters a score of times or more, and had seen as much of prison life as almost any man in the country – "Softy, where's my next crib? I'm going to Portsmouth".

"Well," replied he, "you'd better go to where I said I come from today – anything does for them, you know – Storrington. You has as much gruel there as you want – 'taint bad skilly, either. Matey," he added; "if you can 'cadge' a brown (beg a penny) or two tomorrow, and keep 'em dark till ye gets to Petworth, ye can buy as much 'grub' in the house as ye'likes, cold meat and enough to fill ye – on the quiet, you know. Gad's truth, I'd feed a feed there two nights ago for 1½d. I tried cadging from house to house down in the town for two hours last night, and never got a — farthing. It's frightful slack is trade now; gets nothing but bread anywhere's"; and with this doleful lament, "Softy" laid down his head amongst the straw and endeavoured to sleep.[i]

Gradually the conversation died down, and most seemed to sleep except for two "pals" next to the reporter who discussed their plans for the next day. He sat up and surveyed the room. It had been recently white-washed and clean straw was thickly spread along the whole length of the room with a burning hot pipe running outside the footboard:

I counted about thirteen shaggy heads, some pushed quite out of the blankets into the midst of the straw, and others completely lost sight of under the coverlet. Some were lying on their backs as straight and motionless as though laid out in readiness for burial, while the knees of others were barely an inch from their chins. A general snoring match seemed about to be commenced, when the door was once more opened, and the old porter again appeared on the scene, this time bearing in front of him a half bushel basket, containing the six ounces of bread to each inmate, which had been referred to in the previous conversation as "stark naked".

"Wake up, my men; wake up, will you," called out the old fellow, passing down the passage until he reached its extreme end, where, after administering a sharp knock on the knees of the last casual to arouse him, he tossed a lump of bread into his lap. By this time all were awake, and it was a strange sight to see the eagerness with which some, not withstanding the manifold curses they heaped on the "stark naked" character of their entertainment, grasped the "six ounces" which the parish allots as the evening repast to the able-bodied vagrant. My turn came, and into my lap came flung a huge piece of dry bread,

---

[i] With workhouses being only one day's tramp from each other, the "bush telegraph" warning of bad conditions, or publicizing the fact that a supply of oakum had run out in a particular workhouse, took approximately three days. Scribbled messages – a kind of tramps' "Facebook" – also helped spread the word.

which for the sake of appearance, I began to eat, though almost before I had tasted it, its difference from that to which I had previously been accustomed, had driven away the little appetite I had gained in a self-imposed fast.

"D'ye call that six ounces, ye old spalpeen?" said one, pushing up his "stark naked" into the porters' face, "ye – false-weighted curmudgeon".

"There's a little bit; I think it belongs to you, my man," said the porter, tossing him another piece.

I could not eat mine, and so, after making a motion to one further down, I tossed him the remainder, reserving to myself but a small portion of the crust.

The old porter then lifted the can in the corner, and picking up the tin from the place where it had fallen, brought a drink of water to each of us, remarking, in answer to the question whether he had "shut up shop", "Yes, my man; the Guardians' orders is to close at six, but we lets you in till eight, ar'ter which none is allowed admission, by orders".

"Then they may die of the cold, I s'pose," said one.

"That's nothing to us, my man," responded the old porter; and then, putting the can again in its place in the corner, he vanished, and we saw him no more till the following morning. Directly he had left, however, another old gent appeared, who was greeted with loud shouts of welcome.

"Good night, Mr Jenkins, good night; hope you're quite well. Ain't dead yet, then," resounded from several voices.

"Dead!" responded the jovial individual referred to; "not I; worth a dozen dead 'uns yet!" jumping about in proof of his assertion; and then, passing down the passage to where the lamp was standing, he took it up, and after recognizing several of the inmates, and bringing them more water, he passed out, with many a "Good night, Mr Jenkins," following him from those whom he had left in total darkness. This was, as it seemed to me, about half-past eight, and it would be less than ten hours, at the very least before the following day dawned, during the whole of which time we were left in utter darkness, which was the cause of frightful oaths on the part of all the genuine vagrants, and I myself could not help thinking that it was a most dangerous proceeding on the part of the authorities to leave without a light of any sort a body of men of such desperate character as those in whose company I was. Apart from being dangerous, it was an unnecessarily cruel thing to do, for there was the contingency – however remote it might be – that one of us might have been seized with illness – cholera, perhaps – before the morrow.

After the irritation caused by this had somewhat subsided, conversation was again resumed, and the fellow on my left told us how he had "lagged" a coat last winter, adding, "If I see 'ere a shirt hanging in a back yard tomorrow, here's a mate as wants some clean linen, and is no wise particular about being 'lagged' for it, either," which sentiment seemed to be general among all present, if the vociferous applause with which it was received may be taken as a trustworthy criterion. Another, after telling me how he had "cadged a doss" (begged enough money to pay for a bed), said he had met old Joe, who, it appeared, was an acquaintance of some of those present, and who the speaker said had just come back, after having spent ten years in Bermuda as a convict, and who was determined on "cracking a crib" that very night. Another, further down, started a song, seemingly a parody on Robert Burns' well-known song, "A man's a man for a that," the chorus of which appeared to be worded thus:

"Then d---- the p'leese, the 'beaks,' and all,
We'll 'crack the crib' for all that,"

the last line varying in every verse; and so the game was continued for about an hour, perhaps, till nature asserted her claims, and one by one the shouters grew less, until, after a loudly-expressed wish that there might be "a fall of two foot of snow afore morning," from the only one of the company who really seemed in search of work, the remaining ones fell asleep, and I was left wide awake, unable to see my hand a few inches from my eyes, with the certain prospect of at least nine hours elapsing before a ray of light would visit our domicile. The strangeness of my situation kept me awake for some time, but the darkness was beginning to take its natural effect on me, and I was just on the point of dozing off when,

"There, you —, take that," in a startingly loud tone, accompanied by a terrific thwack, and followed by a loud squeal, awoke me, and all the others.

"What's up, mate? Anybody scragged" (hung or killed), shouted all of us.

"Nothing but a — mouse a gnawing at my cheek, but I 'slewed' him I guess," responded the individual, a man who stood over six feet without either stockings or shoes; and my attention having been thus forcibly drawn to the matter, I could now clearly understand the meaning of the sounds that occasionally met my ears from underneath the straw on which I was lying.

Another of our bedfellows seemed also to have experienced discomfort from another source, and "S'help me," he shouted, "I'll roast 'em," and getting up in bed, he coolly took off his shirt, and turning it inside out, gave it a good shaking, and then put it on wrong side outwards.

I, too, felt a peculiar uneasy, crawling sensation about my body, though I did not take such summary measures for the removal of the cause of it as did my quondam companion. Besides this, I had a horribly nasty feeling at my lips, the consequence of my questionable bath; and the smell of the shirt was anything but pleasant. However, all this is to be ascribed, perhaps, to the fact of my being what I was an "amateur casual".

I had now, too begun to get a little warm, and the company having once again dozed off, I soon was, I am forced to think, myself in the "land of dreams," for the next time I awoke I found the door, immediately opposite which I was lying, wide open, and a most uncomfortable cold air rushing in direct upon me. I half jumped up in bed, but could neither see nor hear anything. I sat and listened, until being able to stand it no longer I tumble out, and in doing so caught hold of the hot pipe that skirted the footboard, and falling backwards struck my head a violent blow against the boards of the row of beds above me. Down I fell on top of someone's knees, and immediately was saluted with a volley of curses from a voice which I recognised as "Softy's,

"Fell down on you," said I, " that's what I'm up to;" and after explaining the cause to his expressed satisfaction, once more essayed, and this time successfully, to get over the footboard, and alighting with my naked feet on the icy bricks, passed out of the door, across the yard, into the place fitted up for a closet. In a few moments I was once more crouching between my blanket, and could devote my attention to my companions, who were, with one exception, that of the rheumatic "grenadier," all enjoying that repose which a long day's march renders so welcome, though ever and anon there was, I might say, a prevalency of volley and file-firing in the matter of short, dry, "churchyard" coughs, most distressing to hear. Not being in the least sleepy, I called out –

"Anybody awake, mates?"

"Here's one as can't get a ha'porth of sleep, through this cursed leg of mine. What luck, matey," asked a voice from the corner, which I recognized as that of the above individual.

"None at all. What's your little emag?" I responded ("emag" is back slang for "game!").

"Same here – the day's gone by when you could knock a half-boozey farmer down and finger his plush. Them things that runs on posts, and them 'ere iron rails, matey, has done away with all that;" here he ceased; and being utterly without any material to force a conversation, I found myself once again dozing and dreaming (for no complaint was uttered in my hearing against the "bed," the "board" being the only subject of animadversion). Here I must have slept two or three hours, for presently I awoke with quite a start to find some straggling rays of light coming in through the little windows, which face due east. I lay and listened, and soon found that several of the others were awake and discussing the operations of the coming day.

One after another woke up, and again a general conversation took place, mainly upon the different directions' of the day's tramp, and other matters of but little interest, till one of the doors was opened and the old porter appearing, called out, "Now, my men; now, my men; it's time to get up." A general rise followed, heads shot out from under blankets, or from amongst the straw, pieces of which, like porcupine quills, stood out from some of the shaggy hair. While some were rubbing their eyes and stretching to wake themselves, and one was propounding the question, "I say, Joe, where shall we be this day week?" to which the answer was returned, " — if I know, and I don't care, either." "Softy," who had been wide awake some time, sprung up, and was the first to see the outside of the shed after our incarceration of thirteen hours! Viz. from half-past six on the preceding evening till half-past seven, the time, as it afterwards appeared, that we rose. Three or four others, out of their turn, sprung up, and darted out of the door, amid the hisses and groans of those re-maining.

"You're young on the road, ain't you matey?" said one who appeared in no great hurry to leave his couch, to me, as I sat up, waiting for my legitimate turn.

"Yes, I am; and I've had enough of it already," I replied, hastily jumping up, glad to escape further interrogation. Out of the door, into the yard on the cold frozen bricks with the bare feet I ran, and having selected my bundle, found myself again in the stove-room, in company with two others, arraying myself in the suit I have previously described, in doing which I unfortunately let a penny fall on the brick floor, for the possession of which I had to give an account amidst the ill-concealed envy of my companions. Again, on bare feet, I crossed the yard to where the boots were placed in a row, and selecting mine, which were, I confess, the worst of the lot – indeed, my "get up," on the whole, erred somewhat considerably on the side of poverty, in its soiled, woe-begone aspect – I put them on, and stood waiting for further orders, looking round at my companions, who appeared a most promiscuous party.

"Misfortune make strange bedfellows," and although I was but quasi unfortunate, the old adage in my case proved a true one. Great hulking men, in blouses, bearing upon them the marks of many a long tramp; little villainous looking fellows, carrying in their features the word thief as plain as possible, and others, like "Softy," long-life journeyers in the paths of crime and vice, formerly the majority of those with whom I had passed the night. I stood waiting, for two had already obtained possession of the buckets of warm water which had been placed in the yard for the use of those who wished for a slight wash before proceeding on their day's journey, and several others were crowding round, impatient for their turn, but having no wish to enjoy this "creature comfort," I stood there apparently idly leaning against one of the posts, when the old porter seeing this, came round to me, saying-

"You can go now, young man; all of you can go now;" and so several of us again recrossed the yard, and knocking at the office door, were each supplied with a much smaller piece of "stark naked" than that of the previous night, which was received with loudly-expressed dissatisfaction by all, except myself. Out of the yard door I went, munching my piece of dry bread as I passed out, in order to keep up appearances, until I reached the "Seven Dials," down one of the roads converging into which I ran, till meeting a fly, which was not there entirely by accident, I jumped in, and soon found myself "at home," where, after another bath, this time with clean water, and a most acceptable replenishment of the inner man, I sat me down to pen my experiences of "A Night in the Casual Ward of Brighton Workhouse".

* * *

The week after the article appeared, Sattin was summoned to the Guardians' meeting and questioned about its accuracy. His main criticism was that the nightshirts given to vagrants were white and not blue and that the bathroom was five yards rather than twenty yards from the ward. Overall though, the Guardians were not too displeased, because the reporter confirmed what they had long suspected: that the majority of tramps were, in his words, like "Softy" – "long-life journeyers in the paths of crime and vice". The public, too, distrusted them because no one knew where wandering men and women had their homes or their origin, and they evoked little sympathy from Victorian philanthropists.

The young reporter's findings were consistent with what other under-cover journalists found: that many occupants of the tramps' ward were part of the criminal fraternity or professional beggars, but that there was an honest minority who were genuinely physically or mentally ill and had nowhere else to go. And this minority did not mind being searched and giving up their possessions on arrival as to have them during the night would have invited robbery.

The reporter had also found being locked up for thirteen hours in complete darkness with potentially dangerous or sick people an unnerving experience. His description of the conditions, ie filthy water, vermin and loose straw, tallied exactly with those in the letters from the Church Hill inmates to the Poor Law Board, previously noted. Norman Longmate, in his book *The Workhouse*, claimed that the other inmates of workhouses themselves often dreaded the tramps because of their yelling, shouting and disorder. At Church Hill, as we have seen, the casual ward was eventually a good distance from the main building. However, in the new workhouse being built at Elm Grove, the casual wards were going to be near the main entrance.

It was always accepted that the casual wards would be the most uncomfortable accommodation in a workhouse because of the great antipathy towards vagrants. The workhouse chaplain at Church Hill, in his speech at the laying of the foundation stone in Elm Grove, had talked about the "present comfortable state of the inmates", which was taken to mean the longer term ones. However, there is evidence to suggest that for at least one type of inmate, the pauper lunatic, life there was anything but comfortable.

Chapter Seven

CHURCH HILL AND THE SUSSEX LUNATIC ASYLUM

In the 1820s Brighton had sent its pauper lunatics to an asylum in Ringmer, but by 1831 the asylum had refused to take any more and had decided to concentrate on private patients. This meant that between 1831 and 1859 there were no licensed asylums in Sussex for the insane poor. Like other parishes, Brighton was forced to send them to badly run private asylums in London, chiefly Hoxton House and Bethnal Green Asylum. In 1834 Brighton had seven paupers in the former and two in the latter and was paying 10s a week per head plus clothes. In 1850 Church Hill received a licence to have a ward for pauper lunatics considered not to be dangerous. However, when the lunacy commissioners visited two years later they found three lunatics in the infirmary "under restraint" – tied up or shackled – who should have been in an asylum. In 1854, Brighton was still paying for 54 of its parishioners to be kept in the Bethnal Green asylum.

Two years later, Philip Passmore, the governor, was recording that:

William Hill is a very violent man. About a fortnight ago he attempted to take liberties with a female in the workhouse. She ran from him and he followed her and threatened to split her head in two. He was removed to the workhouse infirmary because he was not considered safe to be in any part of the house and the surgeon ordered it. I do no think him a proper subject to be in a workhouse and think it would be dangerous to the inmates if he were placed in an able-bodied ward. I think it would not be safe to leave him with any females.[1]

The surgeon, Richard Rugg, also admitted that "I am afraid of him and everyone else in the house is. He tried to strangle an infirmary inmate."[2] But Hill eventually calmed down and was allowed to stay. In 1857, the Poor Law Board received an unusual petition[3] of complaint from a former inmate, Emma Newman – whose husband had deserted her – about Rugg's treatment of her in the workhouse. It was written in verse form. Overleaf are some extracts.

When mind and body was overtasked
For poor relief I sometimes ask'd
Of a hard-hearted overseer [i]
To help me with my children dear.

And Bowridge [ii] to my lodging came
And graceless things to me did name.
I told him I could not do so
But to the workhouse I must go.

There with a conscience clear as day
To my God I still can pray,
Then with a feeling born of hell
They did what was too bad to tell.

They shut me up with prostitutes
Who in my presence were abject mutes,
So then before the Board I went
And boldly ask'd of them what they meant

Fifteen shillings they gave to me
And sent me out immediately
And gave one then to understand
That from the overseer's hand

Three shillings weekly I should receive
My great distress this to relieve,
But when for that I did apply
The deputy assistant did me deny.

He said by Mr Thorncroft's word
She that was ordered by the Board
Then what could a poor creature do
But to the house again must go.

Their Surgeon Rugg gave me to use
The stuff that did my soul abuse
A poison gargle for my throat
'For frequent use' on the bottle wrote.

————————————

[i] Thorncroft.

[ii] Chairman of the Board of Guardians.

Twas then I felt most awful pain
And of the same I did complain.
My heart was like a boiling pot,
My blood ran through me scalding hot,

And strange sensations in my head
When I laid me down in bed.
Look at this gargle Sir, I said,
I think tis that effects my head.

He said that I must quiet keep,
But stranger still I could not sleep.
Look at this gargle, I said again,
For I do feel such awful pain.

Nonsense, he said, you are only nervous.
To look at that was not his purpose –
His purpose was to poison me,
To gratify my enemy.

And then their hellish deed to screen
They sent me off to Bethnal Green,
And when at Bethnal I arrived
They thought how well they had contrived

To keep it all as black as night
By shutting me up out of sight.
Five months there I was confined
Midst poor insane of every kind,

But how I envied everyone,
For none like me were so undone,
My natural steps for ever gone
And my body is undone.

All is so strange I cannot pray,
Only to die, but then I fear
My soul's not fitter to appear
In the presence of that God

Who holds aloft the mighty rod
But cursed be that wicked man
That carried out this hellish plan,
And may my shadow haunt his way
At midnight and so in sunny day.

The Poor Law Board wrote to the Guardians asking for more information about her. They replied that she had been admitted in a "highly nervous" state in February 1856 and had been readmitted as insane a few weeks later. She had tried to hang herself and was sent to Bethnal Green in June. Since November she had been staying with friends in Eastbourne who were being paid eight shillings a week to look after her by the Brighton Guardians.

In another case, in 1860, John Dickinson wrote to the Board claiming he had been kidnapped the previous July. When two policemen came for him he thought they were taking him to the town hall, where the police station was. Instead, he found himself in the workhouse infirmary, suspected of being of "unsound mind". He "escaped" twenty-eight hours later and found that all his furniture had been sold in his absence. Other inmates had told him that it was not unusual for their neighbours to conspire against them.

* * *

The Sussex Lunatic Asylum, the county public asylum for pauper lunatics, opened to a great fanfare in Haywards Heath in July 1859. Victorian reformers believed they had at last found a solution to the problem of mental illness in society. If the sick person could be removed from the environment which had nurtured their illness and placed in a quiet refuge where gentleness reigned, added to a healthy diet, therapeutic work, education and music, a cure was possible. But these progressive ideas came at a cost. It was sometimes three or four times more expensive to keep a pauper lunatic in an asylum than in a workhouse. By law, however, workhouses could not keep dangerous lunatics for more than fourteen days before transferring them to an asylum. Although parishes could save money by keeping them longer, a dangerous lunatic could disrupt the workhouse regime. Nevertheless, the *Lancet* [4] had reported in 1844 that out of 17,000 pauper lunatics only 4,500 were being kept in public asylums and that the majority were languishing in workhouses where there was no proper segregation from the sane, and worst of all, no treatment.

The first medical superintendent of the Sussex Lunatic Asylum was Charles Lockhart Robertson, born into an eminent medical family in Edinburgh. There could not have been a greater contrast between him, in terms of education and culture, and the average nineteenth century workhouse governor. He was paid four or five times more than the latter and was a member of several prominent London gentlemen's clubs.

Robertson was a progressive doctor and deplored the ill-treatment of patients. Shortly after the asylum opened, Robertson was complaining about the state of the patients arriving from Church Hill. In August 1859 Mrs Groves, a 49-year-old Mormon and labourer's wife who died after twelve days:

> … was literally covered with vermin, bruises and sores. Her clothing was so filthy that I sent it to the oven to be burnt.[5]

He also publicly complained about the state of a Mrs Mercer who came from the "Brighton Union, her hair crawling with vermin…and the skin chafed from her dirty habits in the attention of the calls of nature".[6] She too died after a few days. The following year Robertson wrote to Mr Hollis, a Brighton magistrate and Guardian on their workhouse [lunacy] visitors' committee, about a twenty-six-year-old married man who had arrived from the workhouse on 13th April 1860, and sent a copy of it to the Lunacy Commission:

> My dear Sir,
> I think it right to acquaint you that a patient has this day been admitted from the Brighton Workhouse in a shameful state, his limbs and shoulders marked with bruises from blows and the lower part of his back excoriated with being allowed to lie in his urine unchanged. The man is quiet – in a state of chronic mania. His name is John Mockford, a house painter and decorator…. Serious fault in my opinion lies on the authorities at the Workhouse to permit an un-fortunate lunatic to be so abused; the blows and injuries are of recent state, I should say within a week. The excoriation may be of a fortnight or three weeks' standing.[7]

Mockford died five days later. Richard Rugg, the workhouse medical officer, wrote to the lunacy commissioners, informing them that Mockford had been well until a week before his transfer to the asylum, when he had had a "fit of mania" due to his mother not taking him out for his monthly outing. Rugg said he was so upset he had to be put under restraint – a strait-jacket. He added that "there were no more bruises upon his body than what might naturally be expected under the circumstances, and that the Guardians, myself and the Overseer have [since] examined his body, and quite concur with me that the Superintendent has grossly exaggerated the facts of the case".[8]

The visiting lunacy committee of the workhouse produced a report of their visit which concluded that Mockford had only had bruises of a "trifling nature" on his admission to the asylum, and that they were largely self-inflicted. Furthermore, they claimed that in twenty years of sending their patients to the London asylums they had not received one complaint about the state of the patients when delivered, yet since the opening of the Sussex Asylum complaints had been frequent. (The Brighton Guardians had never wanted to contribute towards the new county asylum, but had become a borough just too late to exclude their participation. They had resented the fact that although they paid a quarter of its running costs because of the high number of their patients there, they had no say in its management).

Robertson countered that Brighton had previously sent most of their patients to the notorious private asylum in Bethnal Green, which was the cheapest as well as one of the worst in the country and had been used by Sussex magistrates for at least two decades as a receptacle for county lunatics, but at the expense of the lunatics' parish of legal settlement: "Mr Thorncroft went there as a patron, and yearly added to the profits of that miserable speculation in suffering and disease by the Brighton patients whom he sent there." And he wrote that "so evident had Mockford been subject to blows, that when spoken to or approached he always held up his arm to protect himself and shrank back. He had a worn emaciated aspect and was quite unable to swallow any solid food the few days he survived his removal here".[9] Robertson made a mistake by not having an inquest, and the dispute faded away but left an enormous amount of ill feeling between the asylum and the workhouse. The year Mockford died, a lunacy commissioner, Mr Lutridge, described the Brighton workhouse infirmary as presenting "an aspect of discomfort".[10]

Apart from anything else, a large proportion of people coming from workhouses to asylums were suffering from serious physical illness or neglect. Admission to an asylum was in the hands of workhouse guardians and local magistrates, and these were usually lay people who had little medical knowledge. The medical superintendents of asylums could only make recommendations.

The following year, perhaps in a spirit of reconciliation, Robertson invited the Brighton Guardians to the asylum's second anniversary celebration on 25th July 1861. Seven came, accompanied by the workhouse juvenile band. After giving a performance on the platform of Brighton station while waiting for the Haywards Heath train, the fifteen-strong band in neat blouses and caps and their master, a Mr Thunder, arrived at the asylum just in time to hear the sermon in the chapel by the Venerable Archdeacon Otter of Lewes. It included the lines "My God, my God, why hast thou forsaken me".

* * *

In May 1863 the visiting lunacy committee of the workhouse was itself under fire in an anonymous letter entitled "Egregious Pieces of Humbug":

> I allude to the quarterly visits of some 12 or 14 gentlemen to see that our pauper lunatics are well taken care...these visits by a numerous body of strangers – for the Directors and Guardians are appointed on the Lunacy Committee, quarterly by turns – are invariably attended by bad effects on the patients. Is it not monstrous, that the parties should go on a party of mischief, and then tax the rate-payers with the expenses attending it, to the tune of £40 to £50 a year. Fresh faces irritate patients, and by all means let those children feed themselves.
> Yours truly
> SCRUTATOR [11]

The committee had eaten extravagant lunches at the parish's expense on the days of their visits. Possibly with memories of the scandal about the "feasting and guzzling"of the 1830s, the Guardians sensibly decided to reduce the committee to three members.

The peace between Robertson and the workhouse proved to be temporary. He was soon objecting to the visits of the man who, in the workhouse chaplain's words, had "a thin crust of severity", the assistant overseer, Samuel Thorncroft. Like the Guardians, as a parish officer, Thorncroft was allowed to regularly visit Brighton's patients but had no right to interfere in the management of the asylum. Robertson claimed he was rude and that his visits unsettled patients. A few years earlier a pauper, Liz Willard, had described Thorncroft as "a nasty old brute who she would like to meet on a dark night". Later on he was to be taken to court by a parish clerk who claimed that Thorncroft had aggressively hauled him out of a toilet at the town hall, claiming he had priority! Even some of his admirers admitted he was "uncouth and sharp". But whatever character defects he may have had, Thorncroft was a hero to many ratepayers for keeping the cost of relief to a minimum.

In August 1863 Thorncroft was censored by Brighton workhouse's own lunacy committee for his behaviour when visiting the county asylum, and "this was not the first, second or third time that Mr Thorncroft had behaved rudely to persons".[12] According to Robertson, he had upset one female patient so much that she had became agitated and upset and had to be removed from the room. The argumentative Thorncroft was then asked to leave by Robertson, which he did – but not before telling him that his knowledge was equal to that of any medical man.

However, in 1864, the asylum itself was under attack after a male patient, James Snashall, died there soon after been admitted from the workhouse. At the workhouse infirmary a wardsman, William Weller, admitted that Snashall had become so violent they had put him in a straitjacket for six or seven hours. He had even threatened to run Weller through with a knife. The removal clerk, William Smith, had taken Snashall to the asylum. He claimed he was very quiet on the journey but had become very noisy on arrival. Once there, part of his treatment had involved being left wrapped up in a wet sheet overnight and given digitalis. After being sick he had died a couple of days later with bruises on his body, probably inflicted during the struggle to get him into the wet sheet. At the inquest, demanded by his family and held at the Northern Tavern in Brighton, the jury returned a verdict of 'death from apoplexy', but added that there had been a "great dereliction of duty somewhere at the asylum".

Afterwards some of the Brighton Guardians pursued the matter further. At a meeting, Mr Woollett, who owned the biggest ironmongers in Brighton, declared that:

> ....there was something loose in the management of the Asylum....and that it was not quite clear to him that death had not either resulted from violence or from some gross neglect on the part of the officers of the Asylum.[13]

An enquiry by the visiting committee of the asylum was set up, and it came to the conclusion that "there was no foundation whatsoever for the charges made against the asylum". Other scandals involving the two institutions followed, with each alleging mistreatment of patients by the other. However, after a while an uneasy peace between the asylum and the Brighton workhouse broke out; perhaps a grudging acceptance that they had to get on.

Meanwhile, at Church Hill, pauper lunatics who were not considered to be violent often found themselves being forcibly commuted between there and the local prison. In 1865, a lunacy commissioner visited Mrs Anne Murphy, who had just been admitted to the workhouse from Lewes prison:

> I found her in fair bodily health, suitably dressed. Her left arm had been amputated near the shoulder joint in an accident in a cotton mill. She said she was born in Preston in Lancashire; that her parents were both dead, and that her brothers and sisters had emigrated to Australia. After the loss of her arm she endeavoured to maintain herself by hawking light articles of dress for sale in the rural districts of Cumberland and Westmoreland. Having earned about £3 she set out from Preston to London about a year ago, and made her way to the metropolis where her money soon became exhausted. She drifted down to Brighton about six months ago, and has since begged for subsistence, and for doing so has been sent to prison no less than seven times. On the last occasion she was committed for a month, but was kept in gaol a fortnight beyond the time she ought to have been discharged…Her delusions are very various and very manifest. She thinks that she has £50 in her possession, and that men follow her to obtain it – and that she is pursued by enemies, and has chloroform given to her by men who want her fortune – and that the bread has been adulterated to prevent her becoming pregnant.[14]

The following year, 1866, Robertson was still recording the admittance of patients who arrived in a dying state[15] from Sussex workhouses. The following men came from Church Hill:

Initials	Age	Admission	Death	Cause	Condition on Admittance
S.B.	42	Jan 5th	Jan 10th	Melancholia	Very feeble/Much reduced
J.S.	31	Jan 26th	April 22nd	Epilepsy	Reduced
J.W.	37	April 26th	May 1st	Acute mania	Much reduced from refusal of food
T.B.	41	Jan 16th	July 12th	General paresis	Reduced/Last stage of disease
E.B.	27	Oct 27th	Dec 27th	Phthisis	Reduced/Last stage

After being admitted in such a deplorable physical state, any chance of a cure was out of the question.

In October 1866 a reporter from the *Brighton Gazette*[16] paid a visit to the asylum and described some of the Brighton patients:

…it was pleasing to witness a party engaged at a game of cribbage and another assembled round a bagatelle board. A friend (one of the party) taking up the cue and failing to make a score was greeted with much glee by Johnny H., accompanied with the remark "He don't know how to play". Poor Johnny, the asylum I am afraid will be his only home, unless when the new Brighton workhouse is completed, he becomes an occupant of that portion…Another, H.B., admitted November, 1865, immediately afterwards addressed me, "I am glad to see you, I am quite comfortable; but it is an imposition upon the Brighton ratepayers to keep me here, but I am quite well. Do what you can to get me home." Poor fellow, I knew him as a steady, industrious man, working for an auctioneer…He was a passenger in the train which came to grief in the Clayton Tunnel [i]…

Another (C.P.) admitted 1861, seemed rational. He jumped down the deep Brighton Workhouse well without injuring himself. He is very industrious, but fancies everyone is robbing him, and is watched, fearing suicide. W.D., nearly 50 years of age, an old pie-man, looked well, and in the New Workhouse will probably end his days…H.F. (whose father with difficulty has recently been compelled by the Assistant-Overseer and authorities to contribute 5s. weekly towards his maintenance) looks wretched.

From Brighton I ascertained there were 47 male inmates…All the males having conversational powers stated that they were comfortable and, in contrast to the females, few asked to be removed…Of the females, 62 in number, chargeable to Brighton, I was particularly struck on their being made known to me, with their loquacity and vituperativeness, and I am under the belief that there were more bad cases than with the males…I returned to Brighton deploring the sad affliction of the inmates, but pleased beyond expression with the comfortable home, in every respect, provided for them.

The reporter's observation that the female patients wanted to go home while the male patients were relatively relaxed was an interesting one. It may have been because women were more vulnerable to asylum incarceration

---

[i] Two trains collided in the tunnel on 25th August 1861, killing 23 and injuring 176. At the time it was the worst disaster ever on the British railway system.

(for economic reasons) than men, and that they suffered more from being away from their families.

Despite the overwhelmingly superior living conditions in the asylum compared with the workhouse, Robertson admitted in October 1867 that:

> ...the aged, imbecile and demented lunatics prefer the workhouse to county asylums, partly from the greater freedom from discipline (from enforced order and cleanliness, baths etc.) which they enjoy, partly from the association with sane patients there instead of the insane, and partly because it is situated near their own Parish and family...The truth is that the insane poor who are sufficiently sane to argue the point, are constantly asking to be sent back to the Union [workhouse].[17]

* * *

One of the last entertainments held at Church Hill was the New Year's Treat of 1866. The dining room had been decorated with evergreens and lamps and a stage erected. The chairman, Lt Col Moorsom, and many of the Guardians with members of their families and friends were there. Most of the entertainment was provided by the staff and volunteers:

> Songs such as "Sleep, gentle lady" and comic songs were sang, among which "A Horrible Tale" by Mr Darling produced much merriment and a hearty encore; and the singing of the refrain, "Three merry souls are we," convulsed the whole room with laughter...Mr Jordan sung the "Village Blacksmith" with his customary good taste, and the ladies took their share in the performance with considerable skill and success... Among the instrumental performers, Miss Gates played a grand march from Faust on the pianoforte with much skill and ability, although the room and the position were ill adapted to give effect to the instrument. Miss Brooks [assistant-matron] sang "Jessie's Dream" in a very pleasing manner and also the duet, "What are the wild waves saying?" with Mr Bull; and her sister, Miss M.A. Brooks, sung "The Bashful Man" with considerable taste and humour. Master Tester played a solo on the cornet very cleverly; Mr Goble some sweet airs on the baritone; and Mr W Smith (of the Assistant-Overseers office) volunteered a spirited little solo on the violin, and also a song of a highly amusing character...[18]

During the interval, the inmates were provided with cake, coffee and other refreshments while the Guardians, their families and friends were given more substantial refreshments. The inmates were allowed to stay up after their customary bedtime and at the end of the evening were given oranges. This annual entertainment had been instigated by Sattin in his belief that kindness could be more beneficial than severity.

It was ironic that Moorsom, who had caught a fever during the Crimean War and had never fully recovered, would not live to see the new workhouse open. He died in San Remo, Italy, in March 1867 at the age of 55. He was still officially chairman of the Guardians. One of his colleagues quoted Shakespeare in a eulogy to him:

> *A sweeter and lovelier gentleman*
> *Fram'd in the prodigality of nature*

At the same time the Guardians decided to put a tablet over the grave of a nurse, Sophia Todman. She had been employed at the industrial schools but had temporarily been transferred – for extra money – to the workhouse infirmary when there had been an outbreak of smallpox. Todman had volunteered to sleep in a bed next to a seriously ill patient and had caught the disease herself. The inscription read:

> Erected by the Directors and Guardians of the Parish of Brighton in memory of Sophia Todman who nobly sacrificed her life in the faithful discharge of her duties as nurse to the sick poor at the Workhouse at a time of great emergency.

*   *   *

In 1864, the Guardians had chosen the lowest[i] tender of £30,500 for the construction of the new workhouse by a contractor, Jabez Reynolds. The Poor Law Board put as much pressure as it could to get it built quickly, and gave its opinions about its construction. It advised strongly rather than insisted on changes. Although it had to sanction appointments at the industrial schools, it had no power to do so at the new workhouse, which was covered by a new Act of Parliament.

From the correspondence between the Guardians and the Poor Law Board, it is clear that they often resisted its recommendations. For example, in April 1867 the Board wrote enquiring whether they had acted on the 1865

---

[i] The highest was by W. Henshaw: £46,240.

House of Commons recommendation that quinine, cod liver oil and other expensive medicine should be introduced into the workhouse. The Guardians replied that they had had no complaints from the poor and so had not acted upon it yet. But the Poor Law Board did complain about the iron bars on the windows of the lunacy wards, which it believed were quite unnecessary for chronic harmless lunatics and only tended to foster the idea of confinement and a prison in the mind of the inmates. The Guardians surprisingly asked Dr Robertson's advice, and he persuaded them to have window frames made of iron and wood which were already fitted at the asylum.

In the month before the Elm Grove workhouse opened in 1867, ratepayers could get tickets from the parochial offices to visit. Children had to be accompanied by parents or guardians. At least 12,000 people took advantage of the opportunity to tour the building before it opened.

With their removal to the new workhouse, the pauper inmates were once again being moved up a hill to the edge of town. Once again they would describe where they were going as a "howling wilderness". In its first ten years, life at Church Hill had been bearable. It had been spacious, the diet tolerable and the work relatively light and productive. It was surrounded by open fields, and one imagines the inmates had been able to watch the festivities and gunnery practice of the Royal Artillery adjacent to the site. Church Hill had opened with ninety-five inmates. Now it was overcrowded and cramped with an average of 829, including the children at the industrial schools in Woodingdean. With perhaps some trepidation, they were going to a new home where the intention was eventually to apply the workhouse "test" to the full.

PART TWO

Chapter Eight

ELM GROVE, THE EARLY
YEARS 1867–70

Between 12th September and 21st September 1867 all the inmates were removed from Church Hill to the new 'House' without ceremony. As they straggled along on the last part of the journey up the steep three-quarter-mile hill of Elm Grove – the women in blue striped worsted dresses and the men in grey worsted suits – a crowd of onlookers stood on either side of the road. Some waved at their relatives and friends. Others gloomily looked on with tears in their eyes. But the worst sight was that of the caravan of carts which carried the infirm, the elderly, the sick and the babies to their destination. What was their future to be? Of the 529 paupers who entered their new home, only 38 were considered to be able-bodied and 28 children and infants were under four. At the same time, 2,273 paupers in the town were receiving outdoor relief.

Near the entrance of the premises were the male and female casual wards – with bathrooms under cover – and the porter's lodge. The main building was 318 feet long and 50 feet high. In the centre of the front there was a clock tower[i] bearing the date '1866' and over the entrance hall a big sign, 'Brighton Workhouse'. The aged, infirm and "good characters" were to be accommodated at the front of the building and the rest at the back. The men occupied the various floors on the north side, the women those on the south. Iron gates divided the sexes at the end of each wide and lofty corridor and other gates shut off the able-bodied of either sex from the aged and infirm:

> Entering by the main entrance one commences in the basement where there are shoemakers and tailors workshops and cutting rooms; aged women's day rooms where poor old dames can sit and gossip, snuff or stitch away the remnant of their lives in airy apartments with a good look out over the town and country; day rooms for able bodied women, lavatories and the like. There are

---

[i] A clock was donated by a Mrs G. Pym-Reading in 1873.

similar apartments for the men…and on either side of the coal cellars, refractory wards wherein those whom reason cannot teach must be content to remain for a while incarcerated.[1]

On the ground floor were dormitories, the governor's office, a waiting room and a committee room. There were also a dozen bedrooms and a spacious sitting room for aged married couples, a 70ft by 45ft dining-room, and a bakehouse with twelve large ovens. On the first floor there were dormitories and also staff accommodation for the senior officials, while the top floor contained more inmate dormitories.

The chapel was in the east part of the building. It could accommodate 636 and was lit with two gas star chandeliers. To the south of the main building were two buildings, the "asylum", containing two wards for lunatics, and the infirmary:

> …In close proximity are the male and female airing grounds. These are encircled by a high wall which some say is unnecessarily high and blocks out the view of the surrounding countryside. Others contend that it is not sufficiently high to prevent ill-judged friends from passing spirits or other things contrary to the regulations of the House…There are also rooms for infants, destined for those poor little ones too young to be separated from their mothers… Around these areas are other stores such as a firewood store. Also carpenters and wheel-wrights' workshops, stabling, hay loft, stand for the Parish Hearse, oakum rooms, stone breaking sheds etc.[2]

The surrounding high walls emphasized the separation and loss of freedom. At the far north-eastern corner of the site was a building containing the Fever and Foul wards [for sexual diseases], with an "airtight disinfecting room". The overall accommodation was as follows:

Workhouse proper

Able-bodied men 135	Smallpox ward men 14
Able-bodied women 107	Smallpox ward women 14
Aged and infirm men 102	Lunatic wards 50
Aged and infirm women 121	Infirmary:
Aged couples 24	Men 100
Children under two 20	Women 150
Fever ward men 12	
Fever ward women 12	**TOTAL 861**

The figures show what function a mid-Victorian workhouse really had: it was a general hospital for sick paupers, a lunatic asylum, a maternity hospital, an old peoples' home, an infectious disease centre, a last refuge for the homeless and unemployed, and a nursery as much as a place where the able-bodied inmates had to work. Even this last group was divided into two groups:

Class A – those partially disabled men and youths of good character unfit to do task work but who could work in maintaining the building.
Class B – able-bodied proper and those of indifferent character and troublesome both old and young, constantly taking their discharge without good reason – to do task work.

The harder the tasks, so the Guardians believed, the more likely those who could possibly leave would do so. Compared to the Sussex Lunatic Asylum with its 100 acres of land – a ratio of four patients per acre – the workhouse's accommodation, when full, was squeezed into just seven acres, a ratio of 123 inmates per acre.

ig 12 *The new workhouse at Elm Grove (now Brighton General Hospital).*

Edward Sattin was given £50 for the extra duties the move entailed although one Guardian questioned the payment complaining that he had magnificent furnished rooms and an enormous salary. He asked why Sattin should get the bonus and not other members of staff. Stung by the criticism, Sattin wrote an open letter "to the ratepayers". He claimed the payment was for "many special and anxious services, extending over a period of eight years". These included extra auditing tasks and a vast increase in paperwork:

> …then followed the preparation for the Schools, the sheets, beds and blankets which were all prepared at the Workhouse for that Institution. Then for two years contagious disease existed in the Workhouse, and for which extra wards had to be fitted up; in fact, during the whole period of my appointment, it had been a constant struggle to make the old House meet its requirements.
>
> I would now speak as to my "first class tradesman's accommodation". Without at all seeking to disparage the rooms, I very much question the possibility of finding a tenant for them, with the din incident to the being surrounded by 300 or 400 inmates, and the greater portion of those passing and repassing your door three times a day. Let the objector be, as I have unfortunately been, sick from anxiety and worry, and he would then differently estimate my EVERY comfort.
>
> …Few persons are, I expect, aware of the "enormous salary" apportioned to me for the care of the average number of 600 persons, and the distribution of provisions etc, amounting to £10,000 a-year; in fact, all visitors to this Institution…feel utterly astonished when informed of its amount, viz., 34s per week of seven days – and each day a day and a half long – and rations; out of which I repay 7s 6d per week towards the maintenance of my little children. This payment, contrasted with the salary and duties of the Governor of Lewes Gaol (about £350 a year), will, I believe, leave a strong balance in my favour.[3]

Sattin had some justification for his annoyance. In 1866 there had been a severe outbreak of smallpox – an acute contagious viral disease that could kill or leave permanent scars if untreated – in the town. At one time there had been 150 cases in the workhouse infirmary wards. Many of those admitted were not paupers, but people admitted to check the spread of the disease in the districts where it had originated. This was followed by an outbreak of cholera – the epidemic most feared – and the infirmary wards were thrown open to everyone in the town who had the disease. While the medical officer, Dr Richards, had eventually been rewarded with a large salary increase, Sattin's had remained the same.

Meanwhile, there were huge, regular public sales held at the Old Ship Hotel, where valuable plots of land and fixtures and fittings from the old workhouse site were sold. The land was in a prime position for new villas and only five minutes away from Brighton railway station. Some of the Guardians also bought plots. By the time all the grounds of the old workhouse were sold and the new one built, the Guardians had made a profit of almost nine thousand pounds. The Poor Law Board insisted the surplus could be used only for improvements to the new workhouse and not for a reduction of the rates.

*   *   *

Admission to the Elm Grove workhouse was by an order signed by the clerk on the Guardians behalf or from the relieving officer or overseer. Only in an emergency could the master or matron permit a pauper to enter. If you just turned up without an order you were unlikely to be admitted. Sick paupers needed the signature of a medical officer to be admitted into the infirmary or lunacy wards, which were frequently staffed by elderly female inmates.

Once an order was made applicants had to come within six days. After the long walk up Elm Grove, they would have to pull the heavy iron bell handle outside the gate and be let in by the porter. From the porter's lodge, they were taken to the reception room [receiving ward], searched and medically examined before being deloused, washed and clothed in workhouse clothing and allocated a ward. Their own clothes were put into storage and returned when they left. Any money found on them had to be given up; if not they could be sent to prison for ten days.

Then the family was split up. Children under three were taken to the nursery; the older children to the quarantine ward where they would stay a minimum of twenty-one days before being transferred to the Warren Farm Industrial Schools. The adults were taken to the main block. After going up the cold stone steps that led to the first floor they were separated into male and female dormitories and day rooms. "In the dining room and in the Chapel on Sundays they might catch sight of each other but only from a distance...From this time the family would never be gathered all together until, if they managed to leave the house, they met outside the house".[4]

If an elderly couple were not lucky enough to be one of the twelve couples with their own rooms at Elm Grove, their fate was not unlike that of a couple forced into a workhouse by "that gaunt wolf Poverty and Sickness", described by a poet[5] in the 1860s:

There are but two retreats that beggars crave,
The parish workhouse and the pauper's grave.
[the aged couple] slowly took their solitary way,
Mocked by a gibing mob of cruel fears,
And at the workhouse gate with clasped hands,
Parted for ever "by the law's commands".

No, not for ever! Duly once a week,
When the sad pauper prisoners come to pray
In the dull chapel-room, barred like a gaol,
And scarcely lit by the dull sun's dim ray,
They saw each other for one little space,
What though they gazed upon each other's face.

It was a weekly death to part again,
Yet while the droning voices mumbled on
They sat and joined their hands across the aisle
As in the happy days for ever gone,
The angels looking from their homes above,
Smiled on that pure, imperishable love.

Almost together – but a week apart
The old folks died, unpitied and unwept;
Eternal calm upon each dead face came,
A calm – majestic as on kings that slept.
Strange that the jargon of the doctor's art,
Disdains to classify "the broken heart".

But e'en[i] the grave did not unite the two,
Apart they lay beneath the rank green grass,
In the damp churchyard's coldest, dreariest place,
The same black yew-tree shadowed them. Alas!
The poor have but few mourners, yet the dew
Hung in big tears on flowers that o'er them grew.

Half an hour after the bell rang for rising at 5.30am – 5.00am in summer – the paupers' names (including the sick) were called out by the master and matron and they had to answer. At mealtimes their food had to be weighed by the taskmasters. Every pauper had the right to have his food weighed in front of him if he believed it was under the set weight. If inmates arrived late at the dining room they were refused admission.

Work was divided into "task work" (oakum picking and breaking stones) and "household" work (maintaining and cleaning the workhouse and organizing meals). The men predominantly chopped wood, tended the grounds or did task work. The women spent their time cleaning, sewing, doing laundry work, cooking and helping in the infirmary, but also sometimes had to pick oakum like the men. All Class B able-bodied inmates were expected to do task work. It was left to the master to decide who came into this category, and old age did not necessarily mean exemption. On Sundays, Good Friday and Christmas day no work was done except cooking and the household work. All inmates had to be in bed by 8.30pm in winter and 9pm in summer.

No card games or any form of gambling was allowed and "printed paper of indecent tendencies" were prohibited. Friends were allowed to visit only with the permission of the master, and a visiting room was kept for that purpose. In theory any pauper could leave the workhouse as long as they gave reasonable notice, usually 48 hours, but their families had to go with them. In practice, paupers were often refused their discharge if it was thought they would not be able to survive outside. If they left without permission they faced criminal prosecution. For the older or infirm inmates the workhouse often became their home for life.

---

[i] Even.

The *Brighton Gazette* [6] recorded the first Christmas at Elm Grove:

The walls and pillars of the chapel were simply yet gracefully festooned, and the communion table appropriately decorated with floral devices and the most appropriate mottoes, in evergreens, "Immanuel," "God with us." Nothing could be more pleasing than the scrupulously neat and clean appearance of the house, and the general air of comfort pervading the establishment. At one o'clock the bell rang for dinner which was served in the dining-hall; here, also, we found the busy and tasteful hands of the ladies of the household had applied themselves with much affect to the work of decoration, the hall being tastefully decorated with wreaths and baskets of flowers. In this work the Matron, Mrs Sattin, was actively engaged, and in it she was assisted by the willing hands of Miss Sartain [the assistant matron].

As we said, the bell was rung – it didn't require ringing twice; soon one half of the hall was filled by the female and the other half by the male inmates – the total number being about 300 or 400. There are some 670 inmates but some were in the infirmary, some elsewhere. Those who were mustered in the dining hall had not long to wait. Grace was said by the Chaplain – The Rev. J. Image – "Relieve, O Lord, the wants of others and give us grateful hearts". At the head of the room, behind fragrant joints, were well-known forms [the Guardians], partially metamorphosed by tuck aprons and turned-up sleeves, including Mr Flowers, Mr Cutten (didn't he cut'm) and others. These, armed with fierce carving knives, plunged to the dissection of savoury and fragrant joints. 900lbs. of roast beef and roast mutton vanished in a twinkling from beneath their blades, with 37 immense dishes of roasted potatoes…Then followed 230 plum puddings, each 4lbs. weight – which being duly quartered, afforded the allowance to each inmate. Meanwhile, Mr Flowers was busy as a tapster, a pint of mild ale for dinner was followed by another pint of strong ale, which the inmates were allowed to carry to their wards, together with supplies of tobacco and snuff to those who required them. Extra stimulants were administered to the sick, at the discretion of the doctor…the general feeling must have been, one of thankfulness that such an Institution exists and is so admirably managed.

The scene in the article above, of the Guardians helping out with the distribution of the Christmas dinner, was one played out in workhouses all over the country. However, not all paupers may have appreciated this charity. The great Victorian social commentator, George R. Sims, wrote a famous poem, extracts of which show a different perception:

Christmas Day in the Workhouse

It is Christmas Day in the workhouse,
And the cold bare walls are bright
With garlands of green and holly,
And the place is a pleasant sight;
For with clean-washed hands and faces,
In a long and hungry line
The paupers sit at the tables
For this is the hour they dine.

And the guardians and their ladies,
Although the wind is east,
Have come in their furs and wrappers,
To watch their charges feast;
To smile and be condescending,
Put pudding on pauper plates,
To be hosts at the workhouse banquet
They've paid for – with their rates.

Oh, the paupers are meek and lowly
With their "Thank'ee kindly, mum's"
So long as they fill their stomachs,
What matters it whence it comes?
But one of the old men mutters,
And pushes his plate aside;
"Great God!" he cries, "but it chokes me!
For this is the day she died."

The guardians gazed in horror,
The master's face went white;
"Did a pauper refuse the pudding?"
Could their ears believe aright?
Then the ladies clutched their husbands,
Thinking the man would die,
Struck by a bolt, or something,
By the outraged One on high.

But the pauper sat for a moment,
Then rose 'mid a silence grim,
For the others had ceased to chatter
And trembled in every limb.
He looked at the guardians' ladies,
Then, eying their lords, he said,
I eat not the food of villains
Whose hands are foul and red;

"Whose victims cry for vengeance
From their dank, unhallowed graves."
"He's drunk!" said the workhouse master,
"Or else he's mad and raves."
"Not drunk or mad," cried the pauper,
"But only a hunted beast,
Who, torn by the hounds and mangled,
Declines the vultures' feast.

"Keep your hands off me, curse you!
Hear me right out to the end,
You come here to see how paupers
The season of Christmas spend.
You come here to watch us feeding,
As they watch the captured beast.
Hear why a penniless pauper
Spits on your paltry feast."

The old man then recounts how he had lost his wife, Nancy, the previous
Christmas because she had refused to come to the workhouse and had died
of starvation. The last verse went:

"There, get ye gone to your dinners;
Don't mind me in the least;
Think of the happy paupers
Eating your Christmas feast;
And when you recount their blessings
In your smug parochial way,
Say what you did for me, too
Only last Christmas Day."

*   *   *

The power of the church was all pervasive in workhouses. From the twice daily prayers and regular services to the scriptural texts printed on the walls to remind the inmates that they were lucky to be there, religion was everywhere. God was their only salvation. The main Christian theme was the moral one that made the distinction between the deserving and the undeserving poor. It tied in with the Christian value that denounced the latter for being improvident and of being responsible for their poverty. Their punishment was to be sent to the able-bodied wards of the work-house. On the surface, the workhouse chaplain was an ally of the master and the guardians. In practice, though, there were often clashes of authority particularly between the guardians and the chaplain.

Religious provision for paupers was often a contentious issue especially if it was seen as a challenge to Protestantism. In 1864, the chairman of the Guardians, Lt Col Moorsom, a Roman Catholic, had caused controversy by donating ten religious prints to the industrial schools, an action according to one Guardian that should not have been allowed in a Church of England institution where Anglicanism was dominant. One consequence of the move to Elm Grove was that some of the churches the non-denominational paupers were allowed to visit on a Sunday were further away. They were allowed out only at the discretion of the master, except for one category: Roman Catholics, who had a right to worship in their own church. Sattin believed that inmates were changing to that religion purely to get out of the workhouse on Sundays. In particular, he felt that one local Catholic priest, Neil Crispin, was trying to buy their consciences. When Sattin was asked: "Does he give money to the people in the workhouse?" he had replied, "I have no doubt he does – that's what they visit him for." [7]

A colourful text between the beams of the chapel at Elm Grove. (Laurie Keen.)

Allegedly, Crispin gave them money which they spent in the nearest beer house.

Sometimes paupers were discharging themselves, then converting to Catholicism and returning. From Crispin's point of view, "men were being driven into destitution to carry out a lawful dictate of conscience".[8] One pauper called Humphrey, who claimed he had converted to Catholicism, was stopped from going out on Sundays. The workhouse visiting committee said that he "must furnish stronger and more reliable evidence of a change in his religious views". Furthermore, they would "not allow them [the paupers] to an influence which they have neither the capacity to understand nor the power to resist".[9] After Sattin confiscated some books Crispin had sent to a pauper, George Dorman, Sattin said "Dorman had better not think of changing his religion for it would only cause confusion in the workhouse".

Crispin constantly demanded that the Guardians provide Catholic schooling for Catholic children and not keep them at Warren Farm. The Local Government Board supported Crispin and the Brighton Guardians usually reluctantly acceded to this demand although it always meant extra expense. However, they did insist they would only pay for the children's education at Catholic schools till they were fourteen. After that, they would have to return to the industrial schools unless they found work. The above committee called Crispin "the most troublesome priest in the land".

* * *

In February 1868, for the first time, Mrs Nye Chart, the owner of the Brighton Theatre Royal, offered to allow aged workhouse inmates and children free admittance to watch the Christmas pantomime. Her offer was turned down. The Guardians argued they did not want to give inmates something that many of those outside could not afford to experience. One Guardian, Mr Ireland, claimed that:

> He had a great deal to do with the children of the poor of Brighton and he had seen the greatest evils follow from holding out such attractions as the theatre...The children of the schools had plenty of out of door exercise and once or twice a year, and also the old folks of the Workhouse, had rational entertainment, which he thought was quite as much as persons in their station of life ought to expect and as much as the board ought to afford.[10]

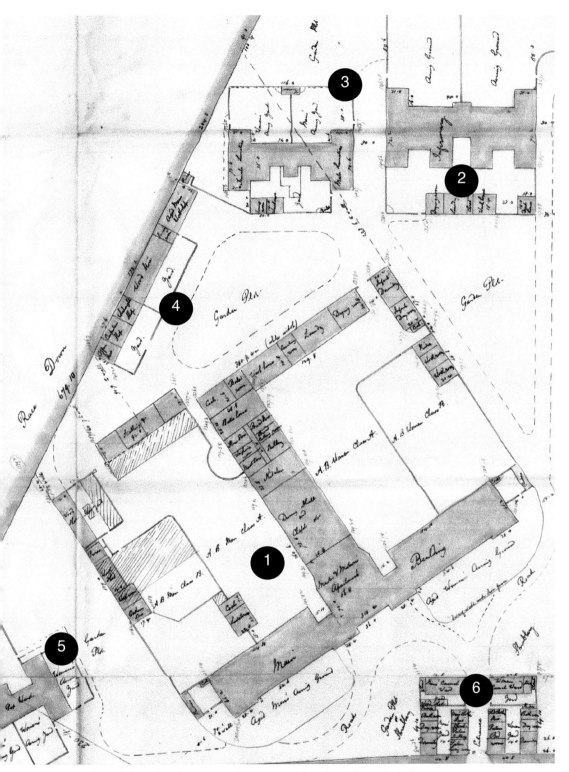

3 13 *Original plan of the Elm Grove workhouse. 1. Main building. 2. Infirmary.*
Lunacy wards. 4.Workshops. 5 Fever wards. 6. Casual wards.

The Guardians did allow Brighton railway station to have a container so that passengers could leave their old newspapers for the inmates. And there was a collection box at the *Brighton Gazette* for people to donate money towards the old peoples' treats. However, as the new workhouse was further away from the railway station, fewer of the aged inmates [over 60s] were able to go on their annual trip to the Swiss Gardens, Shoreham, because of the climb up Elm Grove and the extra cost of transport to the station.

Fig 14 The matron, Mrs Sattin, with an aged couple.

In the same month of Nye Chart's offer, 267 casuals were admitted to the workhouse in one week and one Guardian believed it was becoming "a nursery for the idle of the town". Sattin too agreed that "idlers" were coming to the casual wards rather than the wayfarer and recommended that either the Guardians made the regime more stringent or enlarged the accommodation.

The new workhouse was soon receiving praise. In the visitors' book Rev E.H. Abbey, the chairman of the Derby Board of Guardians, called it "an unrivalled house". He said that "everything appears to be conducted in the most admirable manner".[11] In May, 1868, J.J. Henley, a Poor Law inspector, described the place as "scrupulously clean and the whole establishment in excellent order. This has been the case on my previous visits. The only complaint was from a 66 year old man who was on an able-bodied diet".[12] A Mr G. Brooke, a guardian of Holborn, said the Elm Grove workhouse was superior to any he had seen and R.J. Werner, from Frankfurt, Germany, wrote:

Having been visiting many similar institutions in various countries, I feel bound to say I have nowhere ever met with so much order and cleanliness, and in my humble opinion the whole arrangements cannot be more perfect. [13]

Obviously, the workhouse was well prepared for these pre-arranged visits. Despite the praise, some of the inmates were less impressed. In 1870 an inmate, Henry House, in a long letter, complained bitterly about being bullied by five sixteen year old youths – whom he accused of playing cards – and being mistreated by staff. According to the Guardians, the youths were not blameless but the latter allegation was "very untruthful and grossly exaggerated". Sattin wrote a report:

> … These lads were to me always most respectful and on punishing them at times on complaint of House, they respectfully requested me to make enquiries as to whether the troubles did not originate from him; his meddlesome manner and cantankerous tongue. He produced several towels torn down the middle and said they were done by the lads. He is malicious enough to do such a thing. He teased one of them about wetting the bed. Other inmates said they were "in heaven" when he was removed…The playing of cards, if done at all, is done by stealth. I know that if a lad tosses a button in the air he would call it gambling. His [House's] vision is, in fact, distorted by his quarter of a century's residence in a workhouse.[14]

Sattin explained that he had tried House in different wards in the eleven years he had been the master and everyone had complained. He had had to remove him from the old convalescent wards in Church Hill for being drunk and then from the Class A ward to the Class B one – where the regime was tougher – because he had quarrelled so much. Sattin concluded:

> To order this man back into the Class A ward would be a fatal blow to my authority and a great injustice to the other inmates. I have been nearly eleven years Master of this Workhouse and not once has my conduct been called into question and I do feel that this is a most frivolous and vexatious complaint from a very unworthy person.[15]

As the youths had defaced the rules about disorderly conduct and had threatened House they were given imprisonment of between seven and ten days. However, Sattin got his wish and House remained in the Class B ward.

Another complainant was James Rubens, aged 24. He had come to Brighton to look for work and had a wife and child in London. After two weeks in the workhouse he had asked to leave, but Sattin had told him he would "hear when they think proper". In his letter to the Poor Law Board Rubens complained about a "starvation diet, that he was expected to work like a horse and that there was uncivility when he went before the Guardians". He had asked if he could return to London because he was frightened of missing a winter's work. Instead, his wife and child had been admitted into the workhouse. He had discharged himself but after walking nine miles had returned and been re-admitted. Sattin wrote that Rubens was "troublesome and insolent in his demeanour...The Guardians so far from wishing to keep him in the workhouse would be only too glad to pass him to his parish without delay". [16]

In November 1870, James Miles, in the infirmary, protested about the medical treatment for his poisoned hand and wrote that the food was not enough for a four year old. He claimed that "if we complain, we only get threatened". The Guardians replied that his allegations were "utterly untrue" and that "he had since been removed and they were heartily glad to be rid of such an ungrateful (as well as untruthful) inmate". [17]

That same month, the workhouse received its worst ever publicity when a letter from an inmate in the infirmary, Charles Tourle, was published in a national newspaper, *Lloyds Weekly*. Three years earlier the same newspaper had published a letter from Henry Hiles, "a poor afflicted and ill-used man":

My poor though trifling request was only for three weeks outdoor relief, till I could get a little stronger after my severe illness so as to go to work again if I could get it. They have in the most unfeeling, and, as I consider, unjust manner, refused it to me, although I had the parish doctor's certificate (their own doctor) to say I was, and should be unable to work for a month or more through debility caused by my late illness. I deem it right to make known to a Christian public this most unfeeling treatment in a Christian country where, by law, the poor are to be fed who are unable by misfortune to procure their own bread.

Hiles went on to say he had been treated very badly by Thorncroft. In his defence, Thorncroft claimed he had twice ordered the family into the work-house but they had refused to go. The Guardians condemned Hiles for going to the press, and believed he had just been trying to get some "sympathy" money from charities. Although an enquiry had exonerated Thorncroft, he had threatened to go to a solicitor when a local newspaper, the *Brighton Times*, flooded the town with placards announcing: "Serious Charge against Mr Thorncroft, the Assistant Overseer".

What made Tourle's letter more scandalous, though, was that he was, unlike Hiles, an inmate. Tourle explained that it was "the word of a poor pauper against that of the Guardians", and that "they are not going to say anything injurious to themselves".

A BRIGHTON CASUAL WARD

...they tell you plainly "you don't come here to live, you come here to die". They take the greatest comfort that you don't have any comforts here. Their chief study is to insult you and abuse you in every way, and try to make you unhappy until the end of your miserable existence: for sympathy, kindness, or civility are things quite unknown in a workhouse, and they care just as much about your life as they do of a dog's...I have been a patient here more than 12 months, suffering from rheumatic gout. In the spring of this year I got much better and took my discharge; but after a few days I got much worse again, and I went to the relieving officer to get an order for re-admission, and they refused to give one. At the time I was very ill, for I could hardly get one leg before the other, but after the usual amount of bullying they gave me an order for the casual ward, and I took it, so with great difficulty I made my way there. Here they put me into a bath, and there was not a dry towel to wipe myself with, for about 30 tramps had used it before me. Then they gave me a coarse dirty shirt to put on that was full of vermin, and a nasty filthy rag to cover me, that some scores of tramps had previously used. What with my pains and torments of vermin I got no sleep, and as I could not walk I had to crawl on the cold bricks, to get to a water-closet. In this state they kept me seven days and nights; and there were many more poor fellows lying here besides myself, suffering from various kinds of diseases – some with bad legs, the Itch, ague, and fevers; some had been here much longer than I had.

I should think the Poor Law Board would never sanction this, to make a hospital of a casual ward. But how should they know this, unless someone has the spirit to give them the information? On the seventh day I suppose they thought they had punished me enough here in this kennel. Then they took me to the fever ward, but I had no fever myself. I remained here about a month, when all at once I was seized with another very severe attack of rheumatic fever. Here is fine treatment again! They kept me seven days with no medicine and no nourishment, for I could not eat the usual diet, and I was ordered nothing else...

At last I asked the doctor if I didn't require some medicine, and he told me he did not know what to give me; he could do no good. I was then ordered to the infirmary, and then they began to see my wants. Here I have lingered on ever since, in a very cold ward with a very small fire to keep you warm; and about three weeks ago I had another severe attack of rheumatic fever. It is quite useless to make any complaints to anyone connected with these places, for they all uphold one another in all their doings. If you make any report they lead you the life of a dog afterwards, and you may as well be in your grave out of the way. I think, Mr Editor, it is high time for the Poor Law Board to bestir themselves and adopt some measures to give us poor paupers some protection from all this ill-usage as the same as our hospitals, our prisons, and our convict establishments where no officers or servants are allowed to ill use you. It would greatly deter all connected with a workhouse if they had an inspector or visitor to look after them; and I would suggest that some person should be appointed, whose duty it should be to visit at least once a week, and hear all complaints, if any, from the patients.

    Charles Tourle

    Brighton Workhouse Infirmary

The Guardian's visiting committee went to see him and declared that "his opinions were based on hearsay" and that "there was not a particle of truth in them". He told them he was not "referring to this workhouse" and yet he admitted he had never been to any other. However, they decided to remove the wardswoman from her post in the infirmary as she had been "too strict" in not putting more coal on the fire. Then they delved into Tourle's past. In their report they claimed Tourle[i] had owned a newspaper shop in Edward Street, near the workhouse, but had been sentenced to two years in prison for publishing obscene writing. He had also co-habited with a woman named Brown, who, with her three children (by Tourle), had afterwards become chargeable to the parish.

The workhouse chaplain, J. Image, sprang to its defence:

…I have been in the habit of seeing him[Tourle] every week, and talking with him, and he never even intimated to me that he was other than most comfort-able…He never expressed to me a complaint either as regards medicine, food or warmth…After I had read the charges, I asked him why he had written it, and why he had not represented to me or to the Governor, or to some of the

---

[i] In the 1881 census he is described as a "general labourer".

Guardians, the inconveniences which he represented himself to have been subjected to; and his answer was that he knew I should not believe him, because all parties connected with the house held together, and that it was no use for any of the inmates to complain, for they were sure to be ill-treated in consequence…I told him that I could not believe his statement in the letter and he said 'I did not expect that you would, for you are all alike' and that it was necessary to some independent inspector unconnected with the house, should come and see how shamefully the patients were treated, with other observations to the same effect…My own impression is that there is no foundation whatever for the complaints he has made.[19]

And rather surprisingly, Neil Crispin, "that troublesome priest", wrote a letter of support to Sattin:

I believe the Brighton Workhouse will bear any inspection at any hour of the day or night and that I have witnessed with sincere admiration the faithful and efficient manner in which you and Mrs Sattin have always discharged the responsible duties of your office.[20]

The Guardians produced a complimentary report written by the Poor Law inspector, Hawley, from the previous April. Some doubted whether Tourle could have written the letter himself and believed that it had been "worked up" by the editor of *Lloyds Weekly*[i], which they described as a "disreputable paper". The Guardians sent the paper a copy of their report.

In the end, the Local Government Board decided no further investigation was necessary. But not everyone was happy with this. One letter to the Board from a Brighton resident asked for an enquiry and doubted the Guardians version of events. He said he was "expressing the general feeling of the Parish".[21]

A common theme running through the complaints from Tourle, Rubens, and Miles, apart from the poor diet and treatment, had been that complaining to the workhouse staff and the Guardians was futile and only led to further mistreatment. Later that year, a rather different kind of complaint was received by the Guardians from a local woman. She complained about her husband spending money on drink all summer and on beating her.

---

[i] One workhouse, St Mary's in Southampton, had banned it because of its criticism of workhouses.

She protested that:

You entice poor women's husbands into the Workhouse by giving them better food and lodging than they can get for themselves. What do you suppose, sir, fishermen live on, except on some of the worser kinds of fish they can't sell. It is very seldom they have any butchers meat...As soon as winter comes every year my old man sells off our few sticks of furniture and goes into the House because it is more comfortable than it is at home during the cold weather, and if I try and prevent him he knocks me down. You should not allow yourself to be imposed upon by rogues also such as small shopkeepers who go for relief for their children. My mother makes us take all the things out of the window when the relieving officer is coming, to pretend we have got nothing and as soon as he is gone we put it all back again.

Brighton has been in the habit of feeding the paupers better than any other place and though not so much better now, still as good as the best and better than many shopkeepers who only have meat on Sundays. Should not entice them away by giving them better than they received at home. The Workhouse ought to have fishing boats SO THE FISHERMEN could be sent to catch fish to feed all the Workhouse people.

Anonymous [22]

* * *

During this period, we see the precarious nature of life. In February 1868, Richard Ewer, a forty-three year old grocer of Waterloo Street, failed in business and had a mental breakdown. In July, after he had not eaten for a fortnight, a policeman took him to the workhouse. He was so weak he had to be carried in and was placed in the lunatic ward. He was not seen by a doctor, however, and died twelve hours later. At the inquest, held at the workhouse, a verdict of death through fever and exhaustion was given and the coroner recommended that in future such serious cases should be seen sooner by a doctor. Not long after, George Bone, a former hotel keeper who cleaned the workhouse windows, took his ladder into a toilet and hanged himself.

In September 1868 a young couple from Hackney came to Brighton looking for work but ended up in the workhouse. The wife, only 18, was pregnant and gave birth to a child. Five months later it died and the medical officer decided not to have an inquest, but the father demanded one. The inquest revealed the mother had not had sufficient breast milk to feed the child and that she had only been allowed to see it four times a day to suckle although babies were allowed to sleep with their mothers at night. There were 17 children in the nursery and an inmate, Ann Dunstall, had assisted the head nurse. To keep them warm from the draughts, frocks were often thrown over the babies. The jury brought in a verdict of "accidental suffocation" and said that an inmate was not competent to look after children. There were to be no properly trained nurses at the workhouse till 1892. It is interesting to note that at no time did the newspaper reports give the name or sex of the child.

That year, in a letter to the *Lancet*, a doctor connected to the workhouse, E.F. Russell,[23] reported that from March 1862 to March 1868, there had been 223 babies delivered to forty-five married women and 178 single women in the lying-in wards which were separate from the infirmary. Of these only one woman had died. Most of the single women were servant girls, some "off the town" and a few with syphilis. Many of the married women had been deserted by their husbands. After praising this low death rate, he alluded to the "dark side", which was that one in six of these babies had died, for which he could offer no explanation.

In June 1870, a smallpox epidemic hit Brighton when 271 cases occurred within three months and conditions in the workhouse infirmary became cramped. The medical officer, Dr Richards, took charge and at the height of the epidemic the fifty fever ward beds were full. It was staffed by the only paid nurse, Mrs H. aged 40, and inmate assistants. Unfortunately, she contracted the disease and died four days later. Richards' assistant, Dr Harris Ross said of her:

> I never met with a more kind, attentive, painstaking and hard-working nurse in the whole of my professional experience.[24]

Three other officers also contracted the disease. Dr Ross vaccinated all the other staff and patients, and no other cases occurred. In all, 29 inmates died during the outbreak, which he considered to be a far lower death rate than in the London hospitals. The following year, a nurse, Emily Richards, refused to work with smallpox cases and was sacked.

Two important figures connected with the workhouse died in 1870, the assistant-overseer, Samuel Thorncroft, and the vicar of Brighton, Rev Henry Wagner. The controversial Thorncroft, the scourge of those seeking relief for almost fifty years, suffered a mental breakdown and died under the delusion that he was the Emperor of France. The stern Wagner, so influential as an *ex-officio* Guardian since 1824, left a lasting legacy of £500 towards "treats" for the aged of the workhouse and the children of the industrial schools. The interest on the money was used annually for that purpose.

The decade ended with the Local Government Board taking over from the Poor Law Board, and it began to have more say in the running of the Brighton workhouse. With almost 5 per cent of the town receiving relief, the Guardians decided to turn to another solution to the overcrowding, lack of work and the bleak future for paupers. It had been a proposal tried before. Now it was being tried again on a larger scale.

Number of Paupers relieved in each of the following weeks in the year 1870 as compared with 1869.

	Indoor	Outdoor	Total	Increase in 1870	Increase per cent in 1870
1st week Jan 1870	1,007	3,328	4,335		
Ditto, 1869	943	2,653	3,596	739	20.5
1st week Feb 1870	1,083	4,832	5,915		
Ditto, 1869	981	2,838	3,819	2,096	55
1st week Mar 1870	1,015	4,197	5,212		
Ditto, 1869	954	2,720	3,674	1,538	42
1st week April 1870	872	2,991	3,863		
Ditto 1869	868	2,480	3,348	515	18.3

Table showing the dramatic increase in outdoor relief in the winter of 1870. [25]

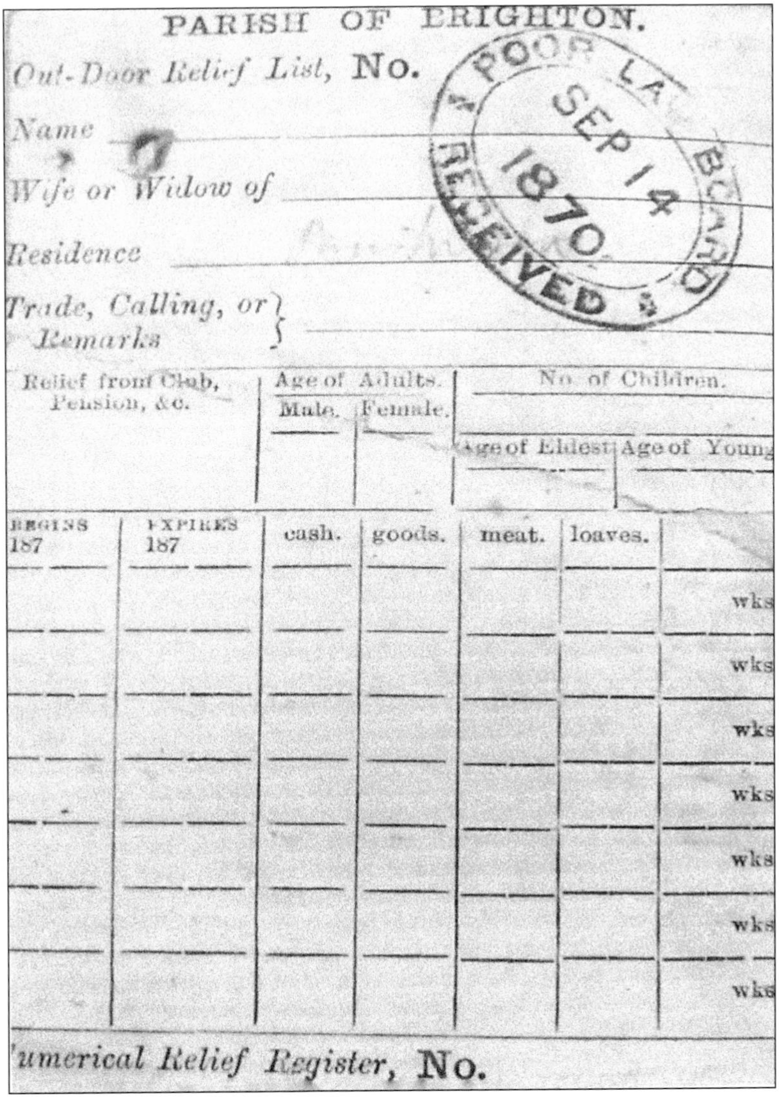

PARISH OF BRIGHTON.

Out-Door Relief List, **No.**

Name

Wife or Widow of

Residence

Trade, Calling, or }
Remarks }

POOR LAW BOARD
RECEIVED
SEP 14
1870

Relief from Club, Pension, &c.	Age of Adults.		No. of Children.			
	Male.	Female.				
			Age of Eldest	Age of Young		

BEGINS 187	EXPIRES 187	cash.	goods.	meat.	loaves.	
						wks
						wks
						wks
						wks
						wks
						wks
						wks

Numerical Relief Register, **No.**

Fig 15 Outdoor relief voucher.

Chapter Nine

FEARING GOD AND KEEPING THE COMMANDMENTS

On 2nd May, 1871, a large group of excited children from the industrial schools sat round the solicitors' table in the magistrates' room at Brighton town hall. They were nervously facing magistrates sitting on raised chairs on a platform. The chief of the magistrates, Mr Begge, asked them individually to stand up and say whether they wanted to emigate to Canada. All but one said "yes". A sister of one boy, William Hall, did not want him to go so far away and asked if he could work with her husband who was a trawlerman. She asked Begge if he could come back if he did not like it there. He replied only after a few years and only if he had the means to do so. As William had been left chargeable to the parish by his father, he said she had no say in the matter.

Begge told her that as the boy wanted to go, he was better off going. He then made a short speech:

> He was sorry to see so many good, healthy and respectable looking young people go away from England. But there could be no question that this was the best thing that could possibly happen to them. He had but little doubt that in a few years the boys would all be happy, independent and prosperous men. He firmly believed that if they lived they would be so. It was a very different country. They would find the sky bluer, the lakes very large; the summer much hotter; and the winter very much colder. The climate, however was exceedingly healthy, and the inhabitants were some of the finest and noblest people on the face of this earth. If they should be happy and successful, they should always remember one thing – it was through the good people of Brighton that they were sent out and it was Brighton in England which gave them their first start in life.[1]

Begge handed each child a shilling. The children returned thanks with a military salute and were marched away. In nine days time, thirty-six of them – including one girl – with other emigrants from the town would be going to Liverpool to catch the steamer *Nestorian*, bound for Canada.

* * *

In the early 1830s, with the collapse of rural economies and the great distress among the labouring classes alarming property owners in the county – incendiarism was rife – the Earl of Egremont had started to sponsor the emigration of poor families in Sussex to Canada, Australia and the USA. With the increasing industrialisation of society, and an increasing population, many of whom were reliant on poor relief, more and more people found themselves unemployed or under-employed. Emigration was seen as a way of removing excess population and leaving more space to those who remained. In that decade, under the patronage of the Earl of Egremont, 404 people from Sussex had left for Canada and the USA under the Petworth Emigration Scheme but it had ceased at his death in 1837.

Between 1836 and 1846, 14,000 paupers had been assisted by their parishes to emigrate. Some were from the Brighton workhouse. In 1830s, the Guardians had sanctioned the emigration of four young workhouse women, Harriet Piper (16), Elizabeth Goldsmith (22), Ellie Barnett (17) and Mary Cook (20) to Tasmania. They were each supplied with a box of clothes, a knife and fork and a Bible. The total cost of sending them was £13 each, which was a long-term saving on the £10 a year the girls would cost if they remained where they were. At the time the Guardians congratulated themselves on easing the burden to the ratepayers. However, the following year they received a letter from one of the passengers claiming the girls had had to sell their clothes during the voyage to buy food and had slept with the sailors on board the *Strathfieldsaye* all the way to the island. One of the girls was now working as a prostitute on the streets of Sydney. Some Guardians laughed as they heard the letter read out, as their intention had been to reform the girls by removing them away from their "bad connexions". They laughed less when they received another letter, this time from the secretary of the Emigration Board, which criticized the girls' behaviour and concluded by saying they wanted no more female paupers from the parish.

The Poor Law Commission would only sanction expenditure for emigration to the colonies, so the Guardians had occasionally to find other funds apart from the poor rate. In 1841, they gave a pauper widow £40 to emigrate to Ohio, USA, with her five children. In 1844, they gave Ann Mills £5 towards her fare to New York where her daughter lived. The following year they helped send a convict's wife, Mary Jenner, to Australia to join her husband. However, six years later they were refusing to give an "honest" unemployed bricklayer and his family of six, of Eastern Road, any help with their fare of £40 to go to Australia. They only offered to buy his family clothes. His friends raised his fare and the Guardians then refused to provide any clothing. The man applied for outdoor relief until his ship sailed but was told to take his family to the workhouse. An exasperated ratepayer complained:

> The cost of this family of seven for one year [at the workhouse] is £140, and this annual charge might be for years tied like a millstone round the neck of the parish instead of, by a trifling aid from the Poor rates, getting rid of the family altogether. [2]

The Guardians rarely heard back from the emigrants, although in 1836 they had received a grateful letter from a Canadian emigrant, Adolphus Graefenstein, who had left the workhouse two or three years earlier. He had thanked them and had written: "We have no master to order us. We all work alike, the rich as well as the poor man". He asked them to send him a woman from the workhouse whom he could marry. There is no evidence they did.

In 1849 and 1852 two large groups from Brighton had gone to Australia. The first had been Baptists from the Ebenezer Chapel on Richmond Hill who had deeply resented the imposition of compulsory church rates and had wanted to set up a separate community in their new land. The second group, almost 200 in strength, had mainly consisted of young, single men and tradesmen attracted by the discovery of gold near Melbourne in 1851. As letters from emigrants to their families showed, Australia could be fraught with dangers. Not least were the extreme heat, the cold nights and the lack of accommodation. Disease was rife. Most of the gold diggers found themselves living in tents. And there was an additional danger. On their way back with their gold from the "diggings" they were often bushwacked and robbed by bushrangers. One of the young men who had gone to seek his fortune had been Richards, the son-in law of King, the governor of the workhouse. He had run an eating house in the town and had left his wife and five children behind in Brighton to join the gold rush. His final letter home had been completed by a friend. It announced his death from dysentery in February 1853.

However, not all the Brighton emigrants had been voluntary. Between 1789 and 1867 nearly 2,000 people sentenced in Sussex courts had been transported to Australia. (see M.J. Burchall, *Sussex Convicts Transported to*

Australia, 1789-1867).[3] This included two workhouse girls, Sophia Clifton, aged seventeen, and Olive King, who, after being charged with absconding and stealing their workhouse uniforms and 7s worth of clothes in 1839, had been sentenced to be transported to Australia for fourteen years.

At the beginning of the 1870s, with the steady rise of the numbers on relief and with little hope for a pauper child's future, the Brighton Guardians sought emigration as a long-term solution. If they could be sent to a land of plenty, everyone would benefit. Early in 1871 the Brighton branch of the Juvenile Emigration Society [part of the National Emigration League] based in an office in Ship Street and run by a group of ladies, decided to organise emigration to Canada. They relied heavily on donations although the Guardians had the power to give £10 to any adult pauper who wanted to emigrate and a lesser sum to the children. One of the ladies, Miss Crisp, went to visit the children at the industrial schools in Woodingdean. She found that thirty-six boys and one girl wanted to emigrate. By law, any child under the age of sixteen who was deemed "orphaned or deserted" had to be brought before the magistrates to swear that they really wanted to

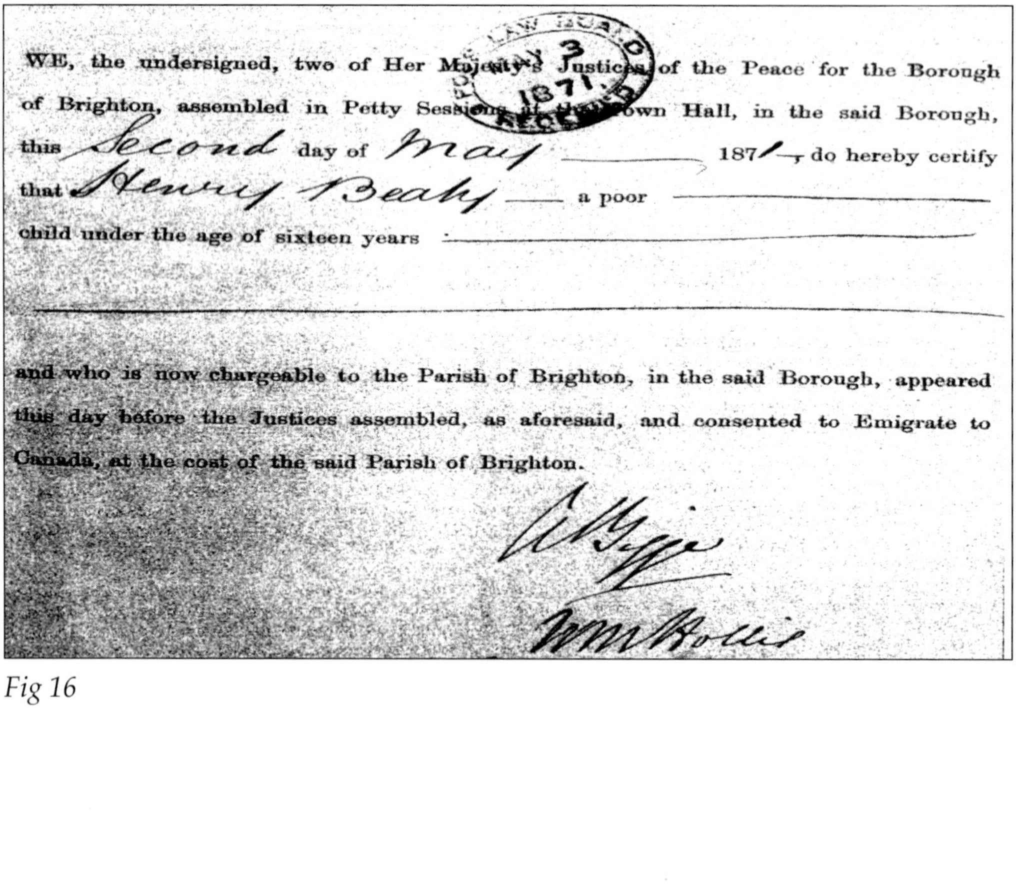
WE, the undersigned, two of Her Majesty's Justices of the Peace for the Borough of Brighton, assembled in Petty Sessions at the Town Hall, in the said Borough, this Second day of May 1871, do hereby certify that Henry Beaty a poor child under the age of sixteen years

and who is now chargeable to the Parish of Brighton, in the said Borough, appeared this day before the Justices assembled, as aforesaid, and consented to Emigrate to Canada, at the cost of the said Parish of Brighton.

Fig 16

go. However, the Local Government Board had decided that all the children must go before a magistrate, even those with parents.

* * *

On the eve of their departure, at 2.30pm on May 10th 1871, seventy-seven children and sixteen adult emigrants made their way through a large crowd gathered outside the town hall in Bartholomews (where it is now) to a large upper room. Each carried small bundles containing clothes and parting gifts from friends, their trunks having been sent in advance. "The boys from the industrial schools were without exception, smart, healthy and intelligent looking lads". While the meeting was assembling "Miss Crisp was to be observed moving hither and thither giving a kind word here, a cheering look there, and a hearty shake of the hand yonder to some boy who had a more thoughtful air than some of his more courageous confreres".[4]

The ceremony opened with a written message from George Duddell, the treasurer of the National Emigration League: "Say goodbye to one and all for me, and urge upon them to write home occasionally, enabling me to inform their benevolent friends in Brighton of their whereabouts and doings in the far West". After a few words from the mayor, in which he believed "each would individually promote his own welfare," the vicar of Brighton, Rev Dr John Hannah, exhorted them:

> … above all to be truthful; to be just to the masters who might be placed over them in Canada; and if they made a promise to remain with certain employers for a given period, to stick to that promise and let no one tempt them to break faith with their masters or induce them to go away before each term of service had expired.

Addressing the boys, he emphasized the importance of sobriety and told them that "fearing God and keeping his commandments was the one great duty of man". Then he addressed the girls and hoped that "when they were far away in the west, they would preserve that spirit of English purity which ought to be the salt of the land". (*Cheers.*) When he had finished, the intending emigrants marched in single file to the platform where they were each presented with a small parcel containing copies of the Holy Bible and the Book of Common Prayer. The boys from the industrial schools then acknowledged the vicar's gift with a military salute.

One Guardian congratulated those going out, as they would have a better chance of becoming wealthy, and also congratulated those who remained, saying there would be more room for them. Mr Hepple Hall, a twenty-year resident in Canada, gave them practical advice and reminded them that "if they would be successful they must be industrious". Next, Miss Crisp gave a number of books to Sattin and Mrs Gower, the matron of the industrial schools, to distribute. Their names were inscribed in each. Another Guardian gave the boys some games to play on the Atlantic crossing. Proceedings were finished by the singing of a hymn composed especially for the occasion. It was printed in mauve ink upon cards with the Brighton arms, dated March 10th, 1871, as a memento. The first verse went:

> We are going, O our father,
> Far from friends and native land.
> Oh! be thou our guide and Guardian,
> Lead us by Thy loving hand.
> Bring us safely o'er the ocean
> To the far Canadian strand.

As the young emigrants, some in tears, left the town hall in vans decorated with flags, they were cheered by a large crowd which lined the route from North Street to Queens Road. At the station, as the town band played on the platform, they took their seats in second class carriages of an express train to London. The platform was crowded with their sad looking friends and local dignitaries:

A few minutes prior to the starting of the train Miss Crisp, radiant with pleasant smiles, passed along the platform. No sooner was she observed than hearty juvenile cheers greeted her, and many were the hands thrust from the windows of the carriages with which a bid good bye to the kind benefactress. Many who were at the station were also at the Town Hall. Flowers and another Guardian, Mr Phillips, were each standing on a carriage step whilst their hands were being shaken in such a violent way by the youngsters as to suggest a fear lest the arms of the respected gents would be pulled from their respective sockets. Perhaps one of the most affecting sights was that where a young girl, apparently a sister, was fondly caressing a little boy of between fourteen and sixteen years of age; and this was possibly rivalled by the genuine heartiness of feeling evinced between two youthful companions who were about to be separated, certainly for a long period of time, and possibly for ever in this world. At length the signal was sounded for the train to start; the shrill whistle of the engine was immediately succeeded by "Auld Lang Syne" from the band, amid the cheers of the spectators and the waving of hats and hankies, the train with its living burden glided out of the station, and the emigrants had entered upon a journey the undertaking of which, it is to be hoped, they may never have cause to regret.

Edward Sattin and Mr Gower, the superintendent of the schools, accompanied the emigrants to Liverpool. Afterwards, the former sent this report to the Guardians:

…The arrangements made for the journey through to Liverpool were very good; but some misunderstanding took place at Euston Sq station, as we were directed to leave the carriages in which we had so far journeyed; and having to keep a lot of exuberant young spirits together for an hour in that large place was necessarily a somewhat anxious task. Advantage was taken of the interval to distribute the pies etc. provided by kind friends. The carriages in which we had left Brighton were, however, attached to the mail train, and in these we all arrived safely at Liverpool at about 3.30am and were very shortly after accosted by a person from Messrs Allans' office, who, in a most courteous and friendly manner, provided for the immediate transfer of the passengers and luggage to the very handsome and commodious vessel.

It seemed to me, as we traversed at that early hour, the silent streets of that great town, a very solemn thing, and I could not help feeling sad about it, although the brave young hearts who were so soon to part from what had been to them both home and friends, never flinched or faltered. At the last farewell, a few glistening eyes showed that the feelings were with difficulty restrained. Having seen them served on board with hot rolls and butter and hot coffee, I left the ship to arrange in Canada, of the several small sums, amounting in aggregate to over £24, which had been deposited with Miss Crisp for that purpose.

The agent who accompanied the Brighton emigrants remained on board until the departure of the vessel, which took place at about four o'clock in the afternoon. May the undertaking, so far auspiciously accomplished, receive the Divine blessing is the earnest wish of,

Gentlemen, Your faithful servant,

Edward Sattin.

The Nestorian.

The children were going on what could be a perilous journey on the grey, rolling North Atlantic. Although the journey took on average eleven days by steamer, ice, fog and seasickness could make it a miserable experience. Sometimes a boat could be stuck in ice for weeks on end, and frequently it was necessary to wait hours and days for fog to lift. Passengers could also be kept below deck in the crowded steerage for long periods during a storm.

When Sattin got back to Brighton, he found more adult paupers from the workhouse requesting to emigrate the following year: Liza Barnett 16, Liz Moors 18, Mary Ann Hart 31, Eliza Mcnoughton 24, Susan Richards 19, Charles Croucher 17, James French 17, William Rawley 17, Horace Fairbrother 17 and William Hart 19. He forwarded their names to the Local Government Board who wanted to know whether they were of "good character". With the exception of Horace Fairbrother, he said they were. His name was withdrawn.

Rev Herring of Clerkenwell was organising the next trip and explained that once landed they would have a free passage right to their destination. He sent a price list to the Guardians and an itinerary:

Assisted Passage of £6 5s for all over 8 years
£3 2s 6d for all under 8 years
£1 is for babies

The price included everything from London to Quebec. Once there, the Canadian government were offering free passage up country from Quebec:

Our party assembles at Euston at 8pm on 28 June. All wear a little piece of red ribbon and oldest clothes for voyage. If you give me names, ages and trades I would suggest certain favourable localities. There is a little book sent which is really valuable for all to study before going...You may rely that I will do all in my power for the guardians and the emigrants, as deeply interested in this class of emigrants, and believe the guardians will find a permanent benefit thereby.

"Clerkenwell & Royal Canadian Emigration Society – SS Scandinavian"

The emigrants would meet the emigration agent in Quebec and if no work was found, they would be sent to James Walker of Hamilton, Ontario, who reputedly was successful at finding employers. Alfred Morris, clerk to the Guardians, received permission to buy new outfits for the pauper emigrants. One family, Charles Cowley, and his wife and four children, aged 5 to 11, received £20 from the Guardians and the rest from friends to enable them to go. The previous year the parish had spent £6 10s 3d in cash and £3 3s 10d in kind on the family.

By April 1872 Miss Crisp had another 42 names, including adults – mainly labourers – who wanted to go to Canada. On May 1st they assembled at the town hall for the farewell speeches. Again, the vicar of Brighton warned them to "fear God and keep his Commandments; for this is the whole duty of man. The bible was the centre of knowledge and the prayer book was the central force of their grace. They must not separate religion from their duties".

The mayor talked about the advantages of emigration to a big, sparsely populated country and warned them not to stow away as "a wicked rascal is now probably reaping his deserts, having been sent to prison for three months. [One boy on the *Nestorian* had hidden on the boat and returned]. He reminded them that they were being sent out at great expense; and that in you this town's character is at stake in common with that of those kind benefactors who have supported you (*loud applause*)".

Another Guardian, Mr Penney, told the emigrants that drinking was the curse of the country and that it made people "paupers, lunatics and prisoners". If people didn't drink, emigration would not be necessary.

The mayor interrupted: "I think you are a little out of order, Sir; we are not met to discuss the temperance question".

Penney finished his speech by giving every emigrant 2s and a paper containing some facts about the temperance question. Then Miss Crisp rose:

> ...I have been to Canada and I know what a country it is. I have seen how well all the lads get on there; what nice farms they have; and what nice homes they get...I hope you will all follow the advice of the good vicar; that you will fear God and set His law before you; thus you will be good and useful men here, and finally be happy for ever. (*Loud applause.*)

The emigrants were given oranges, buns and little presents from ladies. They left the town hall and were taken in cabs and vans to the railway station. Again, there were sad scenes on the platform. At least this time the party only had to get to the London Docks, where the steamship *Scotland* was bound for Quebec.

In 1873, twenty-two workhouse inmates "of good character" – twelve men and ten women – plus six of their children, including Elizabeth Goodridge from the industrial schools, were sponsored by the Guardians to go to Canada. Paupers on outdoor relief such as a widow, Ann Cork, and her two small children, also received money from the Guardians towards their costs. But before she was allowed to go, the Local Government Board wanted to know "for what purposes did she emigrate and was she of good character and how can she maintain herself and her children when she arrived". The Emigration Society gave assurances that she had relatives there who would find her a position.

At the farewell speech at the town hall for these fresh emigrants, the mayor dismissed the rumour that some of the ships were "unworthy of carrying passengers". He also warned them:

> ...it was quite likely that some of them were thinking that they would not have to work so hard in Canada as here; that they would have an easy time of it, and that, indeed, they would earn so much money in one week as not to need to work the next. He wished to undeceive them upon this matter. They would have to work as hard in Canada as in England. If they did not work hard in Canada, there was but little possibility of their getting a living or of being useful to anybody. (*Applause*)...

He finished by asking them to send back encouraging accounts so that it would stimulate others to want to go. Then he gave them all a copy of *The Pilgrims Progress*. The vicar of Brighton continued the farewell speeches:

The emigrants would follow in the steps of men who had carried away to the West many treasures from their native land. Let it be the privilege of the emigrants to carry treasures only, and not what the Indians calls "the white man's vices". (*Applause.*) In the new world, let them practice self-denial, let them take out thoughts of God and religion; and let it not be said that we have sent our vices to those distant parts. Be sober & temperate, chaste and true, upright, honest, and straightforward in their work. Don't drive a hard bargain with their new masters... Another thing, have a steeliness of purpose, with pertinacity of resolution; do not turn back when once they have put their hand to the plough. That was a lesson they especially required. We sometimes hear of people becoming cowardly and wanting to turn back and come home again, forgetting the troubles from which they were released; thus cowardly turning from a course when they should have been brave and noble. (*Applause.*)

You must persevere and not give in at the first difficulty. Women may be weaker for the rough work of this world, but their influence we are glad to know, is even stronger and purer for the work of heaven. Female emigrants must be the salt of society. As is purity to the woman, so is bravery to the man; her bond of honour is to be chaste and pure; his to be brave and noble. Let both endeavour, each in their own sphere, to fill up the great ideas which together constitute our Christian society – purity joined with strength; chastity and love joined with energy and firmness of purpose. Carry with you the old religion of England. Be true servants of our great Master Christ and show that they wish to carry on his work in the world. (*Applause.*)

In his speech, a local dignitary, Sir John Cordy Burrows, questioned whether the country might be a loser by sending them away. He wanted the Emigration Society "to look at those who had lost character and caste at home but who might be amenable to education, love and kindliness". Sattin again accompanied the emigrants to Liverpool.

In 1874, among the emigrants to Canada were Thomas Lee, a fifty-eight-year-old labourer, his fifty-seven-year-old wife and two children aged 10 and 12, who were classified as "irremovable poor". They had been on outdoor relief for years. The same year a housepainter, John Boon, his wife and six children were given £20 worth of clothing by the parish for their emigration to Wellington, New Zealand. Despite being taken to the departure depot, weeks later a Guardian saw one of the children playing in the town in his new clothes!

* * *

We know little about what happened to most of these emigrants. The girl from the schools who went in 1871 wrote back in 1872 asking if her sister could join her. And in 1873, Henry Camfield, a lad who had emigrated from the workhouse, wrote to Sattin:

> Canada is a fine country. Clothes, tea and sugar are dear but meat is cheap. I would like to be remembered to my old comrades and to thank the Guardians and the Master, which had been the making of me.

Camfield wrote that when the emigrants had arrived in Hamilton, they had been beseiged by people wanting their services. He had been picked by a doctor and was now earning good money. One emigrant wrote warning that newcomers might not like Canada for the first two years. Later on, in 1881, another boy emigrant, George Complin, who had left the workhouse in 1871, came and visited the Guardians. He had become a successful rep of a large firm in London and travelled throughout USA and Canada. His parents had deserted him when he was four and he had been sent to the workhouse. He had come back to try and find out about his parentage.

On the surface, sending child paupers to Canada to escape the poverty of their homeland may have seemed like a good idea. The reality was somewhat different. A damning independent report by an experienced senior Poor Law inspector, sixty-five-year-old Andrew Doyle, written in 1874 and published the following year, led to the Local Government Board suspending the emigration of workhouse children for the next nineteen years.

Doyle had spent six months on his own touring Canada and visiting 400 placed children. He found that many were used to replace paid labour and were living in appalling conditions. Like Henry Camfield above, on arrival the children were often herded into a town hall, lined up for "viewing" against a wall and then selected by the locals who came in one by one. Brothers and sister were often separated. It was reminiscent of the selection of black slaves in the American southern states and of convict assignment placements in Australia and Tasmania.

Most of the girls were taken as domestic servants and the boys as cheap farm labour, much like the former parish apprenticeship system for pauper children. Often they faced long train journeys after embarkation as most of their employers lived in remote, isolated countryside, miles from anywhere. Doyle found that the reception homes were dirty, that there was little training or education, almost no facilities for the sick and no efficient personal supervison. Many of the children had never had anyone to see them since they arrived.

Doyle claimed that the older pauper children were exposed to the greatest of dangers and young girls were often abused by the families. The climate could be harsh and the days long, sunless and lonely, especially in the winter. And it was extremely difficult for them to maintain contact with friends and family back in England. Doyle believed workhouse child emigrants struggled more than the waifs and strays or "arab" street children who had not come from the workhouse. The former had been used to a very structured environment, so found it more difficult to fend for themselves. Some of the emigrant children had absconded and no one knew where they were. Doyle wrote that:

> Canadians wouldn't send their own children for service in such conditions and that the children were collected without the slightest reference to their fitness for emigration…The Guardians [of workhouses] wanted to get rid of them at a cheap rate. [5]

Also quite damning was Doyle's finding that one "philanthropic lady", Miss Maria Rye, who ran an emigration scheme for workhouse girls, may have been making a profit of £4 to £5 on each child who emigrated. She had received money both from the workhouse authorities and a bonus of £1 from the Ontario Government. The hon secretary of a Canadian charity set up to help immigrants, J.E. Pell, complained in a letter that their children's homes were full and that:

> the continuance of Miss Rye's work is keeping this country overflowing with pauperism…There are families upon families in our cities – men, women, boys, and girls – in destitution and want for lack of employment, and there are hundreds longing to get back to England. [6]

Doyle ended his report by recommending that only children under five should be considered for child emigration. At least then they would be given a proper education before working.

One Canadian newspaper called the children the "refuse of the workhouse" while the Canadian government's own report recommended a Canadian inspectorate. (The USA would not accept pauper children at the expense of the municipal or government authorities.) And in the 1880s all workhouse children were inspected annually by a Canadian government inspector. The Brighton Guardians, like others, had needed to release space in their workhouse for others. Pauper child emigration had appeared to be an attractive proposition. In their view, it was healthier and cheaper than bringing children up at the ratepayers' expense and they hoped it would save them from destitution and crime but it did not, as Doyle had found out, necessarily save them from exploitation.

The Guardians occasionally were prompted to find out what happened to a child emigrant. In 1872, the Local Government Board had received a letter from Thomas Armitage of the Royal Hospital, Chelsea. He complained that his thirteen-year-old son, Thomas, had not been "deserted" and that the Guardians had sent him to Canada without his knowledge. The Guardians did launch an enquiry and found that Thomas had been hired by a farmer who lived near Hamilton. Despite, the temporary suspension of pauper child emigration to Canada, between 1870 and 1920, 80,000 British children emigrated to Canada. And the emigration of Brighton adult paupers receiving either indoor or outdoor relief to Canada continued.

One Brighton emigrant we do know about was Henry Wooldridge who was born illegitimately in the Church Hill workhouse on April 15th, 1855,[i] five years before his mother, Sarah Wooldridge, married John Reading, a blind hawker whom we shall meet later. Although Sarah was listed as still being in the workhouse on the 1861 census, Henry was not listed. On the 1871 census, he was living at 80 Egremont Street, Brighton, with the Sheedy family from Ireland and five other young people. He was apparently employed as a general labourer. Two years later it was recorded that, under the auspices of Barnardo's, he was sent to Ontario, Canada, by the Brighton Guardians. Under the name of Henry Reading, he departed on the *Nestorian* from Liverpool with a party of unaccompanied young people.

The ship docked at Quebec on May 20th 1873. From there he went to live in Hamilton, Ontario. Twelve years later, under the surname of Wooldridge, Henry married Caroline Sweet. He worked as a painter but soon after his marriage was hired as a coachman and found employment with the Counsell family.

---

[i] There were usually more illegitimate births than legitimate in the Brighton Workhouses. From 1862–1868 there were 45 legitimate and 177 illegitimate births.

Henry and Caroline had two children. In 1911, after twenty-six years employment with the Counsells, Henry left his position and found work as a labourer. Three years later he was working as a machinist. In 1921, he was described as an engineer and later became a boiler operative.

Henry retired from his job in 1929 and died in 1935. Caroline, died the following year. Henry's obituary appeared in the *Hamilton Spectator*:

Henry Wooldridge

An old and highly esteemed resident of this city, Henry Wooldridge, husband of Caroline Sweet, died early this morning at his residence, 114 Augusta street, after a lengthy illness. Mr. Wooldridge was born in Brighton, England, and had resided in this city for the last 60 years. For many years he was an employee of the late C. M. Counsell. Left to mourn his death, besides his widow, is one daughter, Mrs. Thomas Manewell, jun. The funeral will take place from the above address Monday afternoon at 3.30 o'clock. Interment will be in Hamilton cemetery.

Chapter Ten

INDUSTRIAL SCHOOLS FOR SCANDAL
1862–1880

From the very first, scandals involving staff at Warren Farm became routine. Unlike workhouse staff who in theory could be reappointed every year when there was a change of Guardians, the appointments at the schools were permanent, lifetime positions. All decisions had to be sanctioned by the Poor Law Board, later the Local Government Board. This made getting rid of unsuitable employees more difficult. The schools had their own chaplain, teachers, bandmaster and farm bailiff. However, it soon became apparent that it was understaffed and that the initial figure of 142 children would grow rapidly, almost doubling within five years.

The children had eighteen hours of education a week and were unsupervised for 4½ hours every day. In 1863 a nineteen-year-old boy, John Saunders, the porter, who also worked in the superintendent's office, was appointed drill master to look after the boys after school, because, as one Guardian claimed:

> there was a great want of someone to look after them [the boys] when out of school; there was no one to take care of them at such times, and they became dirty and careless …The children were not in such good condition now as when they left the Workhouse…[1] They must bear in mind that these were industrial schools, where the children not only learnt lessons but applied themselves to industrial occupations; and thus it followed that the whole of them were not in school at one time, and that the schoolmaster and schoolmistress were in the school very many hours a day…The Chaplain bore especial testimony to the unwearied zeal and industry of the female teacher; he said she very often appeared to be completely exhausted...and when she was quite finished she was so exhausted that it would be quite improper, quite inhuman, to expect her to keep charge of the children in her leisure hours.[2]

A month later, the assistant-laundress was asked to "drill" the girls.

In July 1863, the master tailor, William Appleby, absconded after facing a charge of indecently assaulting one of the boys. Then the farm bailiff, cook and dairywoman resigned. Before the latter left she wrote to the Guardians about her workload:

> I am surprised at seeing in the papers that the dairywoman is to spend part of her time in the laundry, and not one word has been spoken to her about it. What time has she to spare, for her time is fully occupied now: the dairy, chimney twice a week, receive the children, salt down all meat, and doing the chief part of her washing, attend to the grate and the chimney. Mornings up soon after 4 o'clock, at work two hours before the other officers are at work, and at work after theirs is done. And if you want to put more work upon her, you must increase her salary. She will not have anything to do with the laundry.
> C.M Elsey [3]

In 1864, the schoolmaster, William Tubb, told the Guardians that girls had complained to him about Superintendent Hales' "immoral tendencies". Although the schools had only been open for twenty-one months, Tubb said he had heard more reports about these "tendencies" than in his three years at Church Hill. Hales punished the girls and accused Tubb of employing two of the boys as servants, one of them being kept out of school for nine months. The Guardians tried to sack Tubb, claiming the children's writing had deteriorated, but he refused to go. They appealed to the Poor Law Board. Tubb wrote to them explaining his workload. He claimed he was up at 5.30 am and had to take the children to bathe two and a half miles away. He taught for six and a half hours a day and supervised meals and took prayers three times a day. On Sundays he conducted the music. He complained that Hales had taken his school monitors away but that he (Tubbs) had "no complaint as I am constituted for hard work". [4] However, he did describe the boys' playground as an "acre of mud" and accused Hales of spending most of his time reading the newspapers, smoking and chewing gum. The Board backed the Guardians. Tubb and his wife – who worked as the schoolmistress – were sacked.

In 1865 Hales' wife Margaret, the matron, was certified insane after trying to poison him and others and was taken to Bethlem Asylum in London as a private patient. She was replaced by Mrs Wheatcroft, a relative, who was an unpopular figure. The following year, Thomas Hales was asking for an increase in salary as it was "no small amount of self-sacrifice to isolate oneself entirely from all society, as it is necessary to do here". The

Guardians decided not to give him one but let him off paying for the keep of two of his three children.

By 1867 there were more than 250 children and John Saunders, still acting as a porter/drill master, was appointed to the post of assistant schoolmaster. Unsurprisingly, Edward Smith, the Poor Law commissioner who visited that year, found a deficiency in teaching and that the children were unclean and had few chairs to sit on. He also recommended the Guardians give an alternative to rice pudding every day.

* * *

In February 1868, early one morning, two fourteen-year-old sons of agricultural workers, Charles Avis and William Allen, and three other boys managed to get into the locked building that housed the entrance to the well. They started to let each other up and down on the winch, sitting on a "donkey".[i] Tragically, while Avis and Allen were on it, the boy holding the rope let it go and they fell 500 feet to the top shelf. Their skulls were completely knocked off. Hales was woken up at 5am by the engineer with the news. It took over six hours to retrieve the bodies. The inquest revealed that the room housing the well had not been locked.[ii]

A few years later, a six year-old child, Ellen Vasey, also had a tragic accident:

> …some of the children were swinging on a gate in the girls' yard which had been left open during the passage of a horse and cart from one part of premises to another. The girl in question thrust her head between the gate and the gatepost. At that moment another girl moved the gate and the child was killed instantaneously.[5]

The medical officer did not even bother to report the death to the Guardians, and he was reprimanded at the inquest.

---

[i] A couple of pieces of board on which the workmen lowered themselves in order to do maintenance.

[ii] The boys had not been the first casualties of the well since the schools opened. The previous year a workman, Ben Brown, had fallen down it and been killed.

By the winter of 1868, the schools were already full, with almost 276 children, and plans were made to have an extension to accommodate sixty boys and thirteen girls. Many children arrived in a dreadful state. Often the term "bad head" was used in their admission notes to describe head lice. Once there, conditions were poor. At meal times food was served half an hour before it was eaten. Stone cold rice became normal for those served first. And there was little entertainment apart from the occasional magic lantern show. Offers of free admission for the children to the circus and pantomime were turned down. Invitations to the Aquarium were also rejected by the Guardians, who argued that working men who worked all year could not afford their own children to go. The summer treats now were sometimes held in the nearby Happy Valley in Woodingdean rather than at the more inviting Swiss Gardens at Shoreham.

The following year, Superintendent Hales resigned to take a more lucrative job. As it was a joint appointment, Mrs Wheatcroft – described by some Guardians as "old and inefficient" – went with him. They were replaced by Alfred Gower and his wife Agnes, who had come from the Eversham workhouse. The Guardians also appointed a new drill master, George Hunt, even though he had apparently behaved badly at his previous post at Paddington workhouse. Hunt did not last long and resigned in 1870, saying he had received harsh treatment from Alfred Gower. His successor, Bancroft, absconded two years later.

Some of the staff were very young. Two teenagers, Thomas Hardy and Caroline Streater, were appointed assistants to the schoolmaster at 6d a week plus lodgings, rations and clothing. Another fifteen-year-old girl, Alice Gillette, was dismissed as a pupil teacher but allowed to stay until a domestic situation came up rather than be sent to the workhouse. It is no wonder that the government inspector, Wyndham Holgate, was critical of the teachers. Because of their isolation and low pay, it was difficult to get good ones. He believed the Guardians needed to offer higher wages.

The children's education was often intermittent if their parents were in the workhouse. When the parents took their discharge so did their children, and this could happen several times a year. If they completed their education the girls, aged 14–16, usually left to go into service. The boys, if they were lucky, joined a military band or the services or became farm workers. For those children who could not find work or were disabled or ill, their likely destination was the workhouse.

The Guardians started to "examine"[question] the children every six months to discover their parentage. One year they found that 38 had fathers and 20 had mothers in Brighton; 12 had fathers and 45 had mothers in the workhouse; two children had both parents in the workhouse and six had parents in the Sussex Lunatic Asylum. The rest of the children, more than half, were orphans.[6]

In September 1871, a widow, Elizabeth Private, brought her four children to Brighton and then disappeared. They were taken to the industrial schools. Shortly afterwards, Neil Crispin, the Catholic priest, wrote to the

Fig 17

157

Guardians demanding that as they were Catholics they must be transferred to Catholic schools. [i] They refused, believing that she had deliberately absconded in an attempt to make them send her children to these schools – which had higher maintenance charges. They discovered that when she and her children had been in the Eastbourne workhouse she had been registered as a Catholic, but they had been described as "Protestant", and that their father, when alive, had been registered as a Protestant. They made strenuous efforts to track down Elizabeth Private but said they would only transfer the children if the Local Government Board insisted. They argued that, as she herself had not applied for her children to be transferred, they did not have to act, so the children remained at the schools.

Efforts to trace those who had deserted their families were often made through the *Poor Law Union's Gazette,* which since 1857 had published information about "Deserters of Families". For example, that year they gave a detailed description of William King, 27, a ribbon weaver, who was being sought by the Nuneaton Union. Included in it was the fact that he had "a mole near the left shoulder blade, a mole near the left breast, and a brown mark on the left side." [7] A ten shilling reward was offered for information leading to his apprehension. The journal was particularly read by casual ward staff.

After a series of complaints against the superintendent, Alfred Gower, he resigned along with his wife in 1876 to work at the Clapham asylum. They were succeeded by Mr and Mrs Crook who had been the schoolmaster and schoolmistress at the schools since 1870. He was thirty and she was twenty-seven. They were relieved of their teaching duties and were replaced by lowly qualified teachers. The following May, Dr Mouat, a medical inspector from the Local Government Board wrote the following report:

> The situation and construction of the schools are so excellent that a high standard of health should prevail throughout the institution, and yet ringworm has persistently prevailed for a considerable length of time, and many of the children even now suffer from chilblains. They should not have chilblains in the Spring. The causes are: the want of proper hospital accommodation, the disposal of excrement and the imperfect means of washing…The washing

---

[i] Catholic girls and boys over seven went to the Holy Trinity Orphanage, Tunbridge Wells, and some girls also went to the Convent Orphanage in Norwood.

ARRANGEMENTS ARE EVERYWHERE OBJECTIONABLE. They need a swimming bath, more towels, brushes etc...And the present play grounds are in no way good. They need more grass...I regard an expenditure devoted to the improvement of the physical strength and growth of these children to be the truest and best. The object is to make healthy men and women of them, to enable them to earn an honest livelihood, and to prevent their ever again relapsing into pauperism or becoming the progenitors of another generation of paupers who would certainly be inferior to themselves in all physical and moral characteristics of the class to which they belong.[8]

Mouat found that the "infirmary accommodation was so bad of its kind that it should be prohibited as soon as an alternative was available". The small stuffy wards could not be properly ventilated. The younger children were packed in couples into beds not two-and-a-half feet in width. There were also no proper receiving wards.

The Guardians reacted by ordering an additional supply of towels, basins, baths, brushes and combs, and instituted a weekly medical inspection. They instructed their architect/surveyor George Maynard to have the sewage carried a further 400ft from the premises. However, they insisted that the children did not need grass as they could play on the Downs. As for the sick, they usually transferred the serious cases to the workhouse, but they would consider building an extra storey for them. The Guardians' visiting committee concluded that:

there is not more infirmity amongst the children of their schools than what may be termed the normal conditions of the pauper constitution, and which is mainly caused by the dissolute and drunken habits of their progenitors. [9]

However, the Guardians' own confidence in the schools was undermined by two highly critical letters they received from two members of staff. After they had instigated their own enquiry into their allegations they instructed their clerk, Alfred Morris, to write to the Local Government Board:

...the management of the schools is inefficient and it also clearly shows that there is not simply an absence of harmony amongst the officers of the establishment generally, but that animosity and discord prevail amongst a majority of them to such an extent as to render it impossible they should discharge their duties properly... The evidence amounts to over 100 pages. I am therefore directed to request that you will be pleased to order an official enquiry into the whole matter. [10]

One of the letters had been sent in by the sewing mistress, Clara Brown. According to her, life there was unbearable. The food was so insufficient that she "often went to bed without a crust for supper". The matron was "abusive and foul mouthed" and the two governesses were "screaming and tipsy". A few Sundays ago the laundress, on leaving the hall, had said "If that ball of wax and leather (meaning the shoemaker) cuts me such lumps of fat again I'll slap him in his bloody chops again".

The cook, Mrs Yard, complained directly about the superintendent, Mr Crook, and his wife:

> ...because I spoke for the good of these poor children I am crushed and trodden down [by them]. I can't make the rations last because the staff take them...[11]

Clara Brown eventually resigned and Mr Edmond Wodehouse, a Local Government Board inspector, conducted an enquiry into the following allegations:

> Mr George Crook, general inefficiency in the running of the school.
> Mrs Ada Crook, general inefficiency and intemperate habits.
> Miss Annie Donovan, schoolmistress, alleged intemperate habits.
> Miss Ellen Hills, infant schoolmistress, alleged intemperate habits.

Wodehouse met the Guardians and the Crooks, who were represented by a solicitor. The press was banned. Wodehouse found Donovan and Hills guilty of being drunk on brandy and having to be helped to bed. Donovan had even sent a pupil to Brighton to buy the brandy. Mrs Crooks' drunkenness was substantiated by many witnesses, including the occasion when she had had to be carried back intoxicated from the nearby Happy Valley after a treat for the children. She had frequently sent people into Brighton to obtain wine and spirits and had daily visited a neighbouring beer shop only a hundred yards away. Wodehouse concluded that "she has an excitable and hysterical disposition". He recommended all four should resign, and that it was not a good idea to have paid officers from women taken from the workhouse ie. the cook and the housemaid. It was better to get staff elsewhere even if it meant paying higher wages. The Crooks were given two months' notice and were replaced by Mr and Mrs Newsome whose daughter, Frances, was also appointed infant school mistress. She had been the only applicant for the post.

William Newsome combined the roles of superintendent and schoolteacher and initiated small improvements. He ordered a sewing machine for the girls and persuaded the Guardians to get a master shoemaker to teach the boys not just how to repair shoes but how to make them. He also visited boys from the band who had found positions on *HMS Implacable*.

* * *

The biggest scandal, one that made national headlines, concerned the schools' chaplain, Rev Henry Dodwell, who was appointed in May 1868. Dodwell was born in Middlesex in 1825. His father was a solicitor and, according to Dodwell, led an idle and unsteady life and died at the age of 39 from alcoholism. After attending Bedford Grammar School, Dodwell went to Oxford University as a classics scholar. Later he taught at the prestigious Cheltenham College. The students there found him to be "a man of impulse, fiery disposition with an inability to control his temper", but he was a passionate teacher. A year later he was dismissed for undisclosed reasons.

In 1858 Dodwell took religious orders and once ordained he went to work at a private school in Kensington. He married his wife, Elizabeth, in 1865 and for the next couple of years was mainly employed as a tutor. In May 1868, Dodwell, aged 43, succeeded Rev Allen as chaplain to the industrial schools. He had been the only candidate to apply. The Guardians who interviewed him described his views as "moderate". He was expected to visit the schools three times a week and to hold a service once on a Sunday and twice in the week and to examine the children. The salary was £75 per annum. He moved to 7, Bristol Terrace in Brighton. It was here that he published his first work, *Corrections of the Public Schools' Latin Primer*.

When Mr Hales and Mrs Wheatcroft resigned, Dodwell offered to combine the roles of chaplain and superintendent, as he had "practical knowledge of farming and considerable experience in the management of boys". The Guardians rejected his offer. In July 1869, he was unsuccessfully asking for an increase of salary because "the physical labour was greater than anticipated and that Brighton was the dearest place in the country to live in, even dearer than London".

In November 1871, Dodwell again requested an increase in salary. At a meeting, a Guardian said he thought Dodwell was "the worst paid man in Brighton". Another said he was "a good plain, practical preacher and well

adapted for his office. The chaplain was the right man in the right place".
Dodwell was also congratulated because few of the children had returned
to the schools during his chaplaincy. His salary was increased to £95 per
annum. Mr Flowers, the chairman of the Guardians, even wrote him a
complimentary letter.

A year later the Guardians asked Dodwell to take a Sunday morning
service instead of an evening one. Surprisingly, he wrote directly to the
Local Government Board complaining about an "augmentation of duties"
and asking if he was obliged to do morning services on Sundays which had
not been part of his contract. Furious that he had gone over their heads, the
Guardians were "surprised that a university man should show so little
common sense" in not complaining to them first. They admitted that a
morning service had not been written into his contract, but that at the
interview they had told him they expected it. They needed morning services
because the staff could not return in time for an evening one after a day
out. According to the Guardians, Dodwell had often held services in the
morning in his first year but recently had been frequently absent from taking
any Sunday services, and they had had to ask him to provide a substitute.
And they had their own grievance: Dodwell's predecessor had regularly
visited the children after they had left the schools, but he had shown no
interest in doing so.

The Local Government Board ruled it was up to the Guardians to settle
the matter. By the end of the year the Guardians were claiming he was "not
a fit and proper person" for the post and should resign. They added that he
"was in antagonism with almost everyone at the school". A few months
later Dodwell was citing the "real" reason for the Guardians' request. They
had employed a female of an "immodest conduct" at the schools and he
did not believe the superintendent and matron should have to tolerate her.
When he had protested to the Guardians they had brought up the idea of
a morning service. Furthermore, Dodwell complained about the Guardians
recruiting staff from among the inmates of the workhouse and about
immorality at the schools. From then, relations between Dodwell and the
Guardians deteriorated. He was now being treated as a figure of fun. At a
meeting when one Guardian asked "What shall we do with another letter
from Dodwell?" another shouted out, "Put it in the fire!"

The Local Government Board agreed he should be removed. Dodwell
demanded a public enquiry. He then, in the words of one of the Guardians,

"wrote a very offensive and insolent communication to the vice chairmen and … set an example of insubordination to those placed under his spiritual care".[12] They decided that Dodwell was "not a fit and proper person as in his communications he has used language more fitted to a gas stoker or kitchen maid", and they again asked him to resign. He refused, and the Guardians wrote to the Board asking for him to be removed. Weeks later, the Local Government Board wrote again warning him that if he didn't resign he would have to be removed.

Dodwell accused the clerk to the Guardians, Alfred Morris, of making false statements in the chaplain's report book. At their next meeting, they called the charges "absurd and ridiculous". Morris joked that if he got one year's hard labour, the Guardians deserved seven years' penal servitude! (*Applause and laughter.*) They declined to have any more communication with Dodwell. Finally, in March 1873, the Local Government Board demanded his immediate removal. Four days later he left. Although gone, he persisted with his allegations:

> ….they appointed a woman with two illegitimate children (one in the school; the other in the workhouse) to be in office over children. She had already been sent to prison for striking Sattin, the Master of the Brighton Workhouse. Secondly, that they had appointed a man as an engineer who had been noted as a drunkard for twenty years. He had left the boys in charge of the boiler for 48 hours almost causing it to blow up…[13]

The Guardians admitted that there had been problems of morality two years earlier but these had been investigated and the staff cautioned. In 1869, as they had had no applications for the post of laundress, they had appointed Anne Waller from the workhouse. They had known she had previously been sent to prison for ten days for "refractory behaviour" while there. They also admitted that the engineer had been an inmate of the workhouse as well.

Although dismissed, the Dodwell controversy refused to go away and, strangely, the Local Government Board instituted a private enquiry *after* he had been dismissed. An editorial in the *Brighton Guardian* complained about the Guardians discussing Dodwell at their meetings only after the reporters had left, and demanded a public enquiry into his dismissal. It concluded that "it was the manner of his allegation, not the allegation itself, which brought his removal". Many people in Brighton felt Dodwell had been unfairly treated. The letter below, dated March 29th 1873 and addressed to the Guardians, was signed by many important local clergy, including Aaron Augustus Morgan, the Shakespearean scholar, and Rev Allfree, the vicar of St. John's Brighton:

> We the undersigned clergy and ratepayers have reason to fear that the Rev Henry John Dodwell has not been fairly dealt with seeing that, in defiance of the principle that a man should be felt to be innocent until proved guilty, he has been removed at your special request from his office without a public enquiry, and without any satisfactory reason being assigned for his removal… We are informed by the Rev. H.J Dodwell that although the Visiting Committee's book shows no entry complaining of dereliction of duty on his part for a space of four years and a half, your report yet speaks of 'the repeated absence of the Chaplain'.

The letter also complained about the Local Government Board's inspector who had conducted the enquiry without the press or Dodwell or any nominated representative being present and about his findings remaining undisclosed. Such a proceeding was "manifestly indefensible and unjust", and they demanded a public enquiry. In April, Allfree asked the Guardians to postpone appointing anyone in Dodwell's place until a memorial with 42 signatures was presented to the Local Government Board. Ignoring his request, the Guardians quickly appointed Rev William Augustus Tooth, who was described by one Guardian as "one of the most unprepossessing men he ever saw".

The Guardians told the Poor Law inspector, that although they were against employing former inmates from the workhouse in the schools, "they were driven to make these appointments out of urgent necessity after frequent advertisements". [14] Furthermore, they had already dispensed with the woman – only a temporary appointment – about whom Dodwell had complained. They told the inspector that Dodwell "should have remonstrated against these appointments at the time". Instead, he had allowed four years to lapse before he had said anything. They thought his real motive was to force a public enquiry.

In the autumn of 1873, Dodwell sent a petition to the Lord Chancellor claiming the Guardians had made false returns. The following summer he brought a libel action against them claiming £2,000 in damages and that:

an officer under colour of teaching one of the girls to sing, kept her up several times till ten or past the hour; he was forced to acknowledge to the committee and Mr Morris, the clerk, that he had nursed her and kissed her but not till she was 14. The Guardians kept him at the Schools for another month and let him leave with good testimonials…The sole cause of my treatment was that on learning that the Guardians were placing in office to train children women sent to gaol for theft and other misconduct and having illegitimate children at the schools your supplicant remonstrated also about the virtuous woman, the matron, being forced to receive back to her dinner table a man and woman whom she caught in a bedroom almost in the very act of copulation.[15]

All Dodwell's attempts to get an enquiry failed, despite a series of costly legal actions. In January 1875, he found employment as headmaster of Colyton grammar school in Devon. But again things went badly wrong for him. After only a year he was dismissed for abusive and drunk behaviour. In 1877 he wrote to the Local Government Board claiming that it was hard for him to get employment and asked for compensation for being unfairly dismissed from his Brighton post. Again he was rejected. He wrote to a friend:

For about four years I have been able to think of nothing else by day or night fearing that if my health entirely failed I should have to take refuge in the workhouse…but I will not go to the workhouse except through the gate of the dock and if by so doing my case is placed before reflecting people of England and I sink, I must sink. [16]

In February 1878, the Brighton Guardians received the surprising news that Dodwell had been committed to trial for shooting at Sir George Jessel, the Master of the Rolls, in London. The judge had continually turned down his request for legal redress against the Guardians for losing his "lifetime position".

At his trial at the Old Bailey, it transpired that Dodwell, by now almost penniless with a wife and four young children to feed, in one last desperate act to highlight his grievances against the Guardians had fired a ball of paper at the judge. He had missed but had given the judge a nasty shock. During the proceedings, at which he defended himself, he called as one of his witnesses the former matron of the industrial schools, Agnes Gower. However, when he started to ask her about his dismissal, the questions were ruled inadmissible. Despite an articulate defence and without any medical evidence, the jury found Dodwell "not guilty" on the grounds of insanity, and he was detained indefinitely "at Her Majesty's pleasure". Ironically, if he had pleaded guilty he probably would have received a short prison sentence.

In chains, the former chaplain to the industrial schools was taken by steam train to a red-brick gothic railway station situated in a small village. There he was placed in the hands of three attendants who seated him in a horse-driven carriage. The vehicle slowly made its way through narrow winding lanes. At the summit of a high-ridge it arrived at an imposing red brick mansion surrounded by a huge 17ft wall with iron spikes and broken glass. Massive thick green outer doors were swung open for the carriage and were quickly slammed closed and bolted hard. Ten yards on it passed through another set of heavy gates. Dodwell was ordered to step out and was searched. His chains were removed and papers were handed over. He was taken to the admissions block and given a registration number. He was bathed, handed a uniform and a cloak of black serge and a peaked cap like that of an American Pullman porter. Dodwell was now formally one of the five hundred inmates of Broadmoor Lunatic Asylum. [i]

* * *

Despite the difficulties of the first eighteen years, many believed the children were still better off away from the workhouse. In February 1879 the Guardians finally allowed the children to attend the pantomime at Mrs Nye Chart's Theatre Royal. The *Brighton Herald* [17] reported their march to the theatre with the band:

> ...the long light-hearted, and nimble footed files of boys and girls – the boys first, the girls afterwards. It was evident that the children were healthy, happy and well-looked after. They were no longer squalid and depressed as in olden times. Older Brightonians will recall children and adults mixed up together on one contaminating mess. The chief feature was the 20 in the band. The style in which these stout little fellows, some as young as 11 years, and the oldest no more than 13 – marched and played was one to stir the hearts of the most phlegmatic. Some of the instruments were nearly as big as the players of them; but the little fellows blew and marched with a vigour and an élan that would have done credit to any band of her majesty services.

---

[i] See Appendix 2 to find out what happened to Dodwell.

In March 1879, Dr Mouat, the government inspector, returned to the schools to see whether any of his complaints of two years earlier had been rectified. He was horrified to find that things were worse. He described the infirmary as "the worst of its kind" where the children were herded together like "sheep in a fold and it was terribly overcrowded and stuffy". The younger children were packed into bed in couples and nearly 20 per cent were ill. Forty-six were in the infirmary and nine boys with contagious disease were in the workhouse. There was just one bath for 105 girls and one for 150 boys, but they were in complete disrepair, covered in rust and unfit for use. The children were not being given the full diet, and suet pudding was served with potatoes, which Mouat felt needed treacle to make it more palateable. He believed that to:

> ...aggregate them [the children] together in ill-ventilated wards of which the air is doubly tainted, not to wash them thoroughly at all times, and to underfeed them, is certainly to cause the progressive development of their ringworm, skin infections, ophthalmia [which was highly infectious and could cause temporary blindness], enlarged glands and similar affections under which so many of them labour.[18]

He found that the infant's ward toilet was so close to the chapel that the smells infiltrated it during divine service. Mouat concluded that:

> The vitality of pauper children is naturally low when they are admitted to the Schools, hence they need if possible better hygiene and conditions in the way of cleanliness, plenty of air, sufficiently protective clothing, and abundance and variety of plain wholesome food than children born and bred in more favourable conditions...That's why street arabs and inmates of Reformatories are stronger and more robust than pauper children proper.[19]

Mouat believed they needed a proper detached receiving ward, a better infirmary and better bathing facilities. He thought the schools could be an "excellent model of its kind" and that "I regard expenditure in this direction to be the truest and wisest economy". The Guardians did try and address some of the problems and improved the diet, including more meat to the girls which they had found was necessary once they had allowed them to do gymnastics like the boys. Previously, a long swing had been their only amusement.

By March 1880, there were 288 children in the schools and superintendent Newsome's emphasis was on industrial training. During the last twelve months the children had made 8,454 articles as opposed to 3,809 the previous year. The shoemaker's shop was now making 1,000 boots a year and the girls were making more clothes than the schools needed. [20]

Chapter Eleven

ELM GROVE: 1871–1880
THE DESERVING POOR

The early years at the new workhouse were undoubtedly difficult ones for Edward Sattin. He often felt unappreciated and certainly underpaid. In June 1871, he was earning £130 per annum plus rations. This was almost half the salary of the master of the Lambeth workhouse, which he had visited in 1869. Perhaps fearful of losing him, the Guardians increased his wage to £160 p.a. but said he had to pay maintenance charges for his six children. Because of this, he was actually £4 12s a year worse off. This was to be his last increase for eleven years.

In 1871, Sattin was complaining about the "most troublesome youths over 16 and able-bodied men" and recorded in his journal that:

> This class as a rule enters the House in a most wretched condition. Being at the lowest ebb and frequently with a bad character, they get to feel that everyone's hand is against them and they are consequently, reckless. Penal tasks have been assigned and exacted with great trouble and loss, but have brought no diminution of inmates…It was better to assign them a fixed sum to be earned, they can keep half and receive funds when leave… Forfit all or most if they misbehave. Any clothing required on leaving should not be given but be earned. I think this would improve morally the men and benefit the taxpayer.[1]

His suggestions were rejected. During this period he was frequently sending inmates before the magistrates for refusing to work. In November, 1871, two inmates were sent to prison for "disgraceful and outrageous conduct in the chapel". One of the Guardians suggested he should punish the paupers himself but Sattin replied it was impractical.

On hearing, in 1872, that the Guardians were contemplating changing the annual treat for the aged inmates from the Swiss Gardens, Shoreham, to the Tivoli Gardens – a pleasure ground near Preston Park – Sattin recorded their disappointment and asked the Guardians to reconsider their decision. Some Guardians felt he had overstepped the mark. The main advantage of the Tivoli Gardens was its closeness – cheaper transport costs – and that no alcohol was sold there. However, the owner of the Swiss Gardens, Mr Goodchild, was threatening to withdraw his offer of free entrance to the children from the industrial schools if the aged paupers were barred.

At a meeting, one Guardian claimed the aged paupers liked the Swiss Gardens because of the bar, not for the attractions, and that they returned drunk. Another said the old ladies had to be locked up in the railway carriage on the way, and that between Shoreham Station and the Swiss Gardens, Guardians had to be sent ahead to stand in front of all the pubs to prevent entry. Another believed it did not matter where they went as "a day's pleasure was a day's liberty, a day's freedom from the restraint and shackles of the workhouse, combined with as many luxuries and personal comforts the Guardians could provide out of their own pockets".

In a heated and sometimes hilarious debate, insults were exchanged with one Guardian calling another "contemptible" for saying the inmates did not deserve any treats because they had been "improvident", an attitude he believed more appropriate to the 1820s and 1830s. Another said it was not their duty to sit in judgement, especially as in the past some of the Guardians had arrived at the Swiss Gardens just in time for lunch! The motion to let the aged go to the Swiss Gardens was narrowly won by 14 votes to 12. When 400 inmates went that summer, they were described as a "division of the Brighton Poor" as crowds watched vehicles decorated with bunting unload them at the railway station. There were more flags at Shoreham where they were met by Goodchild and Sattin. They had ham, lamb and beef for lunch. One reporter went with them:

> Glancing round the tables on the lawn, we miss old faces we have seen at the Shoreham Gardens "festive board" in years gone by. On enquiring we are told –"Dead" and so "paupers" pass away unknown, and in most cases, uncared for ...To mention one instance: Boorman, an old cress-seller whose cry of "young water cresses," was once familiar in all parts of the town, was some three years or so back compelled to go to "the House" with his wife. He has joined in the "annual treat" for two or three seasons. On Wednesday, he was not to be seen by "outside" frequenters and on enquiry, "Oh, he's dead three months. His wife, poor girl only lived a few days after him. [2]

The day passed off without incident. However, the issue of drink was to cause the biggest outbreak of disobedience during Sattin's period of office.

In May 1873, without consulting the Guardians' visiting committee, the workhouse medical officer, Dr Richards, decided to ban all alcohol except for medical purposes, thus penalizing the paupers usually rewarded with beer for work and the aged and sick who regularly received it. Sattin agreed with the ban as he believed the supply of beer had been abused, with those who did not like selling it to others. Forty or fifty female paupers initially went on strike and eight were eventually sent to prison. Sattin recorded what happened:

On being informed by the task-mistress that the women had refused to do their usual work, I went to the ward and enquired of each woman if she persisted in such refusal, stating that, if so I should take her before the magistrates. All went to work but the eight who were dealt with, as reported in the refractory journal. I hope the board in the present crisis express their intention to support me in preserving order, and that the inmates

Fig 18 *W. Lambert Payne, one of the Guardians who voted to allow the aged inmates their summer treat at the Swiss Gardens.*

shall clearly understand that they cannot make terms; but that each one is bound to render service to the full extent of his or her ability, in return for the diet and lodging which in the several classes is provided, and that complaints shall be made to the committee whose province it is to attend to such matters. I think it right to state that all the women who today were sent to prison, being employed in the laundry did, in consequence of the discontinuance of the allowing of half pint of ale daily, on Monday, instead of soup for dinner, receive Australian meat, bread, and potatoes, and on Friday, meat and potatoes were given instead of soup. One of the women stated that she had dry bread only for dinner twice a week, because she could not eat Australian meat or pea soup, and as I was not prepared or authorized to study her (as I consider) dainty appetite, she had to, of course, fall back upon bread…Another able-bodied woman expresses her determination to die rather than eat Australian meat. I mention these cases to show the difficulty experienced in dealing, as a rule, with the discontented people who fall here. There are, I am pleased to say, exceptions. It is only fair to myself to state that during the time – nearly fourteen years – that I have had the charge of your workhouse I have never been reproved for harshness or neglect, and that I study to observe a strict impartiality, between the inmates and the ratepayers who support them. Had I discouraged Mr Richards' proposition, I felt, and still feel, that I should not deserve to be the Master of the Brighton workhouse. The dietaries have not been printed since the alterations made at the time when the order for reconstructing the Board came into effect. I submit copies of them with the suggestion that they should be considered and, if approved, that a sufficient number of copies be printed, to distribute freely among the house, so that no misunderstanding shall exist.[3]

The eight female strikers were aged between seventeen and fifty-three. The two youngest were given 14 days' hard labour in Lewes Prison while among the others, Rose Cecil – who had three illegitimate children – received 21 days' hard labour. One of them, Liz Marshall, was discharged when she agreed to work.

The Guardians supported Sattin in his actions because "if the Guardians did not support the Master in cases of insubordination, the whole mass of people in the workhouse might rise, and the Master would not be safe in the building". [4] One Guardian recalled that when he had lived in Tunbridge Wells there had been riots in the workhouse and the police had been called in regularly. He believed the inmates at Brighton had too much respect for Sattin.

Only a week after the ban, Dr Richards was claiming that the inmates had "rosy cheeks". Nevertheless, complaints about it started to come from all over town. Even one of the Guardians declared that the medical officer had exceeded his power as "beer was a national beverage not a luxury and that it was part of the diet". A town councillor, William Wood, wrote to the Local Government Board:

The Medical Officer has decreed no wine, spirits and beer to the aged and infirm. Can you permit me to ask the question? Have the Guardians the power if they see fit to restore the said beer to the dietary notwithstanding that the medical officer may deem it unnecessary? Beer has been allowed since January 1850.[5]

The Board replied that it was up to the Guardians. In July, the Poor Law inspector Murray Browne reported that the beer had been stopped to the "considerable dissatisfaction of the working inmates". After a nine-week trial period some Guardians claimed that "the discipline and management of the house has improved". Others, however, believed that more paupers on their weekly afternoon leave had come back drunk since it had started. To great cheers, at a meeting the Guardians passed a resolution to allow the aged and infirm inmates half a pint of beer daily. Not that the quality was the highest. On one occasion, Sattin asked the contractor to change two kilderkins [i] of beer because it resembled vinegar. The contractor refused but it was still served up to the aged inmates.

A few years later a Guardian, Rev Jehu Martin, a staunch temperance movement supporter, won a motion to give the workhouse staff extra money [ii] instead of their beer allowance. Not long after, the order was revoked as the Guardians discovered it was more expensive.

* * *

In the week ending 9th December 1871, there were 4,022 paupers receiving outdoor relief and Hawley, the Poor Law inspector, insisted that the Guardians should only give it in extreme cases and must apply the workhouse "test" more stringently. In 1874, forty years after the Poor Law Amendment Act, the Brighton Guardians finally agreed. After consulting Mr H. Longley, a Poor Law inspector, they formulated their own rules and put the notice overleaf all over town, especially in places where paupers gathered.

---

[i] Kilderkin = 18 gallons.

[ii] 1s 6d per week for males and 1s 3d for females.

Regulations as to Out-Door Relief – Notice [6]

1. Outdoor relief will in future be regarded as an indulgence, to be granted in certain instances to persons of proved respectability, whose destitution has arisen from no fault of their own.

2. Persons whose destitution is the result of intemperance and improvidence will be relieved, with their families, inside the Workhouse.

3. An applicant for relief will have to satisfy the Guardians that, when he was able to work, he made every reasonable effort, by thrift and economy, to provide against times of sickness and adversity. Should the applicant fail to make this clear, out-door relief will be refused, and he, with his family, will be required to enter the Workhouse.

4. The visitors of the out-door poor shall in future visit the homes of all able-bodied widows, and all persons receiving relief on account of temporary sickness, at uncertain intervals (as far as practicable) once a fortnight; and the old and infirm cases, once a month. A record of each visit shall be duly noted in the application and report book, for the information of the Guardians, when the pauper appears before them.

5. Out-door relief will not be granted to single able-bodied men, or to single able-bodied women.

6. No able-bodied widow, having less than two children dependent on her, shall be eligible for outdoor relief, except during the first six months of her widowhood.

7. Outdoor relief will not, except in special cases, be granted to any woman deserted by her husband, during the first six months after desertion.

27/8/1874

By the end of the year those on outdoor relief had dropped to 3,232. At the same time, the number of those refusing to go into the workhouse rose dramatically. In one week in January 1875, out of seventy-three orders for the workhouse only three paupers accepted. And in a week in November that year, only one out of forty-nine paupers took up their place. By the end of 1877, there were 1,762 on outdoor relief and the population of the workhouse had increased only slightly. [i]

---

[i] Seeing the results, soon other Unions were asking the Brighton Guardians for a copy of their rules, although there was a general decrease in pauperism due to the increase of trade.

So, what was happening to the paupers who were denied outdoor relief but who were refusing to go into the workhouse? There were several residential charities such as the Brighton Home for Female Penitents (1855) and the Brighton Home for Destitute Boys (1871), but they offered help to a very few. The only alternative for a pauper who did not want to go into the workhouse was to appeal for temporary relief from individuals or small charities. Recently discovered records of the "Mendicity Society", better known as the "Charity Organisation Society" [COS], gives us an idea of how much poverty there was in this period. Formed in 1872 and briefly based at 108 Church Street before moving to 182 Edward Street,[i] it was affiliated to the London Society for Organizing Charitable Relief and Repressing Mendicity.

It was formed "to correct the great social evil of undeserving people receiving relief which should be given to the real deserving poor".[7] It was based on the premise that careless indiscrimate charity was harmful. In their rules, COS advised and provided charitable agencies or individuals with information in order to relieve the "deserving" poor and expose the "undeserving" and the fraudulent. Although the charity gave small grants and loans to paupers its main purpose was to act as a channel of communication between the poor of Brighton and other charities and wealthy individuals offering relief. COS had paid agents and voluntary agents who investigated applicants by visiting their homes or talking to various people who might know them. They were to "examine every case by its merits, where no known agency, to help to adopt the method most likely to save the applicant from pauperism and if already a pauper, raise him into honest self-dependence". Its objective was also to "by legal proceedings, repress all mendicity". In this it co-operated with the Guardians, the town council and the magistrates.

Between January and June 1872, the Society received over 200 applications for help from families, probably representing over a thousand people. Apart from requests for food and clothing, it received applications for money. Richard Gray, who went about with "a music on wheels, the fun of the fair" wanted money towards the £18 he still needed to take his wife and three children to Canada. He had lost a leg at Sebastopol in the Crimean

---

[i] Later on it moved to 11 Guildford Road.

War and was constantly out of work. He had friends and relatives in the colony and was confident of finding "constant employment at good wages".[8] The Society gave him £1 on condition that other money was forthcoming.

Sometimes, Edward Sattin would refer a discharged pauper from the workhouse if he felt they had a good character and may need temporary help. However, even his recommendation was no guarantee of success. On one occasion he recommended help be given to William Carson, a labourer with a wife and three children who had recently been discharged. They had behaved well in the workhouse but the Society turned them down. Referrals could be made by wealthy men and women, vicars, town councillors and local dignitaries. It could also be done by self-referral. In January, Lucy Miles, aged 32, who had five children, saw the charity's poster outside the office and went in. She wanted assistance till her husband got work. The agent wrote:

> I made enquiries respecting Lucy Miles and found their home in a most destitute state. They have no bed only a bag of straw to lay on and the children lay on a few bags in the corner of the room. Although they are poor the children are kept clean. They have not been to school for this last three months, not being able to pay for them. I have seen Mr Hunt [the employer] and the only work he will have for him [the husband] will be to help unload a vessel. Mr Hooper gave me a shilling with that I bought some bread and they were very thankful for it. I strongly recommended them to go to the Union [the workhouse]. "Ten shillings granted". [9]

The applicants included failed businessmen, musicians, hawkers, tradesmen down on their luck, the old, the sick, the blind, the disabled, widows and more contentiously, the professional beggar. James Ridley applied to "get a little assistance as the money from the Parish is not quite enough to live on".[10] Harriet Reeves wanted a "little assistance till her husband finds work".[11] John Richardson "spent all the winter in the workhouse, wants money to take out a new license [for hawking] so he may be able to carry out his regular occupation".[12] "James Whitehead, aged 75, wants some money to get some timber to make picture frames. He applied to the Parish but refused to go into the workhouse".[13]

Seventy-four year old Sarah Wells:

> wants assistance for two or three weeks till she gets work. She mends umbrellas and does needlework. She has applied to the Parish and refused an order to the Workhouse.
> "Ineligible".[14]

After the application, an agent from the charity visited the pauper's home to do an assessment. They usually described the conditions they found as "passable" or "destitute". They also found out if the pauper was known to the police or the parish authorities. If they were given a "good character" by their enquiries, temporary relief in kind or money could be granted. For example:

> Caroline Tucker, a widow with two children wants nine shillings to pay the bread bill. Mrs Walker gave her a good character.
> "Accepted." [15]

Most applications for help were turned down. Some who refused to go into the workhouse were often referred on to the "clergyman of the district". Others were simply written off as "undeserving" or "ineligible". Quite often it was the wife who applied rather than the husband:

> Ellen Knight, 24, wants a little assistance till she can get work. Her husband, Thomas, a butcher, drinks. His wife said that he applied to the Parish but refused to go into the Workhouse. The wife stated he went home and lit his pipe with the order!
> "Undeserving."[16]

Charles Linsted, a servant, asked for his fare to get to London where he could get work. The agent wrote in his case notes:

> He is a strong able man, able to walk to London.
> " Dismissed."[17]

Edmund Walters, a seventeen year old labourer, had lost his mother when he was twelve. He and another boy had tramped the country for three years. He was then locked up at Croydon for begging and sent to Byfleet Industrial School for two years. He tried to join the Navy but was turned down because of heart disease. Since then he had lived by begging. Despite good references from his old schoolmaster and the police, he was not given any assistance. Another pauper, Thomas Keen, had lost his left leg at the knee in a thrashing machine and had tramped the country. He applied for the five shillings necessary to buy a hawker's license but was turned down. There was a suspicion that often hawking was used as a cloak for professional begging.

In May 1872 James Norris, a "chair-man", applied for six shillings to buy new tyres for his chair despite earning fifteen shillings a week. He had a wife and three children. The agent wrote:

> The Reverend Mr Salmon states he believes this to be a deserving case. He gave him a pair of boots. The reason they are so destitute at the moment is they have been summoned for arrears of rent. Bears a good character. He relieved him on several occasions.[18]

Norris was granted the money. Two years later he was applying for some help towards the forty pounds needed to get a new chair:

> At present his chair was so old and shabby, people would not engage him if there was another chair on the stand. He wants to sell the old one for £8 and to have a petition to collect the remainder.[19]

The agent recommended some "ladies" could assist him in raising the eight pounds necessary for his old chair to be repaired. However, seven years later it appeared that he had managed to buy a new one and was now asking the Society for money for new wire wheels to replace the old wooden ones. He was referred to the Benevolent Loan Fund. Albert Draycott, a shoemaker with three children, wanted some money:

> to help him over tonight and tomorrow morning. The Reverend Hooper gave the agent half a crown to buy tea, sugar, butter and to pay the lodgings.[20]

The charity was always on the look out for fraudulent paupers. In March 1872 Anne Nichols, aged 29, applied for money to emigrate to Australia with her husband and two children. The charity agent discovered she had been begging from wealthy ladies in Sussex Square and had invented various hard luck stories. In her letters she had used different names. Her stories ranged from claiming her son had sunstroke to pretending her daughter was near confinement and needed money for medical treatment.

She variously claimed to have had five to eight children. Over the years the agents described her as "a thorough impostor who lived by imposing on charitable persons".[21] In 1905, the charity was recording that "we have been asked 41 times for information respecting her by ladies and gentlemen to whom she has applied for charity". Several times she was given 'hard labour' for begging until finally dying of pneumonia in 1906.

Another well-known beggar, Sarah Lennard, aged 44 with four children, promised in 1872 that she would "never send begging letters again" if the Society helped her. But she was known as a professional "troublesome beggar" and seems to have been on charity most of her life. Her parish relief was stopped in 1898 but she was still applying in 1902. Vicars' wives, such as the wife of the vicar of Brighton, J.J. Hannah, were often bombarded with requests for help. Her husband, was clearly becoming exasperated and in 1886 wrote respecting Sarah:

> It strikes me that it is time she receives a little kind attention from the Charity Organisation Society. [22]

Many of the applicants were paupers who spent their whole lives either begging or in the workhouse. When there was no work that was the choice. Some made applications to the Society over a period of thirty years. For those making fraudulent claims, it could backfire. Hannah Shirley "who already receives a great deal of charity"[23] was reported to the Guardians after applying for help. They stopped her outdoor relief for a few years and reinstated it in the 1880s. Often a pauper on outdoor relief would be threatened with its stoppage if they continued begging. However, the Society rarely brought legal proceedings to bear against fraudulent beggars, as most philanthropists were rich women who did not want to appear in court and admit that they had been taken in by "outrageous stories". Apart from local rich people, sometimes celebrities visiting the town, like Bram Stoker, the author of *Dracula*, received begging letters and requested COS to investigate.

For the year ending 30th September 1872, COS had received £86 6s in donations and £285 14s in subscriptions. Interestingly, it had paid out £166 13s 4d in salaries and wages and only £85 16s 7d in grants to paupers, of which £24 1s 8d was spent on bread – figures that substantiated the impression that it was very difficult to obtain help from the Society, whose initials some critics claimed stood for 'Cringe or Starve'. The other impression is that there was a great amount of individual charity on the part of rich ladies and the clergy. In January 1872 the Society refused help to Ellen Small, an invalid, because she was constantly receiving help from Mrs Gaulty of Sussex Square. And the following month Susan Reeves, with eight children, was applying for "some little assistance till Friday when she will have her husband's wages". The agent wrote:

> Bought her some food. The Reverend Dr. Hannah is paying one month's schooling for the two oldest boys – one has no shoes to go in. [24]

The case studies illustrate how many paupers were refusing to go into the workhouse. They also show that even full time work and parish relief sometimes did not provide enough to live on. In chapter eight we saw how Henry Wooldridge had emigrated to Canada in May 1873 and had become a respected figure in his local community. Just over a year earlier, his blind step-father, John Reading, a hawker of matches, wrote to a Mrs Fox because "he had heard she was good to the poor". He was still married to Henry's mother, Sarah, and had four children: Anne (8), Charles (4), Sarah (2) and Martha (2 mths). Mrs Fox contacted COS whose agent wrote:

> John Reading wants a little assistance, he does not want to go into the workhouse. His wife occasionally gets a little charring, but since her last confinement she has not been able to work. The home is in a destitute state. The Rev. Snowdon Smith has relieved them on several occasions. He says the best thing they can do is to go into the workhouse. He gave me one shilling to give to the wife. They are well known to the Parish authorities. They received Parish relief during the wife's confinement and now have an order for the workhouse. [25]

They received no help and soon the whole family went into the workhouse and stayed there till the autumn of 1873. Over the next few years John regularly applied to COS for help. The agents recorded:

> 1873 December: No school for children since they came out four months ago. Guardians have since given them two orders for the workhouse. Miss Johnson, seeing the children running around in a destitute condition, she sent them a loaf of bread and an investigating ticket [to give to the Mendicity Society]. "Told to go into the workhouse".

> 1874 June: Asked for three pairs of boots so his children could attend school. Lost his youngest child. His general circumstances are much the same but lately

I have often seen him return home at night the worse for drink. His wife is looking after a furnished house in Percivale Terrace. The Guardians adhere to their previous decision to offer him an order for the house.
"Referred to Parish."

The next year, an Ada Bright, wrote to COS:

A woman of the name of Reading has been to see me today concerning placing a boy of hers in the Brighton Boys Home and we are anxious to know if her statement is correct. She says she is too delicate to work herself and her husband is nearly blind and also unable to work and that she has three children to support. Will you let me know if it is an urgent case and one desirable to be taken into the Destitute Boys Home.

A COS agent received the following letter from a Miss Emmett of 12 Eaton Place:

The wife is a most respectable woman and has supported her husband for some time by charring as he is unable to work himself. Mrs Reading has worked for some years at Miss Hill's, 10 Eaton Place, and very often for myself. I have never met a more trustworthy woman. She is now ill and does not know how the rent is to be paid…If you could do anything for her I would be much obliged.

The charity recommended that the boys be sent to a boys home but did not grant any money to the family. Nine years later, in 1884, Miss Emmett sent Mrs Reading to COS to apply for some temporary relief. An agent recorded that:

Her husband still sells matches and a fortnight ago the Guardians granted him a pair of boots. Applicant has lately been poorly and suffering from rheumatism, but will be able to work next week. Her son Charles is in Canada. Daughter Sarah in service in London. The eldest, Anne, is dead and the parents appear very poor.
"Granted 2/6"

That is the last entry about John Reading and his family in the COS records. He was still working as a hawker in 1891 and died alone of "senile decay" in the Elm Grove workhouse in November 1902. He was seventy-six.

By November 1881, the *Brighton Guardian* was reporting that the Charity Organisation Society had made 5,065 enquiries into claimants and that it had relieved 33,398 "wayfarers" with bread. [26] Twenty years after it was formed it was investigating four times as many cases as it had done in its first year. [i]

*　*　*

The Mendicity Society's records make it clear that many paupers were risking starvation – there were frequent newspaper reports of dead bodies being found in the street – rather than entering the workhouse despite claims, in this period, that it was one of the best. A Frenchman, Charles Morbeau, who visited in September 1873, wrote in the visitors' book:

> I can only express my profound admiration for the care bestowed on the old and sick. The exceptionally fine position of the House, the capital arrangement of the different branches of work in it, the perfect systems which are employed, guarantee to the poor a well-being which it seems impossible to surpass.

The following year, Louisa Twining, on her first visit to Elm Grove was "very impressed at the improvements [in respect of Church Hill]" although she also recorded that "I should like to see more lady and genteel visitors admitted to read and cheer the inmates". [27] Rev Dr Hamilton believed there was "hardly room for improvement". The medical officer of the Leicester Union wrote: "I have not inspected any workhouse with greater pleasure and satisfaction". A Mr Mackness from Oxfordshire wrote that "it is beautifully clean. One of the best public homes I ever saw and the food is beautiful such is fitted for anyone". [28] And yet on the same day he wrote that the Guardians received a letter from a "ratepayer" which stated he had met two former inmates who told him that they had "not enough food to satisfy their hunger". [29] As the letter was not signed, the Guardians ignored it. Hawley, the Poor Law inspector, also praised the workhouse regularly all except one part, the part reserved for pauper lunatics.

*　*　*

---

[i] 271 in 1872, 1,007 in 1892 (*Brighton Guardian* 30/11/1892).

In the new workhouse there was a separate building for the lunatics adjoining the infirmary and it was known as the "asylum". It consisted of two floors with 25 patients on each. No distinction was made between lunatics and imbeciles, and even people with epilepsy were placed there. The inmates' only exercise was a walk once or twice a week and an annual treat at the Swiss Gardens in Shoreham.

Within two years of opening, the Lunacy Commissioners found sixty-five lunatics being supervised by a married couple assisted by an able-bodied person of each sex. They reported that the court yards for exercise were too small and that the hot taps were dangerous and had already caused fatal accidents. The following year there were seventy-five lunatics and the Commissioners said they needed more exercise. The Guardians claimed they were taken over the Downs in the summer and played cricket. Seventeen men worked in the garden, wood sheds or wards, and fifteen women in needlework or the laundry. The diet was described as "liberal" and the patients had meat every day. Everyone was bathed once a fortnight although it was recommended that they should be bathed weekly in the summer.

In 1873, there were 103 lunatics. Ninety-nine were in special wards while the rest were in the body of the house or in the infirmary. The inspector, Mr Hawley, wrote:

I suggest that greater attention should be given to their amusement and more means of recreation provided…there are said to be some books, but none were to be seen. Neither were there any papers, games or illustrated periodicals. It is asserted that such things would be destroyed if left about, but the Guardians only have to visit the County Asylum to see the fallacy of this statement. They would find in every ward – even those for the most excited class – an abundance of flowers, books and games constantly accessible, but no destruction ever takes place…The infirmary rooms are on the top floor and it was from one of these rooms that Mathew Henry Phillips, committed suicide by jumping through the closed windows. The windows only open six inches but the panes are large. It is best to take cases of melancholy straight to the asylum thus complying with the provisions of the law and giving the patients a far better chance of cure by affording them early treatment for their malady. The banisters are low and dangerous for suicidal or even epileptic cases – something should be done about this or there will be another fatal accident. Also, the handles of the taps should be removed and be fitted with a key to be kept by the attendant…The wards were clean but flock pillows should be substituted for the straw ones…There are paid attendants, man and wife in each division who are both assisted by three ordinary inmates. I had no complaints of harsh treatment and had every reason to think that the patients were kindly treated.[30]

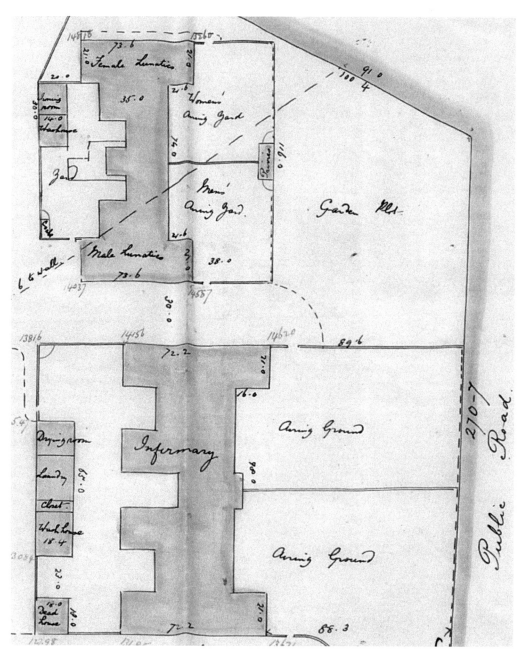

Fig 19 Original plan showing the lunatic wards and the infirmary.

The Guardians agreed to take on board the complaints and the following year the Commissioners found that there was a "fair supply of books," although beer had been withdrawn at dinner.

* * *

Meanwhile, letters of complaint about the workhouse from inmates to the Local Government Board continued on a regular basis. In March 1873, John Hinds, an ex-soldier, who had been granted a pension of 1s per day for life, wrote:

> I have been nearly five months in the workhouse. I was compelled to come in here through ill health. I am sixty-two years of age. The authorities here have charged me seven shillings per week for my whole time here. I am a single man and no one but myself for them to support. I receive nothing but the ordinary house diets. Please can you tell me whether they are entitled to all my money.[31]

The Guardians told the Board they had paid for his wife's funeral and that he had been there 173 days. They had received £6 2s from him but had spent £8 18s 6d. They told the Board that he had already left and had no grounds for complaint.

Another pensioner, William Woods, also complained they were taking his pension. The Guardians showed that in one eight-month period he had been admitted and discharged eight times. According to them, he had been in the habit of drawing his pension monthly, spending it and then going to the workhouse until another payment of his pension was due. They added that he had been in trouble with the police and that they (the Guardians) had a right to his pension. Two years later, the Local Government Board received another letter from an inmate:

> I am unfortunately nearly blind consequently I have been for some time a patient at intermittent periods chargeable to this parish. I entered the workhouse in about the month of Aug 1875 and remained an inmate until the 10th day instant when I took my discharge hoping to be able to maintain myself away from this place during the summer, however I was not able to do as I had intended consequently I had to return here, which I did on the 19th May having been absent nine days. I am of the Roman Catholic religion and as such Roman Catholics have always been allowed to attend St Joseph's Roman Catholic church in Elm Grove on a Sunday morning but on presenting myself on Sunday morning last as usual for that purpose I was informed by the

master of this House that I should not be allowed to go out again for 6 weeks or two months. The alleged reason being that I had discharged myself from the workhouse and had come back again.

I was ordered before the committee of Guardians at their meeting here yesterday and was told by one of them that the master had power to do as he liked in the matter. I respectfully beg to draw your attention to the fact that there is no infringement of the rules of the workhouse alleged against me but I am simply informed that my leave is stopped because I took my discharge and came back again and the Guardians say the master has power to do just as he likes in the matter. I beg to ask whether this is in accordance with the law of the county or the directions of your honourable Board and shall be grateful if you will be pleased to direct that my leave of absence be not stopped in the future.

I am your most humble servant, Stephen Martin [32]

The Guardians informed the Board that Stephen Martin had applied for and had been granted leave on 26 April and had not returned till 9pm, some time after his leave had expired. "On 19 May, he having no apparent means of maintaining himself applied for and obtained his discharge". He was readmitted later that day. On Sunday he was told by Sattin that it was usual under the circumstances to require a month's residence before complying with such a request and that his behaviour was not such as to induce the master to relax that custom. On 28 May, he did not apply to attend the Roman Catholic chapel although he was allowed to. Their report concluded that "Stephen Martin has been, and is, a troublesome inmate, and the Guardians have reason to believe that when leave is granted to him, he stays only for a very limited portion of time".[33] Other complaints came from sick inmates who alleged they were being placed in the able-bodied wards where the food was inferior.

* * *

Under Edward Sattin, entertainment for the inmates undoubtedly improved. In the New Year treat of January 1875, the whole of his family – his wife and six children – appeared in a theatrical production, "Fairyland", and members of the Brighton Athletics Club did a display on the horizontal bars which soon became an annual event. That summer the aged inmates, in a fleet of carriages, were taken to see "Wombwells' Menagerie" at the

Queen's Park cricket ground. The collection contained lion cubs, leopards, two Abyssinian elephants, a panther and a troupe of performing hyenas. On their return they were given extras of beer and tobacco and were entertained by the industrial schools band. Later, the inmates were given lectures on the life of Bunyan, with illustrations on *Pilgrim's Progress* displayed by limelight by Rev T. Lawson.

That year there was an outcry when Elizabeth, one of Sattin's daughters, was appointed to be assistant matron. She had being doing the job for free since June 1873 and was to be paid £20 per annum plus board, washing and lodging. One Guardian opposed the appointment as she was only seventeen years of age. A national newspaper, the *Daily Mail* [34] also had objections:

> The question has been suggested to us whether the Guardians did wisely in appointing a mere child to the responsible position of assistant matron...She is so inexperienced in the ways of Nature and humanity...should an epidemic occur in the House, or should, indeed individual illness prostrate the mother, is a girl of 17 summers sufficiently old and experienced to take command of the female side of a large workhouse such that of Brighton? Under the most favourable circumstances the duties of matron of such a house are arduous, and embrace, amidst their many phases, emergencies which required the knowledge and experience of a mother. And can we expect such service from a young girl like this? We say this in no spirit of unkindness; but we feel it our duty to warn the guardians of the risk they are running, for if in the moment of emergency things should go wrong, the fault will immediately be with the young officer, but the burden of responsibility will unquestionably rest upon those who appointed her...

The Guardians once again reacted angrily to any kind of outside interference, especially from the newspapers and did not change their decision. Sattin was grateful:

18th January 1875

We beg to thank you for having shown the confidence that you have in us by appointing our daughter assistant to the Matron, the only objection expressed thereto being her age; this will, only too rapidly, be remedied. Nothing has occurred during the time she has discharged her duties to cause any doubt, as we would not, for our own reputation's sake, have permitted her to have taken the office unless we were assured that she was equal to it. We have both of us very early in life borne serious responsibilities – the Matron when only fourteen years of age had, through the sickness of her mother, then a Workhouse Matron, to discharge all her mother's duties, and she continued to do so for four years; during two years of such period her mother was wholly confined to her bedroom. I know of an instance where, on the death of her mother, a young person, a year younger than my daughter, was elected Matron … You made no situation for my daughter, but have aided to mine and her mother's comfort by allowing her to discharge the duties instead of forcing a stranger upon us. I think it is only right to state the following facts, which are not known to the new Guardians. Since the resignation of Miss Brooks, a former assistant of the Matron in 1866, who, in consequence of her being able to play the organ and conduct the singing in the Workhouse Chapel, received £30 per annum, we have had no official who could render us that service, and we were depending on voluntary assistance until 1869, since when my daughter has discharged those duties without any cost to the parish.

Gentlemen, you have added another link to bind us to your service, and we are pleased to subscribe ourselves faithfully yours,

Edward Sattin, Master, Emma Sattin, Matron. [35]

Later on, when one of his sons, Arthur, who acted as his assistant and storekeeper, was given a large rise, one Guardian, Thomas Berry, claimed he was unfit for the post and had been 'smuggled in' by his father.

In 1877, the whole town was rocked by a scandal involving the medical officer for the workhouse and the schools, Dr David Richards, and his assistant, Dr Harris Ross, who had been in partnership with him. Richards' wife sued him for divorce on the grounds of cruelty and adultery. In the evidence, his maid, Charlotte Hunt, said that Richards had offered her a gold watch if she went to bed with him. Other witnesses said he had been locked inside the cook's bedroom, and two other servants gave evidence about him staying away and his violent temper. Perhaps most damning of all, "five females of loose character deposed to Richards having been intimate with them in different places of the town".

Richard's wife also said he had attacked her several times when drunk – including throwing a knife at her – and on one occasion had cut open the family cat. Richard's denied the charges and said the cat had been a spiteful creature which had dug its claws into him and he had stabbed it lightly back in retaliation! He also claimed Dr Ross was having an affair with his wife and that she had been seen going into his bedroom in her nightdress and they had been caught in a stable together. The jury found Richards not guilty of cruelty but guilty of adultery and Mrs Richards was granted a divorce.

Richards resigned five years later at the age of 47 with heart trouble. He had been the medical officer since 1864. He had not been very conscientious and his lack of record keeping, particularly in regards to the discharging and deaths of "lunatic" paupers, was repeatedly criticized by government inspectors who wanted to know what happened to those who ceased to be on the list. He was replaced by Dr Douglas Ross, aged 29, the brother of Dr Harris Ross who had been cited in Richards' divorce case.

* * *

Although by 1877, the numbers on outdoor relief had dropped dramatically due to the stricter application of the Poor Law by the Guardians, and those in the workhouse had only increased slightly, the number of casuals continued to rise fast, with over five hundred coming every week. Some ratepayers accused the Guardians of treating the casuals better than in other workhouses. At Elm Grove they had a mattress, blanket, a rug and nightshirt. At other places, they were often treated worse than criminals and only had bare boards to sleep on. In Sattin's *Master's Journal* dated 16 January 1877, he responded to a letter which had appeared in the *Sussex Daily News* the day before, which had claimed that the Guardians' "stupid good nature" attracted the casuals:

> The true reason for the appearance of vagrants here is no doubt [because] it is a fashionable resort…The fact is casual wards are too plentiful, frequently only three or four miles apart, they should be attached to the police stations – a reasonable day's journey from each other – and with power to prosecute as vagabonds those who were found to be continually making use of them. Although I should like to see separate cells here for vagrants, as it would materially assist in the superintendence, yet I do not hope from them the extinction of the vagrant. Brighton for the vagrant, like a sugar cask for flies, has too many attractions independent of its casual ward. [36]

Sattin believed the Mendicity Society, instead of supplementing the relief given by the Guardians, should "take the whole charge of the troublesome community" [the casuals] and that:

> my firm conviction is that all labour should be made as profitable as possible. The pounding of stones which used to cost us about 30s to produce what was with difficulty sold for 5s, is to my mind simply brutalizing; and it should be borne in mind that it is a task which can only be assigned to the able man. We

have had ample proof that by employing the inmates profitably behaviour improves, and the number able to work does not increase. Until within the last few weeks we have had barely sufficient to do the work required.

The Guardians had tried to decrease the numbers by threatening casuals with detention if they demanded admission night after night. But according to the relieving officer, Mr Pearce, the professional tramps:

simply laughed at it, and would, after having been detained two days, present themselves on the evening of the day of their discharge for another order for admission, undeterred by the prospect of having to undergo the same penalty again. [37]

The Guardians had also tried the experiment of detaining a vagrant on Sunday if he had arrived on the Saturday but they found that this had been an inducement – the numbers increased – rather than a deterrent, and they abandoned the plan. So, acting partly on Sattin's suggestion, the Guardians decided that casuals should get their admission orders from the police station at The Level and place Pearce there. The rise in numbers was checked and started to fall temporarily.

The Guardians resolved to erect additional wards for casuals on the separate cell system which were designed to prevent "riotous behaviour" and to isolate them. Some critics argued some casuals might actually prefer this. The Local Government Board insisted that each cell must have a bed board, an inexpensive night stool, an earth commode and a "pull" to call the attendant's attention. There was to be provision for work in the cells and one bath to eight vagrants.

By the end of the decade still nothing had been done and the Guardians decided to lease three acres of land – with power to purchase it within ten years for the sum of £2,400 – and build a new block of vagrants' wards on the separate cell system for 100 male vagrants and also a block of wards for 120 female adult imbeciles and child imbeciles under 12. The vagrant wards would comprise of three separate blocks all connected by a corridor. There would be 80 sleeping cells in the two storey block, 39 with work cells attached, exclusively for male vagrants. The cells were to be 8ft by 4ft 6in and were to be warmed by hot water pipes. The present male casual wards were to be adapted for female casuals. These would increase the workhouse accommodation by 207 to 1,068.

The single cell system in operation in a London workhouse circa 1860.

From 1877 to 1880, the "great depression" of the late 1870s, resulted in the workhouse numbers increasing to just over 950 inmates. And suicides such as that of the sixty year old Emma Newman, who hanged herself with a handkerchief after just two weeks, became more common. Despite this, in one meeting in June 1880, according to the *Argus*,[38] the Guardians spent time congratulating themselves on their achievements and voted to improve the clerk and committee rooms in the workhouse at the end of which, the paper noted "there was no other business":

> And yet, reader, this very week, and for several past weeks, there is and has been an outcry, with statistics backing it up, to the effect that in Brighton and most of the surrounding parts, pauperism and begging and vagrancy have increased in some instances nearly 50 per cent and the above meeting was a meeting of our "Guardians of the Poor".

The decade ended with the Guardians rejecting Mrs Nye Chart of the Theatre Royal's invitation to the aged inmates to attend the Christmas pantomime in the New Year. With snow still on the ground after terrible snowstorms, it was deemed too difficult to take them there and back to the workhouse. This added to the Guardians' unpopularity. Two years before there had been a scandal when it had been revealed that paupers' names were chalked on their coffins to save money. The names were often smudged or unrecognizible due to rain and their relatives were often uncertain if they were following their own relative or a stranger to the grave:

> What a contrast between the splendour and gaiety of Brighton and this melancholy picture of a pauper's funeral in the same town where the poor relatives follow the wrong coffin because the Guardians have chalked it to save 6d. [39]

In a powerful editorial, the *Brighton Guardian* [40] described a pauper's life:

> His shelter is an act of charity, his food is a gift, his clothes are bestowed upon him by the Union – his flesh if he has any on his bones belongs to the ratepayers; his flickering life is the property of the Parish; his smile if he were capable of it might seem a sign of over-indulgence in the eyes of some grim Guardian who would reduce his dietary. Without hope, without one gleam of pride, without one ray of human satisfaction, wondering why he lived, regretting that he ever did – gazing with glassy eye alike on the mist and rain, or even sunlight, which is to him hardly less melancholy – he wants to die; just like an abandoned horse whose master, too tender to kill him, has left standing under some leafless tree until he falls dead. And when the end of the pauper comes, all that will mark his exit from life will be a chalk scrawled upon his coffin.

The Guardians decided to have the names and dates painted on the coffins. But the inmates still had the job of measuring the bodies for the coffins and bearing them by foot to the extra-mural cemetery in Lewes Road: several posts were erected there where they could rest the coffins. Thomas Noel, a poet who died in Brighton in 1861, left a memorable poem:

The Pauper's Drive

There's a grim one-horse hearse in a jolly round trot,
To the church yard a pauper is going, I wot;
The road it is rough, and the hearse has no springs;
And, hark to the dirge which the mad driver sings;
Rattle his bones over the stones!
He's only a pauper, whom nobody owns!

Oh, where are the mourners? Alas! There are none,
He has left not a gap in the world, now he's gone.
Not a tear in the eye of a child, woman, or man;
To the grave with his carcass as fast as you can;
Rattle his bones over the stones!
He's only a pauper, whom nobody owns!

What a jolting and creaking and splashing and din!
The whip how it cracks! And the wheels how they spin!
How the dirt, right and left, o'er the hedges is hurled!
The pauper at length makes a noise in the world!
Rattle his bones over the stones!
He's only a pauper, whom nobody owns!

Poor pauper defunct! He has made some approach
To gentility, now that he's stretched in a coach!
He's taking a drive in his carriage at last!
But it will not be long, if he goes on so fast;
Rattle his bones over the stones!
He's only a pauper, whom nobody owns!

You bumpkins! Who stare at your brother conveyed,
Behold what respect to a cloddy is paid!
And be joyful to think, when by death you're laid low,
You've a chance to the grave like a gemman to go!
Rattle his bones over the stones!
He's only a pauper, whom nobody owns!

But a truce to this strain; for my soul it is sad,
To think that a heart in humanity clad
Should make' like the brute, such a desolate end,
And depart from the light without leaving a friend.
Bear softly his bones over the stones:
Though a pauper, he's one whom his Maker yet owns!

By the New Poor Law Act of 1834, governors of workhouses were allowed to dispose of any "unclaimed bodies" as they saw fit. In 1880, the Brighton workhouse began to sell bodies to a medical school – and it is in this way that over a hundred paupers from Brighton ended up in a cemetery in a famous university town.

Fig 20 'The House on the Hill' (The Penny Illustrated *8/8/1874).*

Chapter Twelve

INDUSTRIAL SCHOOLS
1881–1900

Almost twenty years after the schools had first opened, Warren Farm was still cut off and isolated and William Newsome, the superintendent and head schoolteacher since 1878, found it almost impossible to hold onto staff. Often teachers did not return after the school holidays. For many of the children of course, there were no school holidays, for they had no home to return to. They had no playing fields and on summer afternoons could be seen scampering over the Downs like a flock of South Downs lambs. In winter the wind often swept across the Downs shrieking against the building and driving the rain against the windows in torrents, trapping the children and staff inside. For this reason Newsome started up a debating society in the winter months, and one of the first debates was "Poverty and its Prevention"!

The children still went to the Swiss Gardens in Shoreham for their annual summer treat, although one year Newsome stopped it after complaining that at the previous one a hundred uninvited guests had eaten their food. Very occasionally they went to the Chinese Gardens in Hurstpierpoint for tea. At Christmas there was an annual prize-giving, usually attended by the mayor of Brighton, when the girls were said to be particularly smart in their dresses of dark blue serge with red braided collars. All children had separate clothes for school, work and play.

By far the most successful part of the schools were the two bands which frequently received requests to perform publicly, although the Guardians were cautious about letting them out. On one occasion Mrs Haycroft, the first female elected Brighton Guardian, did not want them to appear at a Sunday school exhibition as it "might indulge them and excite jealousy amongst the other children" and that "they had more sunshine than those belonging to the parents of the very poorest classes". She and other Guardians believed it was wrong to put pauper children on display as it advertised "improvidence". These arguments were often angrily contested by other Guardians. The medical officer advised that the bands, with an average age of ten, should not play any full concerts of two hours in public.

In 1880, the Local Government Board had decided that fourteen-year-olds who passed exams could withdraw from education to be in the industrial sector of the schools: to train in needlework, shoemaking, tailoring, cooking, gardening, dairy farming and musical training. Prior to this date no child left before the age of fourteen and many stayed till they were sixteen. Now, under Newsome's dictum that "every child should receive such industrial training which will enable it to lead an honest and industrial life",[i] children sometimes left at thirteen. This led to the number of children falling from over 300 to 230 during the decade and the Guardians starting to take children from other Unions. One boy from outside Brighton, many years later, recalled his experience:

I shall never forget the heartache of that first day in the institution, and although a kindly nurse, who knew something of my family and the hard fate which had befallen us, tried to soften the blow to my boyish mind, I felt as though the sun had gone out, and that there was nothing else in life worth living for. At the first opportunity I stole away to my little straw bed which had been allotted to me in the long dormitory, and burying my face in the bed-clothes, gave myself over to the grief which tore my heart. I feel now, as I think of it, though it is over thirty years ago, the gentle touch of the hand of that nurse, whose approach I had not heard, as she lifted me to my feet with a word of sympathy and encouragement, telling me to be a little man and learn to face my troubles bravely, for everything was bound to come right in the end. Although her voice had the harshness which one usually finds in institution officials, I believe her heart was pure gold, and though I have, long since forgotten her name – if ever I knew it – her memory is still a bright spot in a very dark and dismal page of my life.

There was an arrangement between the Guardians of that town and the Brighton Guardians, by which some of the children who came under their care were transferred to the Warren Farm School, and I was one of the fortunate boys chosen for this change. I only had about two months at the local work-house, but, in spite of the kindness of the Master and the nurse who had charge of the children's ward, it was a time of horror to my young mind. I remember

----

[i] Newsome wrote these words every year in his superintendent's report.

196

even now with a blush how I felt on the first Sunday morning, when I was fitted out with a suit of ill-fitting corduroys and marched through the town, in which I was so well known, to the church where many of my previous schoolfellows attended. I remember even now, as I passed down the aisle, I heard one of the boys, who had been my playmate, mention my name in an awed whisper as he pointed me out to his parents…But at last the happy day of my departure from that place came, and the little company of half a dozen took the train to Brighton and a happier life.[2]

He also recalled that:

…there was an old lady named Miss Blith – or rather I believe there were two sisters – who at various times of the year paid visits to the school, and always distributed packets of sweets to all the children. I can see her now, coming in at the front door of the school (for I was gate boy at the time), followed by her footman carrying a large leather bag, which I knew from past experience contained small packets of delicious black "bull's eye" peppermint sweets.

* * *

Henry Dodwell's successor at the schools, Rev Tooth – who one Guardian had described as the "most unprepossessing man he ever saw" – was having his own difficulties. In 1880 he wrote a circular to the newspapers appealing for contributions for the children's prizes, as the Guardians provided none. In the letter he claimed, "I do all the good that is done" in the schools. One Guardian thought it was "an act of gross impertinence" and told him to mind his own business and that "he was not their master but their servant". Tooth was forced to apologise and warned not to "write something that does read like one thing and mean another".[3] But it was true that Tooth did award prizes – out of these contributions – every year, usually silver medals to the "best boy on the farm", "the best girl in the kitchen" etc.

Two years later, two female officers fainted with exhaustion in the chapel during one of Tooth's sermons. More than 300 children and staff were present. Alfred Morris, the clerk to the Guardians, in a letter to the Local Government Board, blamed the length and nature of Tooth's service:

That such service consisted of the entire order of morning prayers (the litany excepted), the anti-communion services, sermon, prayer for the church militant, and three or four hymns including one of 24 verses which the officers and children were required to sing all kneeling…That the strain of continuously kneeling from the end of the Creed to the end of Morning Prayer during the reading of the commandments and throughout the long hymn, above referred to, without any support to the hands or back, so far as the officers were concerned produced a feeling of physical exhaustion and consequent faintness...The Guardians will try and improve the ventilation.

Later, when Tooth was interviewed by the *Argus* in 1887[i], he recalled that when he first arrived at the schools he had almost left immediately because the institution was in such a poor state. But, under the Newsomes, it had improved dramatically and Tooth had had a major voluntary role in following the children's progress after they left. He told the newspaper that, in fourteen years, he had been in correspondence with 1,200 ex-pupils. He had received letters from India, Australia, Canada and the USA and had even received a small donation from an old boy living in the Fiji Islands.

When Tooth finally resigned as chaplain in June 1892, some of the Guardians did not want to give him a testimonial and he only received one by one vote. He was succeeded by Rev Seymour Terry. Tooth's main achievement had been to start up an Old Boys Association and in the last few years he had organized a Christmas lunch for as many as a hundred old boys in the town. In 1889, they had presented him with a clock, an umbrella, a walking stick and an illuminated address for "the kindly feeling he has always shown for their welfare...and for his zeal and energy on their behalf since leaving that institution and their entering into life".[4]

Since the Dodwell affair, the Guardians' relationship with local ministers had not been a happy one. When the vicar of Brighton, John Hannah, asked if the industrial schools band could play at a flower show at St Peters Church, they refused. They only reversed their decision after ratepayers complained that the children got very few outings every year.

* * *

Under Newsome, the schools soon began to receive praise. In 1882, the hon secretary of the Female Orphan Society, Mrs Bayle, declared that she had "seldom taken charge of a child [from the schools] so well cared for and

---

[i] 29/1/1887.

looked after". The following year, Rev Robert Blight, a diocesan inspector was reporting that:

> The course of subjects is large and well worked out in every particular. The boys are energetic and full of intelligence. Compares well with public elementary schools. To me it is a real pleasure to pay my annual visit. [5]

But there was a major problem looming. In 1883, John Short, a ratepayer, wrote to the Local Government Board to tell them that:

> …the school master [Newsome] is gone blind and has to be lead about and his son has to do the work for him. Due to his blindness these schools are in a very low state of morality. The officers and teachers are continuously leaving and some under most disgraceful circumstances. Another grave matter is those children suffer dreadful in the winter from colds and chilblains. A grandchild of mine lost two of his toes from chilblains and gangrene, he had to be removed to the workhouse Infirmary, since then the child has died of small pox. Mr Newsome, the schoolmaster, was continuously coming into Brighton attending Masonic meetings, dinners, balls and those schools are four miles out of town and he caught inflammation of the eyes and lost his sight. Mr Newsome being a mason and our Guardians as well, the Guardians are determined to keep him there another five or six years so as to entitle him to superannuation and saddle the ratepayers from two to three thousand pounds which he does not deserve. The Guardians say he is doing a good job but it is impossible. Please send an officer to examine him.

The Local Government Board felt he should resign but were waiting to see if his blindness was hopeless. The following year Edmond Wodehouse, the Poor Law inspector, recalled that:

> …in 1877, the schools were in a very bad condition and I held an enquiry …The chief officers resigned. Conditions have steadily improved under Newsome's care…They have never been in such good order for the last eight years as they are at the present moment. He is a man of great zeal and energy; he bears his affliction with exemplary fortitude and evinces the liveliest interest in all that concerns the welfare of the schools. I can't insist on his resignation although a hopeless case.

In 1886, the *Sussex Daily News* [6] was reporting that Newsome's son, the twenty-six-year-old William junior, an assistant teacher at the schools, had been fined for assault:

He thrashed Alfred Osborne, a youth occupying the post of assistant engineer at the schools. It occurred on 18th May…A servant girl of the defendant asked for coal out of the allotted time after 4.30pm, at five, and Osborne refused. In the evening Newsome ordered him into the playground and violently kicked him when he refused again. Then he slapped him violently on the head. The boy had become an officer of the Guardians. He [Newsome] then procured a cane of exceedingly large dimensions and struck the boy over the head, body and arms. When in the dormitory he wanted someone to undress the boy so he could cane him again. The medical officer said there were 50–60 blows. Last Sunday at the dinner table the defendant offered him two to three guineas if he would hush it up.

Newsome junior was fined the maximum of £5 and costs, although some felt he had been treated leniently. The following month, the same newspaper spoke about "alleged irregularities" at the schools. It claimed that female children were sometimes sent to the superintendent's house in Elm Grove and stayed overnight. The newspaper added:

…a state of discontent, amounting to insubordination has recently manifested itself amongst the officers in the boys department against the Superintendent and the first assistant schoolmaster. Four officers have been sacked and the second assistant schoolmaster and the boys attendant have resigned…The Superintendent should give up the house in Elm Grove…Gross insinuations have been made about the moral character of the two Newsomes…Children had prepared their breakfasts…Improper behaviour! [7]

Before they left, the sacked staff, which included the tailor, the shoemaker, the engineer and Alfred Osborne, went on the rampage, attacking the furniture, walls, dairy utensils and musical instruments. Altogether nine staff either left or were sacked, and several boys absconded. It was ironic that earlier that year Newsome senior had declared that he had a good set of officers.

In September 1887, at a public meeting at The Level, it was unanimously agreed that Newsome junior should have been sacked. It petitioned the Guardians, deploring the Newsomes' behaviour and asking for a local government enquiry into the sackings. The Guardians turned the request down[i] and instigated their own enquiry. One girl withdrew her allegation,

---

[i] The *Evening Argus* had called the request "unEnglish and ungentlemanly".

but they did find that two girls sometimes slept at the Newsome's house when only he and his son were there. Superintendent Newsome claimed that they were sent to "keep the house aired".

At a meeting, one Guardian called the management of the schools "vile", although he later changed it to "bad". Another alleged that government inspectors were often kept walking up and down the grass near Warren Farm until it was put in order and that the Guardians' visiting committee went there at the same time every visit. But Alfred Morris, the clerk, insisted that William Newsome senior had been far superior to his predecessors, and another Guardian thought the schools were in a better condition than at any time since they opened. Instead of the children looking like "miserable little blackguards," they now looked like "decent little people". The Guardians decided to let the Newsomes remain. Not long after, William Newsome junior left for a "better position".

One of the reasons for the large staff turnover, apart from the sackings, was cited in a letter by Alfred Morris to the Local Government Board:

> During the past year, particularly in the Winter and Spring (as well as in previous years) several of the officers of Warren Farm Schools have been more or less disabled through illness from discharging their duties, such illness being caused by the bleak locality, isolated position and distance from the town, and have not been able to procure medical attendance except at a cost which they can ill afford. [8]

Morris suggested, on behalf of the Guardians, that the medical officer, Douglas Ross, be given an extra £40 p.a. to treat the staff as well as the children. The Board assented.

* * *

Under Newsome, as the children began to leave earlier, they were passing through the schools for shorter periods, particularly the girls. The demand for girl servants was three times greater than the supply, and many were sent out at thirteen and fourteen years of age. More boys, too, were leaving to become tailors and shoemakers, one subsequently setting up a "High Class Boot and Shoe Repairs" in Elm Grove near the workhouse.

In the superintendents' report for July 1888, Newsome stated that in the previous year 45 children had been placed in employment: 8 in military bands, 6 with tailors, 5 with shoemakers, 3 as page boys, 3 in business houses, 1 in the post office, 1 in farm labour and 18 in domestic service. The boys could join the bands at fourteen and often favoured playing the clarinet. They went to military regiments at Colchester and even to the Hussars based in Dundalk. Less successful boys were moved on to St Andrews, a boarding house in Brighton for working lads between 14 and 17 years old at a cost of seven shillings a week. In 1889, there were 13 ex-workhouse boys there.

For the girls it was compulsory to do needlework and hand and machine sewing. The needlework room was open three times a day including in the evening. All the girls were expected to spend time there every day. In Newsome's yearly report for 1888 he recorded they had made 234 dresses and repaired 34,000 items. Most girls became nursing assistants or went into domestic service. Usually they went out on a month's trial and were visited by the matron, Marion Newsome. For the first twelve months – a Poor Law requirement – they were monitored by volunteer ladies who each had a section of Brighton to cover. Mrs Newsome also encouraged girls to do cooking, and for those with an aptitude she trained in her own kitchen. The Newsome's regime was geared to trying to suit the capacities of the child to a suitable employment.

The following year, in his report, Newsome contrasted his first full year as superintendent, 1879, with 1889:

1879 –   Total children 279: 171 admitted and 169 discharged.
1889 –   Total children 216: 159 admitted and 164 discharged.

In 1879, eighteen boys – with seven going into bands – and sixteen girls were found employment. Ten years later, twenty-seven boys and twenty-four girls were found employment. Most of the bandboys were also taught shoemaking and tailoring and could now enter the army with either of these professions. Previously, they had been sent to the services without any trade. Newsome was realistic:

It will be readily understood that children leaving these schools can not become proficient tailors, shoemakers, carpenters, engineers in such a short time. But they can obtain situations as improvers, usually expert in hand and machinery sewing.

All children now over the age of 12 spent three hours working and three hours doing schoolwork. The boys had 7½ hours of band practice and six hours drill every week. The changes in training can be seen by the table below:

	1879	1889
Bandboys	25	65
Tailors		27
Shoemakers	6	15
Carpenters	0	2
Stableboys	4	0
Cowboys	2	2
Pig-boys	2	2
Garden boys	21	2
Messengers	4	4
Scrubbers	12	4
Engineers	1	1
Laundresses	6	3
Nurses for Infants	6	4
Housemaids	12	12
Kitchenmaids	3	3
General Servants	3	3
Needleroom	37	16
Total	**151**	**164**

In 1889, as the numbers dropped to 222, the Guardians started to admit "aliens" – children from other authorities – at a higher maintenance rate. On 4 February 1891 the matron, Mrs Marion Newsome, died. As it was a joint appointment, her husband had to resign, eight years after the ratepayer's letter first exposing his blindness. He went to stay with his son. Thirty-six years later, an "old boy", who was admitted shortly before Newsome left, wrote:

I dare say there are many boys who can call to mind his fine upright figure as he groped his way along the corridors of the old school – for he was afflicted with blindness. But that in no way detracted from his efficiency, for he somehow had a wonderful grip of everything that went on in the school, and was, as well, one of nature's gentleman. He ruled with an iron hand in a velvet glove.[9]

There were one hundred and fifty applicants for the joint posts. Thirty-seven-year-old Henry Spooner and his wife Louisa were appointed from Westminister School. According to the above ex-pupil, it did not take Spooner long "to win the hearts of all the boys by his manly bearing and keen sense of justice…There was never a punishment administered which the victims himself would not admit was thoroughly deserved."

In May 1891 the Guardians admitted children from the Petworth Union and the Hailsham Union and took on extra staff. Under Spooner, the diet of the children improved – jam or syrup for supper and roast lamb once a week – and showers were fitted. The staff were now provided with proper bedrooms rather than cubicles. Though the Newsomes had gone, however, the scandals continued, as this letter to the Local Government Board dated 19 April 1893, shows:

> There was a most disgraceful affair took place at the Warren Farm Schools between the schoolmistress and the engineer a few days ago which I venture to think your honourable Board SHOULD ENQUIRE INTO. The matter was "hushed" up and the public was kept in the dark about the whole affair. I, as a large ratepayer, consider that everything in connection with public institutions should be fair and above board and I give you this intimation so that you may make what inquiries you think proper. I have the honour to remain Sir, your obedient servant,
>
> J Crosswell
>
> PS. I should be obliged if you would not disclose my name in this matter if you can possibly help it…keeping my name private in any way you like.

As the writer wanted to remain anonymous, the Local Government Board took no action, although an attractive schoolmistress had abruptly resigned without giving a reason.

The schools were soon full, as the Guardians continued to take children from other Sussex Unions, Croydon and Godstone. Two lady Guardians from the former visited in August 1893:

> We were greatly pleased with their healthy and smart looks, and the improvement. We found the whole establishment in perfect order. [10]

Annually there were now as many as five hundred admissions to the industrial schools as parents increasingly entered and left the workhouse. In October 1894 a block was set aside at the workhouse as a children's hospital and quarantine ward, but children were still spread about the main part of house. In February 1895, J Davy, the Local Government inspector was complaining that "these children are still in the East Ward, receiving no education, and taking up room where I think it is wanted for the better classification of the ordinary inmates…The problem is that if you build quarantine wards at the Schools, it is impossible not to meet other children".

Finally, a quarantine building was opened at the workhouse. [i] It could house a hundred children and consisted of three floors. When the children arrived with their parents they were sent to the middle floor. If they were deemed to be ill they were sent to the top floor, where there was also a maternity ward. If they were well, they were sent to the ground floor and then onto the industrial schools.

In 1895 there were 56 boys and 53 girls considered to be "neglected", and they were placed under the Guardians until the age of 16 and 18 respectively. At this time, according to Rev Head from the Cookham Union:

the children look the picture of health and apparently are well cared for. The visit has been one of the events of my life which will never be forgotten; everything is splendid, and the Superintendent and Matron are the right people in the right place; words cannot express what I feel, and more I cannot say. [11]

In the visit to the Shoreham Gardens that year, they were described as the best behaved children. One old boy later recalled:

It was in 1895 that I found myself playing in a field with other children around about my own age of 7 years, and my earliest recollections commence from this time…Life at school was very dull at that age. I realised that I was an orphan but this did not affect me greatly as I believed in the old adage "what one never has one never misses". The standard of education was very low in those days and badly put over, but I regret now that I dodged whatever I could. However, it had some very good points and nowadays I am grateful for the religious instruction I was given. My aloneness was my spur and created in me an ambition to be somebody and to get somewhere. I saw the masters as the real heroes who exercised at all times the most tremendous patience with us all.

---

[i] November 1899

Mr W. Penfold wrote this in the 1950s after he had had a successful career as a furniture dealer and town councillor.

In 1897, in accordance with the regulations of the Local Government Board, the children were allowed two half days, Wednesday and Saturdays, and one week's holiday at Easter, August and Christmas. For the Queen's diamond jubilee that summer, the Guardians joined in with the sports. There were rifle drills from the boys and dumb-bell displays from the marching girls. "The boys who presented a very comely appearance in their serviceable uniforms, admirably executed a lengthy military drill, including the formation of squares and preparing to receive cavalry". [12] In the tug of war, sixty girls beat fifty boys. The day ended with a cricket match between the boys/masters and the Guardians, who were bowled out for 32 and easily beaten.

*   *   *

In the 1890s more land was acquired for the schools so that the farm could be expanded. [i] There were now nine men working on the farm as opposed to six teaching staff. The Guardians debated whether the older boys should be taught to swim in the public baths in Brighton or should a swimming pool be built at the schools. In the end, they decided to take them to the sea at Ovingdean and hire a man in a boat to prevent them from drowning. Some Guardians did seem to have a genuine interest in the welfare of the children. One, Mr J. Newham, regularly added 5 per cent interest at the end of the year to any savings the children had made.

As the century ended, some educational reformers and guardians began to question the "barrack system" and wanted to encourage the "boarding-out" of pauper children with foster families. They believed that although they were poor, they deserved to be brought up naturally. This approach had been influenced by a report in 1874, written by Mrs Nassau Senior, the first woman Poor Law inspector. She had concluded that pauper children needed more "mothering", especially the girls, and had encouraged boarding-out as a means of escaping the "workhouse taint". Another suggestion was to build "cottage homes", grouped together and containing between twenty

---

[i] In 1900 it had five horses, 27 cows, 113 pigs and 107 poultry (*Brighton Guardian* 2/5/1900).

and thirty children in each of them. The disadvantage of this system was the expense.

A select committee on Pauper Education in 1896 agreed with the reformers. It "unanimously condemned industrial schools on account of the dangers of disease, especially eye and skin infections, which were common when so many children were crowded together, and because of the emotional damage resulting from isolating children from the community and depriving them of individual care and affection". [13] The following year the Local Government Board decreed that no child should do full time industrial training till they were fourteen. The seeds for making education more important were being sown.

One great attraction of "boarding-out" was that it was far cheaper than keeping children in an institution. However, there were disadvantages. Lack of proper supervision of foster homes could result in cruelty and neglect going undetected. Children could also be used as unpaid servants. Finally, it was not always easy to find suitable families. Experience had shown that most of the foster parents in this period had been motivated by money. Indeed, in some cases their sole income had been the outdoor relief they received from Poor Law guardians to look after the children.

By the end of the century, however, Warren Farm, with an average population of 270, was seen as a success story and a fine example of how a well-managed large school could "de-pauperize" its inmates. During the ten years ending 1890, nearly five hundred children had been sent out and "no case of serious misconduct or dishonesty in any boy or girl who had left the schools with a good character and recommended by the superintendent, was known". [14] The chain of a pauper child becoming a pauper adult appeared to have been broken. For now, boarding-out was not seen as a necessary or a desirable option by the Brighton Guardians.

Despite the difficulties of the schools' first forty years, one old boy, Arthur Finch (1889–1894), had fond memories:

> My most pleasant thoughts during my long lifetime have been of the pleasant and happy days I spent at the old school on the Downs at Woodingdean. Opinions have been expressed to me that it must have been a melancholy life – but let me explain…We had excellent schoolmasters who in addition to teaching us took us for the most delightful walks such as to the Falmer Pond and Rottingdean. Further we were instructed in music by the bandmaster (Mr Fry, late of the Royal Marines), while for my part I received tuition in tailoring

by Mr Blades. These people all took a great interest in us and thus our lives were very complete and were an excellent beginning for our future careers. Mine started on July 13th, 1894 in the training ship "St Vincent" as a band boy...An order was given to be obeyed and in our obedience lay the secret of our content and happiness and the success of our careers in the Navy. Our life at Warren Farm had prepared us for this, and I really do thank my old school.

Arthur later fought in the First World War and the Russian Revolution before retiring in 1948.

Chapter Thirteen

THE WORLD OF SHADOWS
1881–1900

In 1881, the medical journal the *Lancet* was declaring that in Brighton "while ample funds are lavished on the principle thoroughfares, and great efforts made to improve what meets the eyes of the visitors, the hidden places are grossly neglected…the back slums were fair without but within full of the tokens of neglect, misery and disease".[1] Two months later it was claiming the town had the highest death-rate from fever of the largest twenty English towns.[2] The journal consistently argued that sickness was one of the most active causes of pauperism. Yet even the sick were reluctant to go to the workhouse. When a seriously ill William Harman was told by his brother to go to the Brighton workhouse infirmary he replied, "I would rather die on a doorstep than go there".[3] Weeks later, partly wrapped in a sail, he was found dying under an arch on the beach.

On the night the 1881 census was conducted, there were 1043 residents in the workhouse including 28 officials and 72 casuals. Four hundred inmates were from Brighton and 232 from other parts of Sussex. The rest came from all over England, from Ireland (38) and even some from France, Prussia, Australia, Malta, Spain and the East Indies. There were 573 males, 442 females, 174 married, 373 widowed, 485 over 60 years and 72 children. The children included those classified as "idiots", child casuals and those in quarantine awaiting transfer to the industrial schools.

The census gives a profile of the workhouse being dominated by the single and the elderly. As females lived longer, one would have expected them to outnumber males. However, as women needed help to care for children if they lacked a husband, there was a greater willingness to grant outdoor relief to women than to men on the part of the Poor Law officers and harsher attitudes towards males. "By the last thirty years of the nineteenth century, only approximately one in four of the able-bodied in receipt of outdoor relief [in England and Wales] was a male".[4] In addition, more "light" occupations were open to women and seasonal unemployment was more likely to result in workhouse residence for males. The only age group where females outnumbered male inmates was in the 15 to 35 range. This was mainly because of the large number of unmarried women.

According to the census some inmates came from mining and manufacturing areas which had been hit hardest during the trade depression of the late 1870s. The vast majority were unskilled workers from occupations such as domestic work (females) and labouring (males). Nevertheless, there was a sprinkling of the professional classes including five teachers, a church warden and an equestrian performer.

The great crisis continued to be the want of accommodation for the large number of vagrants applying night after night. One Sunday, after filling the 156 sleeping bunks provided for male vagrants, Sattin had to put 27 on the floor with rugs in different parts of the house and another 40 in the sheds in the able-bodied store yard. He told the Guardians:

> On visiting the latter place, a sight was presented to me which made me feel that I was not justified in using it for such a purpose. But when people keep sending them, what am I to do? They must send them elsewhere…maybe common lodging house.[5]

It was reported that "Sattin entered into some details which were not fit for publication".[6] In the six months to April 1881 there were 8,013 vagrants, an average of 45 per night. Next year, by a new law, all casuals were to do one full day's work and leave by 9am on the third day. If they came twice in one month they would have to do two days' work. The males were employed wood chopping, stone pounding in the stoneyard and oakum picking, while the women did housework, laundry and oakum picking.

In 1880, the Guardians had asked George Maynard – the architect of the original building – to draw up plans providing for a hundred single cells for the male casuals. This was seen as an effective method of preventing inappropriate communication and an easier way of controlling them. When the Local Government Board examined the plans they declared that the Guardians had been too liberal with their cell space and that Maynard was "not a skilled hand".[i] They asked the Guardians to appoint a more competent

---

[i] Maynard finally retired at the age of 86 in 1888 after holding office since 1847. As he had a country residence and many properties in Brighton, the Guardians did not grant him a pension.

architect, saying "we must correct his gross shortcomings as far as practicable, and need medical input". The plans were only accepted on the condition that accommodation for forty female casuals was also provided. At the same time the Board recommended that a new infirmary was needed for 350 patients and that the old infirmary could be used for female imbeciles and children.

By the end of 1882, there were over a thousand inmates plus casuals in the buildings. Certain parts such as the infirmary, imbecile and foul[i] wards were overfull and almost 10 per cent of females were in the latter. Fewer than 200 inmates were classified as able-bodied. At the same time, there were 4,346 people on outdoor relief, which dropped to 3,231 the following year. In 1884, the relieving officer at The Level police station, who issued admission orders to casuals, was withdrawn, and now these could only be issued at the workhouse between 6–8pm in winter and 7–9pm in summer.

* * *

A reporter from the *Examiner*[7] described the pitiful choice for a father who is out of work, has sold all his furniture, and in one last desperate act goes towards the parochial office:

On the Parish

He hopes to be able to get something to do, he tells her [his wife], and hastening away to escape the piteous cries of his children, he bends his footsteps towards Church Street. Despite the fact that he has been assuring himself over and over again that he is only going to ask for what he is entitled to, a sense of shame seizes him as he enters Church Street and sees other persons on their way to the same bourne as himself. He cannot do it, he says and walks on rapidly with a resolution to make one more application for work. The same result! There is none for him, and despondingly he retraces his steps to the Parochial Office, where he hangs about the portals unable to screw up his courage… It is hardly possible to conceive a more painful position for a man who has hitherto, by steady and honest labour, supported himself in an independent position. He watches his fellow sufferers as they enter the office to obtain the amount of relief awarded to them by the Guardians.

---

[i] For sexual diseases.

The old people generally have the happiest faces of those who pass into the building; for it often happens that the old people are looked after by the district visitors and others who argue, and very rightly, that the aged who are beyond helping themselves should be assisted in preference to the younger poor. They are for the most part women who seek parochial relief, and too often the white cap in the dingy black bonnet, even though the other garments are not of the same sombre hue, tells a story of widowed dependence. Our artisan pictures his wife in that situation, and his heart is wrung with a knowledge that it is a condition into which she may be brought. It is a curious admixture of characters who pass before his notice. The faces of some are sad; others are evidently very ill; some are laughing and chatting together and actually joking about going to receive their "pension"; and still a few more are gloomy and morose. It is with these individuals that our artisan presently wanders into the office and awaits to be questioned concerning his circumstances. He discovers when he has been put through this ordeal that an officer will visit his "home" and test the truth of his statement, and he departs to await this inquiry as patiently as he can.

As he again emerges into the street his attention is drawn to a young widow, apparently, who is just leaving before him. He is induced by some irresistible power within to follow her, and when she stumbles and reels for a moment as he is turning into the Pavilion Parade, he hurries to her side and begs permission to assist her. She accepts his escort across the road, and he insists upon accompanying her up Edward Street. Her protests are of no avail; she is ill, he is convinced, and he will know where she is staying. Why he is anxious to know this he cannot tell, but the young widow, divining that she has his sympathy, discloses to him a depth of misery that is infinitely lower than that to which he and his family have yet sunken. Her husband has just died, and she has two children, one three years old and another who has not yet been twelve months in this world, both of whom are fading away before her eyes, owing to her inability to obtain for them proper nourishment…The faces of the poor creatures who are now visitants of the Parochial Offices bear the impress of many a woeful tale of hardship and misfortune.

According to the Guardians pauperism was decreasing. However, in 1885 the chairman of the Brighton Philanthropic Committee, A.W. Carpenter, wrote to the Guardians to dispute this claim. His committee sent visitors to people who applied for help and so he had a good idea about the real situation:

It is universally reported that there is in all parts of the town considerable more distress than there has ever been for a very long time, caused by the lack of work, particularly in the building trade.[8]

Carpenter said the Guardians spent less on relief now [i] only because of the new policy of offering all applicants an order of admission to the workhouse:

> This is a great deterrent, and in many cases, a cruel one. The Societies, from their experience, have known many cases where families have been literally starving in consequence of the breadwinner being ill; or out of work, and yet they would rather be in this condition than break up their home and go into the Workhouse…Philanthropic societies have stepped in and helped them temporarily…they believe that the Guardians might judiciously and without neglecting the ratepayers, extend a little outdoor relief.

The Guardians' clerk, Alfred Morris, insisted that they did not offer the house to everyone. From 30th September 1884 to 5th May 1885 they had 2,296 applications for relief. Out of these, 1,219 were given money, food and clothes and there were 108 orders for work, 147 orders for medical relief and 32 for burial. They gave 750 orders for the House, of which 569 were granted at their own request and only 181 by the Guardians. In 40 cases they gave no orders at all. Morris believed it was the duty of the Guardians to relieve destitution while the charities relieved distress. But in Carpenter's opinion, by being offered only the house, families were having "the iron of pauperism driven into their souls".[9] His criticism may have had an effect, for the numbers receiving outdoor relief rose slightly the following year and 200 working men were paid 1s a day and a loaf of bread to wheel coke from the workhouse to the schools.

In 1887, a new block for casuals was finally completed at a cost of £5,950. The work cells were equipped with grated openings through which all crushed stone had to be passed. In the new wards, casuals were to have their clothes taken away from them and were given workhouse clothes which had no pockets so as to prevent the smuggling of tobacco etc. into the labour yards. That winter one tramp refused to wear the new clothes and was left naked and swearing. He was taken before the magistrates and charged with "refractory behaviour":

> The prisoner maintained that the regulations of the Local Government Board entitled him to receive his clothes the next morning, and he declined to wear the official suit, and he remained undressed until the windows were opened for the usual ventilation, when he lost his temper.[10]

---

[i] Between 1877 and 1883 expenditure had gone down, due to people being offered the workhouse instead of outdoor relief.

The magistrates asked to see the regulations and discovered that the tramp had been right. They discharged him instead of giving him the usual sentence of two week's hard labour for refractory behaviour. One government inspector claimed that the Brighton magistrates had been wrong "for nothing, not even a cold wind on a bare back can justify the use of bad language".[11]

Fig 21 The outside of some casuals' single cells can still be seen today at the Elm Grove site.

George Cooper, who for the last five years had been taking religious services in the casual wards with the help of employees of Hannington's and YMCA members (who had taken it in turns to play the harmonium), described the new conditions:

When I first went, the floor of the [casual] ward was earth, and often very unpleasant, then a brick one was laid down and now your splendid new ones are open. It is nice to see them in their clean suits and canvas shoes. In the past, I have gone amongst them in their dirt and rags.[12]

In 1887 Mrs Mary Haycraft tried to get a motion passed against the annual summer trip to the Swiss Gardens. She claimed it was mainly the able-bodied who went, which was untrue, and that the inmates got drunk there. For the children:

> she knew those visits to the Shoreham Gardens had been the damnation of the afterlife of some of the girls and boys. They mixed children suddenly with unsuitable acquaintances, and their efforts of years were destroyed. Then some of the younger children were left at the Schools, and were so deprived of a treat.[13]

Haycraft alleged that some of the money for these treats had come out of the rates, as the subscriptions were not enough. She also complained about Guardians inviting friends to lunch at the Gardens: "They got sums of money for poor people, and yet the greater part of it went down the throats of friends." Another Guardian countered that the visit would be no more detrimental to the children any more than it would be to the children of an ordinary family. Haycraft [i] lost the motion unanimously.

That summer, during the week of Queen Victoria's golden jubilee celebrations, subscriptions were raised to pay for fireworks at the workhouse and some inmates were allowed out with their friends for the night. At the same time, processions of the unemployed marched through the town every day. They numbered between a hundred and a hundred and fifty. Five men who collected money in boxes were charged with "wandering abroad to beg" and fined 2s 6d or seven days imprisonment.

Later, there was a series of meetings of the unemployed at The Level, demanding that the council must provide work for them. Most speakers ordered the men to be calm and to protest peacefully. [ii] A delegate from the unemployed, Simmons, claimed that the crowds, about 200, would have been bigger but for the fact that many unemployed were now "working in the house". Simmons claimed the work was menial and that the men were marched about the workhouse by a retired policeman. "They were driven

---

[i] A Guardian, Thomas Berry, had told Haycraft at a previous meeting: "You have such a lot of 'goody-goodies' on the Board that they are too good enough for earth, but not for heaven." (Brighton Examiner 16/7/1886.)

[ii] That November industrial unrest in London had resulted in riots in Trafalgar Square, resulting in three deaths.

like convicts and that the officials kept them stirring, saying, 'Now then, get on; take your hands out of your pocket'." [14]

At the beginning of the winter of 1887, with over 3,000 people on outdoor relief, the Guardians had started to demand work from the able-bodied ones. One hundred and fifty men were employed at the workhouse without being forced to live there.[i] They worked from 8am to 5pm with only bread and soup for lunch. They received two loaves of bread and 1s per day for three days. Sattin noticed that they looked half-starved, and he managed to persuade the Guardians to offer them a breakfast of bread and porridge if they came half an hour earlier. On a bitterly cold day the following February, 108 men out of a total of 127 went on strike. They refused to work outside, "sifting mould", as the ground was frozen and covered with snow. Some of them asked if they could pick oakum inside but were turned down. The men then refused to leave the workhouse: the police were called, and they eventually left peacefully. Next day some of them returned to move the snow. While doing so they complained that the four labour masters had stood jeering at them from a pub.

Eighty men went to the parochial offices to air their grievances to the Guardians. One complaint was that often a potential employer who they saw before they started work at the workhouse would ask them to return at 10am. This led to the men having to jump over the workhouse walls to attend interviews. If they were caught, their bread was stopped and they only received half their money. The Guardians instigated an enquiry which exonerated the labour masters' behaviour, and they made no concessions to the striking men.

* * *

In January 1888, an eighteen year old unmarried pregnant woman, Sabina Tilley, was admitted into the workhouse. On 4th February, she had twins, Edith and Daisy. She left with them on 2nd March, despite pleas from Mrs

---

[i] Before that date, a few individuals on outdoor relief were occasionally required to work at the workhouse. In February 1883 an eighteen-year-old inmate, Arthur Gillam, was picking oakum when an outdoor pauper, Elias Anscombe, 68, porter, also picking oakum, antagonized him by calling him by his nickname "Onions". Gillam then chased Anscombe and stabbed him in the ear. Gillam was sent for trial and received six weeks' hard labour.

Haycraft that she be referred to the "Association of Friendless Girls" which had already helped two hundred young women from the workhouse. Haycraft had asked two ladies from that association to visit Sabina and offer her shelter in one of their little cottages, but she told them she was going to London to marry the father.

A couple of days later a cleaner found the bodies of the twins in a butter basket under the seat of a third class train carriage at New Cross station in London. They appeared to have been suffocated. Sabina was arrested at London Bridge station a few days later and charged with murder. She had been working as a waitress in a restaurant in Holborn. At the inquest she was described as "tall and good looking". She had appeared so distressed at the magistrates' enquiry in London that the *Sussex Daily News* had decided to raise a public subscription for her defence and to support her if she was acquitted. Within a couple of weeks, 1,500 sympathizers from all over Sussex had subscribed over £200 and the newspaper closed the subscription.

Sabina, or "Bina", as she was called by her family and friends, came from a large poor family living in a small village in Somerset. At the age of fourteen she had left and gone to London to stay with a sister and find work. She had found employment as a general servant and then as a waitress in Fulham. All her employers liked and trusted her and said she was particularly fond of children. In January 1888, despite denials, it was obvious she was pregnant and she told her last employer she was returning to Somerset, but instead went to Brighton.

At her trial, officials at the workhouse said she was well behaved and popular. However, the nurses said she did not have enough milk to suckle her twins and that they failed to dissuade her from leaving. She left with only seven shillings after giving a wardswoman two shillings. When she had walked out of the workhouse gates into a barbarous cold east wind, she had been crying and telling staff she did not know how she was going to keep her babies warm. That night she arrived late at night at her former landlady's lodgings in London. She was distressed and alone.

Sabina told the court that after she had left the workhouse she had gone to her lodgings in Brighton and had been shocked to discover that her savings of £2 14s had been stolen from her bonnet box. She told the jury: "I was out of my mind, the children having no clothes and so cold".[15] She sobbed hysterically and said she "had suckled them into my breast until they nearly died" and that they were not quite dead when she put them in the basket. She said that the father was a signalman in Brighton whom she did not want to marry.

The jury after deliberating for only seventy-five minutes, to great applause found her "not guilty", and added that they thought the children had been "accidentally suffocated". The judge threatened to have the court cleared if the applause continued. Sabina appeared dazed and began to cry. After leaving the court Sabina returned with her mother to Somerset and to obscurity, eternally grateful to the public subscription which had paid for her defence.

In truth, Sabina had been very lucky. During the trial it had become fairly obvious that one of her babies had died even before she had discovered that her money, allegedly, had been stolen. She was saved by the extraordinary public sympathy, the sympathy for a poor girl driven by circumstances to go into a workhouse. Interestingly, she was never really pressurized into giving the name of the father.

However, not all the public were sympathetic. Before the trial Mrs Haycraft had complained about people being happy to subscribe money to a sensational case rather than trying to help ordinary workhouse girls. She also criticized the *Sussex Daily News* for raising the subscription. In turn, the newspaper accused her of prejudgement and of "leaving pity at the workhouse gates". It asked why the workhouse could not have done more for Sabina when she had left. The conservative newspaper, the *Brighton and Hove Society*, renamed the *Sussex Daily News* the "Sabina Daily News", and protested about its intention to use the remainder of of the subscription – seventeen pounds after legal expenses had been paid – to help Sabina start a new life. In the end the money was donated to the Sussex County Hospital.

It is interesting that the amount of public sympathy the case raised was in stark contrast to the lack of it for the workhouse girl raped on a placement by a St James Street shoemaker over thirty years earlier. However, there was still a lot of prejudice against workhouse girls. A few years later, when the Guardians tried to place a girl named Florence Mckeown, 14, in one of the Church of England Incorporated Society homes for "waifs and strays", they received a reply stating that the Society's committee "do not think it wise to place a girl so corrupted with others". Its secretary suggested the girl "can be sent to the Society St Saviours Home at Shrewsbury, specially intended for girls of deprived character at a cost of six shillings a week".

Ironically, a few weeks after the death of Sabina's twins, the *Evening Argus* [16] had published the following poem:

A Child of the Poor

A little Hungry mouth;
A tiny shaking form,
Two little naked feet,
Out in the bitter storm,
A tattered bundle of rags and stains,
A beggar from door to door,
A freezing bundle of aches and pains,
A starving Child of the Poor,

Two pleading, tearful eyes
That none will ever miss;
Two little sunken cheeks
That never knew a kiss,
A tattered bundle of rags and stains
Who whines for a crust to eat;
A freezing bundle of aches and pains
A harmless child of the street!

Two tiny purple hands,
A shock of tangled hair,
A little weary head,
A sleep on the pavement bare;
A tattered bundle of rags unblessed
Whose strife is for ever o'er;
A wretched bundle was at rest –
A frozen child of the poor!

* * *

It is obvious that Sabina had been under enormous strain, and was fortunate that she had not ended up in the lunacy wards of the workhouse. With only one toilet for sixty-one females and with child lunatics mixed with adults, conditions there were poor. In June 1881, the lunacy commissioner found that the deaths and discharges had not even been recorded and that not everyone had the required certificate signed by a magistrate and a doctor.

The number of lunatics was steadily increasing: 125 in 1881 and 168 in 1885. That year eighteen males worked in the woodshed and forty females cleaned wards, did sewing and washing. Many lunatics and imbeciles[i] were spread out throughout the house. With the Sussex Lunatic Asylum at Haywards Heath full, a few Brighton patients considered to be harmless were returned to the workhouse. In June 1889 Dr Clifford Allbut, a Lunacy Commissioner, visited and found less than a quarter of the inmates were taken for weekly walks; that sometimes there was only pauper supervison[ii] at nights and that their iron beds were dangerous. He described some of the patients:

> ...Mary Page had delusions of poisoned food and often refuses food, after going 24 hours without food and is losing flesh obviously. Lydia Gane has violent mania. She had just left the padded room which I inspected. She had smashed a large hole in the ceiling by hurling the rubber chamberpot at it repeatedly and the floor was covered with rags and strips of destroyed clothing and bed coverings. She had been parts of seven days in this seclusion generally for the whole of every night. Susan Bailey is suicidal. Ann Walker has delusions of persecution and is probably dangerous. ...There were knives lying on the table where these women were. The attendants do their best to look after these patients and that things have gone on tolerably so far is greatly to their credit but how is it done? I found three women locked up in one dormitory of three beds. Habitually locked up for parts of the day and for all of the night. They and the epileptics are said to be visited every half hour by the inmate nurse but there is no clock on the women's side to prove it. No return of day seclusion is made in respect of the locked up patients. On male side three fully qualified paid attendants for 72 patients...Radical changes must be made in the lunatic department of this workhouse. The airing yard for men is narrow and prison like...High walls being raised with iron fixed on the top...to save attendance [save staff]. Machinery in laundry room not protected.[17]

The Guardians reacted by having two more paid attendants on the female side and tell-tale clocks, and they decided to stop locking up patients.

---

[i] The modern term would be "learning disabilities".

[ii] The inmates received 1s a week plus extras.

220

They said the knives in use were blunt. They agreed to extend airing yards for men and employed able-bodied labourers to do the work. But they argued that the walls were high to "prevent roughs from getting on the wall and annoying the patients not with a view to save attendance." [18] On his next visit Allbut found a great improvement with paid nurses rather than paupers staffing the lunacy wards.

In 1891, the Lunacy inspector found there was no fire escape for the lunatics and that they were watched over by a pauper nightwatchman who was often asleep. He recommended that they had paid staff on at night. He noted that the padded room was rarely used although it had been torn to shreds when it was upholstered and had been replaced by rubber. In 1895 an inspector, Dr Needham, recorded that:

> The patients were neatly dressed and very well cared for. The rooms were bright, cheerful and comfortable and the beds and bedding in excellent order. I have derived a very favourable impression from my visit to this Workhouse of the kindness and care which are bestowed upon its sick inmates. [19]

As Brighton had over three hundred patients in the Sussex Lunatic Asylum and over one hundred and fifty in Elm Grove, the borough started to consider the idea of building a new asylum.

* * *

One of the contributors to Sabina's public subscription was Mrs Nye Chart, the proprietor of the Theatre Royal. Just before the trial, the testimonial overleaf [i] was presented to her by the inmates and officers of the workhouse, in gratitude for her annual invitations to the Christmas pantomime. Some of the words were remarkably candid. The testimonial was richly deserved because for many years she had invited the children, female and male paupers to three separate performances. They were given the best seats in the house and afterwards received fruit, sweets, tobacco or snuff. Sadly, the testimonial's hope that Mrs Nye Chart would live a long life never materialized. She died in 1892 in London at the age of 51.[ii] At her funeral

---

[i] It still hangs in the Theatre Royal, Brighton.

[ii] Probable age. She had been an actress and had claimed to have been born in 1841.

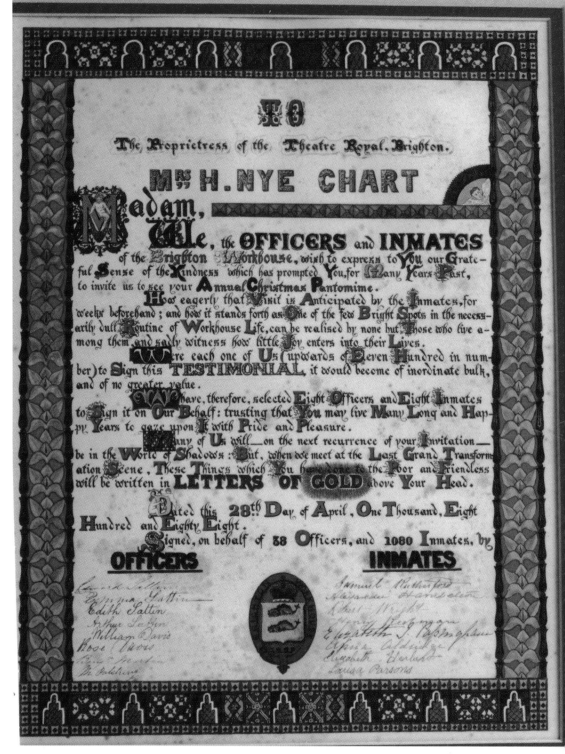

TO
The Proprietress of the Theatre Royal, Brighton.
Mrs H. NYE CHART

Madam,

We, the **OFFICERS** and **INMATES** of the Brighton Workhouse, wish to express to You our Grateful Sense of the Kindness which has prompted You, for Many Years Past, to invite us to see your Annual Christmas Pantomime.

How eagerly that Visit is Anticipated by the Inmates, for weeks beforehand; and how it stands forth as One of the few Bright Spots in the necessarily dull Routine of Workhouse Life, can be realised by none but Those who live among them, and sadly witness how little Joy enters into their Lives.

Were each one of Us (upwards of Eleven Hundred in number) to Sign this **TESTIMONIAL**, it would become of inordinate bulk, and of no greater value.

We have, therefore, selected Eight Officers and Eight Inmates to Sign it on Our Behalf: trusting that You may live Many Long and Happy Years to gaze upon It with Pride and Pleasure.

Many of Us will—on the next recurrence of your Invitation—be in the World of Shadows : But, when we meet at the Last Grand Transformation Scene, These Things which You have done to the Poor and Friendless will be written in **LETTERS OF GOLD** above Your Head.

Dated this 28th Day of April, One Thousand, Eight Hundred and Eighty Eight.

Signed, on behalf of 58 Officers, and 1080 Inmates, by

OFFICERS   **INMATES**

Fig 22

it was said that St Peter's Church could have been filled six times by mourners unable to get a seat inside. After her death it seems that the invitation to workhouse paupers to attend the pantomime at the Theatre Royal was stopped. Instead, by the end of the century they started to be invited to the Eden Theatre in North Road.[i]

Eighteen years after his letter to *Lloyds Weekly* had embarrassed the Guardians, the inmate, Charles Tourle, the ex-bookseller,[ii] was writing to the Local Government Board again. This time he alleged that an infirmary nurse, Miss White, had served medicines out of a dirty cup. Bedridden for the last six years, Tourle claimed he was punished for complaining by being sent to the foul wards and having his broth taken away:

> It appears they make their own laws here themselves without the sanction of the Local Government Board and I humbly ask protection from the abuses I am subjected to on many occasions".[20]

In another letter he accused Sattin of depriving him of a book and letters sent to him: "This Master he has got such a lying tongue". Sattin said that from now on he would open all his letters in his presence. Tourle said it was a prison rule and that the real reason was:

> ... because I am a little relative to him being second cousin – but of late he has no connection with me; he says this because I am a pauper – I am now quite bedridden for the last six years. My son has sent me 2/- in stamps and Sattin has kept them.

In reply, Sattin claimed that the Guardians had ordered him to check Tourle's post because he was sending begging letters to people outside. But there was some truth in Tourle's allegation that he was related to Sattin. His uncle had married Sattin's aunt although this did not make them second cousins.[iii] Charles Tourle's allegations were dismissed both by the Guardians and the Local Government Board. The *Brighton Guardian* gleefully announced "a constant grumbler crushed".[21]

---

[i] It changed its name to the Grand Theatre n 1905.

[ii] Although in the 1881 census he was described as a "general labourer"

[iii] Many thanks to Edward Sattin's relative, Anne Fryer, who investigated Tourle's claim for me.

Another complainant came from a 61 year old man who claimed that:

> according to the regulations laid down I am entitled to be treated as other men of my age namely placed in the body of the house but since my admission I have been in the able-bodied ward, working daily in a shed with the walls saturated with water, picking a task of oakum, then when the work is over – about 6oz of bread and cheese without anything warm to drink for supper so I feel myself justified in appealing to you, as I have paid rates and taxes in this town for 20 years. I now leave my case in your hands feeling satisfied that I shall have my cause justified which I CANNOT here as I applied to the Master, and also the committee, without any notice being taken of my cause.
>
> I remain your humble servant, George William White [22]

As usual, the Guardians were not slow to reply. Although he was 61 years of age, White was "a strong man, married but living apart from his wife, who maintains herself. He has suffered imprisonment for breaking windows when denied access to his wife (whom he has used badly) on her refusing to supply him with money. When out of the workhouse, White is given to drink. He has been an inmate at intervals during the past two years...Since Michaelmas 1887 he has been admitted eleven times and discharged ten...The Medical Officer agrees with the classification. The Visiting Committee have inspected the shed and there is no reasonable grounds for complaint".[23] The Local Government Board saw "no reason to interfere in this matter".

* * *

In 1889, out of a total population of 121,000 in Brighton, there had been 62 births in the workhouse, 58 of them illegitimate. Of the 1,833 deaths in the town, 194 had been in the workhouse.[i] One of these was Caroline Delves, who had been admitted as an "imbecile" in 1835 at the age of eleven. A local paper reported "The End of Dummy" and that she had left two pounds in coins, which was appropriated by the workhouse treasurer.

At Christmas that year, the *Herald* described the workhouse as the "House on the Hill" and its 1,000 inmates as "a huge battalion of crippled, useless and worn out lives, [but it] was as gay as if no such thing as poverty,

---

[i] It contrasted with the Sussex County Hospital, where there were only 84.

untruthfulness, intemperance or idleness was known. There was an excellent dinner and no distinction between the lazy loafer of the nomadic fraternity and the old peoples whose poverty is less, perhaps, their fault than their misfortune".[24] A concert was organized by the inmates and the new chaplain, Heathcote-Smith, put on a farce for the aged.

Meanwhile, the Guardians, in an attempt to deter outdoor relief started to rent 33a Eastern Road as a temporary workhouse extension with three paid staff for the winter months. With a grille in the door, it was restricted to able-bodied married men with two or three children. They worked for eight hours, six days a week and could look for work on the seventh. For lunch they were given 8oz of bread, 2oz of cheese and water. They had to bring their own tea or cocoa. They were paid some money and bread, which they had to take home. The visiting officer came to their homes once a day and reported to the relieving officer.

The majority of those in the temporary workhouse described themselves as labourers, painters and fishermen. They had to pick 3lbs of oakum a day, which was hard work for the inexperienced and involved tying up bundles of oakum and hitting them with a sledgehammer. As the Guardians could not give them work to compete with the labour market outside, they gave the paupers this "test" work instead. From December 1889 to April 1890, ninety-one married men were given orders to go to Eastern Road. Sixty-eight accepted. At the same time, few paupers accepted their orders to go into the workhouse. It is true to say that if every pauper had accepted their order, the workhouse would not have been able to cope with such vast numbers.

On 14th November 1891, Edward Sattin, 66, died from influenza after a short illness. He had been a servant of the Brighton Guardians for thirty-six years, all but four as the master. One newspaper reported that "since the erection of the Elm Grove workhouse, and under their regime complaints have been practically unknown". Inmate correspondence held at the National Archives perhaps contradicts this, but there were relatively few complainants considering the thousands of paupers who passed through the workhouse during his tenure.

Sattin had been accused of nepotism: giving employment to his 17-year-old daughter and to his son Arthur. And the owner of 33a Eastern Road, who was receiving £50 a month in rent from the Guardians, was Joseph

Edward Sattin (1825–1891)

Sattin,[i] described as a carpenter and builder. Sattin had a brother called Joseph and it seems probable that they were the same man. It could also be argued, however, that Sattin might not have lasted so long without surrounding himself with people – his family – that he could trust. Being a master of a workhouse was potentially a dangerous job. The master of the nearby Eastbourne workhouse had been attacked with a knife and some masters had even been shot at. It was not a job for the faint hearted. You needed discipline to run a workhouse but Sattin had a compassionate side as well, no better illustrated than by his recorded sadness at seeing the child pauper emigrants departing Liverpool for Canada in 1871. He certainly was more humane and a better manager than most of his predecessors.

---

[i] When he died in 1900, his father was described as a town councillor. Edward's father had also been a town councillor.

In 1876, one visitor, Lt Col Sussex Lennox, had written:

I have never seen any workhouse home or abroad, so thoroughly well-managed.

And in 1881, another visitor, Rev Wilson-Cook, had recorded that:

Having had opportunities of observing other workhouses, it may not be regarded as presumptious of me to record how very favourably I have been impressed with the appointments and management of the Brighton Workhouse. The perfect order, scrupulous cleanliness and excellent behaviour prevailing throughout reflects no little credit on the wise and kindly authority exercized by the heads of the institution, which seems to have diffused itself amongst all the subordinates until every inmate appears to have been brought under its beneficial influence.[25]

Also on the plus side, Sattin had introduced Christmas festivities for the inmates in 1859 and before he died had persuaded the Guardians in 1889 to allow the able-bodied to attend the summer treats as well:

The grounds in front of the main building were hung with Japanese lanterns and on the grass plots glow-worm lamps were very numerous. These were lit up in the evening, and it may readily be imagined that the illumination had a charming effect. A stage had been erected on the grounds in front of the Infirmary, where a variety entertainment was held during the afternoon which afforded the inmates great enjoyment. The band comprised members from the West Pier, Oxford Theatre of Varieties and Theatre Royal orchestras. A capital motto song was rendered by Mr. Robert Williams, and Professor Edgeio performed some astonishing acrobatic juggling feats. "The Showman" was recited by Mr Arthur Fenwick in his usually effective style…There was a cabinet performance of the "Hassan Asiatic Mystery," and an extraordinary imitation of the cries of various animals and birds was given by Professor B. Sloman from the Oxford Theatre. There were also comic songs, a Punch and Judy show and live music…With the exception of the infirm and sick, who were served in their wards, the inmates partook of tea in the open air at the termination of the entertainments provided for their amusement.

After an interval, the paupers had congregated in the infirmary grounds for a concert given by two of the Sattins and their friends.[26]

Year after year Sattin's whole family had participated in entertaining the inmates on Christmas day. One year the inmates of "Ward 23" had even signed a letter to him and his wife to "acknowledge our gratitude to you and your sons and daughters for the happy days we spent on Christmas day, and all the other kindnesses we receive".[27] Often Edward himself would stand on the stage in the dining room and play charades with the inmates. In 1881, the *Brighton Guardian* had declared that "at no institution in the town is Christmas rendered more attractive or enjoyable than at the Brighton Workhouse".[28] The decorations often included a large wax figure of Father Christmas at the top of the stairs in the main entrance opposite a pretty little fairy cottage illuminated from inside and a huge banner with the words:

> Welcome joy in every clime;
> All hail to thee glad Christmas time.

Another time Sattin had organised a treat at the seaside for the aged inmates. One elderly woman declared "I have lived a good many years on the earth, but I have never before spent such a delightful day".[29]

Sattin and his family also organised the New Year entertainment for the aged paupers. In 1884, 520 had crowded into the dining room, where there was an impromptu stage. The females in neat white caps had sat on one side and the males on the other. They had been entertained by a farce put on by staff, the Sattins and visitors, entitled "The Silent Woman". There had followed a concert in which a song "I'm ninety-five" was sung by one of Sattin's daughters:

> The last named item proved the most taking piece of the programme. It was given in character, and the make-up was admirable. The stooping posture, the palsied limbs, and the tremulous voice, too, were introduced, and were points which appealed strongly to the audience. Many of the old ladies became highly excited, rising from their seats in order that they might lose no item of the impersonation, while many screamed with delight. As Miss Sattin limped off the stage, the applause was deafening, and did not subside until the "grand old lady" had returned to the stage and repeated one of the verses of the ballad.[30]

The first part of Sattin's funeral, which took place in the workhouse chapel, was crowded with inmates as well as dignitaries. It moved on to the Brighton cemetery, where among the floral tributes was a wreath subscribed by the inmates out of the few pence[i] they had occasionally received from friends.

Sattin's family, like so many other masters' families, became wholly involved in the workhouse system. His son Edward went on to become the master at Wolverhampton workhouse. Arthur Sattin became the master at Kettering, and Arthur's sister Mabel an assistant matron there. Sattin's other two daughters, Edith and Elizabeth, also worked as assistant matrons. Elizabeth eventually married Benjamin Saunders, the son of the Guardian, Mr H. Saunders, who had originally proposed Edward Sattin for the master's job. Often the children of workhouse administrators grew up in them, and to a certain extent may have become institutionalised.

As a temporary arrangement, Arthur Sattin took over as master of Elm Grove, assisted by his brother Edward, with their mother, Emma, continuing in the role of matron. In December 1891 there was an outbreak of influenza and extra nurses were brought in from the Royal Sussex County Hospital. Over 150 inmates were affected and six very old inmates died.

Fig 23 The Guardians' brass memorial to Sattin.

---

[i] Sattin had rewarded aged paupers with money for their work or good behaviour.

That Christmas it was reported that there was a general gloom at the workhouse without the presence of Edward Sattin, and the New Year festivities were cancelled. As the year ended Arthur and his mother, Emma, resigned. Without her husband, it was mandatory.

*   *   *

In January 1892, thirty-five year old Valentine Burden and his wife Constance, 34, from the Bath Union were appointed master and matron. Previously he had been the youngest master in the country when, at just 22, he had held that post at a workhouse in Wiltshire. Both his parents had been Poor Law officials in Portsmouth. The Burdens had to pay maintenance for their two children, who could only live in the workhouse till they were fourteen.

One of the first problems Burden faced was the arrival on March 24th of John Bartlett, 51, who had been on the road since Christmas. He had been sleeping in the casual wards in Worcester, Buckinghamshire, Middlesex, Hertfordshire, Surrey, Kent and finally Sussex. His last few stops had been in the following workhouses:

15th March – Redhill
17th March – Cuckfield
18th March – Chailey
21st & 22nd – Lewes
23rd March – Newhaven

He had felt poorly when he had left Lewes, and for good reason: he had smallpox. He was quickly removed to the infirmary and the ward was fumigated. The straw beds were taken out of the casual cells and burned, and then the rugs were fumigated and thoroughly cleaned. In May another casual, William Hayler, arrived with smallpox and was transferred to the sanatorium. He had been on the road for some weeks and had been sleeping in barns in the neighbourhood of Hastings. He had slept in the Firle casual ward just before coming to Brighton. Eight out of the eleven casuals admitted the same night as Hayler were vaccinated but the others refused.

For the first summer treat at the workhouse under the Burdens, most of the entertainers, professional or otherwise, gave their services free. The Band of the Inniskilling Dragoons came, including four ex-members of the schools, and Mr G.W. Kenway, a famous music hall mimic, came down from London. Girls from the Servants Training Hall in Rose Hill, visited the sick wards and sang songs. The aged inmates who could get outside basked in the sunshine and listened to music, ate ham and enjoyed other luxuries such as snuff. The old ladies who did not take snuff were given a parcel of tea and sugar. In the evening, entertainment was provided in the dining hall with the chaplain, Heathcote-Smith, dressed as a red indian. The summer treat finally ended at mid-night.

Despite Sattin's death, Charles Tourle was soon writing to the Local Government Board again in 1892, insisting that Heathcote-Smith had been instructed by Sattin to continue to "make his life uncomfortable".[31] The following year he wrote claiming that the chaplain was insulting him behind his back, but his letters were ignored.

In June 1893, the Local Government Board received a letter from Henry Philips, an ex-inmate of the workhouse, complaining about "my cruel treatment by officials in the Brighton Workhouse" and hoping that the Board would take such steps:

… as you should think fit to prevent any further ill treatment that should cause my health to suffer should I have the misfortune to seek an asylum in the Brighton Workhouse again which I fear I may shortly have to do.

At the beginning of last month while on the sea front I received a sunstroke which necessitated getting an order for the Brighton Workhouse. On arrival at this institution and on seeing and informing the medical officer's assistant that I had received a sunstroke and that I was suffering great pain in my eyes and head, replied to me by asking, "How many glasses of beer does it take to make a sunstroke?", said in a jocular manner. My reply was that it did not. Bathed and sent into the adult able-bodied ward consisting of some very strong rough sort of persons. I had to leave my post as a telegraphist in the Post Office through ill health after 8 years…The following day the Labour Master told me to fetch and carry from the chapel into the yard and sweep large rolls of cocoa-matting. I could only get it halfway down the stairs…thoroughly exhausted and in a fainting condition. The Master asked me what I could do. Tie a few bundles of wood. So did this for two days. Then the Labour Master Mr Elkins asked me to carry cans containing tea and milk which it was physically impossible for me to do. So I asked for and got my discharge. The Labour Master said; "Don't come here again or you will know where you will go." When I left the porter said "You ought to have a thick rope about your back." My prayer is to save me from the officials I have named.[32]

The Guardians said Phillips' allegations were "uncalled for and frivolous." The medical officer, Dr Ross, claimed:

…He is well known to me and from repeated observations I have no hesitation in describing him as a lazy worthless fellow. His wife died in the Workhouse Infirmary and she complained to me many times of his cruel behaviour to her and that she was afraid to live with him any longer and this was corroborated by the clergy and district visitors of the parish of St Martins… he had "an inveterate desire to avoid exertion in any form".[33]

Elkins, the labour master, called him "an exceptionally lazy inmate...his usual practice when given an order is to receive it with great impudence". The porter, Charles Wood, admitted that he had said "a lazy man like you ought to have a piece of rope across your back and be made to do the work".[34] Between March 1890 and May 1893 he had been admitted and discharged nine times. It was in this period that paupers such as Phillips were referred to as the "ins" and "outs". But by far the most serious complaints came from a group of inmates in a letter to the Local Government Board in October 1894:

We the undersigned inmates desire to refer to your notice the following complaints respecting the conduct of the present Master, and also relating to his treatment of the aged inmates of the above institution.

First, is a complaint by George Henry Baker, relating to the quantity of food served for dinner on Wednesdays. The dinner consisting of meat pie and potatoes which the said George Henry Baker received on Wednesday last and he considering it so deficient in quantity took it up to the Master and respectfully asked to have it weighed. The Master refused to do so in a bullying manner and placing the said George Henry Baker under punishment for complaining of his food.

Second is a complaint by James Buckland for the above cause at the same time and place.

Third is also a complaint by George Henry Baker against the Master for refusing to permit him to see the House Committee on his application.

Fourth is a complaint by Henry Vinall, aged 72, who was brutally assaulted by the Master's orders and placed in the insane asylum without the medical officers authority on some frivolous pretence.

Fifth is a complaint by William Breton, aged 85, who mistaking his way to the dining hall was also cruelly ill treated and placed in the insane asylum (without the medical officer's authority.)

Sixth is a complaint by Richard Vernon, aged 72, who was brutally assaulted by the officers on his returning from day's leave. And also for refusing to permit him to see the committee.

Seventh is a complaint by Thomas Page who on the medical officer's order was allowed an infirm diet until released by the master.

Eighth is the complaint generally of the Able Bodied inmates as to the condition of the Receiving ward which is in a detestable condition (formerly a casual ward condemned by the Local Government Board inspectors). The said ward running alive with vermin. Also, putting men to hard labour on their admission to the house without the medical officer certified them able to do so. Also, as to whether it is permissible for the Master to keep a horse and private carriage at the expense of the ratepayers. Also as to the Master returning home to the house on his outings at all hours of the night. And punishing aged inmates (whom he has frightened with his noise) for daring to complain thereof…Also, allowing an inmate, George Payne, carpenter, to leave the premises otherwise than by discharge. For the purpose of doing skilled work at the private residence of a Mr Reed, Surveyor, from the 24th September to 29th consecutively.

Three men who were discharged and employed by a contractor. When returned to do work in the house they were sacked on the master's orders. Thereby causing the said men to be destitute and return to the house as a tax upon the ratepayers. Master took away the old women's tea and sugar on the

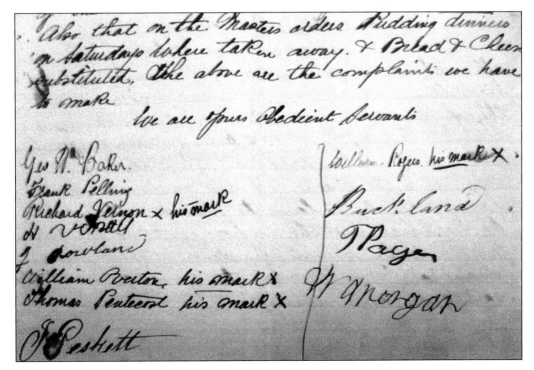

Fig 24 Some of the signatures of the complainants.

plea of extravagance … Also, that on the Masters appointment here, he brought with him from Bath four children, also a domestic servant as his retinue. Also that through the defective bathing facilities, several of the inmates were found infested with vermin. Also that on the Masters' orders [meat] Pudding dinners on Saturday were taken away and bread and cheese substituted.

Signed by 23 inmates, 6 by mark and George Baker.[35]

In their enquiry the Guardians' visiting committee did find that Burden had been remiss in not weighing the food, but that was the only concession they made to the complainants. The Guardians wrote back to the Local Government Board that two of the signatories had since left and would only appear before the committee if they were sent for:

…The letter was prompted by one or two disaffected inmates and that there are no justifiable grounds for the alleged ill treatment by the Master or for the charges against his management of the Workhouse. Your Committee are further of the opinion that in justice to the Master, some of the known antecedents of the following signatories should be laid before your board.[36]

For example, they described Vinall, who had absconded for two days, as an "acute alcoholic, noisy and violent with a black eye". They insisted that Burden's private carriage was, in fact, a dog cart, and that George Payne was a well-conducted inmate who was allowed one day's leave of absence every six weeks.

*   *   *

In the 1890s Local Government Board circulars encouraged administrators to provide the elderly with a better diet, tobacco and more privacy in their sleeping arrangements. In 1892 they decreed an ounce of tobacco be allowed to over 65s – not able-bodied – who were employed on useful work. However, it was left to the discretion of the master. Nevertheless, Burden's withdrawing of tea and sugar from aged females, if true, was going against the general trend of improved conditions for older people in workhouses.

Though the Guardians had defended Burden, soon there were headlines such as "Fracas in Workhouse" and one magistrate censored him with the words that he hoped he would not bring every trivial case before him. It was clear that Burden's regime was much tougher than Sattin's and even staff began to leave more frequently. In 1892 a casual was sentenced to three months for refusing to pick oakum. Next year, another received one month's hard labour for absconding with workhouse clothes. Tobacco and snuff were withdrawn from inmates unless they did "objectionable" work such as removing corpses to the mortuary or extra work such as painting and plastering. There was even another meeting at The Level to protest about this. Despite the complaints, in 1894 a Local Government Board inspector told the Guardians of Tonbridge to visit the Brighton workhouse "as it was near perfection as possible".

In January 1895 Heathcote-Smith, the chaplain who had dressed up as a red indian during a summer treat, made a speech to the Brighton Parliamentary Society. He complained that the house was "cram-full" due to the policy of stopping outdoor relief. He claimed that "now many respectable people who might otherwise have been able to get along outside" [37] were being forced into the house, and that there were over 1,500 inmates, many of whom needed sick room accommodation.

The chairman of the Guardians, W. Bennet, called his remarks untruthful. But Heatcote-Smith insisted that "refusing outdoor relief is often responsible for much hardship and increased rates" [38] and that no allowance was being made for temporary misfortune. However, Bennet insisted that there was accommodation for 823 males and 712 females, and that 705 and 642 were occupied, plus there had been 243 casuals at Christmas. He claimed that at least two thirds of the casuals only came in for the Christmas dinner and then left. Bennet warned the chaplain that he must not make statements like that again.

Heathcote-Smith had started a lending library at the workhouse and had also published a monthly magazine. He often wrote to the newspapers appealing for funds to entertain the inmates or books although with the latter he stressed that "we don't want dry, musty, unreadable rubbish".[39] He also let their readers know that he was not a soft touch: "The grumblers, lazy, and shameless, get plain speech from me and no help until I see they mean seriously to mend their ways".[40]

The vicar of Brighton, Hannah, also gave a talk to the Brighton Parliamentary Society, entitled "What has Christianity done for the Poor?" He argued that the work of the Guardians did not absolve a single individual from the duty of private benevolence:

> To all those poor people, they must behave as gentlemen, testing because they had to listen to so many stale tales. They need infinite patience and must discriminate. Many of the people who come before the Board are "utterly unworthy." They had divine sanction for saying: "If a man will not work, neither shall he eat." You must remember that you are spending other people's money.[41]

As the records of the Mendicity Society showed, Hannah and his wife were often targeted by beggars, and this may account for his uncharitable stance.

In this period, casuals – now more often than not described as "tramps" – were detained for two days and two nights. They were given gruel to eat and milk to drink and were expected to break 2cwt of stone or pick oakum in a single cell. In August 1895 a casual, Thomas Hart, was kept 28 hours in a separate cell after refusing to go to a work cell. When he was brought before the bench, a magistrate said that he had been unfairly treated and discharged him. The much tougher regime for casuals had vastly decreased their numbers. In the four years before the opening of the new block for casuals in 1887, there had been 36,875 tramps admitted. But in the four years to 1891, it had dropped to 17,823.

In 1888, there had been 3,372 people on outdoor relief and 1,369 in the workhouse. By September 1895 there were 1,734 and 1,340 respectively. The fall in oudoor relief was probably due to the stricter application of the workhouse "test". There were still, though, huge numbers of the poor refusing to go to the workhouse. In 1892, the *Brighton Guardian,* in an article "Where the Poor Live", had graphically contrasted the carriages and horses of the rich on the sea-front with the squalid human rabbit-warrens huddled on the hill in behind Edward Street where many families lived in single rooms:

> At the back of Grand Parade, on the darkling hill that frowns upon the valley of Brighton, rises street after street where the poorest of the poor crowd and herd together…Four rotting walls that are positively black with all kinds of vermin, a chair without a seat, a tottering bedstead with a filthy mattress, some wretched rags to serve as coverings for those who have to try and sleep on a gruesome floor…[42]

The article claimed that the woman did most of the work while the man loafed:

> If he gets any money by begging or by cab-running, or kindred occupations, he wastes it on himself. The woman spends her day, earning sometimes not more than two pence-halfpenny an hour, at the exhaustive labour of the washtub. The children…are sent on the streets and woe betide them if they fail, by whatever fault, to contribute at least a few pence towards their daily support. Bread and margarine, dried herrings, and rashers of bacon form the chief food of the poor. The fish and meat are badly cooked over fires made of any old rubbish that hands can be laid on. Is it wonder, therefore, that the people after meals of this kind…resort to the beerhouse and the gin shop for that nourishment which the herring and the bacon have not given them?

The woman drank "to stimulate her overtaxed strength for the exhausting labours of the laundry", while the man drank "as a solace for the misery of his life". The article claimed that the poor preferred living in revolting conditions rather than going to the workhouse, not so much because of the stigma but because they could not get the drink there which they could buy outside. Many town dignitaries believed that pauperism was caused by drink. In Brighton there were 285 beerhouses and 300 public houses. It was said that from the steps of the magistrates' court a young boy could throw a stone into seven licensed houses.

In 1893, a Local Government Board order decreed that a guardian might visit the workhouse of the parish to which he is a guardian any time without seeking the master's permission. However, they could not prevent the master being present during any conversation they might have with the inmates. Two years later the Brighton Guardians moved the parochial administration from the dark and dingy offices of Church Street – where they had been since 1853 – to more comfortable and roomy new offices in Princes Street, which had a frontage of a hundred feet. The paupers were not allowed in the main entrance but through the rear entrances in Steine Gardens. One Guardian contrasted their new accommodation with the "test house" in Eastern Road, which he described as "an abominable place". He said he had been disgusted the first time he had seen it. It had no ventilation and was only heated by gas. The door was locked and the paupers were watched over by "a kind of gaoler".

Two views of the parochial offices, Princes Street, in 2011.

That year a public relief fund for the unemployed was started to provide work for men and relieve families with a few shillings. It received 1,929 applications. One councillor, Dutton Briant, claimed that this represented at least 4,500 people in great distress and that the Guardians had no idea of the extent of pauperism. In 1896 there were 1,718 on outdoor relief, 1,140 in the workhouse and 288 in the schools. Heathcote-Smith, the chaplain, started a "Samaritan Fund" for the workhouse infirmary. He also tried to get a wage increase for himself, asking "in how many places do the Chaplains give up their lives to a work so full of anxious and depressing responsibilities?" [i] Perhaps because of his outspokenness, the Guardians turned him down: he resigned not long afterwards following the death of his wife, and was replaced by Rev Walter Minchin. At his leaving ceremony, Heathcote-Smith's twenty-one-year-old daughter, who had been very active in entertaining the inmates, received a pretty jewel case on a silver plate from a ninety-year-old inmate, Mrs Sarah Harrington, on behalf of the "aged and infirm as a token of their esteem and regard".

In 1897, Alfred Morris, who had started off as a junior clerk in 1844, and clerk to the Guardians since 1857, retired just before his 80th birthday. Benjamin Burfield, his junior for 40 years, took over. During his tenure, perhaps Morris's most stressful time had been when Rev Henry Dodwell had repeatedly burst into his office to complain about his treatment. One old boy from the schools remembered Morris:

> As postboy, it was my daily duty to go over the Downs into Brighton to fetch the letters for the school from the Post Office in Lewes Road, and also to the Guardian's Offices in Church Street. Mr Morris, who was then Clerk to the Guardians, always greeted us boys with a cheery word, and in the winter time always told us to sit by the office fire and have a good warm-up before starting on our journey back to the school.[43]

Morris had almost resigned in protest when the first female Guardian, Mrs Haycroft, had been elected in 1884. One of the last major changes he had witnessed was in 1892, when there had been a vote to have Guardian elections on a ward system. Out of just over 19,000 voters, only 8,375 people had voted, and the proposal had been passed by 1600 votes. So the following year, for the first time, thirty-six Guardians representing twelve

---

[i] The hours, though, were hardly onerous: two hours a day, five days a week and two services on Sunday.

wards were elected, with a third of them retiring every year. A little later, the Guardians, after newspaper criticism, decided to let the public into their meetings, something that was already happening at the council and school board meetings. Worried that it might attract vagrants, they provided only six chairs!

Their chairman, Thomas Rose, wrote a poem which he hoped future historians might say of the Guardians. He was optimistic:

> Then none were for the party,
> But all were for the state;
> And the great men helped the small man,
> And the small man helped the great.
> Contacts were fairly given,
> Relief was wisely doled;
> Those Guardians were like brothers,
> In the brave days of old.[44]

In 1897, it was decided that no pauper inmate should be employed as a nurse on the workhouse wards. By 1898 three new infirmary blocks had been built in the workhouse compound and in this way, after just 31 years in existence, Elm Grove was becoming more and more a hospital. Out of a staff of ninety, thirty-five were now nurses. There were estimated to be 600 sick and bedridden paupers who were either old or handicapped, and the annual mortality rate of 200 reflected the predominance of this group. In the early 1890s the *Brighton Guardian* had started to refer to the workhouse as the "Brighton House of Industry", but with an ageing and sick population the description never caught on. By the end of the decade 30 per cent of all the old people in England and Wales were ending their lives in workhouses. This statistic alone would account for the fear and dread of them felt by older generation after older generation

By now the Local Government Board was taking the hospital side of the establishment more seriously. In 1897, they refused to sanction the appointment of the matron, Mrs Burden, to be the superintendent nurse because she was not trained and yet would be in charge of qualified staff. The medical officer, Dr Ross, wanted her because of her 25 years' experience. The Guardians appointed her, although they eventually did recruit a qualified superintendent. A government medical inspector, Dr Fuller, had visited the infirmary and claimed that it left much to be desired and that twenty patients were in an appalling condition. Ross denied it.

The commemoration day to celebrate Queen Victoria's diamond jubilee in 1897 started at 7.30am with the inmates being given a breakfast of bacon, poached eggs and sausages. For lunch, they had roast lamb and beef on the lawns, followed by pipes, tobacco and snuff. Afterwards there was a Punch and Judy show and a ventriloquist, minstrels, an organist, a pianist and music hall artists to entertain the inmates. One of the more unusual events was an animal race with five contestants: the two cats bolted and the rooster and lamb refused to start, which left a strolling pig as the winner! At midday and after tea more than 1,200 inmates sang the national anthem outside the main building and the whole scene was photographed.

Since 1880, the Brighton Guardians had started to sell "unclaimed bodies" to the school of anatomy attached to Downing College, Cambridge University. "A fee of one guinea was usually paid by the school, as well as the expenses of the coffin, carriage – normally by railway – and eventual burial".[i] Families could also donate corpses in return for having later expenses paid for by the Union. Michael Burchall, in his article, *Brighton*

A workhouse celebration.

[i] *Sussex Family Historian*, vol 18 no. 8.

paupers buried in Cambridge, 1885–1920,[i] has managed to identify 98 of the 104 paupers who, after dissection, were buried at St Benedict's cemetery in Cambridge. Of these 71 were elderly men and 27 were women. Burchall concluded that most "were largely elderly long term inmates of the workhouse, single but more often widowed, with no close family, or family members willing or able to afford a burial, and that the majority had not been Brighton born".[ii] These are truly the forgotten paupers of the Brighton workhouse.

In 1899, with the Boer War – which had begun that year in South Africa – going badly, even some of the workhouse staff were called up, which could lead to their own families having to claim parochial relief. At the Christmas celebrations at Elm Grove, alongside the traditional figure of Santa Claus there was also a model soldier dressed in the colours of the Buffs (East Kent Regiment). At his feet there was an empty drum in which visitors were encouraged to donate money to a local war fund. Above the model's head a flag flew with the words "Dulce et decorum est pro patria mori."[iii] At the entrance to the dining room, there was another inscription: "Success to her Majesty's Forces." Inside, the walls were inscribed with the names of famous soldiers. Outside, even the workhouse clock was draped in the union jack. It is in this atmosphere that almost 1,300 inmates sat down to eat their Christmas lunch.

[i] *Sussex Family Historian*, vol 18 no.8

[ii] idem

[iii] "It is sweet and fitting to die for one's country."

PART THREE

Chapter Fourteen

HARD TIMES 1901–1914

After the death of Queen Victoria on January 22nd, Edwardian Britain – named after the King's reign (1901–1910) and the period up to 1914 – was to become a period of great affluence for a small minority. While the rich seemed to get richer and richer, the poor fell further into poverty. However, this divergence did fan the flames of protest in the form of the emerging Labour Party – created in 1900 – and the women's suffrage movement. Both demanded economic and social changes. It meant that, for the first time, on a widespread scale, the views of women and the working man were being represented.

In Brighton in 1901, 3,761 people were considered to be complete paupers.[i] As a large part of the suburban population of Brighton was included in the Steyning Union, the above figures did not give a complete view of the town's pauperism and were the tip of the iceberg. That year, local charities gave new shoes to 2,332 children from large families living in the town or whose father was dead or unemployed.

In February 1902, the body of a tramp was found in a wagon near the workhouse. He had died from exposure and starvation. It was reported that "there were no traces of food in his stomach and intestines and all fatty matter had disappeared from the tissues of the body". Not long afterwards a chemist from Glasgow, William Mathie, was found dead in similar circumstances. In September, a small female child, name unknown, was found abandoned in Pavilion Gardens and taken to the workhouse by a policeman. When she was undressed a luggage label was found bearing the following words: "Will you take this motherless and homeless child to the Union as her father is dead?" All pauper children – whether they had parents or not – were initially forced to spend time in a block at the workhouse, where there were receiving and quarantine wards, before their transfer to Warren Farm.

---

[i] 423 were in the county lunatic asylum; 283 in the schools, 1,381 on outdoor relief and the rest in the workhouse.

The previous month on August 9th the workhouse had celebrated the coronation of Edward VII. The outside of the building was decorated with 1,700 fairy lamps, although many were blown out by the wind. There were transparent representations of the King, Queen and Prince of Wales, and the letters "E R" were over the entrance. The windows of the children's block were lit up by different coloured lamps, and even the casuals' block was lit up by a crown. Each man received a pipe and tobacco, and the women snuff and tobacco. Punctually at noon they all gathered in front of the workhouse and sang the national anthem. Afterwards, they were entertained with a concert in the dining room by a number of artistes from the Empire Theatre, New Road. It was reportedly ruined by the coughing and sneezing of the inmates. Back at the schools, each child received a coronation medal and 3d in a fancy bag.

In the winter of 1902, unemployment was worse than it had been for nine years, increased by the number of reservists and discharged soldiers from the Boer War.[i] In December, over 2,000 penny dinners were provided to shivering children[ii] and men out of work. The unemployed besieged the town hall and became dependent on the soup [iii] – at a penny a quart [iv] – distributed daily throughout the town. That winter 34,476 quarts of soup were given out. The trade unions urged the government to take more action to help the unemployed. In Brighton a deputation of 90 unemployed people met the Guardians and asked them to provide work. The Guardians replied that they could only relieve destitution and could not by law initiate public works for the relief of unemployment

In the early years of the new century numerous individual charities and funds were set up. For example: the Police-Aided Scheme of Clothing Destitute Children; the Free Meals Society which fed 835 children in one day in October 1904; a New Century Fund for the benefit of the deserving poor of Brighton set up by Edward White, a JP; and the Brighton Distress

---

[i] James Williamson, an early film-maker, made "A Soldier's Return" in 1902. It features a soldier returning from the Boer War only to discover that his mother is in the Brighton workhouse. Although very short, much of the film was shot there. It can be seen at most libraries through the website "Screenonline".

[ii] One boy was found wearing brown paper for warmth.

[iii] The Soup Fund had been in existence since 1835.

[iv] A quart is two pints.

246

Fund, to which over 1500 people applied for help in one week in January 1906. Another charity was set up by John Howard, the director of the Palace Pier. He ran it from an office in Richmond Terrace, had 150 applications per week and was particularly generous to the aged poor. As there were so many subscriptions to charities, the workhouse and Warren Farm treat funds suffered, and for a couple of years the Guardians had to use money from the rates to pay for their treats.

In September 1903, in a major development, the town officially took over the running of the asylum at Haywards Heath and it became known as the Brighton County Borough Asylum. Despite this, the workhouse still retained lunatic wards. Weeks before the changeover, the Guardians had

' WHAT SHALL BE DONE WITH THEM?"

Fig 25 Brighton, January 1905.

been reprimanded over the death of a female lunatic who had died minutes after her reception at the asylum from the workhouse. To save money, she had been transported in a horse-drawn ambulance with two other lunatics and the stress of the journey was thought to have contributed to her death. The Guardians had traditionally hired the cheapest conveyances for these trips, and consequently the drivers made the journey as fast as possible in order to make it profitable. Two months later a male lunatic actually died during his transfer. At the inquest the jury recommended that the Guardians should provide better facilities aboard their vans. Afterwards, rubber protective coverings were placed over some of the rougher edges of their internal compartments.

Later, when the lunacy commissioners visited the lunatic wards they discovered that some of the 122 inmates still had no certificates from either the magistrates or medical officers – they usually had to be signed by both. In other words, they had been dumped there. Perhaps they were a social nuisance or maybe there was no other accommodation available. The males worked on the wards and the females in the laundry and needlework room. They were looked after by two attendants and three nurses in the daytime and by one attendant and two nurses during the night. They had weekly baths and two walks a week. On their visit, the commissioners complained about the dirty windows in the wards and the lack of books and games.

Another major change at the workhouse was in response to the Local Government Board's recommendation at the end of the previous century, that guardians must make a more humane classification of their aged inmates. The Brighton Guardians decided to provide better accommodation for 24 aged men [over sixty] of "good character" on the ground floor of an empty ward. They could now have dinner in their own ward, separate cubicles for sleeping and be granted special leave. Couples were given the right to have separate accommodation, but it very much depended on its availability. Aged men were also given the use of small allotments and supplied with garden seeds. Every year there were to be prizes for the best one judged by a local florist.

There could also be other rewards. One year, casuals set to work digging near the allotments found a tin buried in the soil containing £1 6s 6d – probably hidden by an inmate who had subsequently died. Lastly, no able-bodied man over sixty had to do task work and, for the first time, aged inmates were allowed to smoke in their rooms between 12 and 8pm.

In 1903, the major talking point was the decision of the Guardians not to allow a half pint of beer to the aged inmates at Christmas. The chairman of the workhouse committee, Albert Mellor, turned down the offer of several brewers to supply it free. In a fierce debate, he said he preferred them to donate the money for entertainment. Another Guardian, local businessman Edward Jarvis, said he felt "ale was far better for the old people than to blow themselves out on ginger beer and buns (*laughter*)." Under a heading "No Beer at Brighton", the *Sussex Daily News*[1] reported that:

> Councillor Penfold referred to a teetotal member who had indulged in two or three mince pies at the Workhouse, and had said they were very nice, although brandy was used in them (*laughter*)…Mr J. Page said he felt sure the beer would be sensibly distributed. If the Master knew an inmate was a glutton for beer he would not give him a taste nor even a smell of it (*laughter*)…Mr W Bartlett spoke against the Chairman, the Reverend A Cocks. "Had not the Brighton Medical Officer of Health said that if a man drank regularly it did him harm, but if he got drunk once a fortnight it did him good?"(*loud laughter*)…Someone suggested asking the Master for his opinion.

Fig 26 The Police-Aided Scheme in action.

The free supply of beer was rejected by 17 votes to 8. These votes tended to reflect the strength or otherwise of the local temperance movement. However, it is clear that one way or another beer was available at the workhouse. On one occasion a man delivering coal was caught taking away an empty bottle, filling it with beer at a pub and then bringing it back to the inmates. He was punished by the magistrates.

Edward Jarvis – until he went bankrupt in 1915 [i] – was one of the most vociferous critics of his fellow Guardians. In 1904, he objected to the practice of "outdoor relief in kind" tickets for meat and groceries only being redeemable at one or two stores, often owned by town councillors or friends of Guardians. He thought they should be valid in any butcher's or grocer's in the town. Another time, while watching the delivery of meat at the workhouse, he noticed it was an inferior brand to that which had being paid for; a practice to which he believed Guardians tended to turn a blind eye. His proposal that contractors should be fined £10 every time they delivered lower quality goods was turned down. On another occasion he described the potatoes cooked in their jackets for the inmates as being "not fit for pigs". Jarvis became more and more critical and publicly called the Board of Guardians very corrupt, although he later withdrew a proposal to debate this as it "would damage the fair name of our town".[2] During the meetings, Jarvis often accused his colleagues of "hush and rush", keeping quiet about dubious practices and quickly going onto another subject. Another Guardian, Berry, called Jarvis "a perfect nuisance".

In 1905, ten male paupers between the ages of 17 and 22 emigrated to Canada. The scheme was organized by the Salvation Army Emigration Society. The Guardians paid the £8 fare plus £2 for new clothes. Not everyone was happy with this:

> The Brighton and District Trades' and Labour Council enter a vigorous protest against the Ratepayers' money being expended in the obsolete method of Emigration to solve the question of poverty. The Canadian Government only took those that were physically or mentally fit to open up the barren tracts of land in those parts. They were taking away the very class of people we should keep.[3]

---

[i] This automatically disqualified him from being a Guardian.

Their protests fell on deaf ears, and three years later sixty men, women and children were assisted to emigrate to Canada. Seymour Terry, the chaplain at the industrial schools, believed it was the best solution until the "cause of unemployment is discovered", and he sent the local newspapers positive letters from emigrants. They boasted of plentiful land, work and encouraged people to come. However, his faith in emigration did not go unchallenged. An old Brightonian, William Alfrey, now living in Edmonton, Canada, claimed in a letter that English workmen were not wanted because other nationalities could be hired at lower wages and that the only work they could get was laying railway tracks in the wilderness. He finished his letter by saying "don't come out if you can make a living wage".[4] Another, Samuel Judge, claimed they were all lined up like soldiers when they arrived, and that employers only took a few of them. He advised other Brightonians to stay where they were.

The British representative of the Canadian Trades Congress, Mr W.R. Trotter, wrote that "some of Terry's letters have caused considerable amusement in Canada…He has no knowledge of the cost of living in Canada".[5] It transpired that in one letter a Brightonian in Toronto had boasted about his good wages which in fact turned out to be inferior to that of a roadsweeper. Trotter accused Terry of praising less than starvation wages and that in reality emigrants crowded the entrance to soup kitchens in every city. Thousands were out of work in Canadian cities just as in English ones. Trotter concluded that emigration was no panacea for unemployment.

The Salvation Army, apart from assisting with emigration, was allowed into the workhouse on Sunday afternoons to hold meetings in the sick and able-bodied wards. Other religious or quasi religious groups were also allowed in to take services in various parts of the house. For example, Henry Humphrey from the "Christian Community" conducted gospel services on Sunday evenings. A Guardian, Donovan, claimed that sometimes religious visitors could be a source of annoyance to the inmates:

An inmate of one of the wards had told him that one of the ladies had refused to desist from her preaching when he had asked her to do so as he was not feeling very well, but had gone on to hold him up before the other inmates of the ward as an example of spiritual obstinacy and blindness! [6]

Perhaps they may have agreed with the sentiments of a poem which Norman Longmate in *The Workhouse*, called "probably the last workhouse poem to have survived":

> God bless the squire and his relations
> And keep me in my proper station.
> God made bees, the bees make honey,
> The paupers do the work
> And the Guardians get the money.
> Now I am compelled to sit and hear
> What the parson says while standing here;
> He tells us we are miserable sinners –
> He'd be the same on workhouse dinners.
> But he is fat like well-fed pork,
> He eats and drinks but does no work.
> We hear him promise that when we die
> There'll be great big helpings
> Of pie in the sky.
> Then he shuts his book
> And slings his hook.
> Amen.[7]

Although the early years of the new century were grim, the treats for the aged inmates did not diminish and were regularly publicized. In 1904 the *Evening Argus* reported on their summer outing to Lower Farm, Plumpton. After an early breakfast, at 7.30am the inmates were assembled on the front lawn and given gifts. Then, along with the schools' band, they went by train from Kemp Town to Plumpton. On arrival they were given cakes, lemonade and ginger beer. Later, they had dinner followed by afternoon sports for both men and women:

Among the items were singing, sewing, and stocking darning competitions; bag and bell competition, needle and cotton race; washing competition; fancy costume competition; facial contortion contest, and dancing competition.[8]

Individual charity was also publicized. Mrs Sykes of Carisbroke, Preston Park, and Mrs Penney of "Highcroft" Dyke Road often invited the aged inmates for outings. When one year the weather made it impossible for them to travel, Mrs Penney sent her caterers to the workhouse. A Miss Rendal and Miss Hopson of Clarendon Terrace regularly brought fruit and flowers to the aged. And, on one occasion, a Maori chief, Rangiuia,[i] and friends gave a concert to the old people in the dining hall.

In 1905, Low Warren, a journalist from the *Brighton and Hove Society* newspaper, decided to spend "Christmas Day in the Workhouse"[9]:

> Try and picture what it all means to find yourself when the stream of life is flowing to its ebb, within the walls of "The House on the Hill." To be there and have none of your kith and kin to wish you a Happy Christmas. Poor old men! Poor old women! And yet they seemed so happy…so grateful for all that was done to make their Christmas Day something like the Christmas Day many of them remembered long years ago. But there was just one thing wanting to complete the happiness of all of them: the handshake and kiss of a friend or relative.

Warren found that all the walls, pillars and balustrades had been decked with holly and evergreens and draped with union jacks. He saw "smiling faces everywhere". The visitors, "the friends of the friendless", chatted away with more than a thousand inmates in the dining hall, and a small army of waiters fed them:

> There was a whole roast pig, and endless legs and loins of pork, all grown at Warren Farm. The inmates sat at seven or eight long tables. Old ladies in spotless white caps on one side and the men on the other…Then the doors were thrown open and Father Christmas came in carrying a great brown savoury plum pudding. Their applause made the rafters ring again. One pound was given to each old man and woman. Many ate more. Some drew out their handkerchiefs and stored half away for the morrow.

Warren came away:

> feeling the real Christmas glow of "peace and goodwill to all men." But with it all there was a clutching of the heart strings at remembrance of some of the things I had seen and been told. It was all so pathetic, so-so-very like the story my old friend George R. Sims had painted for us so inimitably in his well known recitation.[ii]

---

[i] He was multi-talented. He could sing in five languages, played the harp, piano and guitar and regularly appeared at the Royal Pavilion.

[ii] "Christmas Day in the Workhouse" on pages 121–122

Newspaper reports on the "treats" could serve to give a stamp of approval to how inmates were treated. However, they could also give a distorted picture of what life was really like for workhouse inmates. The "treats" were only for the aged and the sick, and they were few and far between. There was virtually nothing for the rest except at Christmas time. The reality was that the majority of inmates were imprisoned, for reasons of poverty, in an institution from which they could leave only with permission.

*　*　*

It is in this period that we see more and more families paying maintenance charges to keep their relatives in the workhouse, usually the sick or mentally ill. Since 1883 you did not have to be a pauper to enter a workhouse infirmary and, as conditions in them improved with trained staff, more non-pauper patients were admitted. For example, in 1908, Edward Tatter contributed 7s a week towards the maintenance of his wife. Every week orders would be made against relatives to make a contribution. More often than not the citation on the order was "to be paid in 14 days or proceedings to be taken".[10] However, in cases where it was impossible to obtain the money the orders were "written off".

That year the Guardians decided to appoint a resident medical officer at the workhouse at £120 p.a. to assist Dr Ross and to train probationers in the sick and midwifery wards. When Ross had taken up his post in October 1882 there had been 800 inmates. Now there were 1500 (including Warren Farm children), 650 of whom were sick. Accommodation was built for the new officer, and eventually Dr Duckett was appointed in June 1909. Although the infirmary was increasingly becoming a hospital in its own right, a motion that it should be known as the Brighton infirmary rather than the Brighton Workhouse infirmary was decisively defeated at a Guardian's meeting, as they still considered it to be an integral part of the workhouse.

In February 1907, eighteen married inmates from the able-bodied ward petitioned the Guardians to allow them to leave for a specified period in order to find employment:

You must all be aware of the want of facilities of obtaining work while here and the extreme difficulty a man has with a family on his discharge to obtain the necessary sleeping accommodation for himself and his family even if he has the means at hand. His whole time is spent in this one endeavour, his first consideration and is often the cause of his returning the same day. Applied to the Visiting Committee but allowed no concessions to us. Our aim is to obtain the necessary funds to enable us to get a fresh start in life and so relieve the Guardians of the custody of our families.[11]

The Guardians unanimously rejected their appeal with not a single vote in favour. And they decided to introduce a rule that the "ins" and "outs" – those inmates who came and left frequently – should in future be detained for a further week after asking for their discharge. A couple of years later they relaxed their stance and between 1909 and 1912, 83 married inmates were allowed out to look for work for up to four weeks, although 86 were refused, including those with children in the schools. One man who had found work in Goldstone Villas was allowed to leave his wife and two children and go with one child until he found accommodation for them all. A 67-year-old-man was allowed out to pose as a model between ten and one twice a week. Another inmate was fitted up with a new artificial leg, but at the last moment he declined to leave and so the leg was withdrawn!

Sometimes a family man was given one month's leave of absence to find work on the proviso that once employed he would pay maintenance for his family still in the workhouse. Women with legitimate children were also allowed out on the condition that they paid for their children's upkeep. However, women with illegitimate children were treated differently. In June 1912, despite having an offer of a definite job at the Grand Hotel, Florence Bradick, was not allowed to leave with one child even though she offered to pay 4s per child per week for the other four. The reason: all her children were illegitimate.

Any inmate who absconded or failed to return from leave was, if caught, liable to hard labour in prison. Rewards were offered for their capture. In 1906, Elizabeth Dudeney received £1 reward for the apprehension and conviction of Oliver Hopkins who had deserted his wife and three children. And a Detective Wells of Eastbourne received a reward for the conviction of Richard Buss who had absconded and deserted his children. During this period, as in the 1880s and 1890s, some outdoor relief was granted to men who came to do work in the house but whose families remained outside. It usually lasted from November to March, and they received money, coal, groceries and bread.

In April 1907, there was a "general call-over" – an assessment – of the 1,210 inmates to find anyone who could survive outside with outdoor relief and to weed out those inmates chargeable to other parishes. Over three months all inmates were interviewed individually by the Guardians. They found that only 225 were able-bodied. Of these, most were "unemployable, physically or mentally deficient". The Guardians urged their own visiting committee to see "new admissions" as soon as possible in order to persuade them to take their discharge and seek their own livelihood. At this time, task work for the able-bodied and casual men was:

> The breaking of 7cwt of granite
> The pounding of 2cwt of granite
> The picking of 4lbs of unbeaten oakum
> The picking of 8lbs of beaten oakum
> Nine hours of digging and general labouring or cleaning

The work was often fixed by time. The general labouring – the distribution of wood and coal – was hard and laborious, as the site necessitated a journey of 400 yards. Another task was the cutting and bundling of firewood, usually by partially disabled paupers as a means of employment. On one occasion, when a new lawnmower was required, a Guardian suggested instead that the able-bodied men should cut the fifteen workhouse lawns with shears! His suggestion was defeated. The able-bodied women still picked oakum and did the less palatable cleaning jobs.

* * *

During 1908 and 1909 there was severe national unemployment and distress committees were set up in all areas. In August 1908 the sound of marching feet could be heard as over two hundred unemployed people, "London's Hungry Marchers", started walking from Hyde Park in London to Brighton. Their objective was to publicize the plight of the unemployed. They carried flags and collecting boxes and dragged a small van full of bread. Sometimes the marchers slept on the roadside covered with newspapers for blankets and lit candles and small fires. Their placards read "Work for the Unemployed" and "Working Men stick up for your rights". The marchers arrived in Brighton on a Saturday afternoon. Although according to reports they were orderly and respectful, they were met by the police who steered them away from the seafront and escorted them to the workhouse.

Late in the evening 132 were admitted and given a hot supper of gruel, broth and bread. Some asked for a bath and shirts which they were provided with. According to the newspapers, when they left the next day they expressed their appreciation for their treatment. The marchers split in two, some going to Worthing and some to Newhaven. That evening a seventeen-year-old marcher was found dead on a railway line near the latter. It was thought that he had dropped down from exhaustion and had been hit by a train. His only possession was a new empty purse. At the inquest it transpired that no one knew his name or anything about him.

That year there were rumours – encouraged by certain newspapers – about Brighton being too lavish in poor relief. The chairman of the visiting committee, Councillor Geere, produced a list of those discharging themselves without sufficient reason. Three had been discharged 40 to 50 times

Fig 27 Workhouse officers outside the workhouse in 1907.

during the previous year. He believed they only left for frivolous reasons such as to beg, attend football matches or go to the races. He recommended increasing the breaking of granite to 10cwt and that the amount of oakum picked be increased, too. If the inmates refused they would be put on the punishment diet of bread and water. Further refusal and they would be arrested. He argued that only able-bodied inmates performing disagreeable work should receive any tobacco. His suggestions were adopted by 18 to 1. Subsequently, six male inmates who asked for tobacco for doing painting work were turned down. The local newspapers were jubilant:

> In the Brighton Workhouse there are[sic] a class of able-bodied persons of luxurious habit. They are known as INS and OUTS and use their workhouse as a hotel. They toil neither do they spin. They only sponge. When as an IN, a thirst comes upon them, they become an OUT. They take their discharge and sponge upon old friends, or beg from those who have not had the distinction of coming under that category. Having slaked their thirst, and temporarily exhausted their source of revenue they return to the workhouse – we beg their pardon, their hotel…Some of these gentlemen need the repose of a leather chamber rather than the Workhouse.[12]

The article did not allude to one problem of the "ins" and "outs" which was that those with children were constantly withdrawing them from Warren Farm, thereby interrupting their education. Five years later, the Guardians decided to allow inmates to discharge themselves and leave their children chargeable until the Guardians asked them to be removed. They had to inform the relieving officers of their addresses. Sometimes, the opposite was a problem, i.e. parents obtaining orders of admissions for themselves and children but afterwards only sending their children to the workhouse.

In January 1909, there were 1,809 paupers receiving indoor relief, the highest ever recorded in Brighton,[13] and the town had almost four times the national average of able-bodied inmates. The Guardians set up a special committee – made up of a vicar, a wine merchant, a hotelier and the wife of a furniture dealer – to examine poor relief in the parish, particularly to able-bodied inmates. The committee concluded that they were "loafers, as a rule strong and healthy men, having no trade and a strong dislike for work".[14] Over the preceding six months out of 203 able-bodied men, only 20 had been employed on task work. The rest had done routine housework.

A year later, the master was given the discretion to increase the amount of stone to be broken to 15cwt; stone to be pounded to 4cwt; and unbeaten oakum to be picked to 6lbs. As the campaigning journalist Everard Wyvall, posing as a tramp in 1904, had found out, it was hard enough just to try and break the smallest quantities of granite, which made painful blisters on the hands break out and become bloody. Nevertheless, the *Sussex Daily News* welcomed the news:

> shirkers are to be roped off and are to be compelled to do a fair day's work and weary willie and tired tim will no longer get pork and vegetables for their Sunday dinner…Things were to become less pleasant for those gentry (loafers). They are to work harder and live less luxuriously".[15]

The *Herald* predicted "short shrift for shirkers" and "Guardians stop loafers luxuries".[16] Albert Tindall, a hotelier and Guardian, described the workhouse as "a huge temple of sloth and a palace of idleness".[17] But another Guardian, Pocock, said that he found the attitudes of his colleagues scandalous and cruel. There may have been a small minority of "ins" and "outs" who were taking advantage of the system, but the vast majority were caught in a vicious circle of unemployment and poverty. Although in the short term more of the able-bodied paupers were made to do task work, the figure gradually diminished again.

The attitude of the Guardians towards the able-bodied poor was surprising, as their own investigation in 1907 at the general "call over", as we have seen, had come to the conclusion that few of them could survive outside the workhouse. Two years later a Royal Commission on the Poor Law and the Relief of Distress concluded that workhouse inmates were stunted in growth and poorly nourished. The best "were worse than the worst of the ordinary population" and their mental and physical defects made it impossible for them to survive outside.

The Commission had, in fact, been set up 1905 and had consisted of guardians, local government officers and social reformers such as Beatrice Webb and the future leader of the Labour Party, George Lansbury.[i] For four years the Commission held 200 meetings and questioned 1,300 witnesses as

---

[i] From 1932–1935.

its special investigators were sent all over the country. Beatrice Webb admitted that they had "witnessed terrible sights":

> ...we have seen idiots who are physically offensive or mischievous, or so noisy as to create a disturbance by day and night...We have seen imbeciles annoying the sane and the sane tormenting the imbeciles. We have seen half-witted women nursing the sick, feeble-minded women in charge of the babies... We have seen expectant mothers who have come in for their confinements...working, eating and sleeping in close companionship with idiots and imbeciles of revolting habits and hideous appearance.[i]

The twenty Commissioners were so polarized in their opinions that they ended up by producing majority and minority[ii] reports. The latter, influenced by Webb, believed the Poor Law should be completely abolished and that poverty had structural as well as individual causes. In other words, the state's economic policy had a major responsibility for the causes of poverty and therefore had a duty to prevent it. The majority report, on the other hand, still clung onto the belief that poverty was the fault of the individual, and while it advocated the abolition of the Guardians – to be replaced by public assistance committees – and the end of the mixed workhouse, it wanted to preserve the Poor Law. But both reports agreed that, in terms of the staff:

> The men and women we harnessed to the service of the Workhouse invariably develop an all-embracing indifference to the suffering they cannot alleviate, the insane they cannot enliven, to the virtuous they cannot give courage, to the indolent they cannot correct, and to the vice they cannot punish.'[iii]

As it happened, no legislation followed the reports but the seeds of great social reforms could be found in the minority report. For one of Beatrice Webb's researchers was a young man called William Beveridge, whose report in 1942, during the Second World War, would produce the blueprint for the welfare state.

Over the next six years from 1908–14 the outdoor paupers in Brighton fell by 1,217 (56 per cent) and in the workhouse by 434 (24 per cent). The fall in

---

[i] From Longmate, *The Workhouse*, pages 274–5.

[ii] Considered to be a blueprint for the welfare state in embryo.

[iii] Simon Fowler, *Workhouse*, page 88.

the former was largely because of the Old Age Pension Act introduced in 1908 by the Liberal Government and enacted from January 1909. It was paid to those over 70 by a means test, and anyone in receipt of parish relief was ineligible.[i] Low Warren from the *Brighton and Hove Society*, who had already written about Christmas at the workhouse, witnessed the first pensions paid in Brighton, paid nationwide at post offices to remove the stigma of being relieved by social welfare agencies:

> Entering almost any of the local post offices on New Years Day, one might have noticed 4 or 5 old men and women waiting patiently at the counter, their tired, care-worn faces lighted up with expectation and pleasure. They were waiting for the first instalment of their old age pension. In all some 5,000 of the old folk were entitled to the allowance, but the weather was foggy and depressing and only 1,300 were drawn, many of these even being received by deputies because the rightful owners could not come themselves. Those that did come presented many a curious contrast.
>
> Some, bowed with the weight of years, with tired, patient faces; others upright and astonishingly vigorous, radiating cheerfulness. All seemed to walk with a light step as they hastened home with their precious burden, for although five shillings [ii] is not much in itself, it comes as a godsend to those who are constantly faced with the problems of making both ends meet, while to the even less fortunate it comes in the nature of a safeguard from the workhouse. Some pathetic incidents were witnessed during the day. One old fellow was so overcome with gratitude that he burst into tears, and more than one old woman left the offices striving not to show that she was crying…Another old fellow was so delighted at receiving his five shillings that he trotted out into the street and gave vent to quite a vigorous "Hurrah"… By a thoughtful provision, pensioners are not obliged to draw their money on any particular day, and they are at liberty to save up their coupons, so as to obtain a larger sum later on. Probably few however, are able to afford this.[18]

The Pension Act did not, in the short term, substantially reduce the population of the workhouse. (It was claimed mainly by women who were living in the community). Despite there being 375 inmates over 70, only ten men and six women who left in January 1911 qualified for a pension. In

---

[i] Also excluded were lunatics, ex-prisoners for ten years after their release, perpetual drunkards and those who persistently failed to work – plus you had to earn less than £21 10s a year.

[ii] 7s 6d for married couples.

reality, the fall in the number of pauper inmates just before the First World-War was a national phenomenon. In particular the winter of 1913 was mild and good for trade. It was this that reduced the numbers in Elm Grove, rather than the harsher regime or the introduction of pensions.

* * *

With legitimate and illegitimate births in the workhouse now running at over fifty a year there was urgent need of a new maternity block. Increasingly, the Local Government Board was insisting that any new buildings should be completely separate from the workhouse and infirmary, as in the future they were to have separate administration. In 1910 the daily number of inmates [i] was 1,350, of whom 500 were in the infirmary. The Guardians also decided to appoint a visiting and consultant surgeon for a period of twelve months as an experiment. Dr Ross, the medical officer, who was required to visit three hours a day and to perform minor operations, was still there.

In April 1911 James Pidgeon, the pantryman, was sentenced to one month's imprisonment for stealing butter, margarine and milk worth six shillings. In addition, he lost his pension despite nineteen years of service. At the magistrates' court – which many Guardians attended [ii] – he said he had found it hard to feed his wife and four children on his 10s a week wages and alleged "irregularities" amongst the leading officials. Pidgeon had to live on the premises and his family live outside, but as the Mendicity Society records showed, a full time wage was not necessarily enough to keep a family. His defence lawyer believed that Pidgeon was being made a scape-goat for a lax system of administration.

Ratepayers met to demand an enquiry into the "irregularities." An enquiry ensued with a Local Government Board inspector spending two weeks interviewing staff at the workhouse. It transpired that the master, Valentine Burden, had not only been extremely lax but had himself been receiving meat meant for the paupers. His wife had already resigned through ill health, and with his suspension imminent Burden resigned in

---

[i] Of the older inmates, two women were over a hundred years of age.

[ii] Jarvis contended that some Guardians had also been profiting from the workhouse stores.

May on health grounds suffering from "severe anxiety". John Nicholas, the master's clerk and Burden's daughter, Lillian, who had been the assistant matron, acted up as master and matron. After Burden left almost ten others resigned, in what was described as a general clear out of staff.

Valentine Burden had worked in the workhouse system for 34 years, his wife 37. After he resigned he was taken to court for the "misapplication of a joint of beef weighing 13 lbs." He was found guilty and fined £10 13s plus court costs of £13 8s 8d, which was many times the cost of the meat, or fourteen days imprisonment. But perhaps the worst punishment was the Guardians' refusal to grant him a pension even though he had been their master for twenty years. He may have been lucky though, a ratepayer had

Fig 28 Temporary master and matron, John Nicholas and Lillian Burden.

alleged that almost £30 of meat had been misappropriated by Burden and perhaps by some of the other officers. According to Alfred Bryett, the master's clerk who had been sacked in 1908 for stealing stamps, "all the officials of the workhouse were on the make and that was the only chance I had of making anything." [19]

Burden went into business in Hove. When he died unexpectedly at Victoria Station in 1923, the *Brighton Herald* described him as:

> …something more than a Poor Law Official…A man of expansive, genial temperament. He had a host of friends in the town and he was a figure of some prominence at many gatherings. He seemed a capable and humane Master. [20]

It went on to say that he was a man who did not take criticism easily – as his former inmates would no doubt have testified – and that in his later years at the workhouse there had been mounting criticism about his management of the stores. Earlier on in the century there had been several complaints from inmates about the rough treatment they had received from George Good, the assistant labour master. Although enquiries had found the complaints "ill founded", it was believed that Burden was turning a blind eye to mistreatment. Several inmates had also written to the Local Government Board complaining about his regime.

As with Edward Sattin's family, Burden's two sons followed the family tradition and went into Poor Law service [i] and his widow, Constance, became a Guardian of the Steyning Board. Here it is worth noting that although the majority of workhouse staff did not stay long, those that did stayed for many years. In the year of Burden's resignation, Edward Brunton, the master tailor, and Miss E. Dowdeswell and Emma Brown, charge nurses of the infirmary, resigned after 31 years, 25 years and 35 years respectively.

There were seventy-two applicants for the master/matron posts, and the Guardians appointed Wilfred and Ethel Daking at a salary of £165 and £85 respectively. They had held the same posts at the Stapleton workhouse in Bristol. The 33-year-old Daking had worked in the Poor Law service since he was seventeen. His appointment did not have unanimous approval. One Guardian accused his colleagues of making "their appointments from people who were steeped in Poor Law and reeking of bumbledom". [21] He

---

[i] Reg Burden became master at the Leeds workhouse.

also, along with Jarvis, objected to the appointment of Maria Hodgkins as assistant-matron a few months later. She too came from the Stapleton work-house, and the job had not even been advertised.

The Dakings appointment heralded a stricter regime. From August 1911 to March 1912, Wilf Daking sent 15 men to the courts for failing to perform their allotted tasks. Frank Ward, aged 28, refused to work and was sent to prison for 14 days hard labour. He returned and again refused to work and received another 21 days. Edmund Coelby and Albert Martin refused to do oakum picking and stone breaking and received 10 days' hard labour. Harry Ripley absconded and got three months hard labour. Ben Jasper and Daniel Connally created a disturbance in the dining room, used obscene language and received 10 and 14 days hard labour respectively.

That year, 52 workhouse officials petitioned the Guardians for more variation in their diet and were given permission to choose their food from the stores. New staff were often given one to two month trials but working conditions were poor. Sometimes four nurses had to share a small room and a nurses' home was badly needed. In September 1911, an ex-nursery nurse, Miss Turnbull, made a formal complaint to the Local Government Board about the state of the nursery. She said that there was a shortage of food, a prevalence of illness, insanitary conditions and general misman-agement. The Board sent down their senior medical inspector, Sir Arthur Downes, to investigate. He did find that there was a "want of method" in the feeding but concluded that there was "no foundation for the grave allegations".

Staff asked to form an indoor club for recreation during the winter months "to engender a good feeling and understanding between the officers, and to relieve as far as possible the somewhat depressing routine of their official duties." [22] When, in 1914, an advert was placed for a charge nurse at £35 p.a. plus board and lodgings, there were no applicants. On the other hand, they had 67 applications for the porter's job, which was seen as an important post.

It was the same situation at the schools, where there were no applicants for the position of cook even after it had been advertised four times. On one occasion three women were invited to be interviewed for the post of schoolmistress: all three declined the job after seeing the premises. One temporary schoolmistress left after only one day because no bedroom had been prepared for her. Another time, a schoolmistress had to teach all the girls on her own for two months because it was so difficult to find an assistant. The Guardians started to advertise their posts in the London newspapers.

Daking was soon complaining about inmates trafficking in tobacco, snuff and matches and the able-bodied men walking and smoking in the roadway in the evening. He ordered an unclimbable wrought-iron fencing fixed around their airing ward, and 9ft panels of corrugated steel paling fence to

Fig 29 Mr Gander, the porter, in his porter's lodge.

separate the able-bodied men's yard from the aged yard. Daking discovered that inmates smoked in the night in the basement which the night watchman had not tried to stop. He also found clothing, boots, matches and pipes etc. concealed in their bedding, some of which belonged to the workhouse. One Easter, to deter boys begging outside the workhouse, he had special plain clothes detectives posted there. Daking also clashed with the medical officer, Dr Ross, who had sentenced a patient to one week in bed as a punishment. Daking felt that his authority had been usurped.

The new master found bad practices everywhere. One ward attendant was in the habit of sending an inmate to make bets for him. Another time, Daking discovered new dresses and sheets being smuggled out in a dustbin and that the brandy and wine used for medicinal purposes had a tendency to disappear. Also, a lot of the food ordered had to be returned as unfit for consumption. Often the quality was inferior to the sample sent in by the contractor. One Sunday in June 1912, 360 inmates had diarrhoea after eating the meat. The following month 22 gallons of milk went off.

In this period there were so few able-bodied inmates capable of work that Daking was forced to remove men from the task work of picking oakum to cleaning and scrubbing the institution. And with the decrease in the number of the female inmates capable of work, Daking had to employ a temporary ward "scrubber" at 15s a week plus rations. One of the Guardians, Tindall, wanted to abolish pauper labour in the sick wards, but his proposition was thrown out because of the labour shortage.

In July 1913, a deputation from the Brighton Trades Council made a formal complaint about the aged inmates diet. The Guardians set up a committee to investigate but decided to have no officials from the Trades Council present when they interviewed the inmates. Two Guardians, Mrs E.J. Smith – who was to become one of the first lady magistrates in the town – and George Cooper met with eighty of them in the dining room. They asked those who had complaints to raise their hands. Twenty-six did. They asked how many of these wanted to speak to the committee. Only eleven said "yes". They were aged 66 to 80 and "were severely interrogated at length". [23]

Daking and several of his staff were interviewed. When the committee reported their findings they excluded the press from attending. They answered the allegations point by point.

That dissatisfaction is general amongst the aged inmates owing to the unsatisfactory manner in which the feeding is carried out.
There is a certain amount of dissatisfaction but not general. Few were willing to appear before the Committee.

Since the appointment of the new Master, aged inmates do not receive the allotted weight of food, and in many cases do not get sufficient to eat.
There is absolutely no foundation for this allegation.

From Xmas 1912 to June 1913 the inmates had no green food, i.e. cabbage.
As it was not possible to purchase green food at a reasonable cost both officers and inmates were deprived of this.

That the Wednesday dinner called Barley Broth(soup) is not proper food, so much so that a large number of Inmates refuse to go to the Dining Hall for it, so get no dinner on that day. We are informed that it is uneatable and that most of it is wasted. All gruel left from the previous breakfasts is used in broth, and on Thursday, June 5th, the breakfast gruel on being served was found too bad to eat and was all thrown into the pig tins.
It is disliked by a certain number of Inmates so it will be substituted.[24]

Other complaints were that the meat was overcooked and hard, and even though hungry the inmates refused to eat it; likewise with the black potatoes. The tea was "unworthy of the name, weak and unpalatable" and the aged inmates were forced to have five meals of bread and margarine in succession. The Guardians' committee said it was true that occasionally food might be overcooked, but that the tea and successive meals were within the regulations:

> In conclusion, your committee desire to record this expression of their satisfaction and appreciation of the admirable manner in which the administration of the Workhouse is being carried out under the Supervision of the Master.[25]

Although the formal complaint by the Brighton Trades Council produced few improvements it did, for the first time, show that at last an organisation was giving the inmates a voice; a voice that could no longer be completely ignored.

* * *

In May 1914, proof that official attitudes towards workhouses were changing was symbolized by a change of name. They were to be known as "Poor Law Institutions". The idea was to remove the old stigma clinging to the name. But the change made little difference to public perceptions and they continued to be known as workhouses. To illustrate this, when Dr Duckett, the resident medical officer at Elm Grove, left there were no applicants for his position, and for a week the workhouse with 439 inmates under treatment was without one until a locum arrived.

Another change was the Local Government Board's aim to try to eliminate the able-bodied inmate from workhouses and use paid workers from the outside. When workhouse labour was used for drainage work in Brighton, the Guardian, Tindall, had called it "slave labour". (The utilization of pauper labour without injury to the labour market had always been a problem for the Guardians). There were now only 38 inmates deemed fit for work out of a thousand. However, most ratepayers still believed they should be made to work for their keep. Although the number of inmates was decreasing, the poor rate continued to go up as costs were high due to increases in expenditure and the cost of staffing and the lunacy wards. By now there were 117 staff: 49 admin, 12 artisans, 4 medical/surgical, 42 nurses and ten imbecile attendants.

30 Wilfred Daking, sitting in the centre, next to his wife (in black), with his staff in 1913.

Life inside the workhouse was still harsh and regimented. Electricity had been installed in the main building and one or two wards but the rest were lit by gas. Inmates had to wear coarse uniforms and still needed permission to visit another part of the house including the sick wards and nursery. Every inmate had to get up at 5.45 in the morning, 6.45 in winter, and those who worked had to start at 7am in the summer and 8am in the winter. Everyone had to be in bed by 8pm all year round. The master gave weekly lists to the Guardians of the men and women who wanted to visit their children in the schools. Most were allowed, but occasionally they were refused. And now all able-bodied men – not just the "ins" and "outs" – once they had requested their discharge, were being detained for a further week rather than the one or two days previously required. Lastly, anyone receiving parish relief was still not allowed to vote in a general election.[i]

On August 1st there were 956 inmates in the workhouse – excluding casuals – plus 300 in the schools and 906 receiving outdoor relief. During the week ending August 8th, 533 men occupied the casual wards, 307 of them paying a fee of 4d.[ii] For the foreseeable future these casual numbers would diminish, not because of the fee extracted but because of the 'war to end all wars': the First World War.

---

[i] Universal suffrage was not fully obtained until 1928, although in 1918 all males over 21 were given it.

[ii] A new law said that they were not compelled to take a bath prior to their discharge.

Chapter Fifteen

WARREN FARM 1901–1914

The children from the schools had no Christmas treat in 1901 and due to the economic recession had no outings for two years. But after 1903 these started again with visits to the Brighton Palace Pier, the Crystal Palace and even to Buffalo Bill's Wild West Show in London. A hundred and sixty were taken to the Franco-British exhibition in London, and on another occasion J.H. Thomas MP took 25 of the older girls to the House of Commons and then onto the zoological gardens at Kew. Every year, generous local benefactors donated toys, sports equipment, magazines, sweets and soft drinks to the schools.

In 1906, the Guardians produced a list for adoption of 51 orphaned children living at the schools aged 5–16. The idea was to keep brothers and sisters together. They seemed to have had some success, for six years later their register of deserted children[1] numbered only 26. The register consisted of children who were "deserted", "orphans" or those whose "parents' mode of life was unsatisfactory". The Guardians were responsible for them until they were eighteen. The parents of the "deserted" were often in prison – sometimes for offences against their own children – were mentally ill or the mother was deemed "unsuitable". In the register there are also cases where the child's mother died shortly after given birth in the workhouse.

In 1907, a letter appeared in the local newspapers complaining of children being sent from the workhouse to the schools in a poor state. Some felt the blame laid with Dr Douglas Ross, the medical officer at the workhouse and schools since 1882. Two years later Ross was reprimanded by the Guardians and told to treat the sick children in the schools' infirmary instead of sending them to the workhouse for treatment. Although he received a separate salary for his visits to the former, his attendance was sporadic and he failed to record his medical examinations. He was expected to visit the schools twice a week for a minimum of one hour each time. Instead, his visits sometimes lasted as little as five minutes. The Guardians told Ross he must see all the children, not just the ones requested by the superintendent and matron. They became so exasperated by Ross's lack of conscientiousness that they asked the Local Government Board to send down a health inspector. In October 1909 a Dr Fuller examined 129 boys and 125 girls over the age of four:

> I found a considerable proportion of children suffering with adenoids, enlarged tonsils or some nasal problems.[2]

Fuller also discovered that many of the children were short-sighted and had squints. The worst children were those who had been there the longest. He concluded:

> I would recommend that all the children passing through the quarantine wards at the Workhouse should be examined as to requiring treatment for any of the above conditions…The Guardians are entitled to a detailed report from the Medical Officer about the health of the children in general as well as those who could be helped by surgical or medical treatment.[3]

Two months later, Ross examined all the children and claimed only seventeen were not in perfect health. The visiting committee of the Guardians disagreed, believing that at least sixty more children had tonsil or adenoid problems. Their clerk, Horace Burfield, wrote to the Local Government Board:

> The Medical Officer has entirely failed in the discharge of his duty towards the children and the Guardians. We must have periodic inspections of the children. In our opinion, he sends the children to the Workhouse only to save himself journeys to the Schools…He has on two occasions sent a four year old girl with impetigo[i] from the Sanatorium to the Workhouse and an eleven year old boy with a serious injury to his elbow.[4]

Burfield asked the Board for an enquiry into Ross's conduct. In June, 1910, a Mr Bushells, in his report concluded that:

> There is just cause for complaint in certain matters but not a sacking…It is better to send seriously ill children to the Workhouse because it has better facilities and a residential medical officer.[5]

Reluctantly, Ross agreed to see all the children monthly.

---

[i] A contagious bacterial skin infection.

As a consequence of Bushells' report, in 1911 the Guardians decided to build four receiving wards at the schools, at a cost of £7,745, which could accommodate twenty children each, and a separate hospital with 24 beds. New arrivals would be kept in quarantine for three weeks and the wards were to be run by "foster mothers" – house parents. By the end of the year there was a serious outbreak of diphtheria and the schools had to be isolated. An enquiry into the outbreak concluded that the drainage and sanitation system were in a dreadful state and needed to be repaired. According to the architect who the Guardians consulted, J.W. Hawker, it was dangerous to health and had to be done without delay.

On 10th October 1912, the new receiving homes and hospital were opened by the wife of an MP, Mrs Tyron. So now, children would not have to be quarantined at the workhouse before transfer or be treated in its infirmary. Despite this, in 1914 a Guardian, Mrs Blatch, was still complaining about a sick child being sent to the workhouse infirmary. Apart from anything else, the journey in a closed horse driven van over the rough road between the two institutions was deemed neither good for the staff or a child's health. It was alleged that the fog was so bad at times that the horse's head could disappear altogether from the sight of its rider!

Some Guardians were genuinely concerned about the children. Horace Webb, who later became an important figure in the management of the workhouse, recalled:

My first contact with Warren Farm was in the summer of 1907, when as a young and unimportant member of the late Board of Guardians staff at Princess Street, I was a visitor at a display by the children, and a very happy gathering it was. My immediate impressions were that the every day living conditions were somewhat austere and bare of personal comforts, but subsequent visits very soon convinced me that despite these shortcomings there was at all times a genuine and affectionate care for the children's welfare and happiness by all who were responsible for their well-being…

There was one very strong feature about the Warren Farm in the Guardians' day; each child was known personally to at least one member of the Visiting Committee, and so was able to realize that a "friend" from "outside" took a keen practical interest in his or her welfare by frequent visits, which interest continued when the children went out to make their own ways in the world…Whatever the shortcomings of the general conditions of the old days, they taught self-reliance and initiative.[6]

Meanwhile, the schools' educational standards were coming under fire. In 1905, an inspector, Harrison, found that the boys' schooling was "insufficient" and that their "reading is often indistinct and not very intelligible". The following year he reported that:

> As compared with the boys, the girls are decidedly backward for their ages, even in the case of those who have been for some years in the school...

A few years later, another inspector, Field, found that the boys were doing mainly handwork, gardening, singing drills, walks and music. Whilst the girls:

> ... show very little power in dealing with easy questions in Arithmetic; their compositions consist of reproductions of the ideas and words of others, and when required to write on a simple subject of their own experience, they fail; their instruction in Geography has not resulted in the comprehension of elementary principles, or in a any real knowledge of the map; nor do they observe for themselves in the study of nature.[7]

The schools were still geared towards boys and their careers in military bands. In 1901 eighteen of the boys who left had gone into the military, and that was the average number for the next twenty years. In 1909, the Guardians received a letter from. Lt Col C. de Winton of the Ist Battalion Hampshire Regiment:

> Two boys have recently been enlisted into the battalion from the Warren Farm Schools, and I feel I must write and inform you how very pleased we are with both of them. They are extremely well-behaved, bright, intelligent, and I believe God fearing lads, and my Bandmaster speaks very well of their musical education. They do great credit to the Institution from whence they come and to the Masters who have taught them. We take great care of our enlisted boys. I hope these two will have a happy and successful life in the Ist Hampshire regiment.[8]

Five years later the schools formed their own cadet corp after briefly being part of the Brighton Imperial Cadet Corp. Occasionally boys were sent to the training ship *Exmouth*, a former wooden battleship at Grays in Essex which could accommodate six hundred, where they would train at sea for a month and then be found employment either in the Royal or Merchant Navy. For some of the less able, the Guardians tried to find apprenticeships with tradesmen looking for suitable boys. For example, in 1909 a "bootmaker" from Reading, Charles Pearce, took a fifteen-year-old deaf and dumb boy from the schools as an apprentice "boot improver" for a year. The Guardians had to pay him a premium of £12. In contrast to when workhouse children from Brighton had been sent to Lancashire to work in the cotton mills in the early part of the nineteenth century, a hundred years later public perceptions had changed and there was pressure on the Guardians to ensure that children were not exploited by apprenticeships.

Girls were still mainly taught domestic work, needlework and dairy work, often making pats of butter. They were nearly always sent out to service and swelled the servant classes. Sometimes they were transferred to other institutions. In 1909 Edith May Stallard, aged ten, was given £3 for clothes and sent to the Female Orphan Asylum in Eastern Road. (Girls who were illegitimate were not allowed there.) The other option was adoption. In 1910 a Miss Ellerman asked the Guardians if her brother in South Wales could adopt a girl of six or seven. They replied that they had no girl in the school who they could recommend for adoption. The same year a Mrs May asked the Guardians to pay for a suit of clothes for her daughter because she was taking her out of the schools, but they refused.

On another occasion, the Guardians received a letter from Nellie Carter, formerly an inmate, stating that she would like her brother, Arthur, to live with her grandparents in Sheffield. The Guardians contacted the clerk of the local workhouse to find out if they were respectable. At the same time they interviewed Arthur to make sure he wanted to go. They gave him permission as long as the grandparents sent the fare. The grandparents replied that they had no money, so the Guardians paid in the end.

Child emigration was also an option the Guardians used occasionally. In 1909 they gave £15 8s 4d towards the emigration to Canada of thirteen-year-old Patrick Callaghan, organized by the Catholic Emigration Society. Three years later, a Canadian emigration officer, Hillyards, sent the Guardians a report. Callaghan was working for a farmer for four dollars a month plus board and lodging but received no schooling. Hillyards told the Guardians he was worth at least ten dollars a month and that they should inform the Catholic Emigration Society about the inadequate wages he was receiving. They did.

In 1913, the Guardians started to send boys to a "training farm" prior to their emigration to Canada. It was run by James Fegan, a religious man who had opened homes for destitute boys in London in the 1870s. "In 1911, he had had the idea, innovative and practical, of recreating a Canadian style farm in Britain…All the farming equipment was ordered from Canada so that the boys could be fully trained and experienced in its usage before going out to real Canadian farms." [9] Two years after two brothers from the schools had left Fegan's "camp", the Guardians received a report from a "Canadian Visitor" who had found them working near Ontario:

> Jim is doing alright. Already he is taking to Canadian farming like a native, and I got a very favourable report. He is getting stronger too, and says this country suits him. His employer, Mr Hughes, says he has a lovely disposition and we all like him very much…Billy's personality endears him to all. His brother, George, has already been here for nine years…They are delighted to be together.[10]

During this period, discipline at the schools was harsh. One old boy, George Rapley, later recalled walks to the nearby Happy Valley:

> We passed turnips on the way and a raw turnip was a feast to us. Sometimes we took them back to eat. When the Drill Master arrived he asked us to line up in the dayroom for an inspection. "When he came across a boy with a swollen chest, he said, "Out in front, you." When the inspection was finished there were quite a few boys lined up in front. The fun started when they were told to unbutton their waistcoats; their turnips were falling on the floorboards, thump, thump, thump. They were then told to bend over the wooden form surrounding the dayroom and the Drill Master, using a Sergeant Major's stick, gave each a good hard stroke with it. There were quite a few who stood up for tea that day. The discipline made soldiering child's play to us.[11]

The diet was still poor. The children had no butter or marge at breakfast and little meat in their main meals. One old boy later recalled that he had never tasted tea until he left. They only had water and cocoa (if they were lucky).

From the ages of eight, children could be caned for offences such as dirty habits, laziness, impertinence, disobedience, absconding and stealing. The latter two were the most common crimes. In 1913, the punishment book [12] recorded that Joseph B. received six strokes of the birch in front of all the boys for stealing money. He also received four strokes for making up the bed when the sheets were wet and four strokes for "coarse behaviour" in front of the girls.

In the summer of 1910, the superintendent, Henry Spooner, described as "a man of cheerful, hearty presence with a bluff personality" [13] had retired through ill health. As it was a joint appointment his wife had to resign as well. An old boy[14] who was there in the 1890s reminisced about the couple thirty years later, describing Spooner as "kind and fair":

> Of course, the discipline was fairly rigid; otherwise the morals of the school must have broken down entirely, for it must be remembered that the boys were drawn from all sorts of homes and an inch of latitude would have been at once mistaken for weakness. Anyone who has anything to do with boys will realize how fatal that would have been to law and order.
>
> Then there was Mrs Spooner, who was as good a helpmate as any Master could have had. Keen and shrewd in all matters appertaining to the management of the domestic side of the school, she had the motherly instinct well developed, and there are many men today who will think of her as a good second mother. I am sure the memory of Mr and Mrs Spooner will be treasured by those who came under their care.

They were replaced by Alfred and Ellen Hollingdale, who had come from the Midland Industrial School in Lichfield. Just as at the workhouse, the new management heralded a stricter regime although, concerned about the poor educational performance of the girls, Hollingdale suggested having mixed classes. This would "utilize the teaching, make better progress of the girls, improve the manner of the boys and secure a more natural demeanour of the sexes towards each other." [15] Three years later the classes started to be mixed, and in 1914 the government inspector was reporting that:

> The educational work of the institution has made unmistakeable progress in the last two years. The cheerful bearing of the children and their freedom from institutional restraints are satisfactory and noticeable of their school life.

The same year, a government inspector on domestic subjects came to the conclusion that:

> Domestic subjects were better taught in one of the cottages. In home-like surroundings, girls would get a better idea of the ordinary work of a house than is possible for them to do while carrying out allotted tasks under the supervision of the Institution's Officers.[16]

The Guardians appointed Florence Davis, a qualified teacher of domestic subjects, to do a combined course of cookery and laundry lessons in one of the cottages.

For a minority of Guardians, Warren Farm was becoming more a farm than a place of education. The attached farm regularly made a profit by selling produce to the workhouse and local schools and also sold pigs and calves. Since the turn of the century a herd of twenty-two cows had been kept at the farm. They grazed in fifty acres, necessitating the employment of a bailiff and six farmhands with cottages built for them. The cows produced 60 gallons of milk per day, a third of which was used at the schools, the rest going to the workhouse. The Guardians' visiting committee believed that it was better to keep just a few cows for the children and get most of their milk, as the workhouse did, from a farmer:

> The animals purchased have mostly been young fresh calved cows, which when no longer in milk have been fattened and killed and the beef consumed at the Workhouse. This is a systematic slaughter of young cows, and we do not feel justified in continuing it.

By drastically reducing the number of cows, the Guardians could reduce the land and the staff. One of the Guardians, Dr Whittington, was critical of the visiting committee's interest in the farm. He thought they gave more attention to the cows than to the children, who did not use the farm anyway. He also believed that the terms were too long and the holidays insufficient.

In 1914, a letter from a Guardian, Mrs E.J. Smith, to the Warren Farm committee suggested that:

> children should be taken away from the "barrack" lifestyle and boarded out in separate homes…The Schools were "out of date" and sooner or later must be changed for something more in keeping with the more humane spirit which science and experience show to be necessary in the formation of individual character.[17]

She did not want Warren Farm closed immediately, but wanted the older girls boarded out [fostered] – it was historically easier to find foster parents for girls – as they needed experience of home life. Without it, she believed, they usually drifted back to the workhouse. Nationally, on average 25 per cent of girls from industrial schools ended up in workhouses while only 15 per cent of boys did so. Mrs Smith's pronouncements only emphasized the increasing influence of female guardians. At this time, Brighton had five, who automatically formed a women's committee.

George Rayner, chairman of Brighton and District Trades and Labour Council agreed with Smith, believing that boarding-out would:

> remove them from the stamp of pauperism which is in almost every case branded upon them through the whole of their lives by the present barrack system.[18]

At a meeting, a Guardian, Albert Tindall, said that Warren Farm was only good if you wanted to join the army. Another Guardian, Langmaid-Heal, believed that the "children have no home life there and their individuality is squashed." His remark was met with cries of "rubbish". Rev H. Ross ended the discussion by saying that there was more home life at Warren Farm than at Harrow and Eton.

The schools' visiting committee felt it was not the right time to change. They pointed out that over the last four years, 76 boys had left and they had had satisfactory reports about them all, apart from two unaccounted for. And now that the children no longer had to go to the workhouse before admittance, there was far less stigma. A new law prohibiting any children being kept at the workhouse after the age of three for more than six weeks had led to the immediate transfer of five children to the schools.

Nevertheless, the stigma was still there. One old boy recalled that when the horse drawn bus driven by Charlie Baker made the journey with passengers to and from the workhouse and Warren Farm, there were "looks of gaping curiosity and sometimes disrespect as the public watched it trundle its way to Woodingdean". [19]

With an impending world-shattering disaster about to begin, any changes to the institution were shelved indefinitely.

Chapter Sixteen

THE FIRST WORLD WAR 1901–1914

On August 4th 1914, Britain declared war on Germany and the First World War had begun. Wars sometime accelerated social change or delayed it. What would happen to workhouses? For a short time life in Brighton seemed almost normal. Beethoven's "Eroica" was played twice a day by the municipal orchestra in the Old Steine, despite his German nationality. Then on Tuesday 1st September, under the blue skies and warm sunshine of a summer morning, the reality of war came to the town. Just before 9am, two trains painted a creamy white with a "Red Cross" prominent between their windows arrived at a densely packed railway station. The cry went up: "They are bringing in the wounded!"

The cry went through Brighton…and with the cry went ringing cheers. The noise of the cheering began at the Brighton Railway Station; it ran up the long hill by the railway line and burst out with fresh vigour round the Seven Dials; it sounded along the Dyke-road and culminated in a great shouting and moving scenes at the big Grammar School Hospital.[i]

It was true. The wounded were coming. Brighton was face to face for the first time with the stern ghastly reality of war. Here were men from the stricken field of Mons; men who had lain in the trenches and heard the air around shriek with the bursting shrapnel, and had felt the fierce bite of a tearing bullet. Here were men who had seen the solid wall of the charging German squadrons dashing up to break against them as the sea against the coast headlines – and fresh wave of charging men and fresh waves again, each breaking, each bringing death and destruction. Here were men who had known what it was to stab with the bayonet, who had felt the stab in return; here were men who had lain helpless and wounded among the dying and the dead while the carnage raged around them. They had fought for England; they had bled for England. And now they were coming to us, to Dr Brighton, to be healed and made to know that Brighton knew what they had done for her and were grateful. No wonder that we cheered. It was no wonder that when the thrilling cry first went out

---

[i] The grammar school was renamed "Second Eastern General Hospital". Now it is BHASVIC (Brighton, Hove and Sussex Sixth Form College).

that the people in the Dyke road district sprang from their breakfast tables to see and to cheer. They were taking part in the most moving scene that this generation has known, that God grant no other generation of Brightonians shall ever know. [1]

Each wounded man was examined by a doctor before being transferred to waiting railway vans, a police ambulance and cars offered freely by local residents. Minutes later, as they stopped in front of the grammar school hospital gates, cheers rang out and hats were raised from the waiting crowd by the railings as one by one the wounded appeared. Some walked alone, others were assisted or carried on stretchers; all had bandages on. For nearly two hours the procession continued, with vans coming and going delivering over three hundred wounded:

> Slowly there emerges a stretcher…The figure on it is covered up. You can only see his face. But the crowd with a catch in the sound still cheer. The figure on the stretcher raises an arm and waves it feebly. Magnificent. Let's cheer again. Another stretcher. Silent. The eyes are closed. It is borne in another direction. "The operating room!" whisper the onlookers fearfully. [2]

More than a week later the first victim of the war was buried. Then twenty Germans – mainly waiters and clerks living in the town who had served in the German army – were arrested and marched through the streets escorted by reservists in civvies with fixed bayonets. Notices in hotels and restaurants declared "no Germans need apply". One 83-year-old German who had deserted the German army in 1865 and had lived in Brighton ever since was told to leave the town or be sent to the workhouse. He chose the latter. And as invasion rumours spread, soldiers were placed on the two piers and little fortresses were constructed on the beaches. One immediate effect of the war was the closing of pubs at 10pm on weekdays and 9pm on Sundays. Despite the change, soldiers started to be admitted into the workhouse suffering from the effects of drink.

Soon, fifty sick inmates arrived at Elm Grove from the Newhaven workhouse as that institution made space for the expected casualties. When a recruiting officer came to the workhouse, he found only six inmates fit enough to undergo a medical examination for the services. One of them failed. Seven members of staff joined up, including the stoker, the assistant tailor, the assistant labour master,[i] the drill master and three officials from the schools and many old boys. Then, quite without a warning of any kind, a deputation from the War Office came to see the Guardians on 24th November and informed them that they needed the workhouse as a hospital for wounded Indian troops. When the Guardians queried the decision they were told it was the king's suggestion. They loyally sent a telegram to Lord Kitchener, the secretary of state for war, offering their institution.

The Guardians were now faced with the problem of removing over a thousand paupers and seventy residential staff with two months' notice. Four hundred were on sick wards, seventy on the lunatic wards and many others were old and feeble. The priority was to keep the inmates as near the town as possible. As for the casuals,[ii] it was hoped that local charitable institutions would provide them with tea, bed and breakfast. The Guardians asked the Local Government Board if they could board out the children at Warren Farm and use it for their adult inmates but were turned down. They set up a Special Committee to identify suitable properties, and faced opposition and even abuse over their intentions, but they did have the support of the War Office, which agreed to pay the cost of the removal. They also asked for applications from anyone who was willing to take into their homes relatives and friends in the workhouse – who would be given outdoor relief. It is not recorded how many inmates were eventually dispersed in this way.

Initially, the Guardians asked if they could keep part of the building for their infirmary patients, as the medical officer had said removal might harm their health. But the War Office wanted it all. So Daking and Horace Burfield, the clerk to the Guardians, contacted local estate agents and auctioneers to find out what properties were suitable and available. They visited some the same evening and found that many had not been occupied for a long time and badly needed decorating. They soon faced the

---

[i] The assistant labour master, T. Clements, was soon hit and wounded on the way to Ypres.

[ii] The Local Government Board issed an order closing the casual wards by 19th December 1914.

"not in my backyard" attitude and an unusual situation. As one estate agent said, they had willing tenants but unwilling landlords. A Special Committee member, Mellor, declared that "there was not a single occasion when they had not to fight for possession" [3] for the properties and were forced to settle on the landlord's terms. They would not have accepted those conditions in normal circumstances.

From 4th December, despite petitions from neighbours and opposition from the householders – and even from Hassocks parish council – the occupation went ahead, with the insistence from the owners that their properties had to be returned to them in the same condition. Eventually, by 23rd January 1915, all the 1053 inmates were dispersed to the following properties:

The Downs, Hassocks	59 males, 47 female imbeciles and 11 staff
The Hall, Wivelsfield	45 old men, 75 able-bodied men and 5 staff
The Lawns, Kingsway, Hove	78 aged females, 64 able-bodied females and 8 staff
Sussex House, Norfolk Terrace	193 men and 6 staff
4 &5 Eastern Terrace	84 sick females, 84 males and 21 staff
4,5,6,7 Sussex Square	280 infirm patients and 21 staff
17 Paston place (maternity)	12 patients, 8 infants and 2 staff
24 & 25 Sussex Square	Nurses home, 41 and 4 staff
73 West Street	Master's office, provisions, shoemakers, tailors: 14
8 West Street	Receiving wards, male casuals and 12 staff
70 Sussex Street	Bakehouse and 2 staff
Drill hall, Coombe road	Laundry and 25 staff
Parkside, East Drive, Queens Road,	Master's residence
5 St Georges Mews	Mortuary
Royal Alexandra Hospital	7 sick children

Accommodation for female casuals: Mercantaries Lodging House, Cavendish House. 6d – only lodgings; 1s 6d per night – lodgings , supper & breakfast
4 females and 14 males at the Sanatorium/7 children to the Steyning Union infirmary.

Most of the property owners lived outside the town. For example, Josiah Ritchie, the owner of 4 and 5 Eastern Terrace, lived in Surrey.

Even before the last inmates left, Indian troops were already being brought to the workhouse, which now became known as the Kitchener

Hospital. On 16th January 1915 it was officially handed over to the military authorities. They were getting an old, dilapidated building which had not been painted since 1911. The military complained about the state of the furniture and in particular insisted that the Guardians remove 177 old iron bedsteads. At the last minute, the Guardians tried to take their coal with them, but it was commandeered.

The new military hospital was soon awash with carpenters, glaziers, engineers and bricklayers as the old workhouse was transformed. The dining room and chapel were converted into wards and two kitchens were installed to cater for the requirements of Hindus and Muslims. An operating theatre was also put in. Hoardings and high fences were put up to prevent the public from looking in, and British sentries were stationed on the main iron gates. The various blocks were identified A, B, C etc. to make it easier for the newcomers to find their way around. There were to be 600 staff, mainly Indian, to look after 1,500-2,000[i] patients. "In every corner in the grounds where formerly old folk sat to recall days that were gone, are now to be seen convalescent Indians in hospital suits, long blue overcoats and red turbans, talking merrily in their native tongue."

It was rumoured that the property owners of the "scattered household" had made a lot of money out of the transactions and that Sussex House was receiving double the normal rent. Some Guardians complained that the Special Committee had been extravagant, that Wivelsfield was 2½ miles from anywhere and that the laundry in Coombe Road – which was dealing with 25,000 items per week and had to use two horse-driven vans – could have been outsourced. The immediate effect of the move was the great expense it incurred. The master, Daking, was bought a large car which he nicknamed "Tin Lizzie" to enable him to visit all the properties. Then each establishment had to have a nominal head and more staff employed. At the same time, visiting services like the "haircutter" had to be paid travelling expenses to the establishments out of town. Now, instead of having one kitchen, the "scattered household" had eight, and every building was heated by open fires.

Because the Special Committee had had so little time to find the properties, it soon became apparent that many were not up to scratch and money had

---

[i] Later extended to 2,250.

to be spent on new flooring, plumbing and basic decoration. Edward Jarvis, the irascible Guardian, commented that "the Special Committee seem to have taken pig styes without drainage or anything and they would leave them like palaces". By 1916 the Guardians had claimed almost £12,000 from the War Office to cover their extra expenses, including the £3,200 annual rent they were paying on the properties. Below is the agreement between the latter and the former:

Military Occupation of the Poor Law Premise

It has been agreed that the general basis of the arrangements should be that the Army Council shall make good any additional expenditure falling upon the poor rates as the result of the transfer of the premises to the military authorities, but will not pay rent to the Guardians for the use of their premises and will not pay loan charges upon them…By additional expenditure is meant the amount by which the expenditure has increased by reason of the military occupation of the premises and the items in respect to which the payments will usually be dependable are those set forth in the schedule appended to this circular.

Schedule

1. Principal items in respect to which the Army Council undertake to meet additional expenditure:
    (a) Rates, taxes and insurance.
    (b) Costs of necessary adaption, alteration, maintenance, repairs and re-instatements of the occupied premises.
    (c) Costs of renewal, repairs and additions to furniture, bedding and equipment.
    (d) Remunerations payable to Guardians, to officers, attendants and servants employed in or about the occupied premises.
    (e) Cost of fuel, lighting, washing and other necessaries.
    (f) Cost of conveyance of inmates to accommodation temporarily provided for them, and of their return on the termination of the military occupation.
    (g) The additional cost, if any, of maintaining persons who would, but for the military occupation, have been relieved in the occupied premises.
    (h) Costs of equipment and any necessary alterations and of reinstatement of premises occupied by the Guardians.
2. Consumable stores taken over by the military authorities will be valued and the cost credited to the Guardians.
3. Where the adaptions or repair of the premises involves a considerable structural improvement, a credit of an amount to be agreed between the Guardians and the military authorities; or in default of agreement to be determined by the Local Government Board, will be given to the Army Council in the final settlement of the accounts.[5]

For the inmates, the "scattered household" had both advantages and disadvantages. For example, although conditions for the "imbeciles"[i] were much better in The Downs, a well appointed hotel in Hassocks, it was more difficult for their families and relatives to visit. On the other hand, those living near the seafront received more exercise and it was easier to organize entertainment for smaller groups. In January, a "glee" party[ii] for the female inmates of The Lawns, Kingsway was organized by a Guardian, Mr Lucas, and three hundred aged inmates were taken to the Grand Theatre to see a matinee of "Cinderella". Southdown Motors supplied coaches to collect the inmates from the various institutions and donations paid for the rail fare for those coming from The Hall in Wivelsfield. The following month Daisy Norrish gave a concert to aged men at Sussex House, and Miss Clarence Rendel of Clarendon Terrace organized a drive in the summer and entertained them in her garden. She also gave the inmates of Sussex Square free use of land nearby for tennis and bowling.

In February 1915 a Guardian, Mr Mercer, wrote a letter claiming that prior to the workhouse being taken over some people had raided it and had taken food away for their supper. Furthermore, Daking had been seen giving two chickens to a staff member. When Daking asked for an investigation, Mercer withdrew his allegations. The main complaint of the year came in June when a resident who lived next door to no. 3 Sussex Square complained that a "shower of used wet toilet paper fell upon me from the upper windows of the workhouse next door".[6] An eleven-year-old boy admitted responsibility. At Wivelsfield Green, the locals accused the inmates from The Hall of trespassing on their land looking for mushrooms. But as time passed there were few if any complaints about the inmates in the "scattered houses", and they appear to have been treated kindly by their new neighbours.

Daking reported that initially the paupers welcomed the new accommodation but after a while, despite the improved living conditions, the majority wanted to go back to Elm Grove. They missed the larger community

---

[i] People with learning difficulties.

[ii] Unaccompanied singing by three or more.

and, in some cases, being closer to their families and friends. As war short-ages kicked in, Daking complained about the inferior quality of potatoes the workhouse was getting and about the quality of the frozen and skinned rabbits from Australia and the Russian eggs. He also had to substitute condensed milk for fresh milk and Bovril instead of beef tea for the sick.

With winter approaching, the Guardians received a letter from the Board of Trade warning that, because of the number of miners who had joined up, there would be a coal shortage. Meanwhile, inmates were still sometimes refusing to work and John Wilson, a casual, was given ten days hard labour.

In May 1915 William George, a pay clerk and collector for the Guardians for twenty years, was found guilty of embezzlement after admitting he had kept £25 from a family's maintenance charges he had collected in respect of their relative in the borough asylum at Haywards Heath. His lawyer maintained that "his mind became unhinged through the terrible times we live in". [7] The Guardians asked the magistrates to be as lenient with him as possible as he had already lost his job and pension.[i] Luckily for George, who had a wife and four children to keep, he received a suspended sentence. Meanwhile, when detectives decided to search staff who had just come off duty at the Kitchener Hospital, they discovered that practically everyone had stolen property on them in the form of basic food such as bread. Perhaps, because of the war and staff shortages, the culprits were fined but kept their jobs.

As outdoor relief dropped drastically,[ii] so too did the number of inmates in the first full year of the war. By September 1915, there were 831 inmates and 140 officers which included 49 nurses. However, Daking was continually facing staffing shortages[iii] as more staff joined up, making twenty-eight in all, including two female officers, and he had to use an inmate to drive the ambulance. All enlisted staff were given an allowance to bring up their army pay to their normal wages. Some were difficult to replace, such as the chief engineer and chief cook, and the Guardians asked that Daking and other senior officers be exempted as they were "individually indispensable".

---

[i] Two years later another clerk, Joseph Meredith, would get three months' hard labour for a similar offence.

[ii] It had dropped by 50 per cent in the previous five years.

[iii] Daking complained that he lost many newly qualified nurses who had obtained better positions.

With staff shortages, a 70-year-old man was appointed as temporary assistant baker and a thirty-eight year old Indian from Bombay, Daji Dakwa, was employed to drive the workhouse van. One imagines he may have been an injured soldier from the war.

As a war economy, the tobacco allowance given to elderly inmates on useful work was reduced from one ounce to three quarters. The Guardians decided to meet fortnightly instead of weekly and by the end of the year they were meeting monthly. But wartime did not prevent their annual debate about allowing beer to the aged inmates at Christmas time. A local brewery, Messrs Smithers, was offering two kilderkins[i] of light ale. The house committee by a vote of six to four, declined the offer. At the next meeting, Mr Langmaid-Heal moved that they accepted it:

> He vigorously opposed the statement [by Mr Short] which he said had been made that 75% of the inmates of the institution had been brought there through drink. He suggested that in many cases it was caused by people with thirty shillings a week having to bring up families of twelve or fifteen. "My mother," he said stoutly, "brought up twenty-one children." The statement was acknowledged with a burst of vigorous applause.[8]

Another Guardian, Mr Page, claimed it was not drink that had brought old people to the workhouse but old age and infirmity. One Guardian thought a "kilderkin" was a foreign coin! Rev E.H. Enys "was sorry to think that a public body should be flouting the example of the King", who had forbidden alcohol to be served in any of his houses during the war. Mr R.E. Montague countered:

> First you stop a certain portion of their tobacco, then you take out the sultanas from their pudding on the ground of economy, and now when you are afforded an opportunity of giving them a little extra free of cost, you say no.[9]

To shouts of rubbish, Mr George Cooper, thought that the beer might "tantalize some of those old people who like beer and that they will be very happy at their dinner without it." One Guardian argued that some of those old people who had been allowed out on Christmas day had returned drunk and been a nuisance to others. Another reminded everyone that they

---

[i] A kilderkin is eighteen gallons.

were talking about very weak ale. When it came to the vote, it was 11 voting for and 11 against. The chairman declared the motion to be not carried. However, an amendment by Mr Page that one kilderkin be accepted was passed.

1915 ended with Christmas entertainment being provided for the aged inmates lodging in Sussex Square and Eastern Terrace. To finance it, wealthy local ladies organized an appeal for small subscriptions from residents in and near these roads. The celebrations started at Sussex Square with a group of boys from St Mark's choir who went through the wards singing carols, followed by a piper from the Black Watch:

> At half-past four came tea in the large room at 6, Sussex Square, those who were unable to be present here having the meal served in their wards. The tea was a good substantial one, and consisted of bread-and-butter, potted meat sandwiches, pastries, and plenty of scones and buns and cakes. After tea, an attractive entertainment was carried out. Mr F.R. Growcott, a young actor who was injured at Ypres in "the great push", in some vivid studies of Dickens characters, gave an admirable impersonation of Scrooge from the "Christmas Carol"...In company with Miss Dorothy Forester, a well-known Brighton artiste and a very engaging young actress, he did the Quarrel Scene from "The School for Scandal".[10]

Music followed, including a "lovely little quartet" consisting of a violinist (Master Willie Robertson), a viola player (Mr Mather), a celloist (Lady Tollemache) and a pianist (Miss Rogerson). Afterwards, the inmates were given sweets, tobacco and oranges.

Similar entertainment was provided for the inmates of Eastern Terrace. Several of the Guardians were present, and a list of subscribers and their donations were published in the local press. Afterwards, Rev Hutton and his wife visited all the workhouse "houses" and sang carols. Meanwhile, back at the Kitchener Hospital the sick and wounded troops were being entertained by performers using the stage, scenery and accessories of the old workhouse. By the end of the year 6,000 Indian, 3,000 British troops and hundreds of Belgian refugees had flooded into the town.

* * *

At the beginning of the war, life at Warren Farm carried on much as before. The first Christmas passed with the usual festivities and treats, with one of the Guardians, Albert Mellor, appearing as Father Christmas. At the same time an old boy, Pte A. Tumber, was writing to another in Brighton, describing his Christmas on the Western Front in France. He explained that his unit usually spent three days in the trenches and six days out. They were always covered in mud and it was getting bitterly cold:

> We managed to get hold of a pig and, as we stay in a convent when resting, the sisters cooked the dinner for us. We had a sing song in the evening but no beer…I only wish every old Warren boy at the front had as good a time. It has not been my luck to drop across any of them yet, but I am sure the old school is well represented here and, as of old, will still bear out its good name. On land and on water you will find fruits of its good work.[11]

A few months later, another old boy, Bandsman C. Mcneil of the 4th Worcester Regiment, wrote to a former Guardian in Brighton, Mr W. D. Peskett.[i] Mcneil, serving with the Mediterranean Expeditionary Force, had landed at Gallipoli in June at the start of what would turn out to be the disastrous Dardanelles campaign. He described the bombardment of the Turkish trenches with twenty shells a minute from a hundred guns for one hour as "a splendid sight". The British had managed to capture five lines of trenches:

> I was put on stretcher-bearing duties where there are nearly all our schoolboys including Bone, Blanche (Blaber got wounded, also Welch and Burville junior), Bungary and myself.[12]

A few weeks later he wrote again to Peskett:

Well, Sir, there are not many left in our band from the School and I suppose Bone has told you how the junior Burville's skeleton was found about three weeks back. The poor boy must have strayed a lot on the third day of our action in Gallipoli, because it was on the third day that he was found to be missing. Messor has gone to Malta with appendicitis, and he wrote and said he is getting on all right. Blaber is also at Malta, wounded in the arm and Welch is now in England. He was a very plucky boy and so was Burville,[ii] because on the day we landed he volunteered to go forward to cut a passage through the barbed wire, and it was there that so many of our battalion were killed. But he

---

[i] Probably the future Brighton coroner (1925–1934).

[ii] Sidney Burville died on 28/4/1915. His name is on Brighton's war memorial. His next of kin were unknown.

came though all right until another big action on that fateful third day. I got through all right and am still kicking. I am one of the Worcester's lucky ones and hope my luck continues through the whole campaign.[13]

In January 1915 there was a major scandal. Two young female teachers resigned suddenly, followed by two more shortly afterwards. All had forfeited a month's salary because they had not given notice. According to one of the Guardians, Mr Trill, the superintendent, Hollingdale, had kissed one of them "until she became almost insensible" and had lent an "improper" book, *The Decameron* by Boccaccio, to another. It was rumoured that the book belonged to a town councillor. One Guardian, Montague, said that "the whole town of Brighton is reeking from this scandal"and wanted to know why so many female teachers had resigned in the previous year. Hollingdale admitted his conduct had been "indiscreet". He claimed he had walked over the Downs with one of the females to a "place of amusement" and then on to a restaurant with the full knowledge of his wife. He also admitted kissing another female teacher at the Christmas party. With rumours flying around, the Guardians suspended him. The main accuser, an assistant teacher, had accused him of "persistent undue attention" but she refused to appear before a committee set up to investigate the charges. Neither were the other teachers willing to come forward either personally or with a written statement, as they claimed they had been promised confidentiality. After other staff were interviewed, the committee recommended that Hollingdale resign, but the Local Government Board advised that they needed more direct evidence. In the end, the Board recommended that the suspension, which had lasted five weeks, should be removed and Hollingdale be allowed to carry on.

While he had been away, his wife had covered his duties and was granted a gratuity of five guineas. Some Guardians argued that as he had stayed at the schools and been fully paid during his suspension he should pay the gratuity, but they were outvoted. Hollingdale was a relieved man and was soon asking to be allowed to join up on the condition that if he was killed, his wife could retain her position. The Guardians refused. Hollingdale had tried to join up at the outbreak of war, and one of the Guardians had said that "he should go to the front because he was as good as thirty Germans." [14] That time, his wife had stopped him going as she thought she could not pass a winter without him.

The next inspector's report commented that the work of the schools had been badly affected by so many teachers leaving, and it took a couple of years for the institution to recover. It was obviously a difficult time. Even the chaplain, Cowen, complained about the discipline in the classroom, and in return five teachers wrote a letter complaining about him. So many staff were leaving that there were more vacancies than candidates. Staff conditions were harsh and their food was reduced as well as the children's during the first full year of the war. Even the raisins were taken out of the Christmas plum pudding. However, not everyone appeared to be making a sacrifice. Both Hollingdales had 1½ lbs of bacon each week; 6lbs of meat; 2lbs of fish, and 2lbs of poultry every fortnight. One Guardian said they had so much milk they "were bathing in it".

With more boys and girls leaving because of the great labour shortage, the numbers in the schools dropped from 250 to 180, and other Poor Law Unions were notified about the vacant accommodation. On 28th November 1915 there was a commemoration service for the old boys who had fallen in the war, and that Christmas 32 old boys, many in khaki, and girls came back to visit. By the following June the numbers at Warren Farm had dropped to 164 [i] and three of the four receiving homes were closed. With the farm failing to make a profit for the first time – "swine flu" had killed 45 of their 114 pigs – the Guardians received over a hundred children from the Dover, Eltham and Lewes Unions.[ii] Their only proviso was that their heads must be clean and shaved before admission.

Meanwhile, the Local Government Board urged the Guardians to board all the children out "for a more normal life." [iii] The schools' chaplain, Cowen, agreed and added his opinion that the children needed more "after-care." After a heated debate, the Guardians decided to defer boarding-out until after the war and to extend their tenancy on the farm land. Mrs Blatch, one of the schools' visiting committee – who would later become the first woman councillor in Brighton – resigned, claiming she had lost confidence in the committee, who treated the farm as a hobby. In response, other

---

[i] The "separation allowance" granted to soldiers' children also accounted for the decrease.

[ii] Some institutions were either closed if they were in range of the German guns, such as Dover, or were requisitioned by the War Office for military purposes.

[iii] The Boarding-Out Order of 1911 encouraged Unions to do this.

members justified their decision on the grounds that they could train some of the children in practical farming and that the farm was usually profitable. Hollingdale admitted, though, that the older children did not want to work on the land and had almost to be forced to do so.

The Guardians continued to try and place children in situations, not always with great success. Beatrice B., 15, had been placed in domestic service:

> Beatrice was a pleasant little girl of average intelligence inclined to be shy and deceitful. She was adopted for a year by a clergyman at St Albans and subsequently returned to the Schools.[15]

They also received a report that William C., an apprentice had left his employment in Stoke Newington, London, two years through his three year apprenticeship. They sent Hollingdale to investigate. He discovered that he had joined the Forces, so the Guardians took no further action and did not seek to recover his third year premium from his employer.

In the receiving home that remained open, the chaplain reported that the "children seemed most happy and beautifully fresh and clean." [16] In the infirmary he found only seven children with minor ailments. Under government advice, girls were being taught to make jam, bottle fruits and dry savoury herbs. Boys were being taught gardening and how to keep rabbits. Older boys who worked full time in the shops, farm or garden were given unsupervised leave in Brighton on Saturday afternoons.

It was still difficult to attract staff, and one vacancy for a kitchen maid was advertised four times without any applicants so it was changed to "assistant-cook" with a higher salary. And with suspicion about business exploitation in wartime high, the Guardians even accused one of the town's most famous stores, Hanningtons, of supplying "articles not equal to the samples" when they delivered some sub-standard jerseys. The Guardians told the shop that they would go elsewhere if it happened again.

* * *

There had been no ill effects from the reduced quantity of free beer for the aged at Sussex House over Christmas 1915. Male staff continued to enlist, but not always with the expected outcome. In May 1916, Mr Newell, who was the officer-in-charge at The Hall, Wivelsfield, enlisted but was told that he was unfit for general service in the army. He wanted to return to his job but the Guardians said they would make no application for his return to parochial duties. The following year he did return, but only as a bathroom attendant.

The biggest impact of the war was the effect on the number of casual paupers. Between March 1914–15 there had been 8,173 admitted, approximately 25 per day. But in the year ending March 1916, it had dropped to 2,496, approximately seven per day. The casual wards were at no. 8 West Street, and early on their bread allowance had been reduced from eight to six ounces. Later, the Local Government Board decreed that casual wards in some workhouses should be closed[i] and that they should be provided with ordinary lodgings. Nominally West Street was one of those to be closed, but Daking kept it open, arguing that you could not get the casuals to work in lodgings. He was asked by the Army Council to report fit casuals to the nearest recruiting office but there were few, if any, he could recommend. He now had hardly any inmate labour and found that probationer nurses, after their three year training, were leaving for jobs with better conditions.

Conditions in Brighton were as harsh as ever. An unknown child found in Guildford Street in May 1916 was christened "May Guildford" by Minchin, the workhouse chaplain. Sadly, she died not long after. She was only thirteen months' old. (Whereas foundlings in Oliver Twist were named alphabetically, in Brighton they were named territorially, so a child was named after the location it was found in.) And in September, Lily and Elsie S., ten and three years, were taken from Tichborne Street to the receiving home at the schools but were refused admission because of lice. Although no child over three was meant to be kept in a workhouse, they were taken to the temporary workhouse infirmary in Sussex Square.

As Christmas 1916 approached, the house committee recommended that the sick poor should not have chicken for their Christmas dinner but tripe, and that the normal extras of sweets, tobacco and butter be eliminated. In addition, only 75 per cent of the usual ingredients were to be used in the Christmas pudding. This was to be "their share in the sacrifice" for the war effort.

---

[i] Eastbourne, Hailsham and Newhaven casuals' wards were among those closed.

One of the Guardians, Mr Galliers, was outraged by the committee's recommendation:

> The purpose of the Committee was to decrease the officers' allowance not the inmates' allowances. What would a husband say to his wife if he came home to his dinner on Christmas Day and found a piece of tripe on his plate? The committee ought to have left the matter in the hands of the doctor to say what was suitable for the sick. There are many people, even in a healthy condition, who cannot eat tripe.[17]

Mrs Blatch moved an amendment that six dozen fowls should be ordered for the sick poor. But Councillor Mellor thought they ought to make some sacrifice, and that "boiled mutton with onion sauce would make a very good meal". The amendment was narrowly defeated. The tobacco for the aged poor was also reduced and sweets for the women cut out. After a heated debate, the 36 gallons of light ale donated by Smithers and Sons was accepted.

A revised dietary for the inmates – recommended by the Local Government Board in 1917 – reduced the consumption of bread, meat, potatoes and sugar. And whenever possible, cocoa and coffee were to replace tea. Daking complained it was hard, because of the shortages, to keep to the dietaries but was given permission by the Guardians to buy the supplies where he could instead of using the tendering process. Soon he was buying supplies at a much cheaper rate. The two old workhouses horses, Bob and Dolly, who pulled the ambulances were by now exhausted from visiting the scattered institution. The former died in June on a journey with a nurse and patient in Old Shoreham Rd, from Eastern Terrace to the Steyning Poor Law institution. He had made 192 journeys in three months. A little later, Dolly was sent out to pasture at the schools' farm. They were replaced by three motorized vans.

At the half-yearly call-over, there were only 685 inmates in the "houses" and Daking believed that at least some of the fall could be attributed to the able-bodied "ins" and "outs" having to go to Wivelsfield for relief:

> That in my opinion the walk of 14 miles to the "Hall" has done more to deter the workshy from seeking admission than the task of breaking 10cwt stones in a cell contiguous to his native haunts. Don't let it be known that there is accommodation in town.

Another advantage was the garden at The Hall. It produced £60 profit every year and had good facilities for the chopping and bundling of firewood. With the drop in numbers, some Guardians wanted to give up part of the temporary accommodation to reduce the expense. They were advised by the Local Government Board not to do so.

By the summer of 1917 Brighton was a very different place to when the first injured had arrived in September 1914. Now the early morning trains laden with the wounded regularly shuddered into the town, and the streets were crowded by hundreds of seriously maimed and convalescent men:

> All through the summer blinded soldiers, others who have been deprived of limbs, and those convalescent from wounds or illness spent the chief part of their existence on the piers and the marine frontage, and always with residents and visitors vying with each other in the effort to give to that convalescence all the sustaining help that can come from friendly communion.[18]

After almost three years of the national and local press informing the public that the Germans were on the brink of defeat, the ever growing daily lists of casualties told a different story. The normality of war had crept in:

> War work was now going on in countless directions, flag days, and exhortations to stern endurance and patriotic endeavour, the presence of khaki clad soldiers from all parts of the empire; darkened streets at night; the humming and roaring of planes above – these conditions of war have become commonplace.[19]

Far-stretching queues could be seen daily outside greengrocers. Fewer cars were on the road because of the petrol shortage. Land for the cultivation of vegetables and for allotments was set aside in some of the Brighton and Hove parks, and on some of the Downs estates owned by the town. That summer there were record crowds in Brighton as, apart from holiday makers, the air raids on London had sent thousands flocking to the town as a place of refuge. The pressure on accommodation and food supplies was immense and food supplies were drained. To economize on coal, shops were closing earlier in the winter. However, the first race meeting since August 1914 took place in September to record crowds.

At the same time there was a serious diphtheria epidemic at the industrial schools, and for a while the education classes were suspended. Instead, more manual work was done as the drill ground was dug up to grow food.

Ten boys and twelve girls were regularly employed on the farm, in the gardens and at the dairy. They were given an extra light meal in the evening as a reward. There were regular sales of beef, pork, milk, eggs, butter, vegetables and fruit, and the farm was making an annual profit of £400. There were now 273 children, including 116 from other Unions: Dover, Eltham, Horsham, Lewes and Newhaven. The Eltham Guardians, who had 60 children, sent a complimentary letter to the Guardians saying they were very happy with the children's placements.

The schools granted the bandmaster, Mr L, Wallace, leave to enlist in the army. He was over sixty. And superintendent Hollingdale received a letter from an old boy, a commissioned officer, Lt V. Cherryman, "wishing you and the old school over the Downs the best of luck". [20] The year ended with Rev Cowen resigning as chaplain and being replaced by Rev Morgan. Like Henry Dodwell over forty years earlier, Cowen had fallen out with the Guardians over the times of the religious services. Before he left he made a recommendation:

> I very strongly suggest that considerable benefit would result to the children throughout the Schools if they had a systematic course in "elocution". It would enormously improve their English and articulation. It would give them more confidence in answering and speaking.[21]

At about the same time, George Chance arrived as the resident senior master. He later recalled his first impressions:

> Upon taking up my appointment I was disappointed with the schoolrooms, but the place had a ring of prosperity about it, and the classrooms, though overcrowded with well fed, healthy children, were clean. I thought the girls' hair was subject to lavish attention… Scarlet fever had broken out in the institution and with the closing of school by the Medical Officer we spent much time in the open air.[22]

Chance remembered the overcrowding caused by the influx of evacuated children from Dover and Folkestone – which were in range of the German guns – and the many scares caused by the Zeppelin raids. He believed that "generally, the children were well, and neatly clad, while their physical welfare was well looked after".

* * *

As Brighton entered the last year of the war it was reported that, in January, bootless children could be seen heading for the slums behind Grand Parade. And a £10 reward was offered to anyone who could give information about an abandoned six-week-old baby girl in Kings Road. There was a serious lack of coal in the town, and even the hotels had rationing. In the "scattered houses" the inmates were now receiving tinned meat instead of fresh.

As prices for basic commodities had doubled since the beginning of the war, the salaries of Daking and his wife went up from £190 to £220 and from £100 to £120 per annum respectively, and even nurses' salaries were increased as it became difficult to recruit them. Staff complained about the shortage of food and regularly worked twelve-hour shifts. With the number of inmates falling, the Guardians started to take inmates from other local areas whose workhouses were being used as hospitals. They accepted 40 sick and infirm paupers from the East Preston workhouse (it was being taken over by the army to use as a neurological centre), and another 110 ordinary, aged and able-bodied paupers plus ten children under the age of three.

As the war lingered on there was a possibility that the master, Daking, might have to join up. The medical officer, Dr Ross, who had already lost two sons, successfully requested that another son, Capt Douglas Ross, who had just returned from Italy, could assist him in visiting the various establishments. Even in the last week of the war – the first week of November 1918 – over 500 casualties arrived in Brighton. And then, as quietly as it had begun, the First World War was over:

THE GREAT DELIVERANCE

It came on Monday – that dawning for which aching eyes had been straining through the watches of a night that had seemed as if it would never end. It came on Monday – our Great Deliverance – a deliverance from the carnage, the agony, the deadly peril that had so heavily afflicted us through the darkness of four long years. And, when it came, the Deliverance fell upon us with a swiftness and a splendour that left senses bewildered…the Day of Deliverance had during the final hours been awaited with a tensely eager, yet calm and restrained confidence, born of the unmistakable portents of the time…The signing of the Armistice did not take place until 5 o'clock on the Monday morning, and the news reached Brighton soon after 10 o'clock…At first one was overwhelmed with the solemnity of the situation, very much as one had been overwhelmed by the proclamations on that far away day of August 4, 1914. The tremendous feeling of relief that came to tensely strung feelings moved hundreds to tears even although they were tears of gladness…Men who had sons at the battle front gripped one another's hands, with hearts too full for words, words that were stifled by the sob in the throat.[23]

It was the children, waiting with their flags since the Saturday, who ran out onto the streets first. Then flags appeared on public buildings, hotels, hospitals, roadways, the Piers, the Aquarium, on cars, trams, and on every street and road:

In the humbler quarters of the town, bands of boys and girls, headed by a big flag, supplemented by others of smaller dimensions, paraded the streets to the cheery accompaniment of musical combs, paper trumpets, and sturdy song… With exhilarating chorus and ringing cheers, groups of soldiers made their way along the marine front or through the main thoroughfares with an exuberance of spirits that met with smiling approval on every hand. The ringing chorus of "Sussex by the Sea" poured out sturdily to the rhythmic tramping of many feet filled North street.[24]

Outside the Royal Pavilion, the limbless patients sat outside smoking, their wheelchairs all in a line to join the celebrations. Orchestras played at the two piers. All the national anthems of the Allies were sung. In West Street there was a lot of dancing where "the girls wore the soldiers caps; the soldiers put on the girls' hats" as the police shepherded the cars and buses through the crowds. Symbolically, there now was light everywhere after the gloom people had been accustomed to. However, "thousands who came out were in mourning. There was no shutting the eyes to the shadow of personal bereavement which will not soon pass away." [25]

As a consequence of the war, deaths in Brighton exceeded births for the first time in 1918. And with the casualties at an end there were now new enemies, those of the raging epidemic of influenza and pneumonia. One of the victims was to be Emma Sattin, the former matron of the workhouse and wife of Edward who had died from the same illness.

We do not know how many ex-inmates from workhouses died in the conflict. We only know that John Crown, admitted to Elm Grove as an abandoned baby in August 1898 and who had left in 1915, was one of them.

As he had no known relative and no will, the Guardians claimed his money as they had maintained him for 17 years.

We know more about the casualties who came from industrial schools. Six had won Victoria Crosses, but over 3,500 had been killed and 9,000 wounded.[i] Seventy serving staff had also been killed. After the war, in the Warren Farm chapel, there were 110 names on a memorial roll of honour for those who had fallen during 1914–18. However, it did not include old boys like Frank Dagnolle who died of his wounds two years later. One old boy, Sgt E.G. Mattick, won the French Croix de Guerre and returned to the schools for its presentation. And a Capt J.W. Walter of the Royal Sussex Regiment, on its demobilization, presented a silver-plated cup on an ebonized stand for the "excellent services rendered by so many old boys of the Warren Farm Schools during the Great War".[26] He also sent £1 5s for prizes and suggested the cup could be awarded for sport. Altogether, 53 Poor Law officials from Brighton served in the war, including nine from the schools. Miraculously, there had been only one known fatality: George Stotton, a young farmhand and carter at Warren Farm. When it was over, all but five of the staff decided to return to their old jobs.

Just before the inmates of the Elm Grove workhouse had been dispersed, one of the Guardians, Langmead-Heal, had predicted that they would never return after the war but would be boarded-out. At the industrial schools too, several of the Guardians believed the children needed a taste of home life which was impossible in an institution. Would the Guardians now agree to the principle of boarding-out? There was also another major change in the pipeline. A report by the Royal Commission of 1909 had recommended the abolition of the "Guardians of the Poor" and the transfer of their powers and duties to municipal councils. Although most of the Brighton Guardians were against the change, they admitted that Poor Law officials were held in contempt everywhere. With the first parliamentary elections since the war coming up, when it was suggested that Guardians should urge the Brighton candidates to extol their value, no candidate would, as they knew that to do so would lose them hundreds of votes.

---

[i] *National Archives MH 102/935.*

At the end of the war the future for the Elm Grove workhouse and Warren Farm was uncertain. In the summer of 1914, who could ever have dreamed that within months the vast dining hall and the chapel in the workhouse would be full of beds occupied by wounded Indian soldiers and that the words "Kitchener Hospital for Wounded Indians" would be written in Hindustani under a Red Cross over its old iron gates?

Fig 31.

Chapter Seventeen

ELM GROVE 1919–1930

Two months after the armistice was signed, Brighton was in the grip of the great post-war influenza epidemic, with as many as 78 people dying in one week and schools, including Warren Farm, closing temporarily. And although the war was over, there was still the sound of tramping feet. In January 1919, 7,000 disaffected soldiers marched from a camp at Shoreham to the town hall in Brighton to complain about the slow pace of their demobilization.[i] They were met by the mayor. They told him they were "fed up" wasting their time washing up and cleaning and having to eat biscuits – so hard they broke their teeth – instead of bread. The mayor assured them he would raise their grievances with the Home Office and subsequently the home secretary, Winston Churchill, sent an official to investigate.

In the immediate aftermath of the war, with hundreds of thousands of service men returning home, with food shortages, housing shortages, spiralling inflation and unemployment – so reminiscent of the post-Napoleonic period – it did not need a crystal ball to predict that Poor Law relief resources would be stretched to the limit. Post-war conditions had swallowed up all the advantages of old age pensions which had initially reduced expenditure. However, there were important changes afoot. In 1919, the Local Government Board was replaced by the Ministry of Health, a sign of a more compassionate attitude towards paupers. There was also now the increasing influence of female Guardians, reflecting the progress of the women's suffrage movement – ten out of 33 members in Brighton – and working class members from the up and coming Labour Party. In the past, Guardian meetings had not lacked passion but now they became increasingly fractious affairs.

On 19 July 1919, the inmates in the "scattered household" were given a special diet and extras for the Celebration of Peace Day: 180 aged inmates went on a charabanc[ii] drive and those at Wivelsfield were treated to a tea in

---

[i] Some of the workhouse staff were not demobilized until the autumn of 1919.

[ii] Early form of motor coach.

the dining hall provided by the locals. At Warren Farm there was a bonfire and fireworks followed by a week off and a trip to the Orchards Tea Gardens in Hassocks. Even paupers on outdoor relief received 2s 6d per adult and 1s per child extra. When nine staff also applied for overtime for the celebrations and were granted it, one Guardian, Galliers, commented that "if our employees cough or sneeze they will soon want us to pay for it!" [1] Because of wartime inflation and the payment of war bonuses, expenses had gone up enormously. When the office boy at Elm Grove left for the war he had been on five shillings a week. When he returned the rate was fifteen shillings a week. So, to economize, in December 1919 the Guardians provided none of the usual Christmas "extras" such as tobacco, for their inmates and those on outdoor relief. Curiously though, other authorities did provide "extras" for their non-resident paupers living in Brighton.

With the country still shaken by the devastation of war, there was a surge in warrants for arrests, as parents willfully or out of neglect left their families chargeable to the parish. And money orders were even issued against people who were receiving outdoor relief. For example, a father of sixteen children, with seven of them in the workhouse and an invalid wife at home, was ordered to pay 30s a week for their maintenance. There was also a problem of husbands not returning from overseas after the war. They were not extraditable. On top of that there were the "terrible conditions of the housing shortage, brought about partly by the large number of empty properties in Brighton". [2] The Guardians wanted the council to stop the "scandalous speculation in house properties which was causing so much privation for the poorer classes".

Looking back, it is hard to imagine the extent of the poverty in the post-First World War period which is still, for a very few, in living memory. It was a time when it was not unusual for babies to be abandoned simply because the parents did not have enough money to feed them. One three-month-old baby, John [not his real name], was left by his parents on the doorstep of a woman known to look after children on a farm in a village near Brighton. It was on a dark and cold winter's night. Almost with a sixth sense, the woman had an urge to go and open the door and found the baby in a bundle. She was relieved because, as she told him years later, foxes frequented that area and would surely have eaten him if he had been left any longer. [i]

Edie Burt,[ii] aged 94, remembers the degradation and stigma of being "on the parish" – receiving outdoor relief. Her family was very poor but managed usually to get by. But, on one occasion, her father, who had returned from the war and was out of work, was forced to go and ask for outdoor relief. It was a humiliating experience having to stand in what looked like a police dock and be cross-examined by the Guardians. When he returned home he said "I've never been so embarrassed in my life" and swore that he would never go there again. Once you accepted parish relief, as Edie's mother's neighbour undiplomatically told her, "you are a pauper". Edie, who lived in a turning off Elm Grove, also saw families walking up the steep road heading for the workhouse. They could not afford the tram fare. She remembers that their clothes were "horrible" and that the children looked "so hungry they could hardly walk". She also remembers little children from the workhouse, dressed in blue capes, being taken for donkey cart rides on Sundays and wishing she could have joined them.

As winter approached, local charities were inundated with requests for boots. In December 1919, with roughly 3,000 people registered as unemployed at the labour exchange, a deputation led by Will Evans – a well known railway worker and ex-councillor – attended a Guardians' meeting. He claimed that many of the "scattered households" needed repairs, cleaning and decorating. Evans suggested it would be worthwhile even if only twenty or fifty men and women could be employed. He appealed to the "Guardians as the last resource of the poor to help focus public opinion on the question of unemployment".[3] Government doles and labour exchanges were "blind alleys", and the only remedy was the "quite simple and ridiculous one of work". Some Guardians applauded his speech but legally they could not provide work for the unemployed: although they did employ eleven men at Warren Farm, they could not pay them more than 75 per cent of the wages of council employees. Instead, they agreed to

---

[i] "John" is 91 at the time of writing (March 2011).

[ii] Interview with the author on 9/3/2011.

be more flexible about forcing able-bodied men into the workhouse in order to get relief. They also agreed to provide extras to the inmates of tobacco, bread and cheese for work done.

Evans also suggested that the external painting of the workhouse could be done before the handover. But the Guardians had already put the contract out to tender, and an estimate of £2,000 to renovate and re-instate the workhouse had been accepted. The Guardians themselves urged Brighton Council to give more work to the unemployed as it was better than relief. In 1920 they considered "depauperising" those aged inmates who were employed on work of a useful nature in the households by paying them. However, "in view of the fact that as paid servants it would be necessary to provide separate accommodation, it was impracticable and [we will] defer it until after the re-occupation".[4]

Increasingly, the unemployed were becoming more vocal and sometimes voiced their anger during Guardian meetings. In September, one unemployed man lambasted a Guardian, Rev B.H. Pemberton:

> It is the parsons of this country who are starving us… We are fighting for the lives of our women folk, and the parsons of this country are driving women out to prostitution (*hear, hear!*). We want the Board to pass adequate means of living for the unemployed of the town.[5]

The men demanded the Guardians save them from starvation and warned it would cost more if they sent them to the workhouse. In their turn, most of the Guardians blamed the government and believed the problem of unemployment should be dealt with nationally rather than locally.

Just after the war, Daking and his wife were given huge wage increases due to the extra demands of running the scattered household: from £220 to £350, and from £120 to £262 respectively. Two years later, due to financial pressure, their wages were substantially reduced after going to arbitration, by £50 and £62 in turn, leaving Daking "feeling a bit sore". However, a couple of years later the money was restored. Resident staff also had their monetary ration allowance reduced. No wonder their morale was described as very low. In 1920, one of them wrote to the *Brighton Herald* anonymously, complaining about the seven days a week they had to work, their restrictive liberty and the mentally depressing atmosphere. The letter ended by saying that the staff were no longer willing to put up with these conditions.

In 1918, a Poor Law Workers [i] trade union had been started and by now they had 15,000 members.

While the inmates of Elm Grove were dispersed, complaints were still publicized. Elizabeth New, an inmate in Eastern Terrace, was put to work cooking two weeks after having a baby. Within three days she had a haemorrhage and was still in bed three weeks later. The Guardians decided that no one should have to work for at least four weeks after giving birth. Another complaint was about the treatment of a young woman, Lillian D., who was admitted into Sussex Square. The medical officer, Dr Ross, recorded that:

> This patient was admitted from the town hall as a suspected VD case. Her clothes were in a filthy condition and her body and head verminous. The police informed me she was found wandering abroad in the open, sleeping out on the Madeira Road and in boats on the beach, an immoral girl and an associate of bad companions and was classified by me accordingly. [6]

Lillian wanted to go into the ordinary wards but was kept with the aged inmates. Another inmate, George Good, 58, who claimed he was ill, refused to work and threatened violence when Dr Ross classed him as able-bodied. Good was sent to the magistrates and given hard labour. On another occasion, George Aitchison, the editor of the *Brighton Herald*, reported that an inmate of the infirmary had told him bed-making and the washing of patients started at 3am and sometimes earlier. William Smith, a plasterer, Labour supporter and newly elected Guardian, claimed he had heard patients were often roused at midnight so they could be washed for the following day. Dr Ross replied that it should not have happened before 5am.

Meanwhile, the inmates were frequently asking the Guardians when they would get them back to Elm Grove or "Maison d'Elm Grove" as one newspaper called it! A less respectful term was used by local people: "The Lump on the Hill" or just simply "The Lump". In July 1920 the War Office finally evacuated the premises, but the full re-occupation was to take over a year. The first to return were the inmates of The Hall at Wivelsfield in

---

[i] Later changed to the Poor Law Officers' Union.

October. By Christmas day 1920, there were 725 in the scattered workhouse and 259 children at Warren Farm. The former only showed a slight increase on the end of war figures.[i] But those receiving outdoor relief had gone up from 671 to 1546.[ii] By March 1921 there were 2,732. Disgruntled, often disabled on inadequate pensions, there was a vast army of returning soldiers with no work and little or no hope for the future. Many were forced to live the life of paupers. What dole money they received was impossible to live on, and not all of them received a pension.

One such returning soldier was an ex-officer who had led the men over the top during the war and had been captured. When it had ended he had walked 230 miles from a prisoner of war camp to the nearest neutral territory. Back in England, still suffering from being gassed, he had found it difficult to get a job. Eventually he arrived in Brighton in January 1921 after "tramping" from Ripon, soaked through with the rain, hungry and tired. He went to see a relieving officer. Despite his good war record he was sent straight to the workhouse.

In the summer of 1921 the re-occupation of Elm Grove started in earnest. In May, 93 women and children were removed from The Lawns in Kinsgway, Hove. Next, the occupants from The Downs in Hassocks returned, and in June two hundred patients from Sussex Square. Most of the blocks they came back to had been renovated and repaired, but the facilities were still sub-standard. That summer Daking had to have 81lbs of meat destroyed because of the weather and lack of storage. With the re-opening of the casual wards in September 1921, all the temporary premises had been vacated and there were now 703 inmates and 157 staff at Elm Grove. The Guardians eventually received £95,322 from the Army Council for the expenses of the evacuation and their return. The ratepayers had not had to pay a penny towards the cost.

The return meant staff lay offs. For example, Eli Newell, the officer-in-charge at Wivelsfield, lost his job, as did his sister, Minnie, who had worked as a temporary cook. And those who had worked at the premises outside of Brighton were warned they would be required to move to the town in

---

[i] In the week before the armistice there had been 694 in the scattered workhouse and 189 in the schools.

[ii] Outdoor relief was costing £17,000 a year. (*Brighton Gazette* 4/9/1920.)

order to start the early morning shifts on time. The Guardians resolved that preference would be given to ex-service personnel for future vacancies. Mr Bate the visiting surgeon was reappointed and Dr Fenwick was appointed the resident medical officer.

Once returned, Daking was complaining that there were so few able-bodied females left that he needed to employ staff to help run the laundry. And inmates such as Thomas Norman, the "foul washer", started to agitate to be paid for their services. Another inmate, John Brooker, who drove the workhouse horse-driven van, had a narrow escape when he and his vehicle were blown over in a terrible gale on the top of Race Hill. One month, gales caused the loss of 2,300 roof slates and Daking had to order a 60ft ladder in order to inspect the damage.

As the first Christmas back at the old house approached, one of the paid female ward helpers tried to smuggle out 1½ lbs of cooked bacon and she was reprimanded by Daking. The ever alert Daking also caught a contractor, F. Saunders, delivering only 18cwt 10lbs of coal instead of the 23cwt it said on the invoice. Daking had a weighbridge installed soon after. On another occasion, after a visit from a food inspector, 112 tins of food delivered from the Hockley Hotel had to be destroyed because they had "gone off".

The 1921 Christmas extras for the inmates consisted of one apple and one orange each inmate and some toys for the nursery, sick and "feeble-minded" young children. There was little entertainment. More ominously, the Guardians decided to cut the maximum scale of outdoor relief for adults from 10s to 8s a week. In the New Year they planned to re-introduce "test work", which required outdoor claimants to work for their relief money and vouchers. They had originally introduced it in the 1880s. By May 1922 there were 3,893 on outdoor relief, costing £1,114 a week, and "test work" had begun for 160 of the men. It consisted of clearing away leaves, road sweeping and cleaning beaches. That summer there was so little money in the "Treat Fund", that the treat for the aged inmates' was held within the grounds instead of an outing.

For Christmas 1922, the residents of Elm Grove donated two large Christmas cakes to the workhouse. There was the usual Guardians' debate about accepting free beer from Smithers brewery. One lady member, Miss Turner, said that the young there might get a taste, or a renewed taste, for beer.[i] Other Guardians said it was the drink that had brought the inmates there in the first place. The Labour members William Smith and Ernest Burden – a railway shop employee representing Regency ward, who had been nominated unopposed – stoutly condemned the "slur" upon the inmates. Smith said that his grandmother had lived until she was 93, and during her last twenty-five years had never tasted tea or coffee but had drunk only beer. Burden added that he hoped that at Christmas they took the pips out the oranges because they caused appendicitis! Fortunately for the inmates, they won the argument and beer was permitted. But Daking and his workhouse staff had more than beer to worry about. It was rumoured that four hundred "hunger marchers" were heading their way in the New Year, and these were more assertive men than those who had come in 1908.

* * *

The Guardians had already received a memo from Whitehall saying it was within their discretion to "discharge the hunger marchers at the earliest moment without any detention".[7] On Sunday afternoon on 28th January 1923, 162 of them arrived in Brighton, led by Tom Dingley of Coventry, "commander-in-chief of the Southern Army". Daking was away at the time, but the chief constable of Brighton, Charles Griffin, was there with every available policeman. The marchers were met by the Guardian, William Smith, and local unemployed leaders. They abandoned a plan to hold a meeting at the seafront and headed straight for the workhouse. At the front of the procession was the motto "Workers of all lands unite", printed on a piece of cardboard, followed by a mouth organ band which played "Sussex by the Sea":

> Behind came the hunger marchers wearing red ribbons in caps and coats, with bundles on their backs and carrying stout sticks. Many of them were mere boys, and they looked, as was not surprising, tired and dusty. Some were passably

---

[i] During another meeting she had also objected to Warren Farm children being able to read books – recommended by Hollingdale and the schools' committee – such as *The Bridge of Kisses* and *Married or Single*. One Guardian, looking in the direction of Miss Turner and another female Guardian, had said "Some of you have forgotten what kisses are!"

dressed; others were in a state of dilapidation. The local unemployed organization, with their band, swelled the ranks of the visitors, and banners carried at intervals told the places the hunger marchers had come from – Paisley, Dumbarton, Great Yarmouth, Newcastle-on-Tyne and Poplar. "Give us this day our daily bread" was the motto on one banner and "1914 Mons Star, 1922 Mond's Starvation" on another. Big crowds accompanied the procession, and all the sidestreets on the way up Elm Grove added rivulets of humanity to the main stream, which filled entire breadth of the street and was about 100 yards or so in length. The mouth organ band played energetically – and extremely effectively – most of the way up the long hill with the ominous boom of a big drum as accompanimemt. Collectors were busy with boxes and few refused to give, while copies of a Labour newspaper were freely sold…the police shepherded the procession which was perfectly orderly. [8]

When the marchers arrived at the workhouse, or the "Lloyd George Hotel" [i] as some sarcastically called it, they found the gates were locked. With 50 policemen inside and all available male staff on duty, the marchers asked for hot food which they had been provided with at the Horsham and Cuckfield workhouses. Instead, they were offered bread, cheese, milk and coffee. Their leader, Dingley, thought this was "an insult to our ex-service comrades who had sacrificed themselves for liberty". He sent a deputation to see the Guardians. Whilst they were inside the meeting, a local Labour man, Frank Ingham,[ii] addressed the huge crowd outside advising them to march to the seafront and invade the Hotel Metropole and say to the people there: "We saved you during the war now you pay back something and save us." The marchers rejected his advice and started to sing the "Red Flag" and another song:

> Who won the war?
> Who won the war?
> The next time the enemy's at the door
> Take him in and shake his hand
> Give him a dinner and treat him grand
> What's the use of fighting anymore?

---

[i] Lloyd George, prime minster between 1916 and 1922, had promised "a land fit for heroes".

[ii] He was known as Fearless Frank. Later on he became a Labour councillor, and after he died Ingham Drive in Coldean was named after him.

The Guardians refused to provide hot food, and when the marchers were taken to six large rooms in the casual wards, according to reports, "pandemonium broke out". They started to bang the floor with their heavy sticks and refused to eat the food. According to one Guardian, Marten, these men were "screaming, knocking the doors, frightening the inmates" and "the poor old people were trembling". The marchers went into town, where they were fed at the local Labour HQ and returned to the workhouse at 11pm.

Next morning the Guardians had an emergency meeting to discuss whether hot meals should be granted. Although it was meant to be secret, policemen lined the corridors of the parochial offices in Princes Street just in case of trouble. In a stormy affair, one Guardian claimed the men had plenty of money on them to get board and lodging. Another said if he had enough money he would "spend £20 on these men to get rid of them...We have plenty of our own unemployed in the town, and I am sorry they came!" William Smith said this was no way to treat war heroes and that 140 of the men had fought in France. By 22 votes to 16, a relatively close vote, the Guardians upheld their decision not to give them hot food. Meanwhile, according to the *Brighton Herald*, the marchers were in the town, taking "direct action":

> They stripped themselves of their badges, red ties, and other regalia by which they were distinguishable, and then split up into small batches. They entered eating houses and coffee shops and ordered meals of eggs and bacon. This food they ate, and when asked to pay, informed the shop-keepers that they had better send their bills to the Guardians: "They will pay!" At one shop they devoured eleven rashers of bacon and twenty-two eggs. At one place, in an eating-house in George Street, a party of police arrived in time to find eight or ten hunger marchers refusing to pay for a meal. As soon as the police were sighted, the men bolted in all directions. Unfortunately for him, a Brighton sympathizer was foolish enough to dispute matters with the police. He was quickly clapped into custody and marched off to the police station for obstructing and assaulting the police...Soon afterwards eight or ten handcuffed men, surrounded by police, were seen marching along East Street.[9]

Later, several more marchers were arrested but all were subsequently released.

> On the way to the station they were followed by a large crowd of other hunger-marchers and sympathizers, and the crowd became so dense in East street that all the force who were there in the police station were called out. The crowd was driven into Castle square and eventually dispersed.[10]

In the afternoon there were two large meetings where revolutionary speeches were made. At the Clock Tower, one man declared:

Those of you who didn't know we were coming know we are here now, by —! And all the time they offer us 'casual' food at the Workhouse there will be trouble. We are getting experts at raiding restaurants now. I got twenty-one days in London for it, and we know a little more about it now. I got some eggs and bacon this morning and didn't get 'copped'! Why not stop here? Eggs and bacon are very nice, and a walk along your Front will help me to recuperate! It is your Front, comrades. They're your theatres, your hotels, your houses! And yet we see, 'Keep off the grass!' 'Private ground!' and 'Private Property!' And if you catch a rabbit and are collared, a policeman says, 'This way!' That's the policeman's password. If you're starving you get sent to prison for trying to get a bit of food and if you try to get out of it, you get pinched for attempting to commit suicide! We working men have had enough of it! We're going to put a stop to it. We're going to get something better if we have to give our blood for it." [11]

Another speaker appealed for recruits saying they wanted men who would fight if necessary and not those who were going only to march a few miles and then feel homesick. While the speeches were being made, many of the marchers rattled collecting boxes at the crowd and tried to sell pamphlets. Then they started for the workhouse again:

After the threats that had been made by the leaders, a riot was expected at the Workhouse when the men returned at night. When they straggled up the hill, however, shouting and singing snatches of "The Red Flag" they were met by a very large number of policemen. Fifty or sixty constables lined the route from the gates to the casual wards, and a similar number surrounded the crowd outside. In view of this, those who had uttered such boastful threats evidently thought that discretion was the better part of valour. When the gates were thrown open, they walked in quite quietly.[12]

The chairman of the Brighton Unemployed, Harry Cowley, a chimney sweep by trade, addressed the crowd outside. He was a Robin Hood figure who led a group called the Brighton Vigilantes, who took over empty properties in the town and gave them to homeless families. Cowley told the crowd to go home quietly:

But, remember! I want you to look upon these men as heroes…They are fighting for the cause, and their cause is our cause, and as they will be going away tomorrow, its up to you Brighton unemployed to give them a rousing cheer to send them on their way.[13]

The crowd gradually dispersed. Fifty policemen remained at the workhouse all night. The marchers left the next day at 9.30am. They again refused the breakfast, and as they departed some threw the bread and cheese into the roadway down Elm Grove. They headed for the Labour Institute in London Road for one last meeting before leaving the town. Half headed for Newhaven and the other half to Worthing. At the Newhaven and East Preston workhouses they were provided with hot food, as the Elm Grove workhouse had, in fact, done in 1908. Daking calculated that he had had to pay 651½ hours overtime due to their visit, but the precautions had been necessary. Weeks before, striking Welsh miners had taken over a workhouse near Newport and had locked up its guardians for eighteen hours!

The Brighton sympathizer arrested in the restaurant was fined two pounds by the magistrates, and supporters organized a collection for him. Harry Cowley wrote a letter to the newspapers denouncing the "direct action" of some of the marchers, and informed local shopkeepers that they would be recompensated for any money they had lost. The next time hunger marchers came to Brighton, ten years later, they stayed at the Salvation Army Congress Hall.

* * *

Figs 32 and 33 Harry Cowley in uniform and in working guise as a chimney sweep.

During this decade inmates continued to be admitted in filthy, lice ridden clothes and sometimes were brought in by the police. Often in the admissions book there was a simple citation "clothes stoved" or "clothes all rags, destroyed". However, once admitted there was more flexibility[i] over discharge. For example, Jenny Fabian, a single woman was allowed to take her discharge to enter service and to leave her child at the workhouse for a charge of five shillings a week. On another occasion an inmate was given a pick and shovel on discharge to help him get work. And able-bodied inmates were given passes on alternate days to look for work. Usually if they found a job they were supplied with new clothes.

Penalties for leaving without permission, "absconding", were still harsh. When Catherine Marchant absconded from the able-bodied ward, leaving her ten-month-old child, she was arrested five days later by police and sentenced to one month's hard labour. "Absconding" usually involved taking the workhouse clothes, as the inmates' ones were taken away on arrival, so "stealing" was added to the charge. Workhouse clothes had no names written on them, just a number which corresponded to an inmate's bed. And inmates who just slipped over the wall for one night were often punished with a 24-hour diet of bread and water and kept in a separate room. As well as trying to prevent inmates from getting out – barbed wire was placed on the walls – Daking tried to prevent local boys from climbing on the wall adjoining Pankhurst Avenue and looking into the wards.

On another occasion, Emma Turner, 31, an able-bodied domestic servant with two children of one and seven, who had been an inmate for six years, was given seven days' hard labour for assaulting Amy Loader, a labour mistress. When Daking asked Loader to remove Emma from a room, Emma grabbed her hair from behind and shook her. In court, she said that Loader had "just recently had her knife into me and I have been put on bread and water two or three times". She claimed that she had done her best to leave, but the authorities would not help her. A Guardian commented that "it was disgraceful that she should have behaved in such a way while being maintained at the public expense".

---

[i] Although the Guardians did not accede to every request. One man's request for a week's leave to find work while leaving his wife and child in the workhouse was turned down.

In August 1923, to the embarrassment of some of the Guardians, a picture of aged inmates leaning over the walls begging with their caps out in race week appeared in a London illustrated newspaper. It was known locally as the "Workhouse Stakes"! The old men usually collected £7 to £8, the old ladies £9, and the money was shared among them. It was believed the women got more because they caught the money in aprons rather than caps. A local woman, Joan Malik, 88, remembers her father and others throwing tobacco up to the inmates. And Peter Shannon remembered:

> From the entrance gate in Elm Grove to the top of the hill the flint wall would be FULL of men hanging over and waving their tin mugs to try and get the odd copper or two.[14]

At a meeting, one Guardian said that this practice had been going on for fifty years and that there was no harm in it. However, Albert Mellor, an auctioneer and conservative Guardian who had been on the Board for twenty-five years, tried to have it stopped, but he was overruled. He also complained that there were too many women on the Board and that the current one was the "most incompentent and extravagant he had ever

Race day: the Daily Mirror *observed in August 1923 that 'inmates of the workhouse had a tiring time holding their caps over the walls while the race crowd passed'.*

known". It was true that they were spending more money than ever, but the primary reason, apart from inflation, was due to the complete phasing out of pauper labour in the infirmary.

Under the headline "Old Folk Made Happy", the *Brighton Herald* described the New Year treat of 1924:

> Everything had been done to make everybody happy…The large hall, wherein the festivities were held, had been gaily decorated, and it made the prettiest of pictures. Festoons of flowers hung from the ceilings; brightly coloured ribbons twined themselves round the pillars; balloons, flowers, and all kinds of paper decorations draped the walls, and hidden in all this mass of colour, were many tiny fairy lights which twinkled with charming effect. An excellent stage had been fitted up at the far end of the room, and an arc light threw variegated beams across the hall and over the footlights.

Mottoes such as "Peace and Plenty here abide" were printed in large letters on the walls, and in big red and green letters with a blue and mauve bordering, one read:

> The best of health, the best of luck,
> May you this Christmas know;
> Good fortune take you by the hand,
> And never let you go.[16]

The mottoes were designed and coloured by an inmate, Thomas Harold Moore. H Block, for the mental health patients, was decorated with paper orchids and roses. F Block, for the aged and infirm, had trails of evergreens and red and white flowers, while in D Block one ward whose nursing sister had given each of her patients a present:

> …had been given the appearance of a caravan…with bird cages in brilliant colours, each housing a gay plumaged tropical bird (not living of course) that hung at intervals from the ceiling. There was an electric light in each cage, and when they were lit up the ward was all aglow. There were festoons of greenery overhead and big gilt baskets of poppies and roses and other flowers, while the windows had a seasonable touch of snow.[17]

In the afternoon, the aged men and women were given tea served by the Guardians and their friends:

> After tea there was a jolly entertainment. First of all there was a clever and laughable little sketch entitled "Between the Soup and the Savoury", performed

by the Warren Farm Schoolgirls, with the assistance of Miss Hollingdale, daughter of the Superintendent and Matron. This told of the "high life below stairs," and was admirably staged and acted. The girls' elocution was particularly good…Then the boys from the Warren Farm Schools performed a sketch – a real boy's sketch – called "The Conceited Pirate". The lads entered thoroughly into the rollicking spirit of the piece and the old people thoroughly enjoyed it.

Subsequently there was a capital variety programme of songs, skits, recitations, and dialogues. Several well-known local artistes contributed to this part of the programme. They included Messrs. Clapham and Barnforth, two very humorous entertainers; Mr Harry Taylor, whose "Christmas Waits" and "Current Puns" are well known laughter makers…[18]

Daking's wife, Ethel, an accomplished pianist, also formed an "Institution Trio" with two inmates who played the banjo and violin, and they frequently performed at these "treats". Ethel was affectionately known to the old ladies as 'Bottled Sunshine'. Local cinemas also provided films for the aged inmates. In particular, Charlie Chaplin ones were very popular.

Newspaper reports such as the one above tended to ease the conscience of their readers. They showed how well the town was looking after its poor, but in reality this was a temporary illusion.

* * *

In 1924, Dr Douglas Ross, the medical officer for the workhouse and Warren Farm for the previous 42 years resigned. He had been a controversial figure who the Guardians had attempted unsuccessfully to get rid of on at least one occasion. After the First World War – in which he had lost two sons – he seems to have mellowed and not been involved in so much controversy. When Ross had been appointed in 1882 there had been no other doctor, only five nurses plus inmate help for 1,043 inmates. There were now 747 inmates and 171 staff in the workhouse, including a superintendent nurse and 61 nurses.

Ross had seen the maternity, children's nursery and sick wards, and the adult wards for medical and surgical treatment all built during his term of office, plus an X-ray room. He claimed to have been the first Poor Law medical officer to advocate the appointment of a dentist. At his retirement, Alfred Hollingdale, the schools' superintendent, called him "a sane, level-headed conservative." And Daking reminisced about travelling with him in "Tin Lizzie" to visit the scattered household during the war. When Ross died in Hove in 1937 at the age of 84, one obituary admitted that "his term of office was not undisturbed by storms".[19] He was replaced by Dr Hugh McCurrich, who continued to be responsible for Warren Farm and the Poor Law institution still known by everyone as the workhouse. He was soon complaining about the lack of organization and control in the nursery, where children were often left undressed for a long time before bathing.

The two great issues of the 1920s for the Guardians were the development of the hospital side of the workhouse and the problem of the huge increase in casuals. In 1922, the infirmary was officially approved as a probationary training school for nurses, but there was still no nurses' home which had been first proposed in 1903. And although the nursing side and the workhouse side of the institution were increasingly being separated, they still overlapped. For example, in 1923 Harriet Mary Francis committed suicide shortly after being discharged from the infirmary. Her husband had been told there was nothing wrong with her. According to him the staff had told him that she would be sent to A Block to work as a pauper if he didn't take her away. For this reason sometimes local people, even if they were ill, did not want to go to the infirmary because of its association with the workhouse.

Because of the poor accommodation, many probationer nurses were leaving just weeks into their three-year training. One nurse, Mary Brennan, complained that she shared a room in which she had no chair to put her clothes on. Most nurses slept in curtained cubicles where a shelf was considered to be a luxury. They had little entertainment apart from monthly whist drives and dances in the inmates' dining hall. A Guardian, Mrs Buckwell, described their living conditions as "deplorable."

The nurses in D Block lived on the same floor as their male patients. Their toilets were separated from those of the inmates by a low wooden partition. To have a bath they had to leave the building and cross a windswept courtyard to enter another building. Their food had to be brought to them past toilets used by patients with infectious diseases, and their larders were next to the coal cellars. In fact, many nurses contracted skin diseases and measles. In one draughty bedroom there were six nurses with just a curtain between them for privacy. Above all, the nurses had no escape from the atmosphere of work and the constant crying of the children.

As the *Brighton Herald* observed, "there is no getting away from the fact that the reputation of the Brighton Poor Law Institution from the point of view of the nurses is bad".[20] The Guardians had bitter debates about whether to build a new nurses' home or try and adapt one of the other buildings as the inmate population was falling. The above newspaper was prompted to comment on the "unseemly, personal wrangles" during the meetings, but did not comment on the ideological struggle that was going on between the socialist and conservative Guardians:

> The way certain members lose their tempers with each other and create "scenes" is deplorable…Certain members cannot school themselves into preserving their tempers and cannot avoid calling each other abusive names. [21]

Two of the members they were undoubtedly referring to were the Yorkshireman Albert Mellor, an auctioneer of St James' Street, and William Smith, a plasterer and member of the Labour party. Smith frequently criticized Mellor for the "badgering and bullying of poor people trying to get outdoor relief". Once, while defending a widow, he had accused Mellor and his supporters of sending her husband to the front "for some of you people who stayed at home and made a fortune". On more than one occasion Smith had to be restrained from physically hitting opponents. With a large increase of people being prosecuted for fraudulently claiming relief, Smith had berated his fellow Guardians at a meeting:

> All you can get is "we must think of the rates!" I don't care a jot about the rates. I care more about human life. Do you wonder that people who have to come here through no fault of their own, tell falsehoods, when you know the starvation conditions they exist under? I would do it myself. It is the rotten social conditions that compel these people to come down here and tell these falsehoods. When I look round the Board room, I see a lot of shirkers who have never done any work and don't intend to.[22]

He and the other Labour members had also objected to a practice Mellor defended: that of making applicants for relief stand in a kind of police dock in front of the Guardians. The tension between them exploded in August 1924 over Mellor's proposal to adapt one of the older blocks for a nurses' home. Smith argued that Mellor's proposition was impossible and that Mellor, as "an agent for slum property", ought to know that:

"Don't say too much about slum property," exclaimed Mr Mellor.

"I said 'slum property!' Did you hear me?" shouted Mr Smith.

"Yes, I heard you, you vulgar dog!" replied Mr Mellor.

Mr Smith (angrily): If you call me a dog again, I'll come round and pull your nose.

The vice-chairman of the Board tried to bring Smith to order, but the latter shouted angrily that Mellor had called him a "dirty dog."

Mellor: I did not.
Smith: You did!
Mellor: I did not.
Mrs Smith [Smith's wife]: He called you "a vulgar dog."
Smith: Oh, well, it's the same thing.[23]

Eventually the meeting calmed down. Mellor claimed there was nothing wrong in sleeping in cubicles, as "plenty of people in Brighton are paying two guineas a week for similar cubicles", and endorsed the plan to adapt the old infirmary into a nurses' home. However, Smith asserted that "the staff at the workhouse are sleeping under most filthy and objectionable conditions and that only a new home would suffice".[24]

Later, a Guardian, Mrs Jacklin, visited the infirmary and said she never had such a big shock in her life as when she saw the living cubicles of the nurses. A new Guardian, a chemist, Mr A.J. Franklin, told the Board that "you have got a rotten name all over the country as regards your nurses". He accused them of trying to "make a crystal palace out of a cow shed". Even the Ministry of Health attacked the temporary nurses' plan and insisted they build a proper home. Finally, in November 1926, by a majority of one, the Board voted for a nurses' home, but it would not be completed or opened until 1929, by which time 120 nurses had been sharing two baths. At the same time 250 inmates in the main part of the house were also sharing two baths.

A few months after Mellor's altercation with Smith, he died prematurely after a fall near his business in St James' Street. For twenty-five years he had been the treasurer of the "treat fund" for Warren Farm and for seventeen years in succession he had dressed up as Father Christmas for the children. Some attended his funeral. In his will he bequeathed a box of sweets to every child, and later a portrait of him was unveiled at the schools.

* * *

In this decade we start to see a litany of inmate "accidents" and suicides, although perhaps the increase was due to their being better reported. A 70-year-old inmate, Thomas Townsend, fell 24ft from a first floor toilet window and died. A patient, Sarah Hirsckowitz, 59, jumped from the balcony of E Block and fell 35ft to her death. William Jeffrey, 62, threw himself from the top of A Block. He had been playing cards, and when he left the game had seemed normal. He had fallen 42ft. Matilda Vernon, 35, who had tuberculosis, threw herself from a window on the top floor of F Block. And Arthur Skinner, 55, threw himself from a window on the second floor of A Block. The coroner often brought in verdicts of "unsound minds". Human despair was not classified.

In February 1927 there was an investigation into the stores after it was discovered that out of the first four people stopped leaving the workhouse by the police, three had property of the institution on them. All three were fined by the magistrates and dismissed, despite a petition signed by thirty-six of the staff for mercy in connection with the carpenter, A. Maynard. One of the Guardians, Wellman, believed that "matters at the institute had run riot through a lack of discipline".[25] One assistant labour master was suspended because of "objectionable behaviour to female officers and disgusting conversation with female inmates. When he was around it was difficult to have order in the dining room." [26] And one married temporary relieving officer was dismissed after being found to have issued relief tickets to a fictitious person, "Robert Sims", who was really his mistress. Temptation for corruption on the part of relieving officers was great, sometimes with tragic consequences. One popular officer from the nearby Steyning Union threw himself over the cliff at Roedean during an investigation into his accounts.

Just as in the other institutions, such as the Brighton Borough Mental Hospital, there was an acute local shortage of nurses, and staff started to be recruited from the north, Wales and Ireland. And the death rate started to go up because of road accidents – there were 224 deaths in the first half of 1927. The hospital side of the workhouse was continually expanding with more and more nurses. Now, out of 213 staff, 81 were nurses. But the infirmary constantly had to fight the stigma of being attached to the work-house.

Don Carter, who was born in Brighton in 1920, wrote in his autobiography, *Just One Large Family*:

It seems those for whom the doctors could do no more were sent to the Infirmary, and older people would say to each other "They've sent him/her up the Top," in a hushed voice. They dreaded "the Top". They spoke of it with dread in their voices, but it was nowhere near as bad as they imagined. They looked upon it as an affront to their pride.[27]

Carter may have been right about it being not so bad as people imagined although the suicides told a different story. But for some, the infirmary was providing a reasonable standard of care for poor people. Mrs W. Field wrote to the newspapers, complimenting it for her son's treatment: "The Infirmary is a wonderful place and the treatment he received was a great factor in his speedy recovery. My son tells me he was attended with every care and the staff were most kind to him." [28] Another patient wrote: "Had I been a millionaire, I could not have been better treated." [29] There was now a debate whether the infirmary should become a general hospital.

In October 1927 a Guardian, Albert Tindall, who had been a schoolmaster in his early life before owning a seafront hotel, went to the Stoke Park Colony to study their treatment of the "feeble-minded" and wrote a report. He concluded that:

> It is impossible to close the report without expressing the very deep feeling of dissatisfaction with our own treatment of the feeble-minded in H block. A depressing atmosphere, a mix up of lunatics, epileptics and mental deficients. It can not be right to mix up these three together. Besides there seems little or insufficient attempt to occupy the patients. No agriculture taught which is in the Stoke Park Colony. Walks once a week and exercise round a yard is to me an insufficiency of outdoor life amounting almost to cruelty. No attempt has yet been made to supply adequate institutional treatment. We need to share knowledge with other organizations.[30]

The workhouse system made no distinction between the physically and mentally handicapped. The following January, Dr Ross's successor, Dr McCurrich, went to H Block to see for himself. He found:

> ...no cases of ill treatment or real unhappiness. A.L. aged 55, an epileptic. Was in a grocer shop for 15 years and was originally an apprentice at sea. Lost his jobs on account of his fits. He is apt to be indecent during fits. He was sent back from a colony as unsuitable, probably for this reason. He would like to earn his living but realizes that fits prevent this and therefore is prepared to make the best of things. Has been an inmate for ten years.

Another inmate, L.P. 67, was originally admitted from the Schools. Certified for her own protection. Feeble-minded, poor memory. Not happy here, says all the nurses are kind to her, only wants to go for a change and then return. Has only been out two Sundays and one Tuesday in 27 years but goes to annual retreat and enjoys it.

C.F aged 30 – weak-minded. Runs after men. Has been pregnant once. Certified for her own safety. Happy but would like to go to a good situation if Dr thinks it would be suitable. (He doesn't.)

None of these cases is suitable for discharge. Need open air work. Majority of patients are really happy and at the suggestion of a move they become quite upset. Many women at the thought of a move burst into tears. They look on H block as home. This seems to be a general feeling. Another lavishes her affection on the cats and says they would break their hearts if she left and begged me not to send her away.[31]

The case of L.P., above, was an illustration of how some vulnerable paupers spent their whole lives in workhouses.

McCurrich thought the H Block inmates should be separated into different groups, but that it was not possible because of the lack of staff. He concluded: "The results of my enquiry lead me to believe that on the whole the patients are happy, except for one or two of the higher grade epileptics". Of course, we need to be cautious about his description of the inmates as "happy", for the history of workhouses is full of inmates fearing the consequences of making complaints to figures of authority. And sometimes Guardians were reluctant to send able-bodied "feeble-minded" paupers to separate institutions because they were such an important source of menial labour in the laundry and keeping their own institution clean. Some workhouses would have found it difficult to survive without them. Officials at Elm Grove also benefitted from the service of the inmates, some declaring that they were treated 'like a lord'. "The [married] Superintendents of Imbeciles are said to have spent a life of being waited on hand and foot, with the care of their son being left to an inmate on their Block."[32]

* * *

In 1927, there was surprise when it was discovered that the son of a former lord mayor of London, Sir James Herbert Renals, had "in acute poverty" died in the infirmary. Apparently he had never used his title and had lived in Brighton with his wife and six children. He had been earning his living as an advertising agent:

> Recently, Sir James had found business extremely slack. He was indeed so hard pressed to find money to support his family and himself that he had to obtain parish relief. It is said that before his fatal illness he appeared to be on the verge of starvation.[33]

He had inherited the title but little money twenty years earlier when his father had died. During the war he had offered himself as a transport driver, but had been rejected on medical grounds

> The heir to the title is a little boy named Herbert, aged seven and a half, who is under treatment at the Brighton Borough Sanatorium. When in breaking the news of his father's death to the little fellow, Lady Renals said: "Daddy has gone to heaven," the heir to the title pathetically replied: "I wish I could go with him."…A representative of the "Herald" who visited the deceased's small house found the widow Lady Renals (locally known as Mrs Renals) overcome with grief at her loss, and very anxious at the future of her children, the youngest of whom is only three months old. "I shall work and keep my children,"said Mrs Renals tearfully, but one felt as she was speaking that the mere care of the little ones, even under the most favourable conditions, must necessarily occupy most of her time.

At Sir James' funeral one of the wreaths was signed "Little Dorrit" and "From a few neighbours".

In 1928, with the extension of the new Borough boundary – including Patcham and Preston – Brighton took areas from Steyning and Newhaven. It included seven new electoral wards and covered an area, mainly unpopulated, eight times the previous size.[i] Three new Guardians were to be elected from each, so the Board numbers went up from 36 to 57 and the workhouse received an additional 110 inmates from the Steyning Union. Elm Grove now had a staff of 300, with 910 inmates. At the same time there were 2,315 individuals, including children, receiving outdoor relief. Well over five hundred of the inmates were classified as sick, and an additional resident medical officer was appointed. One surprising fact was that maintenance charges were now more expensive for the workhouse than for the

---

[i] From 1,640 acres to 10,900 acres.

borough asylum, which for much of the nineteenth century was three to four times higher. In 1929, the former cost 30s 3d per week whilst the latter was 24s 6d.

* * *

During the war the Guardians had agreed that the casual wards should eventually be closed. However, post-war, owing to their increase in numbers, Daking had been forced to admit casuals again and on returning to the workhouse, their wards had been re-opened. During the first half of 1921 almost 2,000 casuals had been admitted to the scattered household. In the first six months back at the workhouse, the figure rose to 2,524. Daking believed that:

> The casual worker of today is, generally speaking, of an entirely different character to the pre-war type inasmuch as the majority are ex-servicemen and in my opinion, men willing to work if work could be obtained; and bearing this in mind, I am hoping the Guardians will not revert to the imposition of task work (ie stone breaking and oakum picking) which is plainly of a degrading nature, and moreover, taking a wider view, utterly fails in its object as a deterrent but merely has the effect of driving casuals to areas where the tasks imposed are not so irksome.[35]

Fig 34 First meeting of the enlarged Board of Guardians outside the Royal Pavilion with the mayor.

But the Guardians made no immediate attempt to change task work, although a minority believed the able-bodied should do useful work and be paid for it. Later the government did ban oakum picking and said that if an inmate was forced to do unpleasant work he must be paid half in kind and half in money. After the ban, casuals in Elm Grove were employed chopping and sawing wood, doing garden work and scrubbing and cleaning the casual wards. However, as a punishment they still had to break stones in the casual cells. The Guardians particularly disliked casuals, because they could not claim their pension. One casual had entered one night and been asked to look after the boilers. The next day he slipped over the wall to collect his pension and returned again for another night.

The Ministry of Health started to put pressure on casuals to discourage them from bringing their children. There was a scheme for the adoption of children of vagrants who entered the wards in cases where the parents "are unfit to control them by reason of mental deficiency, their vicious habits or mode of life". [36] In 1926, a Guardian, Mr Brewer, was still reporting that on a bitterly cold winter's day he saw a man, woman and four children, aged eighteen months to seven years leave the casuals ward and setting out to tramp the thirteen miles to the Cuckfield workhouse.

In the 1920s casuals started to be charged one shilling a night for their lodgings, although the first shilling they had was disregarded. Any other money they possessed was collected by the receiving ward attendant and given to the master, who returned it when they left. Since the Pauper Order of 1914, no casual was to be discharged without a mid-day meal. During 1924 a resolution to abolish casual wards because "they involve much expenditure without effecting the reform of the unfortunate people compelled to use them" [37] was defeated at a Guardians' meeting.

By the mid 1920s, casuals appeared to have been staying much more than their legal two nights. In April 1923 Edward Pelling, his wife and children entered the casual wards and were only finally evicted after eight consecutive nights Others were sometimes retained instead of being discharged, and there were rumours about a "Tramp Major" charging other casuals one penny for a basin of tea. "These 'Tramp Majors' took on the duties of supervising the others and, as they were unpaid, provided a cheap source of labour". [38] There were also "trustee" inmates who, like their prison counterparts, gained extra privileges by helping out the staff.

With the New Casual Poor Order of 1925, casuals could now be admitted before 6pm in summer and 4pm in winter. They were still to be searched but were to be bathed in clean warm water and provided with second-hand clothing to work in and night clothing. Their own clothing was to be dried and disinfected when necessary and returned to them when they left. They could now leave at 7.30 am instead of 9 am, which gave them more time either to look for work or to arrive at their next destination. The Brighton Guardians claimed that they had always provided warm water for bathing and had already started to be flexible about admission times, letting casuals in early if it rained.

During the first six months of 1926, the number of casuals had risen to 3,254. And in 1927 the number for the whole year almost reached 10,000. That year, after casuals arrived from the Steyning Union with smallpox, it was decided that all casuals must be vaccinated and separated from the inmates and patients. They were no longer to be allowed to work in the main building and had to work outside. Daking soon complained about them "breaking wind" loudly in the court area. He also lamented that "hitherto I have always had the use of casual labour for window cleaning but now they are no longer employed about the institution". With 1,820 windows to clean, they had saved a lot of expense. He was forced to use an outside agency. One Guardian, Mr Wellman, commented that "they [the paupers] will want waiters with dress suits to wait on them soon". [39] There was always someone ready to imply that workhouse inmates were spoilt.

In January 1928 a casual, Edward Osborne, was admitted with smallpox after arriving from Cuckfield workhouse. He was not seen by the medical officer for two days, in which time 41 other casuals had left Osborne's ward. The chief medical officer of Brighton, Dr Duncan Forbes, reprimanded Dr Hugh McCurrich, the medical officer, and insisted that, for an experiment, from 29th January–30th September 1928 all the casuals must be examined to detect smallpox. In this period, McCurrich and the resident medical officer, Dr Fenwick, examined 8,966 casuals: 8,503 men, 370 women and 93 children.

That May, Daking was asked to do an analysis of the male casuals over a two week period. Out of 687 admitted, he believed that 332 were "habitual tramps", of whom 113 were aged and infirm [60–74 years]; 235 were genuinely seeking work (116 had insurance cards); 118 were mostly young men aged 18–35; and two were children of 14 and 7. Daking believed that the young men "appeared to be without any definite prospects of obtaining work, and merely roamed from one casual ward to another." [40] In the same period twelve married women and eight single women with children were admitted. Over another four week period, 1,510 casuals were admitted of whom, in Daking's opinion, only 328 were genuinely seeking work. He agreed that vagrancy was a big problem.

*　*　*

As the decade drew to an end there was to be a major reform, one that had first been mooted by the 1909 Royal Commission. The government decided that Guardians should be replaced in 1930 by public assistance committees which were to be run by the local authorities. Furthermore, in the long term, it recommended the phasing out of workhouses. The Brighton Guardians were stung by this conclusion, as they believed their workhouse and infirmary were among the best in the country. They claimed the medical service was top class whether you had to pay or not, and that the casual wards were very good. At the same time it was proposed that Warren Farm should be placed in the hands of the council's education committee.

In the summer of 1929 a headline in the *Brighton Herald* declared "Gloom Among Poor Law Inmates". The article asked whether the inmates would get an annual treat under the council. That summer three hundred of them went to the Pleasure Grounds at Hassocks and had sports shows, sideshows and a band playing. The Guardians, too, hired two Southdown coaches for themselves and organized a day out to Windsor, a fraternal outing on the river and a dinner in a hotel.

In December 1929, a meeting to reconstitute the new public assistance committee took place at the town hall. Twenty eight of the new committee were to be members of the council, of which at least two were designated to be women. At the final Christmas under the Guardians, "the wind whistled cold around the Poor Law Institution but inside the "Home on the Hill" all was gay".[41] For the first time there had been no opposition to the free beer. A party was held in the dining room for four hundred aged inmates, nurses and Guardians, followed by a show on the stage. There was nothing for the able-bodied inmates.

A week later, an article in the same newspaper declared:

The future rests with the Council. A movement on their part that might result in authority to substitute a more homelike name than "workhouse", and so eliminate the wretched stigma "pauper" would indeed earn the gratitude of thousands of fellow creatures.[42]

In 1929, the last full year of the Guardians' administration, there had been 2,681 admissions into the workhouse, 15,462 casuals, 80 births and 586 deaths. The population now totalled 936, which included 539 in the infirmary and 397 aged or able-bodied inmates. In January 1930 over a thousand casuals were admitted, three hundred more than in the same month the previous year. They had heard rumours of work in the town. Under new legislation, if they had more than a shilling on them they were now expected to find their own lodgings.

The institution being handed over to the new public assistance committee on April 1st 1930 was a very different place to when it had opened in 1867. Gone were the prison-like dormitories, replaced by wards with radios and record players. Gone were the "feeble" inmates who had attended the sick, to be replaced by trained nurses. And now if an inmate came in with £20 or more, the Guardians could not appropriate more than 75 per cent of it when they left. However, the public stigma remained. There was no waiting room for friends and family to visit patients in the infirmary. Visitors had to wait outside the gates in the rain, were only allowed in two at a time and had to have an admission card. (One Sunday 52 people, including three women with babies, waited outside for their turns in the rain.) And no child under 16 was permitted to visit patients in the infirmary unless there were exceptional circumstances.

At their last ever meeting on 28th March 1930, a Guardian, Franklin, praised the institution where "the patients are treated splendidly in every way. There is an excellent medical, surgical and nursing staff and also a splendid master and matron. We feel proud to hand over the institution in such an excellent state of efficiency to the council." The last business on the agenda, appropriately, dealt with tenders for coffins and funerals!

There was a farewell dinner at the Old Ship Hotel with 120 attending. There were many speeches, including one by Horace Burfield who had been clerk to the Guardians since 1912 and had started as a junior clerk in 1884. He was actually going to stay on for a further month and help the public assistance committee chairman, Horace Webb, with his new job. Eight of the old Guardians were to be co-opted onto the new committee. Daking, told the guests that "when your work is viewed in the light of history, you will probably be found to have left a monument of service that will last for many generations to come".[44] With forty minutes to go before midnight, the Guardians of the poor of Brighton joined hands and sang "Auld Lang Syne":

> It is impossible to escape a certain feeling of emotion in bidding farewell to the Brighton Board of Guardians. They have kept personal watch over every detail of that huge institution, a town in itself, on the top of the hill, with its aged, its infirm, its bedridden, its sick, the leavening of difficult, even dangerous characters among those who have either broken every rule of life or have been broken by life.[46]

Under the new legislation there was provision for making the infirmary into a municipal hospital, for it already had over twice the number of beds as the Royal Sussex County Hospital. But would this change and the passing of the Guardians affect the stigma of pauperism so long associated with the Elm Grove workhouse?

Chapter Eighteen

WARREN FARM 1919–1930

Unlike the workhouse, Warren Farm had not been evacuated during the war and instead had received children from the bomb threatened coastal strip around Dover. By the end of March 1919 there were 229 children in the schools, 103 who belonged to other Unions who could leave at any time. With no bus service to Woodingdean until 1924, the schools remained isolated and it was still difficult to attract staff. The staff accommodation, as the superintendent Alfred Hollingdale admitted, was poor:

> Some [of the rooms] are considerably below the average standard of comfort found in similar institutions in other parts of the country...Only those who spend a winter here can appreciate there are many evenings when it is impossible for officers to go out without a risk of getting thoroughly wet with all its unpleasant consequences...I found that defects of accommodation and catering adversely shortens their term of service.[1]

Female staff had no sitting room and had to share a bedroom. There was no common mess room, and meals had to be brought from the kitchen to various rooms. Hollingdale believed it would be an "economy" to improve staff accommodation. Less money would then have to be spent on advertising for new staff and paying for candidates' travelling expenses, including unsuccessful ones. The teaching staff already wanted parity with teachers employed by Brighton's education committee, but the Guardians, as they so often did, decided to defer it or, in their own words, "lay it on the table". This meant there was always a dearth of candidates for the teaching posts. Hollingdale argued that as two of the receiving rooms were not being used, and because of falling numbers unlikely to be in the future, they could use them to improve staff accommodation, but he was turned down.

Just before the war, there had been a lot of talk about the end of the "barrack" system and the boarding-out of the children. The war undoubtedly delayed this, and for now Warren Farm remained much the same as it had been before. One Guardian, Albert Tindall, complained that the children had "frozen meat faces" and demanded a change. Despite Tindall's contention, the reports on the schools were positive. In October 1919 an assistant diocesan inspector, Rev J.H. Gurney, wrote:

> Very good work is being done in this School and the general standard is above that achieved usually in schools of this character. The teaching is vigorous and effective on the whole and the response on the part of the children is fairly general and effective. The practical application of the teaching is well emphasized and the children are not slow in appreciating this. Altogether, the general tone and discipline are quite good and the influence of the Schools seems to be just what should be desired.[2]

In April 1920, under the headline "Good News for Oliver Twist", the *Brighton Herald* reported that new government regulations meant that the children were to be fed according to their appetites. In reality this never happened. However, they were to get two courses for dinner instead of one. They were also to get "stripe money" [pocket money] for good conduct: 6d for the boys and 3d for the girls. In September, a reporter from the *Brighton Gazette* wrote:

> It is always a pleasure to visit the Schools, which are a model of good management…No one could fail to be impressed by the healthiness of the surroundings, the excellent practical education given the children and the admirable results which follow the kindness and care lavished upon them by the Superintendent and Matron and members of their staff.[3]

He had toured the "spotlessly and meticulously tidy dormitories" with the Guardians, and after the entertainment had gone to the farm "where one or two older boys and girls were seen milking". Three years later the chaplain, Morgan, was recording that "the order and discipline in the Boys' department are excellent just now. They are interested and attentive in what is being taught".[4] And in 1925 Rev Gurney found "a markedly earnest and sincere religious atmosphere in the schools". [5]

The Warren Farm band continued to be much in demand. During the summer season they were asked by the council to play at the Old Steine Gardens every fortnight for two hours on Wednesday evenings. Instead of charging a fee, the children collected money from the public and divided it between their "treat" fund and the band fund. In 1921, the band was asked to play at Preston Park before Edward, the Prince of Wales, who was on his way to the dedication of the Chattri, the Indian Memorial on the Downs where 53 Hindus and Sikhs were cremated during the war.

Throughout the nineteen twenties the summer camps continued, with the boys going for two weeks and then the girls following for the same time. Only the infants remained behind. When the children went to the camp near Rottingdean – where the band played for the public on the White Horse Hotel lawn – the schools hired twenty-two tents and two marquees and local people lent tea urns and cookers. As the children played cricket, football and other games, the fresh air made them hungrier, and Hollingdale ordered more food to be provided. On their return, the boys played an annual cricket match against the Guardians, and usually won quite easily.

Gradually, restrictions on the children were relaxed and the schools were even given a wireless by the mayor and mayoress of Brighton. In 1922, girls over fourteen whose "conduct is good and whose services can be spared" [6] were given leave of absence on Wednesday afternoons. Later, twenty-four of the older girls were sent to have swimming lessons at the North Road swimming pool. And, for the first time, girls were taught hockey. Most still went into domestic service, often at the age of fourteen, and, as Hollingdale himself admitted, were not always treated kindly. The boys continued to enter the military or go into farm work or private service. There was still a militaristic emphasis at Warren Farm, with a miniature rifle range frequently used.

Upon the children leaving, the Guardians started to issue "certificates of good conduct". Sometimes they returned from their placements with the remark "failed to give satisfaction" but they were usually given another chance. On one occasion, Hollingdale placed "a boy over sixteen unable to earn his living because of mental deficiency" into the workhouse. For those unable to find work, it was still often the only option.

For a while, as they had done over hundred years before, the Guardians even considered sending pauper boys to Lancashire again. There was a very large boys' home in St Helens, which supplied apprentices in "glass blowing and rolling industries" to Pilkington Brothers Limited. The boys required two suits and train fares, and would be expected initially to work three eight-hour shifts with a thirty-minute break for food. They were paid by results. Pilkington employed 10,000 staff and provided 80 tennis courts and 80 acres of land for their employees' recreation. Hollingdale went there on a visit with the chairman of the schools committee and was quite impressed. Back at a Guardians' meeting, William Smith said he thought that glass blowing was unsuitable as there was more tuberculosis in that industry than in any others. In 1924 it was recorded that one of the boys who left the schools did go into "glass blowing", so perhaps he was sent to Lancashire.

In January, 1925, the children were visited by the mayor and mayoress of Brighton as they celebrated the new year. There were two hundred and fifty children present, who "made an animated scene as they sat laughing and chattering at the tea-table, where there stood piles of tempting cakes, Christmas crackers, and other novelties." [7] The tea was provided by a local shop, "Leeson and Vokins":

> The Mayor and Mayoress were accorded a rousing reception upon their entry, and his Worship soon found himself pulling Christmas crackers with the delighted youngsters. Visitors were shown round the extensive premises so that they were able to see for themselves the comfortable conditions under which these children live and are taught to become useful citizens.[8]
>
> During the evening selections were played by the Warren Farm Band, under Lieutenant H.M. Carr [the bandmaster] and a capital entertainment was given…Two of the boys, George Rushman and Herbert Smith, appeared in a diverting sketch entitled "The Indian and the Scout", which was followed by another act by Kathleen Dovey, Edna Wells, and Lucy Barton. The artistes who were engaged for the evening were Miss Sylvia Welling, Miss Phyllis Silverman, and Professor Lerrano.

Prizes were given out for, among other things, the best land worker, the best dairy worker and the most popular boy and girl – who were selected by their companions. Hollingdale gave a report on the year. Out of an average number of 237, sixteen boys and sixteen girls had gone into employment found by the schools. Four boys had chosen farm work, six had enlisted into army bands and the remainder were either chauffeurs or servants. One boy had been appointed as an assistant master tailor at another industrial school. All the girls had gone into domestic service. Hollingdale usually kept in touch with his ex-pupils for the first two years, and thirty "old boys and girls" were present at the Christmas festivities. In his speech he told his audience he had received letters from ex-pupils living in New York, Mexico and Indonesia. During 1924,[i] 164 of them had

---

[i] The following year 300 ex-pupils visited Warren Farm.

returned to visit, including one man with two children who had left thirty years earlier. After the speech the children had a supper of ginger beer and buns and so finished "a day to be long remembered at the Warren Farm." [9]

*   *   *

In June 1926, sixty-four years after it had opened, Warren Farm for the first time opened its doors to the public for an exhibition of school work:

The visitors upon entering the boys' school room, examined with interest a large number of models fashioned by the senior and junior classes. There was an excellent model of the school buildings which represented the joint efforts of the juniors. The model was complete, even to the neat paths and flower beds. Another striking model was that of the Cenotaph in Whitehall. The senior boys displayed a number of excellent models, including an unfinished representation of a Shakespearean village. Further down the room young workmen were making boots of sturdy build and nearby, an earnest little carpenter was planing part of a wooden fence.

There were also a large number of very promising maps and sketches, some excellent examples of tailoring work (Edward Cooke, aged twelve, must be complimented upon his invisible patching and the making of a waistcoat) and numerous specimens of needlework by the girls which, to the masculine eye, looked worthy of a costumier's.

The infants had manufactured a diversity of things with the simplest of materials, and their chief d'oeuvre was a big dolls' house of four rooms, complete with inmates and furniture.

The Boy Scouts exhibited interesting specimens of rope-knotting, fretwork, matting, and picture framing. A poem, "The Scouts' Camp" by Harold Hills, aged fourteen, attracted attention by reason of its vigour and freshness. Pride of place on this stall was occupied by a silver cup won by Roy Duly, aged fourteen, in a three rounds' boxing match against Thomas Brooks (Boys' Boxing Club, Brighton) last March when Roy knocked out Thomas in the second round.[10]

After visiting the "airy" dormitories and classroom, Hollingdale took the Guardians and visitors – mainly women – to see the cows being milked and other features of the farm which supplied all the milk, vegetables, eggs and butter needed by the children. The mayor then made a speech in which he praised the school and lamented the fact that, although it was his third visit as mayor, no one yet had called him 'Daddy'!

The farm continued to increase its profits, making £125 in 1924 and £307 in 1925. Pigs were sold at auction, and cows were slaughtered and their carcasses returned to be eaten. Despite the healthy produce consumed, in 1926 there was an outbreak of diphtheria so serious that the medical officer for Brighton, Dr Stott, went to investigate himself. He found that:

> The milk is stored in a room off the playground with the window into the playground and a ventilation just above the ground level of the playground. Dust raised by the children at play is liable to be blown into the milk store.[11]

Stott recommended filters be used which "should lessen the evil."

In 1927, Albert Hollingdale, described as a "jolly, big man" spoke to the Rotary Club and was surprisingly candid:

> It is possible for a school to be unnaturally clean. There must be natural healthy dirt where children are about. Besides, it has a moral value. It reminds us whence we came and what is our ultimate destiny.[12]

Fig 35 Midday rest for the Warren Farm infants in the 1920s.

He explained how, up to the age of 14, children were given an elementary education and were then taught how to earn their own living. He was against the idea of "boarding-out" children because of the financial motive involved and that mixing with ordinary children in a family might make them feel inferior. Instead, Hollingdale was wholeheartedly in favour of the "barrack system":

> In barrack schools all are treated alike; all are happy and healthy and believe in discipline.

He went on to describe how one old boy who had joined the army and had died in Singapore spoke so highly of his time there that his regiment had sent a subscription of £20 to the schools to be spent on the children. Hollingdale did admit though that "the great bulk of the children are necessarily below the average and that they leave the school with a certain stamp upon them. But is that not true of any large school?" Perhaps rather strangely, he compared their "stamp" with the Oxford accent or the Eton manners.

Hollingdale estimated that since 1862, 7,000 children had attended Warren Farm and that now parents had to contribute towards their maintenance according to their means. In 1928, there were 183 children from the parish and 43 from other Unions. That year each was interviewed individually by the Guardians and they all said they were happy.

Bill Stevens' first recollection when he arrived in 1919 was "of a nasty smelly bath, a short back and side and over the top haircut…All I seemed to want to do then until I was sixteen was to get out – I tried twice – but was caught each time, I remember. None the less I did very well, I think, since I learned tailoring, to play several musical instruments, football, cricket and hockey…but above all these achievements I think we were taught to play the game and were thus more fitted to become decent members of society and to cope with the intricacies of "outside" life." [i]

William Oldacre, who arrived at Warren Farm in 1921 as a resident assistant teacher, later remembered that "it had been crowded with children,

---

[i] He left in 1926 and went on to become a businessman.

with a fully stocked farm, and the whole place was pulsating with life". Frank Jones, who arrived as a pupil in 1924, remembered a teacher demonstrating the map of the world by holding up an orange!

The fact that Bill Stevens spent so much time trying to escape gives a hint of the harshness of the regime. Certainly from today's perspective it was a very tough environment in which the children stuck together in order to survive. With the abolition of the guardians in 1930, the schools were to be taken over by the council's education committee, and the future of the "barrack" system, which Hollingdale so admired, would be in doubt.

Chapter Nineteen

A NEW ERA

After the Wall Street Crash of October 1929, the mass unemployment of the nineteen thirties produced the worst crisis in Europe since the Black Death. The "Great Depression" – worsened by wage and benefit cuts – and the threat of another world war engineered by dictators, dominated the decade. Although the former particularly affected the industrial towns and cities, unemployment also hit Brighton badly. Unemployed men like Alfred Davey felt they could not go on any longer. He left a message on a cigarette packet to this effect, went down to the beach and swallowed some iodine. He was spotted by a passer by and taken to hospital. He told the magistrates' court that the public assistance committee had advised his wife to leave him so that she and their child could be maintained on the parish. Davey refused to give an undertaking that he would not try to kill himself again. Sentencing him to six months' hard labour for attempting suicide, the magistrate told him that he was trying "to be a hero in the eyes of the public...Out of kindness to you and to other people concerned we are going to send you to prison." [1]

In 1931, Frank Gray, an ex-Liberal MP and lawyer, graphically described one of the effects of this mass unemployment:

> On every English main road between workhouse and workhouse, on every day in the week except Sundays, may be seen a long-drawn-out procession of unhappy men. This pilgrimage of men passes another group coming in the opposite direction...These men are ill-clad, ill-fed, and evil to look upon. A procession of the ageing, broken and outcast. [i]

He estimated that most of those "on the tramp" looking for work were men but at least five percent were women and sometimes, as overleaf, the whole family was on the road.

***

---

[i] *The Tramp: His Meaning and Being* (1931), p.3.

As Harry Gaston, has pointed out in his well researched book, *A Lingering Fear: East Sussex Hospitals and the Workhouse Legacy* (2009), part of the remit of the new public assistance committees (PAC) was to eliminate the evil of the mixed workhouse, so that, in the future, there would be specialist accommodation for the acute and chronic sick, the aged mental cases and the children. The idea was that the infirmary would become a hospital and the workhouse would eventually be phased out. The Brighton PAC started by designating F Block for the chronic infirm, L Block for the males, C Block for medical cases and C1 for maternity. However, any immediate drastic changes were prevented by the need for "economy".

One of the first decisions the PAC made was to stop selling and sending "unclaimed bodies" to the medical school at Cambridge University. They also resolved to use the old Guardians' rule of compulsory discharge with the utmost caution, deciding that no one should be discharged without a medical examination and deemed physically fit. However, their decision to ban aged inmates from begging on race days in the name of "de-pauperisation" did produce criticism, as many felt it was a kindly and picturesque custom which harmed no one.

A family on the road.

The atmosphere in PAC meetings now was far less confrontational than in the days of the Guardians, and there seems to have been more consensus. The business was concluded much faster, perhaps too fast. One meeting took just two-and-a-half minutes – a record!

In August 1930, there were 1,058 inmates, and already in the first six months of the year there had been 8,603 casuals – a barometer of the hungry thirties – and 273 deaths. For reasons of economy, the summer treat for the aged inmates was suspended for a couple of years, but for the first time, in January 1931, the house committee of the PAC provided the new year treat. The inmates:

> with a philosophy born of vicissitude and endurance, and with a sense of humour which even the hardest knocks of the world have been unable to blunt, threw themselves wholeheartedly into the enjoyment of the moment. They "simply doted" on the sentimental ballads and duets of Miss Ethel Darby and Miss Winifred Morris. They laughed loud and long at the comic antics and the snappy songs of Mr Archie Cresswell and Mr Bert Martin. They joined in choruses, the sexes competing in good natured rivalry. They applauded Mr Cyril Leslie's manipulation of a billiard ball, and laughed at his patter.
>
> When Soermus, the Russian violinist, spoke to them in that fascinating, halting English of his they seemed to sense his sympathy with the lot of the poor. He played intimate little pieces to them, and they loved them. Mr M. Western and Mr Bert James performed a clever illusionist act, mystifying and delighting everyone. When the lights went up "between turns" the hall was revealed as a huge conservatory. Masses of artificial flowers of every hue met the eye everywhere. It was like a scene on the Riviera and this most delightful artistic scheme has been carried out by the inmates and staff.[2]

Free beer, so often contested by the old Guardians, was provided by Tamplins, which had taken over the Smithers brewery in 1928. But the old Guardians were still meeting. Their last clerk, Horace Burfield, had founded an association of ex-Poor Law Guardians, and in March 1931 they celebrated their first anniversary at the Savoy Cinema restaurant in East Street. It was reported to be a cheerful occasion for members who "have, by long practice, become experts in the arts of repartee." [3] The evening ended with entertainment including the singing of "Sally in our Alley" by a guest, Horace Webb, the chairman of the public assistance committee.

As the 1931 New Year began, Dr McCurrich resigned as the medical officer, to be replaced by Dr Ackerman, who only lasted a year before the former resident medical officer, Dr Stanley Firth, was appointed. Firth had himself been born in 1902 in the Wythenshawe workhouse where his parents were master and matron. Ethel Daking had to resign as matron on health grounds, and as it was a joint appointment her husband also had to go. They had been master and matron at Elm Grove for twenty years. At Wilfred Daking's farewell dinner, among the many gifts he received was an easy chair from the inmates. They had clubbed together and had each contributed a penny, a substantial sum from those to whom pennies were a rarity. Five years later Wilfred, aged 59, wearing a pair of new shooting boots, fell down some small steps in his garden and died after an infection.

Forty-nine couples applied to be master/matron and a young couple who had similar posts at the Bedford workhouse, Garnet and Ann Chaplin, were chosen. They promised the committee that this would be their last appointment. Chaplin found an institution very much behind the times, with a horse and two donkeys the main means of transporting goods. The twenty-nine central heating and domestic boilers, which were still being entirely stoked by inmate labour, were over-stoked in the summer and under-stoked in the winter. There was also no night watchman in case of fire, and a non-resident one was soon appointed. Chaplin was particularly concerned about the lack of heating in A Block, where the able-bodied inmates resided:

> In winter the dormitories were extremely cold and during foggy weather the walls streamed with moisture. In fact, there was no exaggeration in stating that pools of water could be seen in corridors and in staircases when such weather prevailed. It naturally followed that the bedding and linen in the dormitories was often damp.[4]

He suggested that if the corridors were heated, this would also warm the dormitories. The Chaplins soon began to transform the place. They started by replacing the dull, depressing, dingy walls, coated with regulation institution dark green, with bright homely colours and ordered more comfortable furniture.

By November 1931 there were still more than a thousand inmates in the institution, of whom at least 50 per cent were considered to be sick. It cost approximately £72,000 a year to run, of which £7,000 was received from relatives and £2,000 from other sources. The maintenance cost was one guinea a week to keep an inmate and £2 3s 6d to keep a patient in the infirmary. With national unemployment increasing, the "dole" from the National Assistance Board was cut by 10 per cent, and over 1,200 people in Brighton were receiving outdoor relief from the PAC, half in money and half in kind. The vouchers of the latter could now be redeemed at almost five hundred shops in the town.

The number of casuals continued to increase, partly because, according to an ex-Guardian, Mr F. Paul, Brighton's casual wards "compared with the best in the country", although it is unclear how many other wards he had seen. In fact, one of the first things the PAC had done was to improve the diet for casuals, relax the searching, provide dayrooms and allow them to smoke. Paul's statement was borne out by a letter from a casual, published in the *Brighton Herald*:

> If I may say it, the institution is run with discipline, tact and good temper by the officers and, as we "down and outs" are in all sorts and conditions, I consider they have a pretty trying time. Anyway, when anyone is up against it, one appreciates the little touch of kindness and there is no distinction made. Everything inside is clean and comfortable as can be expected under the circumstances, and I guarantee they get more work out of the "casuals" than most. I have no axe to grind in writing this, and it is the only way I can acknowledge their kindness.
>
> A.J. (cell 17) [5]

Another letter, from a "grateful down and out", praised Mr Sayers, the reception officer:

> ...who enabled me to jog along again...I would like the same human touch could be found elsewhere, our lives would indeed be happier. My recollections of Brighton Casual Wards with its kindly atmosphere, its comfort and cleanliness, and Mr Sayers and his colleagues therein will be of happiness. [6]

Charles Allen also praised Sayers, "whose patience and courtesy appear so well known everywhere", and the "wonderful treatment" he had received in the infirmary.

Compared with other casual wards, Elm Grove's do seem to have been better. Frank Gray, already mentioned, went 'undercover' in 1930 and, dressed as a tramp, visited several workhouse casual wards. His experience illustrated that some had changed little from when the reporter from the *Brighton Observer* had visited Church Hill in 1866: vermin-infested wards, dirty towels and bathwater that had been used by many. Even the diet was still scarce: instead of bread and water, tramps were now sometimes being given only bread, margarine and unsweetened tea. They were still being locked up for thirteen hours during the night, and after working till eleven the following morning had little chance of finding work. Gray claimed that although the general population had doubled since 1860, the number of tramps had multiplied sixfold.

Because of the relaxed conditions in the casual wards at Elm Grove, they were attracting more people. After paying a shilling, casuals could now have any other money on them returned when they left. For supper they had hot broth and were given a bath and three blankets at night. In the morning they worked in the sheds, the gardens or cleaned. Before they left they had a dinner of meat, cheese, bread and potatoes.

In December 1932 – the month when the worst weather may be expected – 1,196 casuals were admitted. Of these, Chaplin believed that 817 were habitual tramps; 276 young men of no fixed abode; 29 genuine working men; and 74 men over 65 who were incapable of work. Chaplin felt that new types were passing through the casual wards. Some were quite well dressed and looked like clerks, perhaps an indication that unemployment was affecting all classes. Many also came from Ireland, Wales and other depressed areas as unemployment soared.

The PAC, now with 15 ex-Guardian members out of a total of 28, were concerned that with improved conditions and free baths, the casual wards were becoming a better option than the local lodging houses. They noticed that gangs of casuals were arriving at the week-ends. They found that if they did not insist on making them work – with the race course a stone's throw away – they were flooded out on race days[i] and that only work cut their numbers. However, it was very difficult to detain them against their will and few absconding casuals were ever caught. To slow down the increase the PAC told Chaplin to detain casuals – who had no children – for a specific period unless he felt they had a real chance of employment.

---

[i] One committee member, Alderman Wellman, claimed that 200 "race tout casuals" came during race week and used the institution as a hotel, and that it was impossible to get such a large group to work. (*Gazette*, 21/2/1931.)

The PAC also decided to get tough with vagrants who had children. As one member said, "The real and sole reason for these vagrant children being on the road is that of begging…and that the absence of school facilities is a cruelty".[7] They were used as "window dressing" for more profitable begging and the workhouse often had to provide casual children with clothes and boots. The PAC ordered that every casual with children should be visited by a local officer from the National Society for the Protection of Children. If the parents were considered to be neglectful they would be taken to court. But as a vagrant family could only be detained for two days, and only for three nights when it included a Sunday, they were often gone before any legal action for adoption etc. could take place. Nevertheless, after the Children and Young Persons Act of 1933 the number of casual children in workhouses diminished considerably.

The medical officer, Stanley Firth, was required on one day a month to medically examine every casual in the wards at the time of his visit. In 1932 there were 26 cases of scabies – which took three days to treat – in these wards, and Firth felt that some of the other workhouses had been negligent in not properly inspecting their casuals. He did admit though that most casuals disliked medical inspections and even when seriously ill were reluctant to seek help. The PAC wanted to try to persuade the aged and infirm vagrants to give up the road and enter the House. They also wanted to rescue young male casuals from becoming habitual vagrants which in the long term would save the local authority money.

In March 1932 a hostel, the Sussex Home of St Francis, opened at Ticehurst, run by the Brotherhood of St Assissi, precisely for this type of youngster. It offered ten weeks of training in farm, house and garden work to casuals to get them off the road. The PAC resolved to try and send some of their younger casuals there – at a cost of 6s a week – if they had vacancies. This progressive policy signified an important change of attitude, for it meant that these young men were to be helped rather than punished for their poverty.

* * *

If the Government hoped the replacement of guardians by public assistance committees would end criticism of the system, it was sadly mistaken. On 17th September, 1932, this letter appeared in the *Brighton Herald*:

WORKHOUSE OR STARVATION? A POOR LAW OPPRESSION

Sir – From time to time, quarterly reports are given by the Public Assistance Committee containing the statement that a number of people have been given indoor relief. This statement in itself does not convey much. What it itself means in actual practice is that some unemployed men have been told that they must either risk starvation, or be shut up in a workhouse.

A case has recently come to my notice of a man aged about forty, whose only crime is that he cannot find work, and, having drawn outdoor relief in consequence of it, he is now told that all he can have is a ticket for the Workhouse. This man has made every endeavour to find work. He has simply been unsuccessful. If he, or anybody else similarly placed, enters a workhouse what chance has he of ever obtaining work again? Who will give employment to a man dressed in workhouse clothes? How many employers would give a man a job, knowing he had just come out of a Poor Law Institution?

No, it means they have probably got to be shut up in there for the rest of their lives, or take to tramping the roads. That this is an injustice to a man who has been unfortunate enough to be unemployed for a long spell, I think few would deny. But it is also an extra burden upon the ratepayers. It costs many shillings more a week to keep a man in an institution than it does to provide him with outdoor relief. The power which the Public Assistance Committee have to use their discretion as to the form of relief to be given can quite obviously be misused. It would be far better and fairer if a regulation were laid down that workhouse orders should only be given when a man has definitely refused an offer of suitable employment. – W. Chinchen

The letter prompted a reply from the editor of the *Herald*:

House orders are only given in the last resort, when every possible benefit has long been exhausted and outdoor relief has gone on for a very long time – two to three years in some cases. Even then, the "orders" are not given in such cases as would involve the break-up of a family; that is, married men, and even single men who are the support of some dependant, are not subjected to the "House Order" as in some parts of the country. That Brighton goes further in its humane handling of a peculiarly painful and difficult situation may be evidenced by the fact that a man who is in the "House" is given every opportunity to look for likely work, not in the regulation uniform, but in his own clothes.[8]

A few months later in another letter, Chinchen ridiculed the idea that it was easy to get relief, and criticized the way in which claimants had to stand before the committee at the parochial offices in Princes Street – just as in the days of the Guardians – and make their case. Separated by sex, it could be an intimidating atmosphere:

When it is realized that applicants of Poor Relief have to go through forms of degradation and are even placed in a "dock" as though they were criminals it is then seen how utterly ridiculous it is to imagine anybody doing so except through sheer necessity. [9]

Chinchen, a future Brighton councillor, knew what he was talking about, for he regularly claimed outdoor relief for himself in this period. Another letter from Mr Paul, the ex-Guardian, pinpointed the dilemma of the system:

I still retain painful memories of men and women unable to obtain employment, perhaps in cases of some physical disability, being offered a Workhouse order instead of outdoor relief. A member of the late Board, fortunately not on the PAC, would shout "I move a Workhouse order" against every individual, old or young who applied for relief. At times they were merited, however, I recall cases which I considered harsh and inhumane. If outdoor relief is refused in genuine cases and the applicants will not go to the Workhouse, does this not lead to some other alternative? It may lead to crime, yes, or even suicide.[10]

Eileen Jones' parents were caretakers at the parochial offices in Princes Street. She was born there in their flat in 1926, and lived there till she got married. In a "Personal Recollection", she remembered, as a child, what the atmosphere was like for claimants of relief:

There was a massive great hall with a concrete floor with like a drain well in the middle. They used to sit on rough benches in this hall, waiting their turn. Poor people, ill clad, dirty, smelly. I can smell the smell now of unwashed bodies, waiting their turn to see an officer to assess their poor state and what they would be given if they were in need. Whatever they possessed they would sell first and then could get tickets or a chitty for clothing for the children. This is after they had been in what was like a big courtroom in front of like judge and jury. I used to play judge and jury at night in the same room with my brother… I would see the mothers crying with children hanging on weak and hungry…Coming from school, I used to come home to dinner, walking into this building crowded with people. I would pick my way up the stairs, pick a path through them…My food used to choke me they were so hungry.

The PAC decided that those doing "test work" – work in exchange for outdoor relief – should no longer have to clear away leaves in cemeteries and move shingle on beaches. Instead, irrespective of the amount of relief they received, they would be expected to work three or four days a week on allotments in Hollingbury Park. Anything they produced was to go to the Poor Law institution. In November 1932, there were over a thousand cases receiving outdoor relief every week. Two years later the Labour councillors on the PAC wrote a "minority" report criticizing the relief committee. They said that the administration of public assistance was "carried out behind closed doors" and was "means tested", and that "test" work at Hollingbury was ineffective. One councillor, Harris, claimed he knew a widow who had two children and 14s rent a week to pay and was only granted £1 per week. The report said that claimants were treated as criminals as if they had no right to be old and feeble or unemployed. It concluded that however inadequate the relief might be, it must be administered humanely. They wanted Poor Law relief in Brighton to be humanized and "House Orders" only to be given to people without homes, or to people who had nobody to take care of themselves. The minority report criticized the PAC's system of granting only the very lowest possible amount to keep claimants from starvation.

The test work at Hollingbury nurseries owned by the council was also criticized. The report said it was "useless" as a training scheme. A letter [11] to a newspaper by a "working man" in 1935 asked: "What farmer or market gardener would employ a man who has been trained at Hollingbury?" Although receivers of outdoor relief now only had to work there three days, it was work that often dirtied the only clothes they had to look for work in, and they were often working alongside men with full rates of pay. The writer recommended that unemployed men – often broken in health by the last war – would be better getting training in shoemaking or carpentry. He also criticized the cruel "means test" which meant that "if a man earns an odd shilling, he must report the odd shilling and have it deducted". The same applied if his children worked or if he received a service pension. The PAC replied that 53 per cent of claimants were exempted from "test work".

During the 1930s destitute and homeless people often wandered into the local police station, especially between midnight and daylight when the relieving offices were closed. On one occasion a policeman brought a man suffering from memory loss, Albert Allison, to the sick ward. The night porter told him he could only be admitted to the casual ward as he had no medical certificate, so the policeman decided to take him back to the station and let him sleep in the charge room. The chief constable of Brighton complained to the PAC that similar difficulties had arisen before. The master, Chaplin, said that the man should have been admitted into the receiving ward and seen by the medical officer. The problem was that, ordinarily, a doctor's certificate and a three day order were necessary to be admitted into a sick ward.

* * *

In the last six months of 1932 there were 75 births and 258 deaths, the number of inmates averaged 940 and 6,753 casuals were admitted. Throughout the early thirties the institution seems to have been chronically understaffed. Only one barber was employed, and he only had time to give the inmates one shave a week. In February 1932 a letter from a member of staff, "Perplexed", contradicted the PAC's contention that staff only worked eight-hour days. He claimed that on average they worked 140–150 hours per fortnight including some nights. And in July, two nurses, Miss Nash and Mrs Warland, complained verbally about their working conditions in the infirmary but were told they had to put their complaints in writing.

Later, a member of staff was accused of sending anonymous letters to various people – including the master and the newspapers – airing staff grievances at the institution. The committee saw the man, but he denied it. They decided to dictate a letter to him. When they looked at it, it had the same spelling and grammatical mistakes as in one of the letters they had received. The man turned out to be the much complimented Mr Sayers, the reception officer. He admitted writing the letter signed "Perplexed" which had complained about the long hours. Sayers had a good army record and thirteen years of service in the workhouse and lived with his aged mother. The PAC asked him to resign. A letter from the ex-mayor of Deptford and ex-chairman of the Greenwich Guardians [Sayers' former employer], in his defence, said Sayers was seriously ill after having a grave operation and that there was "something wrong with the administration of the institution". He refused to resign and was sacked.

In 1934, Vincent Evans, the general secretary of the Poor Law Officers Union, wrote to the PAC complaining about the "use of inmate labour on work which should properly be performed by the officers in the institution". He claimed that "this was responsible for so much dissatisfaction and loss of prestige amongst institutional staff". The PAC replied that the inmates were employed according to their capacity and ability. They were mainly paid in kind. For example, inmate helpers who prepared the dining hall for weekly concerts were given extra tobacco.

Despite the difficulties, just as at the Brighton Borough Asylum at Haywards Heath, the evidence suggests that some workhouse staff tried to compensate for the drudgery and dullness of the inmates' lives by putting a great deal of effort into entertaining them. In January 1933, the *Herald* reported the celebrations:

Nurses as Pierrettes

...the beautifully decorated dining hall of the Poor Law Institution was surely the gayest of all Brighton theatres that night. Every New Year the staff give the inmates a "treat" but this year they excelled themselves, not only in hospitality, but in the fact that they devised and produced the entertainment themselves. It was a wholly admirable show – bright, up-to-date, full of fun and high spirits, excellently dressed, first-rate as to singing, and even as to dancing...Miss Ederidge's charming rendering of "Good-night Vienna," was made the opportunity for a delightful ensemble of singing and dancing; and Miss Clarke had a very comical "chorus" of men "skivvies" to support her. Mr J. Tongue was an extremely droll comedian; and there was capital comedy too...Serious singing of delightful quality came from Mrs Atkinson, Miss Myatt and Mr Button, and the troupe had a highly efficient pianist in Miss O'Dea.[12]

A large number of inmates, visitors, and local councillors watched. While the speechmaking took place in another room, music was provided in the dining room by Fred Love's Shaftesbury Dance Band. The inmates had a special tea and received tobacco and sweets:

One of the inmates writes: "It is just my wish, as an old crock, to let it be seen that there is someone in this place who would like to say a few words as to how we were all entertained. We were given a nice enjoyable meat tea, which consisted of as much ham and Christmas cake, best butter and tea, as one could wish to eat; also a grand concert which was so kindly got up and given by our staff, which meant weeks of very hard work of their own valuable time given up entirely for our sakes. Then at the interval there were cakes, tobacco and lemonade as well as a bag of apples and oranges at tea time for everyone. I am sure that no one could wish for anything better as a concert. We are all most grateful for what was done for us and also to feel that the Elm Grove Institution is not forgotten. [13]

The inmates were still wearing uniforms: the men in blue with white shirts and red ties, and the women in blue skirts and white blouses. With the election in 1933 of Margaret Hardy as the first woman mayor, one correspondent in the *Herald* was hoping that she would improve the female inmates' clothing:

> I wonder how many trouble to think of the degrading effect it must have for the women inmates to have to be dressed up in those ill-fitting cotton dresses, and also to wear those ill-fitting boots – not forgetting, of course, the depressing effect it must have on relatives and friends who visit the institution. One would almost think they were prisoners...This is 1934 not 1834! – W Winn-Jones [14]

However, the clothes remained the same. Female inmates still generally found it more difficult to leave the institution. On one occasion, one inmate wrote to the committee:

> Could you let me know if I could leave my baby in the nursery until I can get a home for it as I want to have it adopted, and I cannot do anything about it while I am in here. As I cannot get out to see anyone, and could you tell me whether I could apply about adoption. I am expecting the baby any day. My husband wants me to go back with him but he doesn't want the baby, and if I go back with him he may go off again as he has left me twice with other women and it would be impossible to work with another baby. I am quite willing to pay a little each week for its support until I get the home for it. [15]

She was refused, as she already had two children in Warren Farm. On the other hand, a male inmate was allowed to leave his wife and children in the institution while he looked for rooms, on the condition that he reported to the master every Monday morning.

* * *

The PAC were just as vigilant as the Guardians in prosecuting adults who abandoned their families. Alfred Cook left his wife and child at home and disappeared. Several weeks later, the London County Council informed the prosecuting officer at Brighton that they had a single man answering his description in their Westminster workhouse. The officer told the police, who brought him back to Brighton where he was sentenced to one month's hard labour. In another case, William Charles H. was sentenced to three months hard labour:

Whilst an inmate at Brighton with his wife and one child, three other children were in care at Bexhill. The man gave notice of his discharge in November, the children were fetched from Bexhill and he was made to take his children and wife out with him. He expected his wife, with a babe in arms, to walk with him to London. She refused and made him proceed to the Relief Offices, to obtain an order for re-admission of the whole family to the Poor Law Institution. The man refused to take the offered order and left the offices with his family but apparently left them stranded. They were immediately re-admitted and the man subsequently arrested and charged.[16]

And a mother and father were sentenced to one month's hard labour for neglecting their five children who were sent to the schools when they were convicted. When the parents came out they went straight to the magistrates to plead to have their children back. They told the court that they had a tiny wooden bungalow on top of the windswept Downs but had tried to improve it. After paying rent they barely had 9s to pay for everything else and were expecting another baby. The magistrates decided to allow them to keep the eldest and youngest of the children but they had to send the other three to a Dr Barnado's home. Their mother wept. The magistrates told the father if his position improved he could come back and make another application. On another occasion, the PAC repatriated a child back to South Africa after his parents had come to Brighton and left him with a relative. And they also spent £100 in sending an Indian woman and her children back to India after her soldier husband had died.

In April 1934, Garnet Chaplin gave a talk to a local society. He described the institution as a place for the sick and poor which was divided into four sections: house/infirmary/mental wards and casual wards for the aged and destitute of Brighton. He claimed it was one of the biggest in Britain with 1,275 beds and a 75 per cent occupancy rate. The infirmary had 550 beds, 230 of which were occupied by chronic cases. The Royal Sussex County Hospital only had 246. There were 1,150 inmates, some of whom received tobacco, sweets and extra allowances for work. Chaplin believed that:

We get good and bad, but my experience proves that the old Brightonian is really a good fellow, appreciative of anything that is done for his comfort…It was to the regularity of their meals that the inmates owed the long lives they undoubtedly enjoyed.[17]

He told the society that there had been 643 deaths and 199 births in 1933 and that 1,114 casuals came every month. The latter were usually set to work in the woodshed, gardens or cleaning the wards. On average they chopped 200,000 bundles of wood a year. Seemingly a lover of statistics, Chaplin stated that 5,000 eggs and two tons of potatoes were consumed every week.

In 1935 the lunacy wards in H Block were visited by Lady Eva de Paravicini, a magistrate. She found that, despite the brightening up of other wards, the lunacy wards were still painted in a dull green colour and recommended a brighter cream colour. She felt there needed to be a better separation between the quieter and more violent cases, and emphasized in her report that it should only be a temporary place of detention for acute cases. She noted that there was only one padded cell now.

* * *

In early 1935, the public assistance committee decided that the time was right to divide the workhouse into two. From January 1st 1936 the infirmary, now with 700 beds, was to become Brighton Municipal Hospital under the management of the public health committee. The "house" with 442 beds, apart from the casual wards, was to be known as the Elm Grove Home[i] and remain under the PAC. Only 92 of the 152 staff were to be employed at the home, and some of the remaining staff re-allocated to the hospital. To emphasize the change, out went the workhouse titles of "labour master/ mistress", to be replaced by chief male and chief female attendant.

All buildings to the right of the Elm Grove entrance, Blocks C,D,E,F and H, were to be the hospital, whereas the main central building, A Block and the rest of the site were to be the new "home". It was planned that eventually the two institutions would have separate entrances. As a temporary measure, the babies and children of the nursery were transferred to number one receiving home at Warren Farm.

Just as the abolition of the Guardians had been a symbolic step in the eradication of the stigma of the workhouse for the poor, so too did this latest change promise to eradicate it further. However, as Harry Gaston has

---

[i] It was named this in May 1936.

pointed out, "the hospital was not able to throw off its workhouse reputation locally".[18] Edie Burt, quoted in the previous chapter, remembered that her mother refused to go to the hospital because she still thought of it as a workhouse. Gaston also noted that "conditions in the buildings forming the home, almost certainly without exception, were far inferior to those comprising the hospital".[19] For example, all toilet facilities in A Block were outside and J Block (containing 118 women) had only one inside toilet.

Next, the question was, who was to be in charge of the hospital? The master, Garnet Chaplin, was sceptical about the ability of the medical officer, Stanley Firth, to run it: "Medical officers with years spent in academic training were wasting their time in attempting to become efficient administrators of institutions." [20] In fact, although Firth was appointed medical superintendent, Chaplin was appointed to be the hospital's steward as well as retaining his role of master. However, his wife was not made matron of the hospital.[i]

The medical staff now came under the hospital's control although assistant nurses, ambulance drivers and attendants were to be under the home's, although they were available for hospital duties. The medical supplies were to be the responsibility of Stanley Firth, while Chaplin was in charge of the ordinary supplies. And for the first time, all nurses' uniforms were to be made by local contractors instead of being made at the institution.

A few weeks after the changeover, Chaplin made a report to the PAC which was publicized in the *Brighton Gazette* [21] under the headline, "Pleasant Life in 'The House on The Hill" – All About Brighton's Largest Family." He spoke about the nursery children – the under-threes – being taken for daily rides in the donkey cart; the daily walks on the Downs – weather permitting – for the mental patients; and the male patients playing football and cricket. For the aged and infirm who numbered 95 women and 68 men:

> The wireless installation does much to dispel monotony, and the staff is zealous in attention to the patients and doing everything possible to soften the pillow of old age.

But the main beneficiaries of the more compassionate regime were the casuals. After receiving a meal on admission, and after a bath and being provided with dressing gowns:

---

[i] Mrs Rylance was appointed.

356

each man is issued with a clean shirt , and so to bed to sleep on a well-sprung wire mattress bedstead with straw palliase and blankets. The Wards are centrally heated throughout. On the second night of their detention the men have the privilege of remaining up until 8pm for the purpose of reading and games (draughts and dominoes). They are also permitted to take papers and books for reading in bed until the time for "lights out."

The casuals were detained for two nights unless Sunday intervened. Their main work was still wood-chopping and bundling, although they also cleaned the wards and did gardening. Chaplin commented:

I am sure the Committee will realize what a difficult problem is set in keeping the men fully at work, especially as each day sees a fresh group of men whose characters and temperaments are in the main unknown to the Officers.

The casuals' diet was as follows:

Breakfast: 8oz bread, 1oz of margarine or dripping and one pint of tea.
Dinner: 3oz bread, 2oz cooked meat, 2oz cheese, 4oz potatoes and
                4oz vegetables.
Supper: 8oz bread, 1oz margarine or dripping and 1 pint of tea.

On their discharge they were given a mid-day meal of 8oz of bread and 2oz of cheese to take with them in a paper bag.

In the main part of the building, A Block, according to Chaplin, the inmates were primarily old Brightonians, there through destitution. He admitted that none was paid for working, but men and women received tobacco and dry sugar and tea respectively for "work of a disagreeable nature".

The classification of the inmates receives very careful attention. It will be readily seen that proper classification has an important bearing upon the happiness and comfort of the inmates whose characters, temperaments, educational and social up-bringing differ so widely. Frequent leave of absence is granted to the older inmates to enable them to visit their friends. The dietary is exceedingly good; the quantity and quality of the food provided being also very satisfactory and obviously greatly appreciated…Bed-time is 8 o'clock in the winter and 9 o'clock during the summer months. During the months of January and February entertainments are held in the Dining Hall. These entertainments, on an average two per week, are provided by local concert parties and are immensely enjoyed.

It is not clear from Chaplin's statement how he was classifying the inmates in a practical sense. Describing the institution as running with "the smoothness of a well ordered machine", Chaplin gave some statistics. No fewer than 78,000 letters and 22,000 parcels arrived at the porter's lodge every year. The huge number of letters indicated that many of the inmates must have been literate. Approximately, annually, there were 100,000 visitors to the institution or hospital. Two thousand meals were prepared daily and in the last year, 1935, the bakery had produced 82,671 4lb loaves and 17,310lbs of cakes, which were distributed to Warren Farm as well as Elm Grove. Also, 1,712,851 articles had been laundered, double the total dealt with in 1925. No fewer than 2,000 pairs of boots and shoes were repaired and 33 pairs of boots made in the shoemaker's shop. In the tailor's shop 105 coats and jackets, 28 waistcoats and 72 pairs of trousers were made for the staff, and 139 jackets, 90 waistcoats and 196 pairs of trousers for the inmates, in addition to 2,500 repairs. Finally, £75-worth of produce was obtained from the four-acre garden. At the time of Chaplin's report, there were 460 inmates in the home and 390 patients in the municipal hospital.

Given the positive nature of Chaplin's report, it must have been a surprise to the PAC when he and his wife suddenly resigned a month later to

Fig 36 The shoemakers' shop.

run the Kirkdale Home for the Aged in Liverpool. According to one committee member, his departure had only been brought about by "the intereference of other people". In fact, Garnet Chaplin had not wanted to be subservient to the medical officer in respect of the hospital. He had found it a "humiliation" to be under the doctor, and complained about interference from the health committee. Also, he may have seen the prediction in one or two newspapers that the home would eventually be taken over by the municipal hospital, and that nationally workhouses were to be phased out. Compared to their immediate predecessors, the Chaplins had not been there long, but they had made a very favourable impression and had brought about a high state of efficiency. In their last few weeks there were many presentations and tributes to them. In a brightly decorated dining hall, the staff presented them with a silver salver and illuminated address with all the names of the subscribers. They were also given a gift of cutlery by the old ladies of the institution.

Despite Garnet Chaplin's impressive report, and however bearable some of the conditions may have been, the stigma of the workhouse still refused to go away. For, as an elderly lady who lived through this period recently told this author, to be poor in the thirties was a thing of shame and to be in a workhouse was a mark of shame, whichever part you were in.

*   *   *

The PAC decided that it was no longer essential for the matron and master to be man and wife, so they replaced Garnet Chaplin with Mr S. King, the assistant master, who had been at Elm Grove since 1911. At the time of the former's departure there were 400 patients and 200 staff in the hospital, and 600-plus casuals with 140 staff in the home.

In June 1936, with the home becoming increasingly overcrowded, the PAC decided to set up a committee to interview all able-bodied men and women in A Block who were over 50, with a view to their being discharged and granted outdoor relief or other means of assistance. One hundred and forty-eight inmates were interviewed. Twelve said they wanted to be discharged to family and friends. However, on investigation only eight of the latter were prepared to accommodate them. Twenty-six more inmates wanted to be discharged if they could find accommodation. In the end, only seven out of the 148 were discharged, three to friends and four to other accommodation. Undoubtedly, one of the motives for trying to get the inmates to leave was financial as well as a part of social policy. It cost from 25s to 30s a week to keep somebody at the home, whereas outside maintenance charges were only 16s per week.

A Block was still pretty grim. It had a cheerless and barrack-like atmosphere and outside toilets. To have a bath the old men had to go out into the open air, up a windswept flight of steps and along a path to the bathrooms. As the medical officer observed, after a hot bath it was not a sensible journey. And most of the women in A Block were far from physically fit and able. Forty of them were very old and infirm. They lived on the ground floor which was cold, draughty and without central heating.

Despite the experimental closure of the casual wards at Shoreham workhouse, the number of casuals admitted to the home started to fall, no doubt helped by the local Salvation Army facilities and the rise of charities such as the Hostel for the Destitute and Homeless Help Society. Albert Tindall, the ex-Guardian and now a member of the PAC, claimed in a report that "no one has given a satisfactory answer about the 'vanishing tramp'. He prefers the old insanitary buildings to the modern up-to-date wards...Most

Fig 37 The Gazette *caption read, "Well cared for: a glimpse in the Old People's Day Room, where the inmates spend their time sewing and reading by the fireside."* (Gazette 22/3/1936.)

Fig 38 "In the nursery: some of the bonny babies whose welfare receives the attention of a devoted staff." (Gazette 22/2/1936.)

are between 31 and 60." [22] At least by then the casuals were far better at seeking medical advice, and in 1937, 346 casuals asked to see the doctor and 956 were examined at the routine monthly inspections. Of those, 83 received treatment or advice and 23 were admitted into the hospital. They also no longer had to work on Sundays and were the following year given the same food as the other inmates for Christmas.

From Jan 1937, as an experiment, no settlement enquiries (to see which authority were financially responsible for them) were to be made of casuals over 65, to encourage them to give up the road and go into an institution. However, according to the master:

> The elimination of settlement enquiries has proved no inducement to aged and infirm casuals to enter and remain in institutions; they do not take readily to the routine of an institution however much is done for their comfort, and in spite of liberal leave of absence, postpone as long as possible the day when illness or physical defect compels them to finally give up the road.[23]

In January 1937, the mayor of Brighton, councillor John Routley, triumphantly announced at the new year party for the elderly at the Elm

Grove Home, that "Bumble is dead",[i] and that if anyone doubted it they should come and visit it themselves. The inmates had a bumper tea and were entertained by the "Snappy Ten" and the Brighton Corporation Tramways Band. A year later, there were 207 men, 162 women and 18 children in the home, and 48 inmates were receiving treatment in the hospital. The PAC improved the inmates' diet – which hadn't been changed for twenty years – and also allowed the casuals to have the same food. The improvements included:

Breakfast	Porridge three times a week; marmalade once a week; bread and 1oz margarine daily.
Dinner	Pudding to be served six days a week.
Tea	Jam twice weekly with ½oz margarine; cake once a week; bread with 1oz margarine when no jam was served.

Between tea at 5.30pm and breakfast at 7am the able-bodied inmates received no food and so the PAC considered introducing a supper consisting of bread, biscuits, cheese and cake at 7.15pm.

In July 1938, all inmates over 65 were allowed up to 2s pocket money a week to spend on "additional comforts". During the year there was a visit from a health inspector, Miss Hobbs. She found that the inmates were only bathed once a fortnight; that many sheets were dirty, that often the beds and pillows were made of straw and that the bedsteads were very old. There was no drinking water on the dining table and the table cloths were dirty. Of the four hundred paupers in the home, 275 were over 65, and to all intents and purposes the institution was on the way to becoming one large old peoples' home. One member of the PAC, Frank Ingram, said he saw poor old people tramping up the hill because they could not afford a penny for the tram on their afternoon off. Ingram claimed that staff at the workhouse gave preference to those inmates who had money, because "it is a rule of life. Better off people receive better treatment". In fact, it was rumoured that the cooks used to sell food to the inmates with money during the night.

By the end of 1938, 112 men and 30 women in the home were performing work for no financial reward, only extras. Eighty-one of the working men

---

[i] The parish beadle who sends Oliver Twist to pick oakum in the workhouse in Dickens' novel.

were over 65 and seven were in their eighties. They helped with the stoking, in the dining hall and as messengers. Two men worked in the stables and six in H Block, which was now part of the hospital. The women were mainly in the laundry, and ten of them were over eighty. The old workhouse bakery was still supplying all the bread and cakes for the institution, but without inmate labour.

By the end of the decade, although conditions had generally improved in the home, you still needed permission to leave. One man jumped over a wall to post a letter and when he came back was sent to the magistrates where he was given seven days' hard labour. In December 1938 an inmate, Stanley Ward, was transferred by train to London to his Union of settlement. He worked until a few minutes before leaving and was taken by an official, unshaven, unwashed and without a hat or coat. The PAC censored the master, King, for allowing him to go in this condition. They said that there had been "several cases like this, and if travelling on a train with Poor Law officers it discredits the committee". This created "adverse comments about the home, and in future inmates should be properly clothed when discharged" [25] The committee ordered King to excuse inmates task duty on the morning when they were discharged.

* * *

Fig 39 An outing for the aged inmates in the 1930s.

If the First World War had come as a surprise to many, a second world war had been anticipated for some time. As early as October 1937 there had been "black-out" practice in Brighton, and for one night all cars had to have dimmed lights. A year later, ominously, electrically operated air raid sirens were placed on the top of A Block and "work began on adapting D and E Block basements as air raid shelters, and two thousand sandbags and special darkened lamps were purchased for use in the hospital".[26] Anti-gas classes were held, and gas masks were supplied to all inmates, patients and staff. And the bell above the clock was tied up, never to be used again.

The winter of 1938–39 was the coldest for thirty years, and the weather was causing a terrible slump in the building trade. In January 1939 there were demonstrations in Brighton, organized by the National Unemployed Workers Movement (NUWM) which had been founded the previous November. Its banners demanded "Work Not Charity" and declared "Chamberlain Must Go", as unemployment in the town hit 7,000. That month, eight members of the NUWM, led by their leader Anton Miles, entered the Albion Hotel where forty members of the Wine and Food Society were having their dinner. Unfurling banners of "You feast while we starve", they were hurriedly taken downstairs and fed in the staff quarters.

Meanwhile, in Moulescoomb – where 45 per cent of the male population were in the building trade – the vicar, Rev Bransby-Jones, reported that "there were starving people and savage want. Men broken by long spells of unemployment and undernourishment pitiably clad have cried on his doorstep".[27] And the *Gazette* admitted that in north and east Moulescoomb[i] and Whitehawk "poverty, misery and tragedy lies behind the attractive veneer of her [Brighton's] suburbs".[28] It found a serious shortage of food and clothing and when there were six to ten children in a family, unemployment pay was totally inadequate.

---

[i] *Gazette* 24/12/1938.

40 Unemployment demonstrations in Western Road, January 1939.

In the spring the government sent out ration cards. Underground tunnels below the back gardens of Sussex Terrace began to be prepared as bomb shelters. In July, there were black-out and gas mark drills in all Brighton schools, and housewives started to stockpile food. With war looming, the desperate conditions in Brighton were reflected by the sudden increase in casuals once again – 6,827 by 30th June that year.

Chapter Twenty

THE END OF THE FARM?

From 1st April 1930 the industrial schools were to be recognized as a public elementary school and eventually a junior school under the Education Department[i] and to be run by the Warren Farm management committee in place of the Guardians' visiting committee. The new management immediately organized the installation of electricity and issued permits for children to visit their parents. In the short term, they cut back on outings and summer camps[ii] and hinted that the farm might be abolished. In May 1931 Alfred Hollingdale, who had been superintendent since 1910, produced a report on the current state of the institution. For the boys:

> much of the tailoring, shoemaking, gardening and farm work and kitchen work is designed to meet the routine needs of the institution. Their value as vocational education can be increased by the provision of instruction on educational lines, not subordinated to the institution's needs.[1]

He recommended that agriculture and cookery should be taught at Warren Farm or in Brighton, and lessons in "waiting" for those who wanted to work in hotels. For the girls:

> I recommend that a course of Advanced Cookery and Housewifery be provided for girls who have left school…For both boys and girls I recommend two hours general education per week.[2]

However, some of the girls he felt might be better off elsewhere:

> I recommend that Irene H. aged 14 and Doris H. aged 16 years be placed under the care of the Guardianship Society. The former has periodic fits of ungovernable temper which render her a danger to other children and to herself. The latter is incapable of earning her living unless carefully supervised. The Society charges 17/6d per week but any wages earned are credited against

---

[i] Although the PAC was still responsible for it.

[ii] They started to go to Dymchurch again in 1933.

this…Kathleen C. occasionally refused to eat and has been filthy in her habits – in view of her thoroughly bad influence here, better the Magdalen Hospital, Streatham.[3]

The numbers at the schools began to rise dramatically in the early 1930s due to "day scholars" from the local area. By the end of 1932, there were 271 children, including 36 of the latter. There were also five children over sixteen. In January 1933 Hollingdale was declaring that "our old enemy diphtheria has been defeated thanks to three years of immunization advocated by Dr McCurrich." However, there were epidemics of influenza and conjunctivitis, with 104 and 54 cases respectively. In March 1933 a report by Mr J. O'Brien, a Ministry of Health inspector of children's homes, strangely didn't allude to this:

An addition to the staff has just been authorized in the form of the games master who is to be responsible for the organized games of the boys and for their discipline during recreation time. The girls need one now…The premises throughout were in good order, and the children appear to be well-cared for and to live as normal a life as possible in an institution of this size….[4]

A visit by an educational inspector found that "they [the children] are a little shy of oral answering and need encouragement to speak out more… but that the lessons are purposeful". Margaret Hardy, a member of the management committee, said the children were "clean, brightly clad and seemed happy in classes and out of school…at meal times Grace was spoken clearly and with reverence." [5] Dr Firth, the medical officer, recommended a change of diet for the 3–5 year olds:

Porridge on five mornings per week as an option to bread and milk. Fish once per week, none at the moment. Two eggs per week instead of one and the substitution of butter for margarine.[6]

In April 1933 the schools sent 86 of their older children to the Whitehawk senior school, which had just opened, and started to receive more and more junior and infant children from the Woodingdean locality – 81 in total, twenty of whom brought their own food. A Mr Peach was appointed the first headmaster of the junior school. A local author, Peter Mercer, has written:

Warren Farm School did not enjoy a good reputation and at first the village children found it very daunting and many were made miserable by the cold and rather unattractive décor, stone flag floors and the brick paved playground. It was a very austere place, particularly for young children. They also found it strange to sleep on little beds in the school or in the meadows at lunchtimes, a part of the school life emanating from the Victorian times…School started before 9am with an inspection of every boy and girl. The orphan boy always wore grey trousers and black boots. Day pupils were not obliged to wear a uniform and were easily discernible in a crowd.[7]

With the Hollingdales due to retire in 1934, Alfred was asked to report to the committee on the value of the tradesmen. The shoemaker was expected to do repairs and give some technical training to the boys who assisted him. However, Hollingdale thought that they were often "indifferent craftsmen" and that there were so many repairs on a daily basis that it "does not permit a very high standard of work".[8] He concluded that "the educational value of this type of workman is very small". The same applied to the tailor who had so much work to get through that there was

Fig 41 An October plunge for the boys in the open air swimming pool at Warren Farm.

little time for instruction although Hollingdale believed that "the present master tailor is an intelligent man and is an excellent workman and does his best to teach his trade to the boys who assist him".[9] Next, Hollingdale reported that the primary object of the Farm was to:

> provide clean milk of good quality, fresh vegetables, and to dispose of the waste from the Schools economically. It enables a certain number of boys to get some experience of farm work. Their instructor is the working Farm Bailiff – he is a good farmer and an estimable man but the educational value of his teaching is not considerable. He turns out some excellent boys however who readily obtain places as farmhands because they are able to perform minor operations of farming, understand something of the care of stock, horses and poultry and are able to milk so the proof of the pudding may be estimated by the eating thereof. [10]

Hollingdale thought the cook was "an intelligent man, assisted by boys in vegetable preparation and general cookery who has placed many boys." He concluded that:

> Manual or Hand Work is a recognized side of general education and I am of the opinion that were boot repairing, tailoring, farm work and cookery, if under skilled tuition are not only as valuable educationally as any other form of handwork but have the advantage of producing something of material value to the children and the institution.[11]

There was no report about the value of needlework for the girls.

Hollingdale was proud of the schools and was offended when a member of the management committee intimated that the "[Farm] children who go to Whitehawk school are not equal to the rest of the children in attainments". Hollingdale demonstrated that the latest end-of-year exam results showed the children had done quite well, some even coming first. (The fifty boys averaged 16th out of a class of 40; the twenty-eight girls averaged 24th out of 39). And three out of the eight prefects at the Whitehawk senior school were from Warren Farm.

In the Hollingdales last full year, 1933, in the summer alone the children had four steamer trips, two motor coach rides, two excursions to Orchards Tea Garden, Hassocks, and seven picnics apart from the summer camp. A male voice choir had also visited the schools, and trips to the piers had been organized by Margaret Hardy. At Christmas, the children had stockings containing fruit, nuts, sweets and suitable presents, including a present each from the Lewes Road Congregational Church young people's class.

There were also gifts and a Christmas tree from a store, British Home Stores. One of the committee, Horace Webb, acted as Father Christmas. Lunch consisted of pork and beef and plum pudding served by members of the committee, just as the Guardians had before them. In the evening the children themselves provided the entertainment.

In 1934 one of the empty receiving homes was made into a separate and independent remand home despite "serious objections" about it being too close to the schools and the danger of the other children being influenced by bad behaviour. The home had previously been in Ditchling Road. The committee agreed only on the basis that there was a complete and effective separation from the rest of the children. The remand home started with six "delinquents", aged between 9 and 16, who arrived from all over the country. The log book, [12] which covers its ten year history, shows that the boys were constantly escaping and being chased all over the countryside by staff and police. When caught they were often whipped or given the taws – a thong made of leather. By 1938 the numbers had risen to fifteen, and they were doing canework and handicraft. The remand home had separate staff from the schools, but used their nurses when necessary and their food and bedding

Alfred and Ellen Hollingdale retired at the end of October 1934 to take over a private hotel in Herne Bay. They had been at the schools since July 1910. Alfred had had progressive ideas and had introduced mixed classes and the "house" system. George Chance, appointed a senior master in 1917, later recalled that he was kind to the staff. In 1916, when there had been a collection for a memorial tablet for the old Warren Farm boys who had fallen in the War, Hollingdale had made the biggest donation. On another occasion, he had gone to visit an old boy who had caught pneumonia and was languishing in a military hospital in Aldershot. The year he retired, there were 190 children in the schools, 62 of whom attended Whitehawk, and 105 day scholars who came to Warren Farm from the local area. Hollingdale had overseen great changes, for now the institution was more a children's home than a workhouse, more a school than an industrial school. And their famous band had not for a long time been known as the Brighton Workhouse Juvenile Band. In a poignant picture (overleaf), when Henry Carr their popular bandmaster died the following year, the boys lined the cemetery.

Fig 42 Boys from the Warren Farm Industrial Schools Band lining the route at the Lewes Road cemetery at the funeral of their bandmaster, Henry Carr.

Fig 43 The band during the 1930s.

The Hollingdales both received gold watches at their retirement dinner and in Alfred's farewell speech, he said that leaving:

> was like parting from one's own family. I do hope that you will grow up to be good men and women and that you will so manage your affairs that you will be able to enjoy most of the comforts of life and many of the luxuries. I have told you how to do it. Mind you carry out my instructions.[13]

The threat implicit in his last words illustrated the disciplinarian side of his character. One old boy, Frank Jones, remembered all his life how Hollingdale had made all the boys stand outside on a bitterly cold night, dressed only in their nightshirts and forced to hold with raised arms sideways their heavy boots until a boy who had stolen a box of matches owned up.

Hollingdale's record was also tainted by his behaviour towards female teachers and staff who had left in quick succession in 1915. He had been suspended for five weeks and had been very fortunate not to have lost his job. Later on, the author was told that on another occasion he removed a twelve-year-old girl from a coach who was just about to go on an outing and made her sit on his lap in his office. She never spoke about the incident afterwards.

Unlike other posts which sometimes had no applicants at all, the jobs of super-intendent and matron attracted no fewer than ninety-one couples. Five of them were invited for interview, and Ronald and Kathleen Ferriman, from a children's home in Grimsby, were chosen. He was 31, she 29, and they were the youngest of the candidates. Frank Jones later recalled that the Ferrimans' arrival had been like "a breath of fresh air", with the "sun coming into their lives" after the Hollingdales' regime.

Fig 44 The Hollingdales at the time of their retirement.

* * *

In 1935, Ronald Ferriman wrote a comprehensive report about the staff. He reported that the tailor and shoemaker were helped by two boys each in doing repairs and worked 56-hour weeks. The drill master was responsible for the physical welfare for children aged 7–16 and for their cleanliness, as was the girls' attendant for the girls. But Ferriman was not at all happy with Miss P., the infants' attendant who was in charge of the cleanliness and bathing of all children between five and seven years of age:

> In my opinion [she] is not at all suited for the welfare and training of infant children…Abrupt in manner, industrious only when being watched…[14]

She worked a 67½-hour week, and he recommended she be sacked, which she was the following year. He was also unhappy about Mr B., the attendant/yardsmaster, who he felt was unsuitable to be with children.

Ferriman discovered that there were only four teachers available for supervisory duties and asked for them to have uniforms. He also found many "irregularities with the schools accounts", which were the responsibility of his assistant, Mr Puttick, who had been employed there since 1922. He was asked to resign. Lastly, Ferriman said he and his wife found that the "behaviour and manners of a number of children needed much to be desired".[15] Mrs Ferriman also wrote a report in which she concluded that it was necessary to rearrange the domestics. As a result, several of the temporary staff left.

As numbers at the schools dropped to 160 out of an accommodation capacity of 260, the shoemaker was given notice and the remaining leather was transferred to the Elm Grove home. The boys were being taught carpentry, kitchen work, gas and hot water fitting, electrical work, farm and garden work and how to play musical instruments. The girls still mainly learnt needlework and domestic work. The Ferrimans spent time visiting children in service in Littlehampton, Bramber, Worthing and Eastbourne. The children were still subject to abuse and exploitation as cheap labour. On one occasion, Gladys T., who had gone into domestic service, was admitted to the Elm Grove home. The master asked Dr Firth to examine her:

> I did not find any serious injury, but there were bruises on the right upper arm and a bruise on the left upper arm and on her chest. The injuries detailed would be consistent with the girl having been struck with a stick.[16]

The committee decided not to pursue the mistress, but did not send any more girls to her and tried to find Gladys another placement.

With the decrease in numbers, the education committee considered building a new local school, and the future of Warren Farm was in doubt. Public opinion was turning against the centralized treatment of children in institutions and in favour of bringing children up in a more loving and homely environment. The committee looked at three options. One was to board-out [i] [foster] deserted, orphaned or ward-of-the-council children (due to neglect or unfit parents) with foster parents [ii] who would train the children in "honesty, obedience, personal cleanliness and industry". Each child would be provided with a new outfit on leaving the schools. The parents would be responsible for making the children go to school and church. The council would have the power to visit the children at any time and also to take them away from the home if they were not satisfied. Ferriman believed that only twenty-nine out of a possible fifty children would be suitable for boarding-out. They were to be visited at least once every six weeks by members of a boarding-out committee.

The second option was for the older children to go to "scattered homes" in residential areas around the town run by foster mums. Each would have no more than twenty children and would also provide some form of industrial training. They would use local schools and amenities, like children from normal homes.

The third option was for "group homes", containing no more than twelve of the younger children, to be made out of the receiving homes at Warren Farm. The homes would have to be divided from each other by an iron fence. The objection to this last option was that the children would still be stigmatized by their background and by remaining on the site. However, no immediate decision as to the three options was made. But one thing was clear: Warren Farm's days as an institution were numbered.

In October 1937, the management committee decided to hold an enquiry into the continual resignations from the schools, particularly by new staff,

---

[i] London County Councl were already boarding out some of their own children in Moulescoomb.

[ii] Foster parents were ineligible if they had been receiving relief in the previous twelve months.

and complaints against the matron. It soon became clear that there was a lot of tension between the nurses and the attendants. According to the latter, the former thought they were superior. Other staff felt the Ferrimans were too soft, that staff took advantage of them and that the children did not work hard enough. A male member of staff, when asked why so many were leaving, blamed the rumours about Warren Farm closing. But a senior female attendant felt the blame for the resignations lay elsewhere:

Attendant: Some time ago you, the committee, got rid of six officers…There is always the feeling that you are trying to get rid of us. It puts us in a funny position; it makes us feel unsafe.

Miss Dorothy Stringer (committee member): We had good reason.

Attendant: They were very nice girls. Of course there are a lot of petty complaints. You take my job – it is not the one I took on…The children get up at six and they work too long. They spend one hour sweeping the dormitory and dining room before having their breakfast at 7.45. [17]

In its final report the committee concluded that the matron was "tactless" and that there was a "bad attitude of older staff to new ones". As a result of the enquiry two senior staff accused of being "troublemakers" resigned.

Morale among the staff was undoubtedly low. As early as March 1937 there had been headlines about "the end of the Warren Schools". The buildings were increasingly antiquated and obsolete and required a lot of money to modernize. Finally, it was agreed in principle that the schools should close, as Brighton was one of the last boroughs to support the "barrack system". One factor was economic. At the schools it cost 32s a week to keep a child, whereas there were 580 children on outdoor relief whose parents only received two shillings a week per child. One councillor, Mr Major, questioned whether children from the criminal classes would get the necessary control in foster families. Others feared that foster parents would take the children for profit. Another said that "some [children] are innocent little angels, and some are wicked little devils".[19] Generally though, most of the committee members believed the children needed a normal family life.

By January 1938, there were 93 boys and 53 girls, with 31 children attending Whitehawk senior school and 72 attending the day school at Warren Farm. Dr Firth, the medical officer, was critical of the dietary for the children aged 5-16 years. They had no variety and no fresh fruit every week. Only sick children were being given fish and eggs. Although there were fewer and fewer children, more of them were being admitted into the infirmary, 437 in 1937 compared to 361 in 1935, and there were serious outbreaks of mumps. He advised a four week diet rota. Also, he suggested that children who went to bed at 8pm or later should have supper of bread, butter and biscuits.

Firth was asked by the committee if he could explain why in a six months' period in the winter of 1938, twenty-one babies aged between three and eleven months had been transferred from the schools' nursery to the municipal hospital, five of them subsequently dying. He was asked whether he thought "their sojourn at the Farm was in any way prejudicial to their health".[20] Firth replied that they all had suffered from severe colds and coughs and mild influenza, and that in the winter the nursery "left much to be desired." Another factor was the poor staffing levels at the schools. For example, the infirmary nurse had twelve children to look after night and day, and worked 156 hours per week with little time off.

45 *Retirement of Miss M.E. Moore after 33 years as the infant teacher.*

By November 1938, 116 children were already in three scattered homes and Brighton Council passed the following resolution:

That the Warren Farm Schools cease to be used as an institution for the reception and maintenance of poor children; who are to be accommodated in the existing four receiving homes and a pair of homes to be erected at Warren Farm. The hospital at Warren Farm is to be used for new admissions and the treatment of minor cases. The farm is to be discontinued.[21]

The farm was to be sold and everything in it after the crops had been harvested. The staff were to be cut from forty-two to fifteen as fewer would be needed to run the new, foster-style-run homes. Included in the cuts were Mr and Mrs Ferriman and Burchett the bandmaster. That summer, for the first time, the girls and boys went to their summer camp near Rottingdean at the same time as an "economy". As numbers fell to 125, the seamstress was given notice, and it was decided to send the laundry to the municipal hospital. The tailor was also dispensed with and sent to Elm Grove, and other redundancies followed. Now only two girls were helping out with domestic work, compared with twenty, two years earlier.

Fig 46 The infirmary at Warren Farm.

378

Despite the changes, the stigma remained. In August 1938 Mrs Jenner, a teacher at a small local private school, suggested putting up a sign "Woodingdean School for Infants and Juniors":

I don't want the Warren Farm Schools renamed as a whole, only the part which is distinctive as a day school. Many of them [local residents] say we have not even got a school here after paying rates all these years. I point out to them that they have. It is a properly appointed school with properly certificated teachers. They say, "It isn't fair that our children should go to the Warren." The parents have no objection to the children, nor to the teachers, nor to the building, but they have a decided objection to the association of the name. I have nothing at all against the Warren Farm Schools. I think that the children cared for there are wonderfully happy, and wonderfully looked after, as anyone would think who has the slightest knowledge of the Schools and their officers, but the fact remains that people do not understand the drastic changes that have taken place there and still think of it as an Industrial School and reformatory. If the headed paper was "Woodingdean Schools", much heart burning amongst the better type of parents (who have their children's welfare at heart) would be relieved.[22]

Mrs Jenner also went on to say that at the "local branch of the Girl Guides, the other girls stand aloof from them [the girls at the Schools]".

When Warren Farm had opened in 1862 there had been only a few isolated farms in the vicinity. By 1938, the village of Woodingdean had expanded to five hundred premises and over thirty businesses. As the local population grew, so the ratepayers became more vociferous. Already one year, seventy-five ratepayers had sent a petition to the council complaining about the smell of manure in the summer and the smell of the piggeries, situated on the main village road, which emanated from the schools. The piggeries contained 190 pigs and were a main source of profit, so the committee were reluctant to act. However, by January 1938 there had even been representations in parliament from MPs to the Ministry of Health about the smell, and the committee was forced to move the piggeries to the south side of the schools.

In January 1939, with only 119 children at Warren Farm, half the staff were laid off, and with its impending closure at the end of the year, the remainder were told to look for other jobs. In March, ironically, it was decided that there should be no more military training at the schools and the cadet corps was replaced by the boy scouts. It was hoped this would

47 Fig The casualty ward.

'God rest you merry Gentlemen
Let nothing you dismay'

The "Brighton and Hove Herald" extends
to all its readers best wishes for a very
HAPPY CHRISTMAS

Fig 48 Christmas 1937.

make it easier for the boys to mix with others and that they would be more useful to the community. All the animals on the farm were sold and the old carthorse "Prince", aged 27, was put out to pasture after 22 years of service. However, despite the previous year's resolution to close Warren Farm, the outbreak of war delayed it.

Fig 49 The mayor and mayoress at Warren Farm, Christmas 1937.

50 The Ferrimans with the mayoress at a Christmas party.

Shortly before 5am on Friday 1st September, 1¼ million German troops, accompanied by the terrifying roar of Stuka dive bombers, invaded Poland. Later that day, 10,000 bewildered looking child evacuees from London, with gas marks in containers slung around their shoulders, arrived at Brighton station. On 3rd September Neville Chamberlain, the prime minister, declared war on Germany.

Chapter Twenty-one

EVACTUATION AND THE SECOND WORLD WAR

As soon as war was declared, the casual wards (B Block) were taken over as an Air Raid Precautions (ARP) first aid post, while A Block was evacuated in 72 hours and requisitioned as an emergency hospital with 413 beds to accommodate patients from hospitals in vulnerable areas and to provide beds for the expected casualties. However, the chronic infirm, both male and female, remained in J and L Blocks. No patients from the municipal hospital were transferred, and it temporarily took over the Elm Grove home's staff and the porters' lodge.

As they had been empty for some time, parties of cleaners had to be sent to the properties requisitioned and rented for the three hundred A Block evacuees. No. 25 Sussex Square was again one of the properties, and ninety-three aged inmates were sent there. Montpelier Terrace, Vernon Gardens (nos. 4 and 5), and 13 Vernon Terrace accommodated the remainder. All the houses had gardens, which was an obvious advantage. As for the casuals, Horace Webb, the PAC chairman, believed that:

> Gradually they [the tramps] will disappear off the road in war time. The able-bodied of them will be called to the Services and others will be found work when labour becomes short. At least that was the experience of the last war.[1]

The male casuals were sent to the Church Army hostel in St James' Street, where there were no warm baths, and the females and child casuals to 13 Montpelier Crescent. The hostel only agreed to take up to thirty casuals per night, but not the "verminous ones". The casuals still had to report to the Elm Grove home first, which meant a walk up the three-quarter-mile long hill, then traipsing back into town. Often hungry, and in all weathers, it was particulary hard on the young and elderly.

At Warren Farm the evacuation was even quicker. Within forty-eight hours of the outbreak of war, the main building was evacuated – to be used as an emergency hospital by the Ministry of Health – and only thirty children, toddlers between the ages of three and six, and children in the hospital remained on the site. Soon the east wing was adapted to store hospital equipment and the west was re-opened as an elementary school. Sixty-eight of the older boys were placed at 5 and 8 Portland Place and the older girls went to 24 and 25 Sillwood Road. The boys were sent to a variety of schools in the town, including Park Street seniors and Varndean secondary, while the girls were sent to Christ Church senior girls' school and St Margarets junior school. The headmaster at Park Street seniors was soon complaining that the boys were arriving late, although he found that "they were of average intelligence and quite well behaved in class and he would be very sorry to lose them".

The temporary accommodation was much nearer the beach and closer to town life, and it provided a more homely atmosphere for the children, although the dormitories were overcrowded. The newspapers reported that the girls found the shops and the crowds more interesting than the comparative isolation of Warren Farm. When a reporter visited, he found them happily listening to the radio in their recreation room. On the other hand, the boys missed playing football and the open spaces of the Downs, and he believed that half of them would have returned there if given the choice. Overall, "the children were more self-confident because they were brought into contact with the outside world in a way that was not possible at Warren Farm".[2]

The famous Warren Farm band practised in Madeira Drive shelter hall but found it unsuitable. The committee asked if they could practise in a building evacuated by St Dunstans home for the blind in St George's Road. St Dunstan's had evacuated it to avoid paying full rates, and initially refused. The committee appealed to the borough treasurer for exemption because:

> The private houses in Portland Place provide no facilities for recreation for 60 boys and during winter months and inclement weather it is trying for both boys and staff and therefore the facility would be greatly valued.[3]

The treasurer agreed for the boys to use it as long as the waiving of rates was kept "confidential". St Dunstan's agreed that one room could be used for band practice and other recreational purposes and would only charge a nominal fee for electricity.

Back at Warren Farm one of the cottage homes was adapted as a temporary nursery for the nursery children evacuated from Elm Grove. Dr Firth thought they were heathier there than when they had been in G Block because they had practically been confined to indoor life. Now they could run outside and get adequate fresh air. On the farm itself, one labourer was employed to look after the vegetables, potatoes and fruit. The cellars under the building where the vegetables had been stored were used as shelters. Later the farm was taken over by the Sussex Executive Committee and, ironically, piggeries for three hundred pigs were set up there.

For the first Christmas of the war, festivities took place in all the "outposts" of Elm Grove and at the main site, although the tobacco ration and other extras were reduced. The children in the temporary homes returned to the main site for the day and also had far more modest Christmas celebrations.

In February 1940 Dr Stanley Firth, the medical superintendent, was recording that:

> It is interesting to record that many of the old people who have been inmates of the institution for some considerable time, and have become accustomed to the type of accommodation provided in the institution, miss their old surroundings, but persons more recently admitted appreciate the more homely and normal conditions which prevail in the ordinary house. [4]

This observation was reminiscent of the experiences of the evacuated inmates during the First World War. Overall, Firth believed that the temporary accommodation had improved their health. He attributed this to the more normal living routine in a house. Pam Piercey, whose family lived in Sussex Square, remembers that the neighbourhood was expecting no. 25 to be occupied as an RAF officers mess and were surprised when paupers arrived, although they gave them a good welcome. As an eighteen-year-old girl, Pam starting working for the public assistance board in 1942, and one of her jobs was to visit Elm Grove and the temporary accommodation. She remembers seeing the "old boys at Sussex Square shuffling about with suits made of different colours and shoes made by the workhouse shoemaker".[i]

---

[i] Interview with Pam Piercey, April 2010.

Back at the main site, people were still being admitted to the Elm Grove home infirm wards with orders from the relieving officers, and they soon became overcrowded. B Block, originally intended as a first aid post, started to be used as a casualty and out-patients department. In April 1940, it was decided to admit casuals to the receiving wards at Elm Grove now that their numbers had dropped dramatically from more than a hundred a week before the war to thirty-three. The master, Mr King, was still allowed to impose tasks on them, but they could not be detained for more than four hours on the morning following admission and their routine inspection was discontinued.

* * *

The Second World War took many months to directly affect British people and for a while the precautions taken in Brighton during a period known as the "phoney war" – the sealing off of the beaches from the public and the blowing up of parts of the two piers to prevent a surprise landing – seemed exaggerated. However, the evacuation of Dunkirk at the end of May and at the beginning of June 1940 brought the reality of war home to Brighton. Bedraggled and injured soldiers from what was in many ways a miraculous escape from a military disaster, could not be hidden from the public eye, and the municipal hospital received ninety-six casualties from Dunkirk. And later that year, on Saturday September 14th, the loss of fifty-three lives – including children attending the Kemp Town Odeon – when a German bomber offloaded its bombs while being chased by a Spitfire, stunned the town.

That same month, the municipal hospital was vacated. As many patients as possible were sent to their own homes, and maternity cases were sent to Warren Farm. Many others were sent to a hospital in Macclesfield and subsequently to one in Burnley. By the end of the month 168 military and forty-three air raid cases had been admitted to the vacated blocks. Thereafter, the local civilian sick were admitted. Those remaining in Elm Grove home (365 in November 1941), were mainly elderly and infirm, and so there was an extremely high death rate. The medical officer, Firth, declared:

> I am satisfied that the number of deaths is due to the general increase of patients and that most of the increased number admitted are of an acute type which must obviously have a higher mortality rate.[5]

At Warren Farm by March 1941 there were nineteen 3–6 year old children in receiving home no. 1; eighteen 6–10 year old children in receiving home no. 2; eleven children in the infirmary; forty 10–16 year old boys in Portland Place and twenty-seven 7–16 year old girls in Sillwood Road. That month there was a ban on visitors to the Sussex coast, and all the children were to be evacuated, although those with parents had to have their permission. Already, by this time, over two thousand Brighton schoolchildren and some of their teachers had been evacuated to the mining villages and industrial valleys of Yorkshire and were said to be developing a broad Yorkshire accent. It was reported that they enjoyed the more rural life although found the climate harsher.

Eventually fifty-six children from Warren Farm were evacuated to Yorkshire.[i] Thirty-three of them were "adopted" by the committee – those orphaned, deserted or under their control, aged 2–8 years – and often went to ordinary miners families. This enabled the remainder of the children in the requisitioned homes to return to Warren Farm. There was room for eighteen 3–5 year olds to go into the infirmary block, and eighteen each of the older boys and girls to go into nos. 2 and 4 receiving homes.The other homes were for the Elm Grove nursery and the remand home.[ii] The band was discontinued and its instruments were loaned out. After almost eighty years of entertaining the Brighton public, it was never to play again.

There were only seven resident female staff in the schools and it was thought unsuitable that they should have to leave the children in the night to do fire-watching. The committee decided to employ a paid firewatcher and that two of the female staff be called in the event of a fire. During the war old boys and girls were allowed back at Warren Farm during their holidays, and one soldier even spent his Christmas leave there. They were not charged any money as it was considered to be their home. In September 1941 the Ferrimans' posts were terminated as a joint appointment. Mrs Ferriman was re-appointed matron and Ronald was kept on for "useful work" – an executive officer for the feeding and housing of the homeless.

In January 1942, the public assistance committee was renamed the social welfare committee. In 1943 there were 156 deaths out of an average of 374

---

[i] Some of the children ended up being adopted by the familes they stayed with.

[ii] It eventually closed in 1944 and was transferred to Linton House in Hurstpierpoint.

residents at Elm Grove. Thirty-three died alone in December; nine of whom were in their eighties and three in their nineties. The following year, there were 198. Edie Burt, quoted in the previous chapters, remembers visiting her sister in the hospital during the war and seeing a young woman lying in the corridor who had been evacuated during the London Blitz. She recalls that the beds were very close together and that her sister's body was full of sores under her nightgown.

Meanwhile, the old, long-serving workhouse staff at the Elm Grove home were gradually retiring and not being replaced. In April 1941 Frederick Saggers, the master shoemaker, retired after forty-two years service. At his retirement presentation he recalled that when he had first started he had had the help of six skilled inmates. Together they had made and repaired shoes, surgical boots and also boots for people on outdoor relief. He remembered, too, that angry inmates used to throw boots and shoes at him and that the iron pots used for granite pounding had been chained down to prevent inmates throwing them at officials.

In April 1943, a member of the social welfare committee, Mr Horton-Stephens, visited Warren Farm:

> Today I found every member of staff hard at work, washing children, mending clothes that were almost beyond repair, and I cannot speak too highly of the work done and the cheerfulness with which it is undertaken.[6]

By June 1943, there was an average of forty-three children at the schools. Some came in temporarily while their mothers were in confinement. However, its infirmary was often overcrowded and short of staff, and conditions were very poor. In January 1944, Dr Firth found:

> The general health of the children housed in this Home has given cause for some anxiety during the past months, and some of the minor ailments can in some way be attributed to the rather overcrowded conditions. In the interests of the children's safety they were brought down to the ground floor because of the danger of bombs. Now the risks were very small, could they sleep upstairs?[7]

For the moment the children had to remain where they were.

* * *

Towards the end of 1944, after D-Day in June – the start of the Second Front and the invasion of France – conditions in Brighton became more relaxed. In September, the ban on going on the beaches was lifted and in October street lights were allowed back on. Evacuated children started to return to Brighton, including some from Warren Farm. By now there were seventy children in the cottage homes, and their meals arrived ready cooked from Moulescoomb. Six older boys carried the hot food containers to the hot plate in the dining room where volunteers helped out. In August a lady gave a gift of ten shillings to the boys and financed a social evening for them during the holidays. A Dutch refugee donated £5 for toys for the toddlers who she had seen walking in the vicinity. And in December the Wills Tobacco Company sent model aeroplanes and Happy Family cards for the older children.

By Christmas 1944, the social welfare committee resolved that they wanted the children to enjoy the advantages of ordinary home life and to board out the children as soon as they could after the war. At Elm Grove, too, Dr Firth did not want the workhouse inmates to return, because he thought it would undo all the good work the hospital had achieved if they did. He believed the majority of the old people did not want to return, although he admitted that some of them missed walking up and down the corridors. As with the children, he concluded that what they needed were homelike conditions. In December, after discussions between the health committee and social welfare committee, it was decided that the main building of the Elm Grove home A Block should be donated permanently to the municipal hospital, which was currently using it as a maternity hospital. Some of the welfare committee even wanted to build a new hospital altogether in better surroundings. In fact, as early as February 1939 they had tried unsuccessfully to buy forty acres in Stanmer Park for that purpose.

On Boxing Day 1944 the mayor of Brighton's visit to Warren Farm caused a scandal. He found that the passages in the cottages were unheated and that no fires were lit until 9.30am. The children were insufficiently clothed and the overcrowding was so great that they had to eat their meals on their beds. He found 18-month old children sitting up in bed, blue with cold. Following his visit, other councillors came to see how bad the conditions were. One said he felt cold when he went in and felt even colder by the time he came out.

On January 27th 1945 the headline in the *Brighton Herald* was "Warren Farm: A Disgrace to Brighton." It reported that at a town council meeting it was said that "the children were so cold that they were past the 'crying stage'; that they had neither toys nor games or even any furniture; and that in unheated passages sick children ran about with children who were well". Children under three were overcrowded in one cottage and there was not a single pram to take them out. One councillor, Lewis Cohen, declared:

> ... the sooner the babies are taken away the better it will be for Warren Farm and the better for the reputation for Brighton, for it is a disgrace to the town...They need a home where they can be given a chance of getting health and happiness and not be allowed to grow up with stunted bodies and warped minds.[8]

The poor conditions were largely due to the war: a chronic shortage of staff and of reduced rations. It was a particularly bitterly cold winter and on the day of the mayor's visit there had been problems with the heating system. Nonetheless, the conditions were given national publicity when the *Times* also declared that it was "a disgrace to Brighton" and repeated the allegations. The following day, on 3rd February, an editorial in the *Brighton Gazette* declared:

Brighton's unwanted children housed away in the cold and seclusion of the Schools

Although in the opinion of our grandparents who were usually concerned in the selvish well-being of their own off-spring to the exclusion of all others, these buildings may have been ample and suitable accommodation for these children who had no loving parents to care for them, today there are new conceptions abroad implying that the well-being of all children is the responsibility of the community as a whole. We the citizens of Brighton should demand that all the children housed at Warren farm be brought into better and up to date accommodation nearer the centre of the town where they can feel that they are part of the community of Brighton and not just castaways on the starry seas of life thrown up on the Downs at the back of Brighton – out of sight and out of mind – to spend some of the most precious and most valuable years of their lives among the conditions described.

The newspaper also published a photograph showing cots in the hall of the nursery as evidence of overcrowding.

During the next couple of weeks several letters about it were published in the newspapers. A member of the nursery staff, Miss J, Harmer, wrote about the 12½-hour shifts with only two small breaks. But she claimed that:

> The children have never been neglected or ill-treated…We have knitted wool-lies for the children in our off-duty and taken them out in our off duty time. There are plenty of toys and there always have been…I can assure you that no one could be more glad that something is going to be done for us, but no one could have done more than we have for the children and it is most disheartening to hear all this unkind criticism.[10]

A letter from H.O. Steer wanted to know how often the council's committee visited the schools: "I write feelingly on the matter for there still remains in my mind a painful recollection of the time I spent in Warren Farm Schools as a small boy. The scars on my fingers bear witness to the severe chilblains from which I suffered".[11]

A letter from "A Mother" recalled:

> I travelled to the Schools every week for ten years and I never found my loved one cold. She was admitted when nearly four into the home; I always found nice fires and everything to make my kiddy happy…My daughter is a staff nurse in a hospital and married now and I am very grateful for all that was done for her for ten years.[12]

Fig 51 Children in the nursery home playroom at Warren Farm school.

Finally, a letter from an old boy serving in the RAF claimed "the school was used after the last war for those hit financially...We never had to go unreasonably cold".[13]

As a result of all the publicity, letters and parcels were received from all over the country and the local women's institute in Woodingdean offered to help. When an *Argus* reporter visited a few weeks later he found the rooms warm, no shortage of toys and little to complain about. Nevertheless, the Ministry of Health ordered that the social welfare committee build a separate institution for their under-fives, and the committee set aside £9,000 for this project. In truth, they had resolved to do this before the war, but at its outbreak had been forced to postpone it indefinitely.

The overcrowding at Warren Farm was largely due to the requisitioning of the major portion of the main building by the Ministry of Health as an emergency hospital. Another reason was the increasing use of the municipal hospital for sick mothers or those in confinement and whose children were therefore sent to Warren Farm for several weeks. And the staff shortages had not been from the want of trying. Adverts for more staff in the *Public Assistance Journal* had proved fruitless. Whereas there should have been six staff for twenty-four babies, there were only three and one domestic. And there were similar shortages for those children aged three to five and those in the hospital home. As a result of the scandal the council hired three extra staff, and a better stoking system was devised for the heating.

* * *

On 30th April 1945 Hitler committed suicide in his bunker in Berlin. Britain and America had won the war in Europe and the Second World War was virtually over. In Brighton, there had been 198 fatalities, 1,000 casualties and 15,000 houses had been damaged. At the Elm Grove site a bomb had landed on the tennis court between B Block and the medical superintendent's house, causing extensive damage to their roofs. A German plane had also strafed the front of the main building, A Block, where it is said the marks can still be seen today.

Unlike the First World War, where the sudden dramatic collapse of the German army had not been anticipated, the Second World War's end had been expected for several months. Perhaps because of this, it was reported locally that the celebrations lacked the spontaneity and liveliness of the

First World War's. It is also true that some people preferred to listen to events on the radio at home.

In July there was a general election. Just as Lloyd George's coalition had won triumphantly in 1918, Churchill and the Conservative party were expected to win in 1945. Therefore, it came as a shock when Clement Atlee and the Labour party swept to power in a landslide. Most political commentators believed it was because many people did not want to return to the old status quo of the 1930s, a decade dominated by poverty, mass unemployment and a divisive class society.

At a local level, as we have seen, the social administrators did not want the Elm Grove home and the Warren Farm industrial schools to continue. In other words, they wanted to end once and for all the workhouse system. The majority of the home's inmates were spread out in temporary accommodation, as the municipal hospital had appropriated the main building. Now the social welfare committee had to find new quarters for them, for those remaining in the home and for the casuals. And at Warren Farm the evacuee children were beginning to return to the main site which had been woefully neglected during the war. They would also need new accommodation.

But if it was the conditions at the Farm that had caused a scandal in 1945, the following year it was to be those in which the aged were forced to live.

Chapter Twenty-two

THE END OF THE SYSTEM

After the war ended, the social welfare committee immediately went about looking for new comfortably furnished accommodation for inmates over sixty-five. They planned to buy a number of homes and place 35–40 in each of them. For those in the temporary requisitioned houses, returning to the Elm Grove home was not an option, as the main building had been taken over by the hospital. In any case, according to a councillor, Alderman Cooke, it was "a cold and unattractive place for old people to end their lives" [1] and they were happier in their new accommodation. It soon became apparent, though, that there was serious overcrowding in all the homes and in the wards at the Elm Grove home. On hearing that twenty-five old ladies were packed into one small room in Vernon Gardens, the *Brighton Gazette* sent a reporter and photographer along, but they were refused admission. At the other homes too there was serious overcrowding, with beds touching and no space for lockers.

Under the headline: "Overcrowding in Homes for Aged. Conditions a Disgrace" in May 1946 the *Brighton Herald* [2] quoted a councillor, J. Downs, saying "We ought to be ashamed of ourselves for allowing old people to live in such disgraceful conditions" at a meeting of the social welfare committee. He had visited the temporary home for the men in Sussex Square. There had been no fire escape and the residents had been mixed up with casuals. The carpets were threadbare, the linoleum was torn and cracked, the bedrooms had no floor covering and the old men had to sit on hard-backed chairs. There was no lift, making it a physical trial for those who slept on the third and fourth floors. And, due to the lack of accommodation elsewhere, thirty old people at Elm Grove had become prematurely bedridden.

Mrs Ireland, the chairman of the homes sub-committee, paid tribute to the staff "who have done everything possible to make the old people comfortable". She went on to say that they had looked at a possible ninety-two properties but either had not found any suitable or would need a purchasing order to obtain the ones they liked. At the same time many ex-servicemen were finding it difficult to get a house, and this often resulted in them having to put their children into Warren Farm.

Apart from the aged inmates, the other problem for the committee was the casuals. For the quarter ending 30th June 1939 there had been 3,611. This had dropped to only nine in the corresponding quarter for 1944. But by 30th June 1946 the number had risen to 724 and was rising further due to the gradual demobilization after the war.[i] As the old casual wards were now being used as outpatient departments, casuals were being housed immediately in front of the main entrance to the hospital. And some of the old casual work cells were being used as Accident and Emergency accommodation. In February 1946, Dr Firth wrote:

> The arrival of friends and relatives for visiting patients in the evening often coincides with the arrival of the casuals, and this does lead to criticism, and is derogatory to the general atmosphere of a modern hospital. My own opinion is that the habitual vagrant should be discouraged entirely…They should have casual centres on the outskirts of town…Until some national scheme is in place, some local arrangement must be made to avoid them coming to Elm Grove.[3]

But over a year later the casuals were still using the main entrance of the hospital jointly along with the hospital patients. As there were only twenty-two beds available, some were offered emergency accommodation at the Church Army hostel.

In July 1947 local authorities were compelled to offer institutional assistance to "casual wayfarers", and their accommodation was now to be called "reception centres". These were to be not less than thirty miles apart. Despite the name change, there was to be no change of address, and in 1948 Dr Firth was complaining that twenty were coming every night and that sometimes he had to get the police to eject them because of their behaviour. There were serious brawls, broken windows and obscene language, and again he protested to the Ministry of Health about having casuals on hospital premises. He wanted them banned. On one occasion he had had to escort from the porter's lodge a nurse who had felt threatened by them. According to Firth, previously when the casual ward was full the turned-away casuals had often gone away to sleep on The Level, but now new and

---

[i] *Brighton Gazette* 30/6/1946.

aggressive types were trying to climb back over the hospital walls. In May 1949 it was reported that eleven had started a riot, and an exasperated Firth asked the ministry if in the future the casuals could not be sent to Newhaven Downs hospital, but his request was ignored.

In 1947, nos. 4 and 5 Vernon Gardens were bought to provide homes for old ladies, and also a house in Windlesham Road. After inspecting 110 properties, Horace Webb, the director of the social welfare committee, found only two suitable and used a compulsory purchase order to buy them. In one of his last reports, in February 1948, he claimed there was still a waiting list of cases for the hospital infirm wards and that many of these could be accommodated outside in homes for the elderly.

The following year Elmcroft was opened in London Road for sixteen aged male residents. Each had to pay something towards his upkeep according to his means. One of the men, A.B. Westgate, told a reporter that "we are surrounded by luxury which many of us have not been accustomed to for many a day".[4] And another ex-workhouse inmate recalled living in "glorified prisons" and having to break flints to earn his bed and breakfast. They could now have visitors every day and received a daily tobacco allowance. The emphasis was now on quality of life rather than the punishment and detention of the old workhouse system. Later, most of the

Fig 52 Elmcroft.

other aged Elm Grove inmates were placed in homes dotted around the town. Even then, some councillors mooted that perhaps they might be better off in the normal community rather than segregated into homes for the elderly.

The period between the end of the war and the creation of the welfare state, with the National Insurance Act of 1946 and the National Health Service in July 1948, was economically a difficult time. Rationing, energy shortages, a housing shortage and severe winters all added to the gloom. And as the staggered demobilization evolved – some service men were not demobbed till 1947 – more and more people sought outdoor relief. Pam Piercey, who worked at the parochial offices in Princes Street, remembers that:

> The two pay clerks worked in a Dickensian atmosphere, on high stools, at equally high wall mounted desks, recording every payment in huge leather bound ledgers. Payments were made from a little window, to the ever lengthening queue of eager clients in the passageway outside, a queue of such length that it stretched all along the passageway, out of the rear door and into the street beyond, regardless of weather conditions.[5]

Pam remembered the famous "dock" where applicants had to face the committee. The chairman would sit in a huge carved chair, such as a judge would sit in, with four leather chairs either side. The applicants would, from a high up dock, have to plead their case or face a severe reprimand if they had been caught doing part-time work. Pam also recalled that many of the applicants were flea-ridden and obviously in a very impoverished state, and depended on vouchers:

> Chits issued to the poor for food and clothing also had to be checked and prepared for payment. In the case of large firms like the Co-op they were in great numbers but little out-lying shops only had a few. Anything under £5 was paid in cash and known as "Sundry Smalls"...I plotted my way round the town's small shops. This was one of the nicer jobs as shopkeepers were always very pleased to see me.[6]

Pam had to visit the overcrowded geriatric wards in the municipal hospital "that were packed with what to me looked like lines of corpses in cot beds...they [the wards] were considered far too depressing for the employment of the very young nurses". As part of her job she also had to knock on the doors of people in slum houses to collect debts from people who could ill afford to pay. Until the NHS came into being, people were often afraid to be ill because they could not afford a doctor or hospital treatment, so suffered in silence.

Another woman who worked in the almoner's department at the hospital remembers that before the NHS, patients were means-tested [i] once they were admitted and she had to calculate how much they had to pay. She also remembers the Elm Grove home part of the site being very Dickensian and dilapidated.

In 1948, with the founding of the National Health Service, the hospital, with 546 beds, was renamed Brighton General Hospital and it came under the Brighton and Lewes hospital management committee. The hospital was described as "mainly old and in need of considerable reconstruction".[ii] It had now almost lost its last links with the Poor Law and workhouse except that it still had wards for the casuals and the non-sick [chronic infirm]. There were estimated to be over a hundred aged patients there who were not sick. For this reason, despite the coming of the NHS, workhouses that became hospitals never quite lost their stigma for the older members of the community. And the saying about "not wanting to end up in a workhouse" took a long, long time to disappear.

In 1951, a geriatric unit was set up so that those not requiring further treatment but who were unable to go home could stay before their eventual dispersal. Unfortunately, as Gaston has pointed out, geriatric patients remained the poor relations of the hospital world and were always at the end of the queue in terms of any material improvements. Later, female casuals were accommodated at the Vernon Gardens home and provided with shelter on an overnight basis. Meanwhile, until the 1970s there was still a reception centre for male casuals at Elm Grove. David Johnson, a nursing officer at that time, remembered that:

...outside Brighton General was a bus stop and the guys used to have to queue to wait for the workhouse to open at night. I was always fascinated by their way of life. They were never aggressive or abusive. One guy I used to talk to

---

[i] Once the hospital came under the Sussex Provident Scheme in December 1942, people could contribute to this and not have to pay for their treatment after they were admitted.

[ii] Gooch, p. 169

because he had the most wonderful speaking voice. Every six to eight weeks he would be there. He would tell me where he had been and about his family. I missed several buses listening to his stories but when the doors opened for them to go in, he would dash inside.[i]

By all accounts, Brighton General developed into a satisfactory hospital and served the town well. However, it always struggled to get the necessary finances to improve its facilities. By 1986, there were three long-stay wards full with 77 beds. Four years later though, sixty elderly residents were transferred to residential nursing homes. By the early part of the new century, H Block – which had contained the original lunacy wards – still had wards for psychiatric patients and was the last link to the workhouse days.

In 2004 the number of wards was reduced from seven to two. But even then Claire Devereaux, a speech therapist at the Royal Sussex County Hospital, remembers that the older patients were still refusing to go to Brighton General because of its old stigma. Finally, in 2007, the last of the elderly patients were transferred to the Newhaven Rehabilitation Centre and it was no longer used for in-patients. The buildings were now used as outpatient clinics, including for the elderly and the mentally ill, but as a place of treatment rather than containment. The connection with their workhouse past had finally been broken.

* * *

After the war, the policy was to try and board out as many children as possible with foster parents. The schools soon became known as the Warren Farm Homes – an orphanage – as some of the children started to trickle back from Yorkshire. And when the bandmaster, Mr Wells, returned from the Services, he discovered that there was no longer a band. A Sunday school was started by the chaplain, Rev Arthur Whittle, based on "moral instruction as well as church teaching and practices, given both in classes and privately, to try and offset present day trends, eg dishonesty, untruthfulness, impurity and the prevalent desire to get something from life without contributing to society".[7] And as Woodingdean expanded, the chapel was loaned indefinitely to the Woodingdean parish church, and sixteen of

---

[i] Email to author.

the children joined its choir. The idea was to integrate more with the local community.

In 1946 the homes took the overflow from the Elm Grove home nursery so infant cots were soon crowding out the main hall. That summer, for the first time since before the war, seventy children and ten staff went for two weeks in the summer to the children's camp at Dymchurch in Kent. By September there were fifty-one staff for 144 children, with sixty-six children in the main buildings, and it was described as being "hopelessly congested".

In December 1946, Ronald Ferriman went to visit the thirty-three children still boarded out in east Yorkshire. He saw all but three, and covered three hundred miles in his travels. The children had been gone for six years, and Ferriman hardly recognized some of them. He reported that they seemed happy and settled. The major complaint of the foster parents was that the allowance they received was not enough to buy their clothes. The following year, Ferriman went to visit the twenty-three children still in the West Riding of Yorkshire.

Fig 53 A visit from Father Christmas during the first Christmas after the war.

The policy of trying to find good homes for the children extended even to sending them abroad. In 1946, three children, two aged 10 and one aged 11, were sent to the Fairbridge Memorial College in Rhodesia [now Zimbabwe] under a Rhodesian government scheme for children who wanted to emigrate. Their criteria was that the "children must be healthy and possess good natural intelligence". The British government paid half their fare, and friends or local authorities were expected to pay a small amount towards their college fees. The social welfare committee paid for their raincoats and suitcases etc. The children were to have an education geared to filling the professions in the country. In the first year a hundred British children were sent to Rhodesia, each one becoming a ward of the state. Later, other children from Warren Farm were sent there.

At the beginning of 1947, Horace Webb, the director of the social welfare committee, declared that:

> the spirit and will animating the staff is to give the children as much as possible the conditions of good normal homes.[8]

However, the plan to get the children adopted by foster parents was being thwarted by the lack of parents coming forward or the children being unsuitable for boarding-out. That year, they stopped wearing the Warren Farm uniform and those of school age lived in the four cottages run by foster mothers. A major problem was that there was no reception home for the new arrivals, which meant they were mixed straightaway, with healthy children thereby increasing the risk of infection. The committee's plan was to open a new nursery for the under-sixes at Buckingham House, Shoreham, so that one of the four cottage homes could be used as a reception centre. There were also one or two children as old as eighteen still living at Warren Farm. One eighteen-year-old girl was returned there from "service" because of her rudeness, and she was allowed to stay until she found employment in needlework. Ferriman commented that "she has the idea she should be earning a large salary for very little work".[9]

Despite the overcrowded conditions, the children were still enjoying busy Christmas festivities. For 1947, these included a trip to the Curzon cinema (sponsored by the local rotary club), toys presented to them by the Lewes Road Congregational church, a Christmas party, a visit by the mayor and mayoress, a film in the main hall and a pantomime for ninety children paid for by an anonymous donor.

In the new year the Ferrimans started up an "Association of the Old Boys and Girls of the Homes". In March, there was a re-union of a hundred, which included the oldest, a Miss Peacock, who had left the schools sixty-four years earlier. (A previous reunion in 1937 had attracted 60 boys.) There was also an annual newsletter – in which ex-staff and pupils recorded their memories – annual dances and monthly social activities held in the main building. The chairman, William Stevens (1919–1926) believed the "association was a means of contact, through social activities of many kinds, whereby funds could be raised so that any old scholars in genuine need might be given a helping hand; while at the same time the old comradeship which we had at the Schools could be maintained." [10]

In December 1949, the association held its first dance – to raise funds – at the Regent dance hall, where well over a third of the six hundred who attended came from the schools. Soon, the association had 250 names on its books. Writing in the first newsletter, the matron, Kathleen Ferriman, wrote about one of the major changes since the pre-war period:

> There is a change I am not really happy about, and that is the young generation in our care… So much is done for them now, all their pleasures are made for them that the general attitude today is to expect and take everything for granted. This has been more noticeable since the war. Now we have few orphans and all the children have either friends or relatives in the town whom they visit frequently.[11]

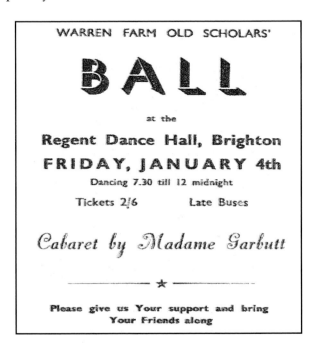

WARREN FARM OLD SCHOLARS'

BALL

at the

Regent Dance Hall, Brighton

FRIDAY, JANUARY 4th

Dancing 7.30 till 12 midnight

Tickets 2/6   Late Buses

Cabaret by Madame Garbutt

———— ★ ————

**Please give us Your support and bring
Your Friends along**

The local Woodingdean community's reaction to Warren Farm still appears to have been mixed. On the one hand, a local woman paid for four of the children to have violin lessons. On the other, in the summer of 1948 Rev Arthur Whittle was greatly regretting that "our children are to be excluded from the participation of a summer fete arranged by the local Community Association for Woodingdean".[12] Whittle, a member himself, had been the only one to vote in favour of the schools' children being included. He had wanted to bridge the gap between them and the village children. "The infantile response was that as the village children were never invited to affairs at the Home, the Community Association would not invite the Home children to the village party (to be paid for by public subscriptions). I greatly regret this attitude. It is unhealthy, divisive and ungrateful. Both Mr and Mrs Ferriman have, with me, served the community without thought to exclusive benefit to the Warren Farm Homes…My efforts to bridge the gap continue." [13]

In June 1948 Whittle was recording that "several of our nine year olds still cannot read" and that admissions to the homes were now reaching "an alarming state".[14] The numbers were being augmented by parents who had no room for their children at home because of the housing shortage. On one occasion the police brought in four children they had found abandoned in a "verminous state". By December there were 160 children and a long waiting list. Some of the town councillors were worried that as fit and sick children were still sleeping side by side, there could be an epidemic which would cause a scandal for Brighton. In fact, not long afterwards 107 children had either influenza or tonsillitis.

In January 1949, officials from the Home Office paid a visit and sent a confidential report to the council. It concluded that there was a lack of qualified supervision of the sick, a lack of iron in the diet of the older babies, a lack of equipment and still no separation of the sick and healthy children. In October, the headline in the *Gazette* was "Warren Farm May be Closed".[15] A large part of it had previously been used as a primary school, but now that the new Woodingdean primary school was opening in October 1949, the premises would no longer be needed for education. The primary school was built on The Meadow, where the children from Warren Farm used to play football and cricket. Now they only had one small field to play in, so there was little space for outdoor recreation.

That month, thirty-eight children under six were taken to Buckingham House, Shoreham, ostensively for a "tea party". They thought they were returning to Warren Farm afterwards. When they saw the coach return without them they were reported to be "inconsolable". However, newspapers reported that they soon adapted to their new surroundings – they had no choice – and efforts were made to get them adopted. This left forty of the older girls in the main building and sixty in the four cottage homes run by foster mums. Some of the former could be boarded-out, but they would need other premises if the main building was to be discontinued. That Christmas, a Father Christmas accompanied by a "fairy princess" arrived in a horse-driven George III coach from the Brighton Acquarium. He had come to distribute presents to the children still there.

Fig 54 New arrivals at Buckingham House, which the Gazette *described as "a home for deprived children".*

By 1950 it was getting increasingly expensive to keep the children at the bleak, unfriendly looking main building at Warren Farm and the four existing cottages.[i] So it was decided to retain the existing cottages, build four more and two homes at Hollingbury and Coldean. Fostering was still seen as the best option but foster parents were reluctant to take boys and some parents were equally reluctant to let their children be fostered.

In the last entry in the official records of the social welfare committee a member reported: "I visited the Homes and Cottages and everything was in good and clean condition and the children very happy." In April 1952, with two scattered homes already finished, there were fifty boys in the cottages, thirty-five girls in the central block and twenty-eight of both sexes in other homes. With its closure imminent, the Ferrimans resigned at the end of October. By then children from the main institution had already been placed in group homes on new housing estates in Woodingdean, Coldean, Hollingbury and Rottingdean. The idea was that they would stay there till they were sixteen, and then go on to hostels.

Ronald and Kathleen Ferriman had worked there since October 1934 and were unhappy about the way Warren Farm had recently been portrayed. As president of the Old Scholars Association, Ronald had made a speech in March to its members in the main building. He said that many of the schools' methods were being followed by the public schools and that:

> I am the last person to say that perhaps this old building has not perhaps outlived its usefulness and that new methods and ideals should not be tried, but why should our Children's Committee and Press decry it as if it were a blot on the landscape? How short lived is the memory and how soon is forgotten the traditions that once belonged to Warren Farm Schools. How often that the prowess of the boys has been praised in boxing, cricket and football activities and how often has the boys' band played in various functions in and around the town and brought pleasure and happiness to thousands.[16]

Rev Whittle, the chaplain, also addressed the members. He told them he was "appalled and utterly disgusted to think that the wonderful work which has been done at the schools should be so casually treated. The wreckers had stood by for a long time with their axes and crowbars. Now

---

[i] £5 3s 10d per child per week.

they had wrecked the institution as such, but they could not take away what it means to you, the wonderful times, the character-forming process and the glorious past." [17] Ferriman and Whittle were particularly angry that the local children's committee had forbidden their association from using any part of the building for its activities in the future. This was its death knell, and it soon folded.

Ferriman's comparison of the methods of Warren Farm to contemporary public boarding

Fig 55 Boxing in the 1930s.

schools had, in a sense, been an accurate one. For these private schools, too, believed in the character forming benefits of living in barrack style accommodation, playing rigorous sport and military drilling in the form of their officer cadet corps.

Fig 56 Sports day, 1936.

On 22nd November 1952, as watching councillors and educationists stood shivering in the cold, the mayor of Brighton, Dorothy Stringer, placed a large key in a well-worn lock and thereby closed the institution as a home for the orphans and unwanted children of Brighton for ever.

She then placed the key in a casket which was inscribed: "Thus marking the passing of an old and the birth of a new epoch in child welfare."

It had lasted 90 years. In a little speech, Miss Stringer talked about how the children had been unwanted and how the cloaks that they had used to wear "stamped them as orphans". She was "carrying out the council's decision to dispense with the old methods of childcare, of which Warren Farm was a symbol for many years".[18]

Fig 57 The mayor, Dorothy Stringer, turns the key in the lock to symbolise the closing of Warren Farm School.

The following week, an "old scholar", Mrs Maude Ohlson, wrote to the *Herald* from her home in Essex denying that they had ever worn cloaks. In her letter, entitled "An Old Girl's Tribute: In Praise of Warren Farm School", she wrote:

> The word unwanted had no place in our vocabulary. Many of the children, like myself, had been placed there because of the death of one parent and the inability of the other to keep a job going and look after a young family at the same time. At least, that was what we were more or less led to believe.

The School under the superintendence of Mr and Mrs Spooner was home to all the children. We were well fed and looked after, and I could go on for pages recounting the very happy times we had. Our education was second to none – witness this letter at the age of seventy and with no other schooling than that received at the home.

I have been a member of the Old Scholar Association since its inception and have travelled down to Hove many times to attend its functions.

It may well be that under modern conditions a 'family' unit is more desirable but I doubt if it will leave the children with the warm feeling and regard which I know so many of us retain for the Warren Farm Schools.

The buildings continued to be used for children, and for many years it was a Catholic school, latterly known as Fitzherbert. John Finnie, who became headmaster there in 1969, remembers taking "old" Warren Farm children round the buildings. They had mixed memories but, although admitting it was a hard life, some looked back with nostalgia and affection for the institution.

The school finally closed in 1987, one hundred and twenty-five years after the pauper children from the Church Hill workhouse had first marched over the Downs and arrived at its gates. In 1994, the main buildings were demolished to make way for the Sussex Nuffield Hospital.

* * *

Website memories of ex-Warren Farm children and their families are very mixed. Some clearly hated their time there and wrote of freezing cold baths and strict discipline carried out in a frightening, bleak building. Others wrote of the character building and comradeship of the place, and the kindness of the staff.

As one woman who went there as a child recently told me, it very much depended on the circumstances before your arrival. According to her, if you had had a very unsettled upbringing, life there did not seem too bad. However, if you had come from a stable family life which had suddenly been disrupted by a death or illness, then life at Warren Farm was hard. But whether a child's experience was bad or good, they formed some kind of attachment to the institution.

One of the earliest recollections – already quoted – came from an anonymous old boy recalling his life there in the 1890s. He wrote an article, "An Appreciation", which was published in the *Brighton Herald* on June 11th 1927. He concluded:

> There are thousands of old boys who, like myself, feel they owe a debt of gratitude to those who were responsible for their training and the inculcation of all those ideals that make life worthwhile. There are so many happy recollections in connection with the years I spent at Warren Farm…Brighton people themselves ought to know what a great boon their school has been, and, I hope, will continue to be, not only to their own poor children but to others from outside their borders. May the old school continue for many years turning out lads and lasses trained in all the things that matter, and prepared to face the world with an assurance that if they play the game they are sure to get on. Brightonians should take a greater interest in such a fine institution, for it is well worth it!

After leaving the land army, Eileen Gander, aged nineteen, came and worked as an assistant housemother at a cottage home. She eventually married the clerk/storekeeper there, Frank Jones, who in 1924 had himself been taken into the workhouse at three months as an illegitimate child, and later had spent his youth at Warren Farm. She remembers that after the war:

> …First I worked in the nursery but could not stand the noise. I asked to go into the boys' cottages and all the children had come from broken, unhappy homes. When it was call-over day, the councillors would come and talk to the boys and ask if they were happy. It was a laugh really because they were not happy. The superintendent would test the dinner and if it satisfied his palate they would have to clean their plate, gristle and everything. The girls used to put food up their knicker legs or pass it the dog…There were no cleaners in the home and the children were allocated so much work before they went to school…
>
> My husband had to scrub a large staircase [when he was a boy there] and emery cloth the brass bannister before the bus picked him up for school. When he was younger they had school in the home… There was a massive high wall that went round this home, and I mean a high wall. No one was allowed out without permission from the office…the children were given a small amount of pocket money called "stripe pay", and unless a boy could show he had got money to go on a bus to see his people, he could not go…The home would say, "We don't send out paupers."

Figs 58 and 59 Two images of Frank Jones: as a boy at Warren Farm in the 1930s and (right of photograph) with his wife Eileen next to the famous well now in front of the Nuffield Hospital at Woodingdean – the site of the former Warren Farm school. The well was originally behind the main building, which was much closer to the road than the present hospital.

With Frank and Eileen is Victor Grand. He had been abandoned as a baby in the Victoria Gardens, Grand Parade – hence his name.

Mary [not her real name] was admitted to Warren Farm, aged five, in 1950, with one sister and two brothers. She was one of sixteen born to biological parents, and was in the main building for two years. Writing in 2009, she recalled:

> It was an awful, horrid, nasty place and it makes me sick to think of it. Horrid things went on there…The main building was a sinister place and a lot of evil went on there. ..Older girls took me out late at night to the toilets and touched me in parts one should not have been touched. Other times they would force my feet onto earwigs that were in the washroom and toilets.
>
> I can still recall the night I was helped from a car and taken in…I can even remember what I was wearing – red coat, red leggings, with a few buttons at the side of the ankles, so you feet slide into them, red bonnet…I can see myself now clutching a hand in the dark…it was raining. That memory has always stayed with me…I was put to bed in a very long room with about ten beds either side of the room which had windows overlooking the front of the horrid building. I think there was a tin locker by each bed. The floor was damp and cold. The wash rooms were horrid, dark, damp and cold. So was the water to wash in…
>
> It was a grey building with lots of windows and had one main door roughly in the centre of the long building. It was very dark outside and I was very frightened and was crying. I was used to sleeping in one bed with my little sister and two brothers. My younger sister often came to my dormitory and sneaked into my bed. If she was caught we were thrashed. We still did it as we needed the comfort from each other. The food was just about food. I had malnutrition and I suffer through it even to this day. I was given shoes that did not fit and my toes are curled to this day. I am so pleased now that this building has gone from the face of this earth.

Mick Toner, born in 1940, described to me how his father was the kind of man who went out for a packet of cigarettes and came back six months later! He remembers how he and his mother were placed in a workhouse in Ireland and then came to Brighton in 1945 at the end of the war. He remembers the pain of being separated from his mother and the pain of not being able to understand, and being placed in one of the cottage homes – where Eileen Jones worked – with eighteen children up to the age of sixteen run by foster mums. On the whole, although it was strict, he believes he was treated kindly there and learnt good values which have stayed with him all his life.

Every morning before going to school the children had to clean the dormitories and other rooms. Afterwards, the children were lined up for inspection. If they were not turned out well the monitors were "told off". The children wore their own distinctive uniforms to the local schools and Mick remembers one mother angrily telling her child not to talk to Warren Farm boys. Mick received 6d a week pocket money and remembers lovely walks to Rottingdean and being given potatoes – sometimes baked, sometimes raw – by German prisoners-of-war working nearby.

More painfully, he remembers his mother on a secret visit telling him not to tell anyone, as by visiting without permission she risked been banned from coming for two months. He also recalls that when he returned from a day out with an apple or an orange, the other children would surround him and say "bags the apple core" or "bags the orange peel". (Because of rationing, fruit was scarce.) Mick left after three years and later spent a year in a Catholic convent which he found to be much worse. After some time at home, he left again and was a pupil at Warren Farm. Looking back more than sixty years later, he still remembers a song the children used to sing when they went on their outings:

> Oh I bought a penny banana
> I put it behind the door
> And when I got up in the morning
> It was dancing on the floor.
> Singing, mummy, daddy, take me home
> From this convalescent home
> I've been here a year or two
> Now I'm coming back to you.
> Give my love to the dear old driver
> Tell him I won't be here any longer
> Hey, ho, here we go
> The driver's drunk and the bus won't go.
> Now we're coming back!
> Now we're coming back!
> Back to the place where we all come from.
> Goodbye church, goodbye steeple
> Goodbye all you funny little people
> Dressed in red, dressed in blue
> I belong to Waterloo.

Here comes the nurse with the red hot poker.
Oh said the patient, that's too hot,
Oh said the nurse, I'm sure it's not!
Hey ho, here we go
The drivers drunk and the bus won't go.
Now we're coming back!
Now we're coming back!
Back to the place we all come from.

CONCLUSION

In the preface I wanted to find out how far Brighton's workhouses resembled the image of the one conjured up by Dickens in *Oliver Twist*. Although none of them exactly mirrored his portrayal, one could say that most of the elements in it (mental and physical cruelty, meanness, impoverished diet, carefully calculated monotony, subtle deprivations and degradations, the cropped hair and standardized rough clothes, uncaring officialdom etc.) appeared at one time or another in the history of the Brighton workhouses. And surely it can not be a coincidence that the one that resembled Dickens' image the most, Church Hill, was the Brighton workhouse at the time he wrote the book.

In 1601 the Elizabethan Poor Law Relief Act had given paupers a legal right to a better life. No person was to be left to die of hunger or cold, and workhouses eventually came into existence to prevent this. In practice, the Act was really aimed at the *deserving* poor and those deemed to be work-shy: the *undeserving* poor. By the 1820s, in the aftermath of the Napoleonic wars, masses of injured and unemployed service men returning to their homes had caused the national poor relief bill to quadruple from £2 million to £8 million in twenty years, and Sussex had the highest poor relief rates in England. The government's response was the Poor Law Amendment Act of 1834 which decreed that the workhouse system must be administered by Unions – groupings of parishes run by a locally elected Board of Guardians. Through a local act, Brighton managed to get exemption from amalgamation.

In the nineteenth century there was a strong Christian belief that poverty was a common fact of life, and incurable. In particular, Anglicanism permeated the workhouse system and gave it a philosophical justification. But too much poverty spelled danger for the wider society. Consequently, the Act's main objective was to force into the workhouse people who were unable to stand on their own two feet outside it. It was hoped that the daunting spectre of the workhouse would spur men on to work hard to maintain their families. If they were given relief outside, it would weaken this resolve. Initially, savings were made, but in the long term workhouses became uneconomic, as institutional relief, involving costly buildings and officials, was always more expensive than outdoor relief.

Brighton's first workhouse, Bartholomews, started off with thirty-five inmates and at least had the benefit of being in the centre of town. When it became overcrowded, almost a third of its residents declined to move to the new workhouse, Church Hill, which was considered to be on the edge of town. After the Act of 1834 conditions in workhouses took a turn for the worse, and Church Hill from around the mid-1830s to the mid-1850s was a brutal, badly run dismal place to live in. And once a decision was made to build a new workhouse with a separate site for the children, the physical conditions there deteriorated even further. Edward Sattin's appointment as governor in 1859 did herald some improvements though, such as the annual entertainments after Christmas for all the inmates, not just for the aged.

Sattin oversaw the transfer of the children to Warren Farm and the adults to the Elm Grove workhouse, both of which were even more on the edge of town than Church Hill had been. On the whole, Elm Grove does not appear to have been a violent institution, more a place of grinding monotony bereft of stimulating activities and entertainment, except at the annual summer treat and at Christmas. The soulless, hard, repetitive work, such as oakum picking, stone breaking and the drudgery of domestic work, epitomized it. Added to this was the regular enforcement of strict silence during rigid meal times, chapel and work. Given the amount of violence in other work-houses, it is surprising that apart from the eight female paupers gaoled for refusing to work after their beer allowance was stopped in the 1870s, there were few acts of organized defiance. Run mainly by inmate labour with job titles such as "foul washer" and "boot improver", Elm Grove seems to have been tightly controlled, and in 1876 it was being described as "one of the best in the land" by a Poor Law inspector. But even the best of the best were still poor by any civilized standards.

From the 1850s onwards, through letters to the Poor Law Board, we start to hear the voice of the inmates as literacy levels improved. Many of the letters – perhaps some written with assistance – complained about being kept unfairly in the casual wards where conditions were deliberately the worst. For those who were permanently kept in them as a punishment, it must have been awful. The voice of the staff was less discernible, and really we hear only those of the senior officers: the chaplains (including the extraordinary Rev Henry Dodwell), the medical officers and the masters. In Warren Farm, from the late nineteenth century onwards, we also hear the voice of the children through personal reminiscences recorded many years later. They may have been subjective, but they do give us a flavour of life there.

With the opening of the industrial schools in 1862, the enforced separation from their children over two years of age must have been a bitter blow for parents. While it may have saved a minority of children from abusive parents, it caused great distress to the majority and in no small way became one of the main criticisms of the workhouse system. Indeed, the medical journal the *Lancet* occasionally cited cases where the separation of a mother from her child was believed to be a major cause of death.

In Warren Farm's case, the prediction that its isolation would mean the children receiving worse medical treatment was borne out with their continuing poor health, ie. chilblains in spring. Almost immediately after it opened there were concerns that the children's welfare had taken a turn for the worse. And conditions for staff were little better, with vacancies often being impossible to fill. Despite its inhospitable environment, the schools somehow did manage to survive the early turbulent scandal-filled years and provided a kind of rudimentary education. And they also managed to engender a spirit of comradeship that by the late 1920s saw up to 300 "old boys" returning to visit annually. This may, however, have been more to do with their attachment to their roots rather than any nostalgia for the regime itself.

By the beginning of the twentieth century the concept of herding children into large institutions was being openly questioned. Their inmates were frequently described as "dull and listless", and even one of the Brighton Guardians[i] in the 1920s described the children at Warren Farm as having "frozen meat faces". Quite apart from the fact that they lacked a family environment and were stigmatizing, these institutions were proving very detrimental to health. Throughout most of its history, skin disease, eye infections and other diseases were commonplace at Warren Farm. Though its closure was first suggested before the First World War, because of economic circumstances it became one of the last industrial schools to close in England.

---

[i] Albert Tindall.

Life at Warren Farm was always much better for the boys than the girls in what was very much a male dominated society. They had a variety of sports, learned to play musical instruments – which most poor families could not afford – and were taught skills such as basic shoemaking. In contrast, not until the last part of its history did girls play any sport, and most of the skills they learned were of a menial nature. These were sometimes not much help when they were placed as servants in small family homes. In Ron Ferriman's speech to the "old scholars" in the last chapter, his praises for the activities of the schools' past all related to the boys. For this reason most of the photographs of the children published in the local newspapers in the 1930s were taken of them.

* * *

However mean and meagre the diet in Brighton's workhouses – and at different times it was considered to be better than the average – nobody physically starved in them. But by the 1840s it was regularly reported in the local newspapers that people would rather starve than enter one, as the harsher aspects of the 1834 Act kicked in. And some did. This is one of the paradoxes of the workhouse system: built to ensure that the Elizebethan Poor Law premise that no one should die of cold or hunger was fulfilled, by their very nature workhouses caused people to suffer this very fate outside their walls. On the other hand, they undoubtedly saved thousands of people from starvation even if the psychological price was high.

In hard times, all sections of the populace – tradesmen, businessmen, skilled and unskilled workers – were susceptible to becoming inmates. And once inmates, they found that instead of being a refuge for the poor man the workhouse was an authoritarian place with punitive rules where they lost their dignity, their liberty and worst of all, all hope. Any material advantages were offset by the psychological damage caused by the splitting up of families – wife from husband, child from parent, brother from sister, young from old etc. And when in the 1870s the Brighton Guardians started to enforce the workhouse "test", the fear of the workhouse grew even greater, as evidenced by the increasing number who refused to enter it even after being turned down for outdoor relief. Despite this, Brightonians on outdoor relief always outnumbered those in the workhouse as it did in all Poor Law Unions. In fact, the majority of paupers – even the able-bodied ones – never saw the inside of a workhouse but survived on parish vouchers, cash grants and charities. For example, in the 1891 census, nationally, only one male in 137 and one female in 187 were in workhouses.[i]

By the end of the nineteenth century, Elm Grove had filled up with the sick, the disabled and the elderly, and there were few able-bodied paupers. In fact, 30 per cent of all old people were ending up in workhouses. Indoor relief was increasingly being given to the weaker members of the community who had no feasible alternative of existing outside. By this time, calling it a "workhouse" was a misnomer, for it was more a hospital, more an old peoples' home. When a young Ernie Mason living in Brighton in the early part of the twentieth century asked his mother what a workhouse was, she replied that it was where poor old people were sent in to die – his own grandmother had ended up in Elm Grove. By and large, by then, workhouses and asylums were gradually becoming institutions for the mentally ill, the physically sick and elderly.

All three of Brighton's workhouses and Warren Farm were a big part of the community, and a lot of tradesmen and businesses relied on them for their livelihoods. Unsurprisingly, the temptation to supply them with substandard goods was great. Within the workhouse, the statement by one member of staff in the early part of the twentieth century that everyone was "on the make" was epitomized by stories of workhouse property being smuggled out in dustcarts. Guardians, too, with their close links to suppliers were not immune from criticism, especially those early Guardians who were accused of "guzzling" at the parish's expense. And some inmates themselves, and some people on oudoor relief, too, did their best to thwart the system whenever they could, arguably out of necessity

The main group that benefited from the workhouse was probably the elderly inmates who were too old to work but who were not bedridden. Time and time again the local Brighton newspapers reported on their new year and summer "treats" and how much the aged inmates enjoyed themselves. These events may have given great pleasure but they were few and far between, and these reports could give a distorted view of workhouse life. The aged were also the main beneficiaries of the individual, often anonymous, charity provided by local people.

---

[i] Quoted in the Lancet 1/4/1893. According to the census there were 102,689 males and 80,024 females in workhouses.

For some, being in a workhouse undoubtedly provided company in their old age. And when Elm Grove was evacuated during the First World War, many of the aged inmates complained that they missed their old home despite living in far superior temporary accommodation. On the whole though, for most non-able-bodied aged inmates the days in the workhouse were long, tedious and spent sitting in barren day rooms.

In many ways the First World War accelerated the end of the workhouse system. When the inmates returned to Elm Grove in 1920–21 it was during an economic depression that, arguably, lasted till the Second World War. And surely the 1920s was one of the worst periods for workhouses. Ex-servicemen who had been traumatized by the slaughter in the trenches during the First World War were now traumatized by unemployment, poverty and hopelessness. Rather than return to Lloyd George's "land fit for heroes", they came back to dole queues, the humiliation of asking for outdoor relief and, if refused, the degradation of the workhouse. This degradation can be seen on the cover of this book, with racegoers in August 1923 trying to avert their eyes from the paupers begging over the walls of the Elm Grove workhouse. Perhaps, too, the little boy walking in the road had been told not to get too close to them.

With the rise of the trade unions and of the Labour party, workhouses were doomed in the long term. For, as the latter pointed out, workhouses seemed to perpetuate poverty and did little to eradicate it. Ironically, on the eve of the Brighton Guardians being disbanded in 1930, the local papers reported that there was great gloom among the older inmates, who feared that their "treats" might suffer with the replacement of the old paternalistic regime by the town council. Fortunately, the public assistance committee continued them.

If the introduction of pensions before the First World War was the first nail in the coffin of the workhouse system, then surely the welfare state after the Second World War was the final one. Large institutions, either for adults or children, were seen as humiliating and counter-productive in that they segregated, isolated and alienated them from society. During the wars they had almost been completely forgotten about. There had obviously been other priorities.

Older Brightonians still remember the last days of Elm Grove. As children they were sometimes threatened with it if they were disobedient.

Some still remember it being called "the Grubber", and Don Carter recalls it being called "the Top". One lady remembers that her father, who was a policeman in the 1930s, used to refer to it as the "Lump on the Hill". Despite it ceasing to be known as a "workhouse" since 1914, when it was called a Poor Law institution, the stigma remained. And although there were examples of kindness and consideration on the part of the staff, they took place against a background of humiliation and degradation. Even now, those older people who remember the days of the workhouse continue to speak of it with fear and loathing. Its very name evokes memories of the poor being terrorized by an uncaring system.

Today[i] the main building from the outside looks exactly as one would expect a Victorian workhouse to look. Its simple exterior has none of the elegance and therapeutic empathy that can be found at the Sussex Lunatic Asylum at Haywards Heath, built eight years earlier. Yet both were equally feared and stigmatized. The thick grey, dull walls of the Elm Grove building made its purpose clear to its pauper residents. This was to be a place of harshness, of grim austerity, of regimentation. Mellowed little by age, it still stands as a memorial to its Victorian values and as a testament to the grim power it once held over the destitute of Brighton. And looking at the clock in the tower, one is reminded of the words of the poet, George Crabbe:

> That large loud clock, which tolls each dreaded hour,
> Those gates and locks and all those signs of power;
> It is a prison, with a milder name,
> Which few inhabit without dread or shame.[ii]

If one looks out over Brighton from the high buildings of the old Elm Grove workhouse one can try to imagine what it was like for those inmates all those years ago. Perhaps they could see where their relatives and friends were still living. Perhaps they could see where they used to work and play. But now as inmates they were completely separated and isolated from their former lives and, if old, would remain so for the rest of their lives.

---

[i] Using the original plan of the workhouse, one can still see the main block, the lunacy wards and the infirmary.

[ii] *The Borough*, by George Crabbe (1810).

Warren Farm was even more a place of isolation, and when it first opened in 1862 must have seemed like the middle of nowhere for the children. All that is left now are the cottages with their small windows which were originally the receiving homes for the new arrivals and, of course, the site of the famous well.

*   *   *

As a general observation, I would have to agree with Longmate's conclusion that "the workhouse represented a bold, ruthless and in some ways successful attempt to solve a problem as old as society itself: the state of needing to be supported by the rest of society".[i] And, on the whole, Brighton did try to look after its poor and provide them with some sort of safety net. Its Guardians were not just grinders of the poor: some defended the ratepayers, some defended the poor and others arbitrated between the two. Their sentiments frequently vacillated, according to their beliefs, from meanness to generosity.[ii] This was no better illustrated than by the years of fierce debate about allowing inmates beer at Christmas. Fortunately, some Guardians did understand that anyone could end up in a workhouse, including themselves. Others strongly believed that their improvident lifestyle had led them to the "house". Just like today's welfare administrators, they were wary of rewarding the scrounger, the undeserving poor.

In all, tens of thousands of Brightonians went into the workhouse and an even higher number received outdoor relief from the parish. Some were born under the Poor Law, lived under the Poor Law and died under the Poor Law. Added to these were the thousands not from Brighton who ended up in its workhouses – the majority of inmates, according to Edward Sattin – and the vast army of tramps/casuals (as many as five hundred a week) who slept there during their travels. Indeed, the majority who stayed at workhouses, however briefly, were these people. Communities were suspicious of them. No one knew who they really were or where they had come from. The names they gave to the porters on their admission

---

[i] *The Workhouse*, Longmate p.14

[ii] Most of the "treats' for the aged inmates and children, apart from the interest on the Wagner legacy of 1870, were paid for out of the Guardians' own pockets.

were often unverifiable. Like gypsies, they were suspected of criminal activity and evoked little public sympathy. For this reason, the Brighton Guardians wanted them to leave as quickly as possible and for a long time did not demand they work in exchange for their lodgings. This only changed when Elm Grove became overcrowded with casuals, no doubt attracted by the leniency of its regime. Of all the inmates, they were the most difficult to control and supervise. Some were undoubtedly criminals, but others were just people down on their luck.

In this book we have met a varied group of people, from Samuel Thorncroft to Edward Sattin, from Charles Tourle to Sabina Tilley, from Albert Mellor to William Smith and, not least, Rev Henry Dodwell and his extraordinary demise. We have also seen how the workhouse, at various times, was in Woodingdean, in Eastern Road, in Elm Grove, in Hove, next to St Nicholas church, in the smart elegant Sussex Square, and even outside the town in Hassocks and Wivelsfield. Wherever you lived the shadow of the work-house was never far away. The legacy of the Brighton workhouses, as with some other workhouses, was, in practical terms, their gradual evolution into a first rate hospital for the town's poor: Brighton General Hospital.

Looking at the modern attempts to deal with the unemployed, some of the arguments have changed little. This book is being written against the background of savage cuts in social welfare at a time when even those in employment are sometimes struggling to make ends meet, and we are once again witnessing attempts to make the unemployed work for their relief. Some of this new welfare to work programme is reminscent of the "test" work imposed on the able-bodied unemployed in the 1880s, 1920s and 1930s. As today, they protested that monotonous and menial work, when done alongside paid workers, rather than raising self-esteem was demoralizing, and compounded the misery of their situation.

There has also been the re-emergence of illnesses associated with poverty, such as rickets in children. In addition, there are plans to re-assess the needs of the sick and disabled. It is almost like the old annual "call-over" days of the Guardians, when they would try and separate the "deserving" from the "undeserving" poor. Modern administrators would do well to remember that although workhouses were effective in reducing the number of able-bodied claimants, the price was the punishment and stigmatization of the very people the state promised to protect: the elderly, the sick, the infirm and poor families. They should also remember that unemployment affects every single sphere of life, and that unavoidable poverty is the result of sickness and misfortune.

In writing this book, whenever I wanted inspiration I turned to Norman Longmate's great book *The Workhouse*, written in 1974. I hope his conclusion will not be forgotten:

> The history of the workhouse surely has much to teach every citizen today: that poverty is a misfortune, not a crime; that human suffering is too high a price to pay for tidy administration; that authority in enclosed communities should be subject to constant scrutiny; that it is better for a dozen spongers to grow fat than for one deserving applicant to be turned away; above all, perhaps, that in all the affairs of life there is no substitute for compassion.

APPENDIX 1

BRIGHTON WORKHOUSE.

We publish below an account of the Receipts and Expenditure of the Governor of the Workhouse for three successive years, commencing on the 25th March 1826, 1827, and 1828. Some of the receipts, under their respective heads, show a considerable increase for articles manufactured and sold. We call the attention of the inhabitants to this subject, particularly of those who are in want of such articles as are made in the workhouse. The employment of the inmates is of the utmost consequence in order to stimulate them to acts of industry, as well as to correct idle habits, and materially assists in maintaining regularity and good discipline. The principal articles made are of very superior kind,—such as whitening, corn sacks, coal sacks and sacking, door mats of any size, rope, twine, lines. &c. and straw bonnets.

Dr. RECEIPTS.	1826.			1827.			1828.		
To paupers, labour	65	9	8	92	9	8	86	5	6
whitening, manufactured and sold	63	19	7½	92	14	1½	100	17	9½
sale of articles made in the sacking and rope manufactory	168	7	0	207	8	7½	343	7	11½
ditto in the straw plait manufact.	24	1	11	22	0	11	45	17	0
sale of vegetables from the garden	174	6	6	228	6	5½	259	2	1
ditto of cows and calves	11	10	1	17	5	0	8	7	6
ditto pigs	49	0	11	80	9	3	109	17	11
cash for James Drake's coffin				18					
sale of fishing net							38	11	6
cash in John Collier's pocket at the time of his death							6	6	
cash re-payment for postage of a letter from Manchester							2		
cash from the treasurers of Directors & Guardians on account							10		
Total	556	15	8½	741	12	0½	992	15	9

PAYMENTS.	1826.			1827.			Cr. 1828.		
By sundry weekly disbursements	227	7	9½	257	19	10½	240	11	11
cash paid on account of the sacking manufactory	85	3	11½	55	15	5	74	8	7
ditto straw plait	43	9	10½	17	9	7	25	19	10
ditto for manure for the garden	17	14	10	8	13	6	10	6	6
ditto for pigs	11	17	0						
ditto for fat sides of pork	15	12	2						
ditto for a cow				16	0	0			
ditto weekly for skim milk							16	16	2½
ditto for furniture on family's leaving the workhouse							4	13	0
ditto Mr. Wisden for shoeing the horse, &c.							2	12	6
ditto Mr. Cully, for brooms and brushes							4	14	6
1 cash paid to labourers employed gardening							106	19	0
ditto making whitening							34	0	0
ditto tailoring							54	5	0
ditto shoe-making							30	17	4
ditto braiding							15	3	10
ditto digging well							7	8	0
ditto blacksmithing							7	10	0
	351	5	7½						
Balance paid Assistant Overseer	205	10	1						
Total	556	15	8½						
				356	3	4½			
Balance paid Treasurers				385	8	8			
Total				741	12	0½			
							636	11	2½
Cash paid Treasurers							352	3	2
Balance in hand							4	1	4½
Total							992	15	9

1 These items for labourers employed, are principally for paupers out of work, sent by the Directors and Guardians to be employed in the respective trades and employments: previous to last year they were paid by the Assistant Overseer, or Deputy Assistant, in lieu of relief.

APPENDIX 2

In Broadmoor, Henry Dodwell continued to protest that he was not insane and that his actions had been a protest against the unfair treatment he had received from the Brighton Guardians. He had many supporters, including two leading psychiatrists, Dr Forbes-Winslow and Dr Winn. They had examined him in Broadmoor and declared they could find no evidence of insanity. His case was even raised in the House of Commons. Dodwell, referring to Broadmoor as the "Brigands Inn" and the staff there as "cut-throats for hire", did not do himself any favours by bombarding the royal family, the archbishop of Canterbury, Prime Minister Gladstone and any other leading figures he could think of with long, obsessive letters about his case. When not writing these he translated hymns and poems into Latin on thin blue Broadmoor toilet paper, some of which were published in the *Ecclesiastical Art Review*.

After a while, Dodwell refused to speak to Dr William Orange, the medical superintendent, and would communicate only through writing. And it was while Orange was reading one of his letters in 1882 that Dodwell attacked him with a stone concealed in a handkerchief. Orange suffered cerebal concussion and was off work for eight months. Dodwell was transferred to a block where the most dangerous criminals were kept. All of his privileges were taken away from him and he was placed in a cell with a chamber pot and a mattress.

Now it was Dodwell against the world. After his attack on Orange the clamour for his release virtually dried up. Even the *Lancet*, which had supported his cause, admitted that "he was not in a state of mind to be a safe member of the outside community". As time passed he became more and more paranoiac, accusing his wife of being unfaithful and of siding with the government against him. He wrote to one daughter that "your mother never once expressed indignation at the behaviour of the Guardians…if you follow such an example, you will be ruined…" In May 1890, he was writing that he felt "deceived and deserted by all my four children…I now fear that I am helpless to get anyone to come near me".

In 1898, with his health failing, Dodwell was transferred to the infirmary block. By this time only his eldest son, Henry, was visiting him. In June 1900 he was dying, and his daughter Sally asked if she could visit him. Too weak to write himself, he dictated a letter to an attendant saying he would only see her on condition that she went to Bow Street magistrates court and "tell the presiding magistrate that for twenty-two years, I am detained on a forged certificate". Sally and her mother still planned to visit him. They were too late. Henry Dodwell, chaplain to the schools for four-and-a-half years, died in Broadmoor lunatic asylum on 15th June 1900. To the end he insisted the Brighton Guardians had robbed him of a "lifetime position".

Dodwell's time in Broadmoor led to the splitting up of his family and his wife being forced to work as a housekeeper. The origin of his downfall lay in his dispute with the Brighton Guardians. Four years after he had left the schools, the Local Government Board enquiry concluded that it was not a good idea to have paid officers from women taken from the workhouse. So, ironically, Dodwell's main complaint was vindicated after his dismissal.

It is difficult to know whether Dodwell was insane or not. He did show all the symptoms of paranoia, and when detained blamed everyone in authority except Queen Victoria for his demise. But he was incarcerated even when old and harmless. Before the liberalisation of the mental health sectioning laws, placing unwanted individuals in asylums was a mechanism by which society could get rid of "undesirables", however well connected they may have been. Perhaps the real reason for Dodwell's detention can be found in Dr Orange's original assessment on his arrival at Broadmoor in 1878:

> He told me that for months before he committed the offence [shooting at Jessel], he had been in the habit of writing to every person whom he found (in the papers) to have a grievance and that with those people he had quite an abundance of correspondence. The risk to society lies in that direction.

Dodwell's legacy is some beautifully handwritten Latin translations, much of them written on thin blue Broadmoor toilet paper, which can now be seen at the Berkshire record office.

CHRONOLOGY

1727 – Bartholomews workhouse opens.

1822 – Church Hill Workhouse opens.

1846 – Poor Law Removal Act – immigrants of more than five years residence become irremoveable.

1862 – Warren Farm Industrial Schools open

1867 – Elm Grove workhouse opens.

1876 – Inspectors give the workhouse a clean bill of health.

1878 – Warren Farm well no longer used.

1887 – New casual wards opened.

1891 – Two new infirmary blocks opened.

1898 – Third infirmary block opened.

1902 – Nurses become professional.

1914 – Workhouse renamed Poor Law Institute.

1915 – Elm Grove becomes a military hospital.

1920 – Elm Grove handed back to the Guardians.

1921 – Re-entry of the inmates.

1922 – Approved as a training school for nurses.

1926 – X-ray and therapeutic department opened in basement of E Block.

1929 – Nurses home built.

1930– Abolition of guardians, to be replaced by public assistance committees. End of the Poor Law and workhouse system.

1934 – Unemployed Assistance Board brought back an alternative form of relief exactly a hundred years after its abolition.

1935 – The infirmary is renamed Brighton Municipal Hospital and the workhouse becomes the Elm Grove Home.

1948 – National Health Service. Hospital renamed Brighton General, and Elm Grove inmates dispersed.

1952 – Warren Farm closes on 22nd November.

BIBLIOGRAPHY

NEWSPAPERS AND JOURNALS

Brighton Argus
Brighton Examiner
Brighton and Hove Society
Brighton Gazette
Brighton Guardian
Brighton Herald
Brighton Observer
Brighton Patriot
Daily Mail
Journal of Mental Science
Poor Law Union Gazette
Sussex Daily News
The Times
The Lancet
Warren Farm Old Scholars Magazine
Workhouse Visiting Society Journal

ARTICLES ABOUT THE POOR LAW AND THE WORKHOUSE

M. Burchall, *Brighton Paupers Buried in Cambridge 1885–1920*,vol.18 no.8 Sussex Family Historian 2009.

R. Grant, *Brighton Paupers*, Sussex Family History, 1995.

J. Jacobs, *Drastic Measures for Sturdy Loafers 1909–1920*, Sussex Archaeological Collections (128) 1990.

P. Piercey, *Proper Poor Law*, unpublished.

R. Tibble, *Charity and Chastity: Brighton Workhouse and the Female Penitent's Home*, The Sussex Genealogist and Local Historian vol 4 no.4.

A. Trimingham, *From Workhouse to General Hospital*, Argus 21/4/2007.

C. Ware, *Relaxation and Amusement for the Poor, Brighton 1854–1914*, dissertation.

Bartlett P., *The Asylum and the Poor Law: the Productive Alliance*, in Melling and Forsythe, Insanity, Institutions and Society, Routledge 1999.

Berry S., *Georgian Brighton*, Phillimore, 2005.

Carter D., *Just one Large Family*, Queenspark, 1992.

Chandler J., *Forty Years in the Wilderness*, London, 1893.

Chance W., *Children Under the Poor Law*, London, 1897.

Choomwattana C., *Opposition to the New Poor Law in Sussex 1835–37*, University of Sussex, unpublished PhD, 1990.

Collins J., *Letters from Australia*, unpublished.

Crompton F., *Workhouse Children*, Sutton, 1997.

Digby A., *Pauper Palaces*, Law Book Co of Australasia, 1978.

Erredge J., *The History of Brighthelmstone*, E. Lewis, 1862.

Farrant S., *Georgian Brighton 1760–1820*, University of Sussex, 1980.

Fowler S., *Workhouse*, The National Archives, 2007.

Gardner J., *Sweet Bells Jangled Out of Tune*, James Gardner, 1999.

Gaston H., *A Lingering Fear: East Sussex Hospitals and the Workhouse Legacy*, Southern Editorial Services, 2009.

Gaston H., *Workhouse to Hospital 1930–48*, Southern Editorial Services,1996.

Gooch G., *A History of Brighton General Hospital*, Phillimore 1980.

Gray, Frank *The Tramp, His Meaning and Being*, London 1931.

Higgs M., *Life at the Victorian/Edwardian Workhouse*, Tempus, 2007.

Hill R., *Underdog Brighton*, Iconoclast, 1991.

Hopper T., *Transformation of Political Conciousness in South-East England 1880–1914*, Brighton PhD. thesis, 1998.

Johnson V., *Diet in Workhouses and Prisons, 1835–1895*, Garland 1985.

Kershaw R. and Sacks J., *New Lives for Old. The Story of Britain's Child Migrants*, The National Archives, 2008.

Kohli M., *The Golden Bridge: Young Emigrants to Canada*, National Heritage Books, 2003.

Longmate N., *The Workhouse*, Temple Smith Ltd. 1974.

Macintosh C., *Aspects of Poverty in Nineteenth Century Brighton with Particular Reference to the Workhouse*, unpublished dissertation, University of Brighton, 2004.

Martin H., *History of Brighton and Environs*, John Beal, 1871.

Mason E., *Working Man: A Century of Hove Memories*, Queenspark 1998.

Mercer P., *The Hunns Mere Pit,the story of Woodingdean and Balsdean*, The Book Guild, 1993.

Mercer P., *Woodingdean, Reflections and the Millenium*

Morrison K., *The Workhouse, A Study of the Poor-Law Buildings in England*, English Heritage 1999.

Nelson I. (ed.) *Hurstpierpoint: Kind and Charitable*, Hurst History Study Group, 2001.

Noakes D., *The Town Beehive: A Young Girl's Lot 1910–1934*, Queenspark, 1975.

QueenSpark Books: *Who Was Harry Cowley?* (1984).

Rose M., *The English Poor Law 1780–1930*, David and Charles, 1971.

Study Group, *Brighton 1837*, Patcham University of the Third Age, 2004.

Twining L., *Recollections of Life and Works*, E.Arnold, 1893.

Waller J., *The Real Oliver Twist*, Icon books, 2005.

Winchester S., *The Surgeon of Crowthorne: A Tale of Madness and the Oxford English Dictionary*, Viking 1998.

RECORD OFFICES

The National Archives

MH 9/3

MH 12/12769 –94

MH 13/21

MH 13/33

MH 14/5

MH 57/102

MH 68/319

MH 68/320

East Sussex County Record Office

AMS 5660

AMS 5889

EMA 25/1 Warren Farm schools management committee minutes (appointed 20/1/30)

R/S 10/1–55 Brighton Guardians' minute book

R/S 11/1–15 Visiting committee minutes. RS 12/1 –Workhouse stock and management committee minutes

R/S 13/1–6

R/S 16/1 Rota minutes

R/S 17/1–3,5,8, 10 Warren Farm schools management committee visiting minutes.

R/S 18/ 1–9 Master's reports

RS 19/1 & 2 Matron's reports

R/S 20/1–3 Warren Farm superintendent's report books

R/S 21/1 Superintendent's report to farm/gardening sub-committee

R/S 22/1-3 Chaplain's report books

R/S 25/ 1–6 Public assistant officer report books

R/S 27/1 Complaints to the Warren Farm committee

R/S 29/1–2 Workhouse schools, admission and discharge

R/S 30/1 Elm Grove admission and discharge 1943–45

R/S 33/1 Receiving ward, female 1927–1930

R/S 37/1 Register of placement of children (Jan 1891–Nov 1935)

R/S 38/1 Register of children under Guardians' control

R/S 39/1 Warren Farm schools log book

R/S 40/1 Punishment book at Warren Farm, January 1913–March 1948

R/S 42/1 Visitors' book – Warren Farm schools visitors' books

R/S 42/3 Guardians' sealed orders 20/2/1871

R/S 48 1-6 PAC correspondence

R/T/3/1-5 Staff records

HB 68/1-2 Reports on Elm Grove home 1935–1948

HOW 34/1,2,7,8,16,17,18,19,20

HOW 37/4,7

HOW 38/1,2,

HOW 39/2,12

PAR 277/1/2/19

PAR 353/32/5/15

PAR 304/32/4/2

ENDNOTES

The National Archives = TNA
East Sussex Record Office= ESRO

PREFACE

1 "An Autobiography and Other Essays"
   (1949) G.M. Trevelyan in "Autobiography
   of an historian".
2 Popular Lectures on the Prevailing
   Diseases of Towns (1848) Brighton.
3 *The Making of the English Working Class* :
   EP Thompson

PART ONE

CHAPTER ONE

1 ESRO How 34/7
2 Ibid
3 ESRO How 34/16
4 ESRO Par 353/32/5/15
5 *Brighton Gazette* 15/3/1821
6 ESRO How 34/18
7 ESRO Q0/EW37 from Michael Burchall's
   "The Sussex Poor 2 1801–1850"

CHAPTER TWO

1 *History, Antiquities and Topography
   of Sussex* (1835) vol. 1 p.151
2 *Brighton Gazette* 26/9/1822
3 ESRO AMS 5660
4 *Brighton Gazette* 19/7/1827
5 *The Parish Chest* p197 by Tate
6 *Brighton Gazette* 9/4/1829
7 Ibid 27/4/1826
8 Rossbret 5 November 2002
<http://www.institutions.org.uk/poor_law
_unions/info/poverty_and_the_poor.htm>
9 ESRO HOW 38/2
10 The *Lancet* 21/5/1842 p 278
11 *Brighton Guardian* 23/3/1836
12 The *Times* 16/2/1842
13 TNA MH12/12769
14 *Brighton Guardian* 16/3/1836
15 *Brighton Patriot* 3/11/1836

16 Ibid
17 *Brighton Patriot* 28/3/1837
18 TNA MH 12/12770
19 *Brighton Gazette* 23/8/1836
20 *Brighton Herald* 20/1/1837
21 Ibid 20/1/1837
22 Ibid 13/3/1834
23 *Brighton Patriot* 24/5/1836
24 *Forty Years in the Wilderness* (1893) by
   John Chandler
25 *Brighton Guardian* 23/12/1840
26 *Brighton Herald* 6/3/1841

CHAPTER THREE

1 *Brighton Patriot* 20/8/1836
2 *Brighton Herald* 23/9/1837
3 Ibid 21/3/1838
4 Ibid 25/1/1845
5 Ibid 18/12/1841
6 *Brighton Guardian* 8/10/1842
7 ESRO HOW 34/1
8 Ibid
9 ESRO How 37/7
10 *Brighton Gazette* 13/1/1848
11 ESRO HOW 34/22
12 *Brighton Observer* 9/1/1957
13 *Brighton Gazette* 8/8/1861
14 Ibid
15 TNA MH 12/12773

CHAPTER FOUR

1 *Brighton Patriot* 13/2/1838
2 *Brighton Herald* 13/1/1849
3 *Brighton Gazette* 2/2/1849
4 *Brighton Herald* 25/6/1859
5 *Brighton Examiner* 19/7/1859
6 Ibid
7 *Brighton Examiner* 31/5/1859
8 *Brighton Herald* 4/6/1859

CHAPTER FIVE

1 TNA MH 12/12773
2 Ibid. Letter dated 4/5/1859

3 *Brighton Gazette* 26/6/1856

4 Ibid 12/8/1858

5 *Brighton Gazette* 31/3/1934 article by Magnus Volk

6 Ibid

7 *Brighton Herald* 16/2/1861

8 *Brighton Guardian* 20/8/1862

9 TNA MH12/12773

10 *Brighton Examiner* 7/3/1864

11 TNA MH 12/12272

12 *Brighton Examiner* 5/7/1864

13 Ibid 9/1/1866

14 Ibid.

15 *Brighton Herald* 13/4/1865

16 *Brighton Gazette* 17/1/1866

17 TNA MH 12.12774

18 TNA MH12/12773

19 TNA MH 12/12774

20 Ibid

21 TNA MH 12/12774

22 Ibid

23 *Brighton Examiner* 18/12/1866

CHAPTER SEVEN

1 TNA MH 12/12773

2 Ibid

3 TNA MH 12/12773 petition dated 6/3/1857

4 The *Lancet* 20/7/1844

5 ESRO HC 7/1 Robertson's Asylum journal 17/8/1859

6 Ibid

7 Ibid 17/8/1860

8 *Brighton Guardian* 25/4/1860

9 ESRO HC 7/1 Robertson's Asylum Journal 23/5/1860

10 *Brighton Herald* 26/5/1860

11 *Brighton Observer* 15/5/1863

12 *Brighton Gazette* 1/12/1863

13 Ibid 10/3/1864

14 TNA MH12/12774

15 ESRO HC2/1 Eighth annual report of the Sussex Lunatic Asylum

16 *Brighton Gazette* 4/10/1866

17 *Journal of Mental Science*, October 1867

18 *Brighton Examiner* 9/1/1866

PART TWO

CHAPTER EIGHT

1 *Brighton Herald* 20/9/1867

2 Ibid

3 Ibid -Letter dated 22/4/1968

4 *Brighton General Hospital* p.37 Janet Gooch

5 Once a Week 28/5/1863

6 *Brighton Gazette* 26/12/1867

7 TNA MH12/ 12775

8 Ibid

9 Ibid

10 *Brighton Guardian* 12/2/1868

11 TNA MH12/12755

12 *Brighton Examiner* 12/2/1868

13 Ibid

14 TNA MH 12/12776

15 Ibid

16 Ibid

17 Ibid

18 *Brighton Examiner* 5/3/1867

19 *Brighton Guardian* 7/12/1870

20 ibid

21 ibid

22 TNA MH12/12776

23 *Lancet* 23/5/1868

24 Ibid - 30/3/1872 p428

CHAPTER NINE

1 *Brighton Guardian* 5/5/1871

2 *Brighton Herald* 13/2/1851

3 Sussex Convicts Transported to Australia – M.J. Burchall(Parish Register Transcription Society CD, 2011)

4 Ibid

5 TNA MH32/20

6 *Children under the Poor Law* p 262 – W Chance.

CHAPTER TEN

1 *Brighton Gazette* 23/7/1863

2 Ibid

3 *Brighton Examiner* 8/9/1863

4 TNA MH12/12774

5 TNA MH 12/12782

6 *Brighton Guardian* 25/10/1876

7 *Poor Law Unions' Gazette* 28/3/1857
8 TNA MH 12/12781
9 Ibid
10 Ibid
11 Ibid
12 Ibid –MH12/12778
13 Ibid
14 Ibid
15 Ibid
16 Broadmoor casenotes (D/H14/D2/1/1/4)
17 *Brighton Herald* 8/2/1879
18 TNA MH12/12782
19 Ibid
20 The *Argus* 12/5/1880

CHAPTER ELEVEN
1 TNA MH12/12776
2 *Brighton Examiner* 30/7/1872
3 *Brighton Guardian* 14/5/1873
4 Ibid – *Brighton Guardian*, Mr Tankard
5 TNA MH12/12778
6 Ibid 30/8/1874
7 Ibid 2/4/1890
8 ESRO AMS 6930/6/124
9 Ibid AMS 6930/6/12
10 Ibid AMS 6930/6/2
11 Ibid AMS 6930/6/16
12 Ibid AMS 6930/6/37
13 Ibid AMS 6930/6/27
14 Ibid AMS 6930/6/38
15 Ibid AMS 6930/6/39
16 Ibid AMS 6930/6/170
17 Ibid AMS 6930/6/23
18 Ibid AMS 6930/6/171
19 Ibid
20 Ibid AMS 6930/6/195
21 Ibid AMS 6930/6/94
22 Ibid AMS 6930/6/67
23 Ibid AMS 6930/6/13
24 Ibid AMS 6930/6/15
25 Ibid AMS 6930/6/104
26 *Brighton Guardian* 30/11/1881
27 Ibid 6/5/1874
28 Ibid 28/5/1875
29 Ibid
30 Ibid
31 TNA MH12/12778

32 Ibid MH12/12779
33 Ibid
34 *Daily Mail* 14/1/1875
35 *Brighton Guardian* 25/1/1875
36 *Brighton Guardian* 17/1/1877
37 Ibid 10/10/1877
38 *Evening Argus* 17/6/1880
39 *Brighton Guardian* 6/3/1878
40 Ibid 13/3/1878

CHAPTER TWELVE
1 *Brighton Guardian* 3/2/1886
2 *Brighton Herald* 11/6/1827
3 *Brighton Argus* 18/1/1881
4 *Brighton Guardian* 9/1/1889
5 *Brighton Examiner* 20/11/1883
6 *Sussex Daily News* 25/5/1887
7 Ibid
8 TNA MH12/12787
9 "An Appreciation" an anonymous article
   in the *Brighton Herald* 11/6/1927.
10 *Brighton Guardian* 16/8/1893
11 *Brighton Examiner* 1895
12 *Brighton Herald* 1/8/1891
13 *The Workhouse* – Simon Fowler, p.1338.
14 *Children Under the Poor Law*, p.130

CHAPTER THIRTEEN
1 The *Lancet* 3/9/1881
2 Ibid 19/11/1881
3 *Brighton Guardian* 12/1887
4 Ibid
5 *Brighton Examiner* 1/3/1891
6 Ibid
7 *Brighton Examiner* 23/12/1884
8 Ibid 15/5/1885
9 Ibid 9/2/1886
10 *Daily News* 3/2/1888 in TNA MH 12/
   12788
11 TNA MH 12/12787
12 Ibid 9/9/1887
13 Ibid 29/4/1887
14 Brighton Herald 17/12/1887
15 Ibid 10/3/1888
16 *Evening Argus* 10/4/1888
17 TNA MH12/12788
18 ibid

19 TNA MH12/12794
20 TNA MH12/12793
21 *Brighton Guardian* 12/6/1889
22 TNA MH12/12788 13/1/1889
23 Ibid
24 *Brighton Herald* 18/12/1889
25 *Brighton Guardian* 24/8/81
26 *Brighton Examiner* 30/8/1889
27 *Brighton Herald* 2/1/1889
28 *Brighton Guardian* 30/12/1881
29 Ibid 24/8/1875
30 *Brighton Guardian* 16/1/1884
31 TNA MH 12/12792
32 TNA MH 12/12793
33 Ibid
34 TNA MH12/12794
35 Ibid
36 Ibid
37 *Brighton Guardian* 23/1/1895
38 *Brighton Examiner* 21/1/1895
39 *Brighton Guardian* 30/9/1891
40 Ibid
41 Ibid
42 Ibid 30/11/1892
43 An Appreciation
44 *Brighton Gazette* 8/10/1949

PART THREE

CHAPTER FOURTEEN
1 *Sussex Daily Express* 22/12/1903
2 ESRO RS 10/12
3 ESRO RS 10/14
4 *Sussex Daily News* 20/5/08
5 *Sussex Daily News* – 6/5/1908
6 *Evening Argus* 1/3/1905
7 *The Workhouse,* by Norman Longmate, page 282
8 *Evening Argus* 18/07/1904
9 *Brighton and Hove Society* 30/12/1905
10 ESRO R/S 13/2
11 Ibid R/S 10/11
12 *Brighton Herald* 7/11/1908
13 "Brighton Guardians and the Workhouse 1909–1914" (Sussex Archaeological Collections 128 p.226.

14 ESRO RS 10/16
15 *Brighton Herald* 4/9/1909
16 *Sussex Daily News* 4/9/1909
17 *Brighton Herald* 26/2/1910
18 *Brighton and Hove Society* 6/1/1909
19 The *Times* 17/7/1908
20 *Brighton Herald* 29/9/1923
21 *Sussex Daily News* 24/5/1911
22 ESRO R/S 20/1
23 Ibid R/S 11/3
24 Ibid R/S 10/25
25 Ibid

CHAPTER FIFTEEN
1 Ibid R/S 38/1
2 Ibid R/S 10/17
3 Ibid
4 Ibid
5 Ibid
6 Warren Farm Old Scholars' Association (OSA) magazine 1951
7 ESRO RS 10/23
8 Ibid RS 10/17
9 New Lives for Old page 77.
10 ESRO R/S 10/41
11 Warren Farm OSA   magazine 1951
12 ESRO R/S 40
13 *Brighton Herald* 4/10/1924
14 *Brighton Herald* "An Appreciation" 11/6/1927
15 ESRO RS 10/23
16 ESRO RS 10/27
17 ESRO RS 10/27
18 Ibid
19 Warren Farm OSA magazine 1950

CHAPTER SIXTEEN
1 *Brighton Herald* 5/9/1914
2 Ibid
3 *Sussex Daily News* 23/12/1914
4 Ibid 9/6/1915
5 *Sussex Daily News* 28/4/1915
6 ESRO R/S .11/14
7 *The Argus*, Mr Lord Thompson, 14/5/1915
8 *Brighton Herald* 25/12/1915
9 Ibid

10 *Brighton Gazette* 29/12/1915
11 Ibid 6/1/1915
12 *Sussex Daily News* 6/7/1915
13 *Brighton Gazette* 11/8/1915
14 Ibid 1/9/1915
15 ESRO R/S 31/7
16 Ibid R/S 22/1
17 *Brighton Herald* 9/12/1916
18 Ibid 29/12/1917
19 Ibid 29/12/1917
20 ESRO R/S 10/34
21 Ibid R/S 21/2
22 Warren Farm OSA magazine 1951
23 *Brighton Herald* 16/11/1918
24 Ibid
25 *Brighton Gazette* 13/11/1918
26 ESRO R/S 17/5

CHAPTER SEVENTEEN
1 *Brighton Gazette* 20/8/1919
2 ESRO R/S 10/38
3 *Brighton Herald* 20/12/1919
4 ESRO R/S 11/16
5 *Brighton Gazette* 21/9/1921
6 ESRO R/S 11/16
7 Ibid R/S 10/42
8 *Brighton Gazette* 31/1/1923
9 Ibid 3/2/1923
10 Ibid
11 Ibid
12 Ibid
13 Ibid
14 Email to author dated 4/10/2008
15 *Brighton Herald* 5/1/1924
16 *Brighton Gazette* 29/12/1923
17 Ibid
18 Ibid 26/12/1928
19 Ibid
20 Ibid 16/10/1937
21 *Brighton Herald* 22/9/1923
22 Ibid
23 *Brighton Gazette* 20/12/1922
24 *Brighton Herald* 25/08/1925
25 Ibid
26 Ibid 5/2/1927
27 ESRO R/S 11/10

28 *Just one Large Family* p.4 (Queenspark 1992)
29 ESRO R/S 13/10
30 *Brighton Herald* 13/3/1930
31 ESRO R/S 11/13
32 Ibid
33 *A History of Brighton General*, Gooch p. 69
34 *Brighton Herald* 8/9/1927
35 *Brighton Gazette* 21/4/1928
36 ESRO R/S 18/5
37 Ibid R/S 11/16
38 Ibid R/S 15/5
39 *A History of Brighton General*, Gooch p. 124
40 *Sussex Daily News* 18/5/27
41 Ibid
42 *Brighton Herald* 4/1/1930
43 Ibid 11/1/1930
44 *Sussex Daily News* 22/1/1930
45 *Brighton Herald* 6/4/1930
46 Ibid

CHAPTER EIGHTEEN
1 ESRO R/S 17/1
2 Ibid R/S 10/1937
3 *Brighton Gazette* 4/9/1920
4 ESRO R/S 22/2
5 ESRO R/S 17/8
6 ESRO R/S 10/42
7 *Brighton Herald* 10/1/1925
8 Ibid
9 Ibid
10 *Brighton Herald* 12/6/1926
11 ESRO R/S 17/8
12 *Brighton Herald* 29/1/1927

CHAPTER NINETEEN
1 *Brighton Herald* 20/10/1934
2 Ibid 3/1/1931
3 Ibid
4 *A History of Brighton General*, Gooch p.143
5 *Brighton Herald* 25/7/1931
6 Ibid 28/10/1933
7 Ibid

8 *Brighton Herald* 17/9/1932
9 Ibid 13/4/1933
10 Ibid 27/4/1933
11 Ibid 7/9/1935
12 Ibid 7/1/1933
13 Ibid
14 Ibid 6/1/1934
15 ESRO R/S 27/1
16 *A History of Brighton General*, Gooch p.144
17 *Brighton Gazette* 7/4/1934
18 *A Lingering Fear*, Gaston p. 41
19 Ibid p. 42
20 *A History of Brighton General*, Gooch p.145
21 *Brighton Gazette* 22/2/1936
22 ESRO R/S 11/14
23 Ibid R/S 25/1
24 *A History of Brighton General*, Gooch p.151
25 ESRO R/S 48/1
26 *A History of Brighton General*, Gooch p.157
27 *Brighton Herald* 28/1/1939
28 *Brighton Gazette* 7/1/1839

CHAPTER TWENTY
1 ESRO EM 25/1
2 Ibid
3 Ibid R/S 20/1
4 Ibid
5 Ibid R/S 42/1
6 Ibid
7 *Reflections and the Millenium* – Peter Mercer, pp 40-41
8 ESRO R/S 20/1
9 Ibid
10 Ibid
11 Ibid
12 Ibid R/S 39/1
13 *Brighton Herald* 3/11/1934
14 ESRO EM 25/1
15 Ibid

16 ESRO HB 68/1
17 ESRO R/S 17/10
18 Ibid
19 *Brighton Herald* 20/3/1937
20 ESRO R/S 48/1
21 ESRO R/S 25/1
22 Ibid R/S 48/3

CHAPTR TWENTY-ONE
1 Ibid 16/9/39
2 *Brighton Gazette* 9/3/1940
3 ESRO R/S 48/3
4 Ibid HB 68/2
5 Ibid HB 68/1
6 Ibid R/S 42/1
7 Ibid HB 68/1
8 *Brighton Gazette* 27/1/1945
9 The *Times* 2/2/1945
10 *Argus* 30/1/1945
11 Ibid 31/1/1945
12 Ibid 12/2/1945
13 Ibid 8/2/1945

CHAPTER TWENTY-TWO
1 *Brighton Gazette* 8/12/1945
2 *Brighton Herald* 18/5/1946
3 ESRO HB 68/1
4 *Brighton Gazette* 17/9/1949
5 "Proper Poor Law" by Pam Piercey (undated).
6 Ibid
7 ESRO R/S 22/3
8 *Brighton Gazette* 18/1/1947
9 ESRO R/S 20/3
10 Warren Farm OSA newsletter 1950
11 Ibid
12 ESRO R/S 22/3
13 Ibid
14 Ibid
15 Ibid
16 *Brighton Gazette* 22/3/1952
17 Ibid
18 ESRO R/S 9/26

FIGURE REFERENCES

Fig 1   ESRO QDP 133
Fig 2   John Erredge's *History of Brighthelmstone* (1862)
Fig 3   ESRO AMS 5660
Fig 4   Official New Poor Law Amendment Act Diet Sheet
Fig 5   *Illustrated London News*. Date unknown.
Fig.6   *Brighton Herald* 2/6/1934
Fig 7   TNA MH 12/12773
Fig 8   TNA MH 12/12773
Figs 9,10,11   Martin Phillips Collection
Fig 12   Mary Evans Library
Fig 13   TNA MH 14/5
Fig 14   Brighton Museum
Figs15,16   TNA MH 12/12776
Fig 18   Chris Horlock collection
Fig 19   TNA MH14/5
Fig 20   Chris Horlock Collection
Fig 21   Brighton Museum
Fig 22   Author's private collection
Fig 23   Brighton Museum
Fig 24   TNA MH12/12794
Figs 25 & 26   Brighton and Hove Society 9/1/1905
Fig 27   Chris Horlock Collection
Figs 28, 29, 30   Brighton Museum
Fig 31   Chris Horlock Collection
Figs 32 & 33 *Who was Harry Cowley?* (Queenspark Books 1984)
Fig 34   *Brighton Herald* 21/4/1928
Fig 35   Chris Horlock Collection
Fig 36   Brighton Museum
Fig 37   *Brighton Gazette* 22/2/1936
Fig 38   Ibid
Fig 39   *Brighton Gazette* 2/7/1936
Fig 40   *Brighton Herald* 7/1/1939
Fig 41   *Brighton Herald* 21/10/1933
Fig 42   *Brighton Herald* 30/11/1935
Fig 43   Margaret Cronin
Fig 44   *Brighton Gazette*   13/10/1934
Fig 45   *Brighton Herald*   4/12/1937
Fig 46   Martin Phillips Collection
Fig 47   *Brighton Herald* 29/12/1934
Fig 48   *Brighton Herald* 25/12/1937
Fig 49   *Brighton Herald* 11/1/1938
Fig 50   Eileen Jones
Fig 51   *Brighton Herald* 3/2/1945
Fig 52   *Brighton Gazette* 17/9/1949
Fig 53   *Brighton Gazette* 29/12/1945
Fig 54   *Brighton Gazette* 15/10/1949
Fig 55   *Brighton Herald* 22/1/1938
Fig 56   *Brighton Herald* 25/7/1936
Fig 57   *Brighton Herald* 29/11/1952
Fig 58 &59   Eileen Jones.

INDEX